This book is dedicated to my daughter
Madeline and my granddaughter Sicily.

Introduction

"Let food be thy medicine!" Truer words have rarely been spoken. In this day and age with the availability of information on how and what to eat to stay healthy, and feel energetic, I will not then bore you with the obvious. These are simply a few suggestions and recipes for those who want to incorporate them into their lives, not any dogmatic set of rules. To each his/her own.

This being said, I try to live by the mantra of "strive for five", meaning I try to get 5 different VEGETABLES into my body every day. Within this, I try to make sure at least one or two of them are a cruciferous vegetable and a green vegetable, such as broccoli, cauliflower, kale, brussel sprouts etc. This is not as difficult as one may think and it is not necessary to eat extremely large amounts of each of them in one meal. As a quick easy example, if you make a hummus and vegetable platter for lunch with sliced English cucumbers, julienned red peppers, julienned carrots, celery stalks and sliced zucchini, that would be five already! If you make a whole grain pasta for dinner and include in the pasta broccoli and mushrooms, that would be 2 more. Fruit is also nutritious, but it is a sugar, a natural sugar, but it is still a sugar. I am not anti-fruit, it is quite delicious and healthy. I just do not include fruits towards my 5 vegetables a day since they are not a vegetable.

I also try to eat as much whole grain as possible. Barilla, Dreamfields and other companies make great high fiber white pastas that do not have the "cardboard" texture associated with most whole wheat pastas. There are tons of whole grain breads on the market. Brown rice is a healthy whole grain, as is quinoa, millet, corn, oats and others. If you prefer white rice, which I often do, or fluffy homemade white rolls, pizza dough etc, I serve those with a lot of vegetables and/or a bean side dish to make up for the lost fiber in the refined grains, such as white rice or white flour breads.

I also want this to be taken into consideration: civilization has sufficed and survived on grain for thousands of years. We would not be here today without the ability of ancient people learning how to grow and harvest grain. This is what took us from being hunter gatherers to stable colonies of people. Asian countries had rice, the Americas had corn, the Europeans had wheat, so on and so forth.

The low carb diets that are out there, in my opinion, are not sustainable and are downright unhealthy in the long run. Protein is not the only component needed in maintaining a healthy body. Protein is in almost every food we eat and overconsumption of protein creates acids in the body that are buffered by calcium to be able to be excreted by the body. In other words, over consumption of protein can possibly lead to osteoperosis and bone problems due to the calcium loss via the buffering. There is a delicate balance between all nutrients. If you can replace some meat and dairy with some vegetables and whole grains, it can't hurt you, it can only help.

I completely understand the argument of "we're all going to die anyways, may as well live it up and eat, smoke and drink what you want and enjoy life". Personally, I would rather not spend the last 20 or 30 years of this life hooked on pills to stay alive and contribute to needless suffering of others. Sure some get lucky and live to 95 with horrible eating and lifestyle habits, but this is a not the norm, so, why roll the dice? You can enjoy life, I eat what I want, and what I want is healthy food and healthy versions of foods that I am familiar with. Nobody is perfect, people are going to indulge and eat less than healthy foods from time to time but if you maintain a good diet 90 percent of the time, you will be just fine.

To switch gears, when I mention sugar as an ingredient in the book, I am referring to organic sugar. The reason for this is that I am not positive if common white sugar is filtered through animal bone anymore. There is much confusion on this issue.

When I refer to specific name brand products in the book, I do so because I have been cooking vegan since 1993 and I have tried most products on the market and I know which ones work the best for vegan cooking. A lot of trial and error has taken place but I have spent plenty of money on good and bad products to differentiate between the two. Any product mentioned in the book that you may have trouble finding at a store can easily be found and ordered online.

I hesitated on writing a cookbook all these years because cooking is very much something that is subjective to taste and hammering down exact recipes is nearly impossible. Use your discression with salt and spices to your taste. Do not be afraid of salt. It is a necessary part of the cooking process to make food delicious. I prefer to use kosher salt and/or sea salt. They are much easier to cook with. Experiment, add different ingredients once you are use to a recipe, make it your own, but at first, follow the exact recipe, so that you can enjoy the dish as the chef intended.

I can not stress enough to ALWAYS ALWAYS ALWAYS taste your food before you serve it to yourself or others, make sure it tastes delicious and not bland, and fix it, if it is bland, with spices, seasonings and necessary ingredients. To me, bland food is the same as bad food. If you're going to work hard on a recipe, make sure that it tastes perfect.

One more thing about what to cook on or with, when I refer to "sheet pans" in recipes, I am referring to a 13x18 inch large sheet pan. A pastry cutter is an instrument that allows you to cut shortening or oil into flour so that it properly gets mixed together. Cutting in the shortening means placing the shortening onto the flour mixture and pushing down over and over with the pastry cutter until the shortening is mixed into the flour mixture completely. Nutritional yeast is not a product used for bread to rise, it is a vegan product that comes in flake form and gives food a savory rich and cheese like flavor. It is high in B vitamins and can be found in health food stores and some grocery stores. I can also not stress enough how much easier a nice non stick frying/saute pan, a sharp knife, a food processor and a digital rice cooker will make your cooking experience.

All of the recipes in the book are 100 percent vegan and plant based. They are all my own developed creations from many years of vegan cooking. My favorite vegan soy chicken patties, Delight Soyfoods brand, are available at some health food stores and online at :

www.delightsoy.com
919 468 1077

 The Maywah company also makes delicious vegan chicken nuggets and tenders. You can find them online.

 *Any ingredient that you do not recognize and you want to know what it is, simply look it up online.

 *You can substitute brown rice pasta or any other gluten free pasta for any recipes in this book involving semolina pasta.

 *For any cookbook questions or to purchase them, contact me at littlesilky@yahoo.com and follow me on Instagram at instagram.com/simpletogourmetvegan74.

Table of Contents

Soups, Starters and Sides

Smoky Coconut Crusted Avocado Cocktail

So simple and elegant, sure to impress anyone who tries it.

1 prepared recipe of my Parmesan Crusted Avocado Fries (page 36), but in place of the parmesan, use 3 Tbs shredded sweetened coconut and 1 tsp of smoked paprika to mix into the panko bread crumbs before breading and frying the avocado
cocktail sauce: 1/2 cup ketchup whisked together with 1.5 Tbs grated jarred horseradish, a pinch of salt, 1/4 tsp garlic powder and 1 tsp vegan worcestershire sauce (if you can not find vegan worcestershire sauce, you can omit it)

Simply place some sauce into a cocktail glass and arrange the cooked avocado around it. Enjoy.

Yield: Serves 3-4

Garlic and Fresh Basil Parmesan Rolls

These are crisp on the top and fluffy on the inside with a
rich parmesan garlic topping.

Make the Basic Dough recipe from page 81. The dough recipe makes 2
balls of dough, but you will only use 1 here.

for the topping: 3 Tbs extra virgin olive oil, 4 cloves chopped garlic, 1 Tbs
chopped fresh basil, 1/4 tsp salt, 1 Tbs Go Veggie brand vegan
parmesan cheese or Follow Your Heart brand vegan parmesan shreds

Line a cookie sheet with foil and then parchment paper. Spray with non
stick spray. Once the dough has risen, do NOT punch down, pinch off golf
ball size pieces and pinch them into round balls. Place on the cookie sheet.
Allow them to touch each other so that they rise into each other, this makes
them very soft. Once your tray is full of balls of dough (should make about
16 rolls). Cover and let rise 2 hours. Preheat the oven to 440 degrees. With
gloves on, mix the topping ingredients and spread over the rolls. Bake for 15
to 20 minutes until browned. Enjoy.

Yield: Serves 6-8

Avocado Rice with Sour Cream and Fresh Chives

I love this rice. It is beyond simple and requires a rice cooker. They are only about $30 for a digital model with a white and brown rice button as well as a "keep warm" button that will keep soups, sauces, gravies and chili's warm in it. A great investment.

1.5 cups jasmine rice
pinch of salt
2 cups water whisked together with 1.5 Tbs of Better Than Bouillon No Chicken Base or Roasted Garlic Base
1 large avocado, peeled and diced
hot sauce to top (optional)
Tofutti brand Sour Cream
1 Tbs chopped fresh chives

Place the rice, salt and the water/no chicken base in the rice cooker. Stir together. Start the rice cooker. When the rice cooker is finished, fluff the rice with a fork and gently fold in the diced avocado. Place servings in a bowl and top with a dollop of Tofutti Sour Cream, the chives and the optional hot sauce.

Yield: Serves 3-5

Rosemary, Grape Tomato, Olive and Caper Focaccia

1 ball of risen dough from the Basic Dough recipe from this book (the dough recipe makes 2 balls of dough, but you will only use 1 here)
1 Tbs olive oil
1/3 cup grape tomatoes cut in half lengthwise
1 Tbs capers
1/4 cup kalamata olives cut in half lengthwise
1/2 tsp rough chopped fresh rosemary
a few pinches of salt
1 Tbs of Follow Your Heart brand vegan parmesan cheese

Take a 12 inch deep dish round baking pan and brush the inside and sides with olive oil. Take your risen dough out of the bowl it rose in and place it on a lightly floured board, do not re knead it. Press it into a circle the size of the pan and place it into the pan. Cover it and let it rise 1.5 hours. Pour the olive oil onto the risen dough and push your fingers into the dough, making several indentions all around the dough. Sprinkle with a little salt and then place on the tomato halves face down, the olive halves face down, the parmesan, rosmary and capers. Heat the oven to 440 degrees and bake for 10 to 13 minutes until golden and place under the broiler the last minute to get it extra golden.

Yield: Serves 3-4

Golden Raisin Balsamic Grilled Pear and Avocado Salad (gluten free)

4 cups of mixed baby greens or chopped fresh baby spinach and iceberg or your favorite salad greens, 2 pears each cut into 4 flat 1/4 inch thick pieces (do not cut into the core), 1 pitted avocado cut in half, 1/3 each cup cooked red kidney beans, peeled sliced carrots, cucumbers and tomatoes and marinated artichokes, a few toasted salted green pepita pumpkin seeds and golden raiains, 1/2 a cup bite size chopped broccoli and 1/3 cup asparagus cut into 1 inch pieces **marinade:** 1/3 cup balsamic vinegar whisked together with 1 Tbs olive oil, 1 tsp sugar, a pinch of salt and garlic powder, a pinch of oregano

Bring 3 inches of water to a boil. Drop in the broccoli and asparagus. Cook 30 seconds and drain and cool them in cold water. Set aside. Place the pear slices and avocado halves (place avocado face down in the marinade) in the maridade and let them marinate 12 minutes while you heat a grill on high for 12 minutes. Grill each side of the pears for 2 minutes and grill the avocado halves about 3 minutes total. Arrange the salad greens on a plate or in a bowl and top with all of the ingredients. *Yield:* Serves 2-3

Soft Pretzels

1 full Basic Dough recipe from this book (it makes 2 balls of dough, you will use them both here), 9 cups of water, boiling, with 1/2 cup of baking soda added into it, pretzel salt or Kosher salt, 2 Tbs melded vegan buttery spread

Heat the oven to 450 degrees. Line a cookie sheet with foil and then parchment paper sprayed with non stick spray. Divide, without re kneading, each ball of dough into 4 equal size pieces on a floured surface (this recipe makes 8 pretzels total). Roll each of the 8 balls into a 24 inch rope. Shape each rope into a U shape and then bring the ends in and over the middle of the U so that it looks like a pretzel. Drop them, by 2, into the boiling baking soda water. Boil each side 1 minute. Remove from the water carefully with a large flat spatula onto a plain sheet pan. Brush each pretzel with a little of the Earth Balance and then sprinkle with the salt. Move them to the sprayed parchment/foil lined pan carefully with the spatula and bake for 15 to 18 minutes or until browned. For the last minute, place then under the broiler to get them even more browned. Remove from oven, brush with a little more of the melted Earth Balance buttery spread and enjoy.

Yield: Makes 8 pretzels

Cucumber and Red Grape Kidney Bean Salad in a Fresh Orange Vinaigrette (gluten free)

1 cup English seedless cucumber sliced into 1/4 inch thick
half moons
1/2 cup seedless red grapes cut in half
1/3 cup peeled carrots cut into thin 1 inch long matchsticks
1/4 cup each small diced
red and green bell peppers
1 cup cooked kidney beans

for the dressing:
1/2 cup fresh squeezed
orange juice whisked together
with a pinch of salt and pepper,
2 Tbs olive oil, 1 Tbs sugar
and 1 Tbs rice wine vinegar

Simply mix all of the ingredients in a large bowl and serve chilled.

Yield: Serves 2-3

Baked Thick Cut Potato Chips (gluten free)

3 medium sized russet
potatoes or 4 medium sized
red potatoes, washed and
cut into 1/4 inch thick disks

for the seasoning:
2 Tbs extra virgin olive oil
1 tsp garlic powder
1/2 tsp black pepper
1/2 tsp dried oregano
1/2 tsp dried basil
1 tsp salt
1/4 tsp red pepper flakes
(optional)

Preheat oven to 400 degrees. Make a baking rack by placing foil along the bottom of a sheet pan. Place a metal cookie cooling rack on top of the foiled pan and spray the rack with non stick spray (this way of baking them keeps the bottoms from burning). In a bowl, mix the cut potatoes and the rest of the ingredients. Place each potato disc on the elevated rack until they are all on the rack. Bake for 25 minutes or until golden. Sprinkle with a little salt and serve.

Yield: Serves 4-6

Mushroom and Leek Wild Rice

This reqires a rice cooker. Aroma makes a good digital one for about 29 dollars, available at any big box store. The chewiness from the wild rice and the richness of the leeks and mushrooms make this a great side dish.

3/4 cup uncooked wild rice, 1 3/4 cup water, 1 Tbs Better Than Bouillon brand Roasted Garlic Base or No Chicken Base, 1/3 cup thinly sliced leeks, 2 cloves minced garlic, 1 cup thinly sliced mushrooms, 2 Tbs Earth Balance brand buttery spread, 1/4 tsp minced fresh thyme, 2 Tbs sliced scallions, 1 Tbs nutritional yeast, 1/2 tsp garlic powder

Place the rice, water, bouillon base and a pinch of salt in a rice cooker. Stir it, close the top and hit the "brown rice" button. Cook it and then completely cool it in the fridge or freezer for about 20 minutes. Heat a large non stick pan for 3 minutes on high. Add in 1 Tbs of the buttery spread, the leeks, scallions, mushrooms, a pinch of salt and the garlic. Sautee 4 minutes and add in the thyme and the rice. Break the rice up with a spatula and cook until heated. Stir in the other Tbs of the buttery spread, garlic powder and the nutritional yeast. Taste for flavor, add salt and pepper if needed. Enjoy.

Yield: Serves 3-4

Beet, Avocado, Red Bean and Spicy Sesame Tamari Tofu Baby Bibb Lettuce Salad

4 cups of chopped baby bibb lettuce (red or green or a combination of both)
1 medium sized beet, peeled, chopped into 3/4 inch triangles about 1/8 inch thick, boiled 6 minutes and then drained and cooled
15 pitted kalamata or pitted Sicilian green olives
1/2 a medium cucumber cut into half moon
1 carrot, peeled and cut into matchsticks
1/2 cup cooked small red beans or kidney beans
1 avocado, pitted, peeled and diced
3/4 block of extra firm tofu that has been frozen, thawed and pressed between your hands until no more water drains out of it, chopped into small cubes

 Toss the tofu cubes in a large bowl with a Tbs of tamari (soy sauce) , a tsp of toasted sesame oil and a 1/4 tsp dried red pepper flakes. Place the lettuce at the bottom of a large salad bowl. Arrange the rest of the ingredients on top of the lettuce greens so that all of the colors of the toppings are equally represented. This is delicious topped with Goddess dressing and served with the Silky Smooth Butternut Squash Bisque and Homemade Pesto Bread Stick recipes from this book.

Yield: Serves 2-4

Creamed Spinach and Kale (gluten free)

2 heads of kale, stemmed and
chopped roughly
6 cups of raw baby spinach
sauce:
3/4 cup vegan mayo
2 Tbs Tofutti brand cream cheese
1/2 a jar marinated artichokes
a pinch of freshly grated nutmeg
3 Tbs nutritional yeast
1 tsp lemon juice
1/2 tsp salt
black pepper to taste

 Heat a large pot of water to a boil. Add in the chopped kale and cook 5 minutes. Add in the spinach and cook another minute. Drain. Be sure to squeeze all of the excess water from the greens. Place all of the sauce ingredients into a food processor. Process until smooth. Add a little water if it is extremely thick. Heat a non stick saute pan for 2 minutes and add in the sauce and the cooked greens. Stir until heated through. Taste for flavor, add more nutritional yeast or salt if needed. Enjoy.

Yield: Serves 3-4

Homemade Limoncello (gluten free)

  This takes a while to develop the flavor, but it is well worth it for this incredible Italian cocktail. I like to serve this in an ice chilled cocktail glass. It is delicious and perfectly lemony and sweet with a little kick from the vodka for a warm summer day or an after dinner drink. It will keep well frozen in the freezer for about a month.

5 lemons, washed very well with the peels carefully peeled off (peeling with a carrot peeler is best, peel thick chunks of skin off of the lemon, trying not to get any of the white part of the lemon in the peels)
1 cup vodka
3 cups of plain water
1 1/4 cup sugar

  Take the lemon peels and place them in a jar with a tight fitting lid. Pour the vodka over them and place the lid on tighyly. Let this sit in a cold, dark place for 30 days (yes, 30 days). After 30 days, place the 3 cups of plain water in a pot and bring to a boil. Add in the 1 1/4 cup sugar. Stir until the sugar is melted. Cool this mixture completely and pour it into a large pitcher. Take a strainer and place it over the top of the pitcher to catch the peels. Pour in the vodka/lemon peel mixture, it will be a gorgeous yellow color. Discard the peels and serve the limoncello ice cold. You can store it in the freezer in a bottle with a tight fitting cap until ready to drink.

Yield: Serves 6-10

Classic Baked Macaroni and Cheese

I have experimented for years trying to perfect vegan macaroni and cheese and this is the best one you will ever eat, guaranteed. Creamy and satisfying.

1 box elbow pasta cooked 5 minutes then drained and cooled (I like Ronzoni brand large elbows or the Dreamfields brand elbows because they have fiber and a great taste). You can use small shells too if you prefer.

cheese sauce:
2 cups plain rice milk
1 1/2 cups water
1/2 cup nutritional
yeast plus
1 Tbs nutritional yeast
1 tsp garlic powder
1.5 tsp lemon juice
1/3 cup flour + 1
Tbs flour
1-2 teaspoons salt
4 Tablespoons Earth
Balance brand soy
free buttery spread
1 package Daiya brand

shredded cheddar, 3 Tbs Follow Your Heart brand shredded parmesan
1 cup of So Delicious brand
cheddar jack shreds for
an optional topping

Mix all ingredients except the pack of Daiya, parmesan and the optional So Delicious cheese, nor the macaroni. Heat over medium heat until butter is melted into the mixture and it starts to thicken slightly. Add the Daiya shreds and parmesan, whisk it all until the cheese is completely melted, takes about 3 minutes. Add more lemon juice, butter or salt if you think it needs it. It should taste rich and a tiny bit tangy.

Preheat oven to 375 degrees. Mix the sauce with the cooked macaroni and pour into a sprayed casserole pan. Bake covered with foil at 375 degrees for 40 minutes, remove foil, top with a cup of So Delicious brand shredded cheddar jack cheese and bake uncovered for another 5 minutes. If not using the extra So Delicious cheese topping, still bake it uncovered for the last 5 minutes in the oven.

Yield: Serves 6-8

Lemon Butter Parmesan and Oregano Grilled Asparagus (gluten free)

1 head of asparagus with the hard bottoms trimmed off, 3 Tbs Earth Balance brand buttery spread, 1 Tbs fresh lemon juice, a few pinches of salt and fresh cracked black pepper, 2 cloves of garlic rough chopped, a few Tbs of Follow Your Heart brand shredded parmesan, 6 fresh minced oregano leaves, 2 Tbs olive oil

Mix the asparagus with the olive oil, minced oregano and a pinch of salt and pepper. Heat the grill on high for 10 minutes. In a pan, melt the Earth Balance buttery spread. Add in the garlic and a pinch of salt. Cook until the garlic barely starts to brown. Add in the lemon juice. Set aside. Place the asparagus on the hot grill. Make sure they are placed across the grates so they do not fall through. Grill each side about 2 minutes. When finished, place on a plate and top with the lemon garlic sauce and the parmesan. Enjoy. *Yield:* Serves 3-4

Purple Carrot and Caramelized Onion Horseradish Hummus (gluten free)

1 medium onion sliced into thin half moons, 2 cloves minced garlic, 1 tsp olive oil, 4 Tbs tahini, 1 Tbs lemon juice 1 cup of purple carrots gently peeled, but keep the purple skin on and cut into medium chunks, 1 tsp horseradish, 1/2 cup cannellini beans, 1/2 to 1 tsp salt or to taste 1/4 tsp garlic powder

Bring a large non stick skillet to a high heat for 2 minutes. Add in the oil and onions. Let them sit, flat in an even layer for 1 minute. Add in the garlic and a pinch of salt, stir them and repeat this 3 or 4 times until they are golden. Set aside. In boiling water, add the carrots into the water and cook about 9 minutes or until soft. Drain them. Add the carrots, onions and the rest of the ingredients into a food processor. Process until very smooth. Taste for flavor, if you want it spicier, add more horseradish. If you want it a little richer, add more tahini, salt or lemon juice. Enjoy.

Yield: Serves 4-6

Crispy Fried Mac and Cheese Balls

3 cups of leftover mac and cheese recipe from this book, cold
3 cups flour
3 cups panko bread crumbs
1/2 cup shredded Daiya brand vegan cheddar cheese
3 Tbs nutritional yeast
1 container of Go Veggie brand vegan grated parmesan cheese
1 tsp salt
1 tsp garlic powder
1 tsp dried oregano
canola oil to fry

Mix the leftover mac and cheese with a 1/2 container of the parmesan cheese, nutritional yeast, 1/2 cup flour, Daiya cheddar cheese, a few pinches of salt and 1/2 cup of the panko bread crumbs. Mix well with your hands until it is not too wet but not too dry. If it seems too wet to roll into balls, add a bit more flour. Roll into one inch balls.

Set up your breading station by placing one cup of flour in a bowl, take another bowl and whisk together 1.5 cups of water with 1.5 cups of flour until you get a pancake type consistency. In a flat casserole dish, mix the remaining panko bread crumbs, parmesan cheese, salt, oregano and garlic powder. Working from left to right, roll the balls in the flour, then the flour/water mixture, and lastly into the panko bread crumb mixture. Do about 6 balls at a time until all are coated.

Heat about 1/2 inch of canola or vegetable oil in a non stick pan on medium high for 3 minutes. When you can dip a mac ball into it and bubbles form around it, they are ready to fry. Cook about 8 at a time, cooking each side about 3 minutes until golden brown. Drain, sprinkle with salt and serve hot. *these go nicely with a vegan ranch, basil aioli or a sweet and sour dipping sauce

Yield: Serves 4-6

Roasted Beet Salad with Mandarin Oranges and Kalamata Olives

2 medium sized beets, peeled and cut into 1/2 inch cubes
1/2 tsp each dried oregano, garlic powder and dried basil, 1 tsp olive oil
1/3 cup kalamata olives, pitted and sliced in half
1/2 cup Mandarin oranges (the kind packed in water, not syrup) washed and drained
3 cups raw baby spinach that has been dropped in boiling water for 1 minute and then
drained, cooled and squeezed dry (this will leave you with about 1/2 cup or less of spinach)
1/3 cup minced celery
for the dressing:
1 Tbs minced shallot, 1 Tbs olive oil
2 Tbs red wine vinegar, 2 Tbs water
1 Tbs each sliced fresh basil and fresh chives
salt and pepper to taste, 1 Tbs maple syrup

For the dressing, simply whisk all of the dressing ingredients together. Set aside. Heat the
oven to 400 degrees. Line a sheet pan with parchment paper. Mix the diced beets with the
teaspoon of olive oil, dried basil and dried oregano, a little salt and pepper and the garlic
powder. Pour them onto sheet pan in an even later and roast for 20 minutes or until the beets
are tender but not mushy. Cool them completely. Mix these with the rest of the salad
ingredients and then toss it all in the dressing. Enjoy chilled. This is tangy, savory and sweet.

Yield: Serves 3-4

Crunchy Fried Dill Pickles with Spicy Brown Mustard, Cholula and Black Pepper Aioli Dipping Sauce

60 dill pickle chips, drained
3 cups panko bread crumbs mixed with 1 tsp garlic powder, 1 tsp salt, 1/2 tsp dried basil and 1/2 tsp dried oregano
2 cups flour
1 cup water
1/2 inch canola or vegetable oil in a large non stick pan

aioli sauce:

simply whisk together 1/4 cup vegan mayo
1 tsp Cholula brand hot sauce (more if you like it spicier)
2 Tbs water
a few pinches of black pepper
pinch of salt
1.5 Tbs spicy brown mustard or Dijon mustard

Set up a breading station of a bowl with 1 cup of flour in it. In a second bowl, whisk together 1 cup of flour with 1 cup of water (this acts as the egg to make the panko stick to the pickles). In a third, flat casserole dish, add the panko bread crumb mixture. Dip the pickles first into the flour. Next, dip them into the flour/water mixture (only do 3 at a time) and then shake them off a little and put them into the panko mix. Coat the pickles all the way. Coat the rest of the pickles. Heat the non stick pan for 3 minutes over high heat. Add in the pickles, about 6 at a time and cook each side until golden. Drain the pickles on a foil lined cookie sheet with a cookie cooling rack placed on top (this will allow you to reheat the pickles if you want to serve them later without burning the bottom and they will also stay crisp). Sprinkle with a little salt and serve with the dipping sauce. Enjoy.

Yield: Serves 3-5

Simple Balsamic Vinaigrette (gluten free)

1/2 cup olive oil, 1/2 cup balsamic vinegar, pinch of salt, 1 tsp dijon mustard, 1 clove garlic, 2.5 Tbs sugar, 1 tsp minced shallot

Place all of the ingredients into a blender and blend until smooth and uniform. If it seems too thin, add a little more oil and blend again.

Yield: Serves 4-8

Stracciatella (gluten free)

Every bit as rich and satisfying as its egg and dairy filled counterpart. An Italian classic.

for the broth:
4 cups water whisked with
2.5 Tbs Better Than Bouillon
brand No Chicken
Base or Roasted Garlic Base
and 2 Tbs nutritional yeast,
1 cup flat leaf baby spinach
cut into thin strips and
salt and pepper to taste

for the egg mixture:
4 Tbs Follow Your Heart
brand Vegan
Egg whisked together
with 4 Tbs Follow
Your Heart brand
Parmesan Shreds
that you have chopped and
1 cup of cold water in a bowl

Heat the broth ingredients to a slow boil. Turn to medium and slowly add in the egg mixture from the bowl you whisked it up in, slowly pour it into the soup, stirring a little with a spoon (not a whisk) with each pour until all is poured out and you have many tiny little egg curds that have formed. Cook 1 more minute until soup is smooth and thickened and serve topped with more of the vegan parmesan.

Yield: Serves 3-4

Sriracha Sausage and Spinach Potato Hash

4 medium size red potatoes cut into small cubes
1/3 cup green bell peppers, medium diced
1/3 cup yellow onion, medium diced
2 cups raw baby spinach
2 cloves garlic, minced
1 Tbs olive oil
1/2 tsp each garlic powder, salt and chili powder
black pepper to taste
2 links of Beyond Meat brand Bratwurst links cut in half and then into half
moons, browned in a non stick pan for 3 minutes on high

Heat a large non stick skillet (make sure it is non stick or this recipe will not work) over high heat for 3 minutes. Add in the olive oil and then the potatoes. Let them sit 2 minutes before stirring them to get a little color on the bottom. Stir and let them sit another 2 minutes, repeat this process 2 more times, then add in the onions, pepper, garlic and salt. Let these cook 3 more minutes. Add the sausage, spinach, garlic powder and chili powder. Stir until the spinach is cooked. Taste for seasoning, add more if needed. Top with Sriracha. Enjoy.

Yield: Serves 4-5

Fried Pesto Stuffed Mushrooms

Crispy and decadent, a crowd favorite. Be sure to use panko bread crumbs for extra crunch.

2 packs white button mushrooms, pop the stems out carefully then set aside and 1 Pesto recipe from this book

Place the pesto in a ziploc bag and cut a small opening in one corner of the bag and pipe the pesto into the stemmed mushrooms. Dip the filled mushrooms individually into a bowl filled with 1 cup of flour, coat well, then into a second bowl filled with 1 cup of flour mixed with 1 cup of water (sort of like a pancake batter). Lastly dip them into a third and flat container like a cookie sheet or casserole dish filled with 2 cups of panko bread crumbs that you mix with 1 teaspoon garlic powder, 1/2 teaspoon dried oregano and 1 teaspoon salt. Once all the mushrooms are coated in bread crumbs, heat an inch of canola oil in a non stick pan over medium heat for 2 minutes then fry the coated mushrooms 2-3 mins per side until golden. Drain on a cookie cooling rack and sprinkle with a little salt after taking out of the oil.
aioli dip: whisk together 1 cup vegan mayo,
1/2 tablespoon red wine vinegar, salt to taste,
3 leaves fresh basil finely chopped and 1/4 cup water.

Yield: Serves 8-12

Sicilian Potato Salad (gluten free)

A tasty side on a warm summer day for a cookout or a picnic. It is much lighter than a traditional mayonaise based potato salad and has a lot of zing from the vinegar and olives. One of my favorites.

1 medium red onion sliced into
thin half moons, 2 Tbs capers rough chopped
1/2 cup grape tomatoes cut in half
1/3 cup pitted kalamata olives
cut in half
1/3 cup pitted green Sicilian
olives cut in half
2 Tbs each fresh chopped parsley and fresh basil
1/4 cup olive oil
whisked together with
1/4 cup red wine vinegar
1 Tbs sugar, 1/4 tsp
dried red pepper flakes and 1/2 tsp salt, 2 medium russet potatoes, peeled and cut into
1/4 inch thick half moons

Boil the potatoes until tender but not mushy, about 8 minutes. Drain but do not rinse them. Let them air cool and dry (this creates a nice texture). Mix all of the ingredients together and add more salt and pepper if needed.

Yield: Serves 3-4

Homemade Spicy Chili Garlic Biang Biang Noodles

These are chewy, spicy and delicious.

1 recipe of the Homemade Egg Past Dough from this book (on page 56), but replace the olive oil in the dough with sesame oil, 2 Tbs sliced scallions for garnish
spicy dressing: mix 1/2 Tbs of Better Than Bouillon brand roasted garlic Base with 2 Tbs hoisin sauce, 1 tsp hot chili garlic paste or sriracha (more if you want it spicier), 1 Tbs water and 1 Tbs sesame oil

Cut the dough into 4 pieces. Roll each ball about 1/4 inch thick and then run through a hand cranked pasta machine starting on level 1 of thickness and keep running it through until you get to the second to last thinness setting (if you have no pasta machine, just roll each piece as thin as you can get it, into about a 15 inch by 4 inch large rectangle. When each ball is rolled out flat, flour them a little and roll each one up from the shorter 4 inch side on up into a cigar shape. Make about 3 to 4 equal cuts into each roll across the 4 inch dough rolls and then unroll each cut piece into a large flat noodle. Boil a large pot of water and boil the noodles for 1 minute, using tongs to stir them around keep them from sticking. Drain and toss in the dressing. Plate and garnish with scallions. Enjoy. *Yield:* Serves 3-4

Garlic Mashed Potatoes (gluten free)

These are deliciously rich and creamy. A great side dish for any meal, including any holiday meal. They go well with the mushroom gravy recipe from this book.

4 medium size russet potatoes, peeled
and cut into medium chunks 6 Tbs
Earth Balance brand vegan butter

2 Tbs Tofutti sour cream
1-2 tsp salt
1/2 tsp black pepper 1/3 to 1/2 cup
plain rice milk, 4 cloves minced garlic
sauteed until browned in a little
olive oil and drained

Bring a large pot of water to a boil. Add in the potatoes and cook them until tender and soft, about 14 minutes. Drain them well and add in the rest of the ingredients. Use a potato masher to mash them or use an electric hand beater to give them a gorgeous and light whipped texture. Add a little more rice milk if they seem too dry. Enjoy.

Yield: Serves 4-8

Creamy Mushroom Soup

5 cups of white button mushrooms or cremini mushrooms, sliced
2 tsp minced fresh garlic
1/2 cup small diced onion
4 Tbs Earth Balance
brand buttery spread
1 Tbs Better Than Bouillon
brand No Chicken Base or Roasted Garlic Base
1 can of coconut milk
1/2 tsp garlic powder
salt and pepper to taste
1/2 tsp fresh thyme, minced
1-2 cups of plain rice milk or almond milk

Bring the buttery spread to a medium heat for 1 minute in a large pot, then add in the mushrooms, garlic and onions with a pinch of salt. Cook for 5 minutes until the mushrooms are soft. Transfer this cooked mixture to a blender and add in the rest of the ingredients besides the rice milk and thyme. Turn on the blender and slowly add the rice milk, a little at a time. When you get a medium thick, smooth consistency, add this back to the cooking pot and add the fresh thyme and add more buttery spread and salt and pepper if needed. Heat and enjoy.

Yield: Serves 3-4

Teriyaki Grilled Pineapple

1 peeled and cored pineapple cut into 1/4 inch thick rings
teriyaki marinade: 2 Tbs dark soy sauce, 2 Tbs regular soy sauce, 1 Tbs brown sugar, 1 Tbs rice vinegar, 1 Tbs vegetable oil and 3 Tbs water

 Place the pineapple slices into a flat glass sided dish and pour the marinade over it. Let it marinate 20 minutes. Heat a grill for 15 minutes on high. Add the marinated pineapple and grill each side 3 minutes. Enjoy. *Yield:* Serves 3-5

Arancini Italian Rice Balls

 Serve these with my Homemade Tomato Sauce recipe.

1 cup arborio risotto rice
2 cups water whisked together with 1.5 Tbs of Better Than Bouillon No Chicken Base, a pinch of salt + salt to taste, 1/2 container of Go Veggie brand vegan parmesan cheese and 1/4 cup nutritional yeast
1 box of panko bread crumbs mixed with 1 tsp salt, 1 tsp garlic powder and 1 tsp dried oregano, 3 cups flour
4 slices of Field Roast brand Chao Cheese stacked and cut into small cubes

 Heat the 2 cups of water/bouillon/nutritional yeast mixture with a pinch of salt. When boiling, add the arborio risotto rice. Stir, cover and turn to low and cook 15 to 20 minutes until cooked. Cool completely. Add to the cooked, cooled rice, 3/4 cup of flour and a little more salt to taste in a large bowl. If it seems too wet, add more flour. Taste for salt and cheesy flavor, it may need more salt, parm or nutritional yeast. Form into golf ball sized balls. Make a well with your thumb in each rice ball and place a cheese stack in the middle of each ball and then form back into a ball until they are all filled. Fill a bowl with 1 cup of flour and coat 5 balls at a time in flour. Take a second bowl and whisk together one cup of flour with one cup of water, whisk well and then dip the balls into this, and finally into a flat dish filled with the panko mixture. Coat the rice balls completely. Heat a 1/2 inch of vegetable oil in a non stick pan over medium heat for 3 minutes. When you can dip a rice ball into it and bubbles form around it, they are ready to cook. Cook 6 to 8 balls at a time and cook each side until golden. Enjoy.   Yield: Serves 6-10

Grilled Vegetables (gluten free)

This is a basic recipe that you can change according to your liking. For instance, you can add lemon pepper seasoning to it, or, if you want it to be Asian inspired, you can omit the cauliflower and add in sliced onions and long cut peeled carrots and use soy sauce and sesame oil for a marinade. I also have a great Chipotle Grilled Vegetable recipe in this book. If you like, you can add some Beyond Meat brand chopped up Bratwurst Sausage to this before grilling as well for more of an entree experience.

1/2 head cauliflower cut into medium size chunks
2 broccoli crowns chopped into medium size florets
1 head asparagus
1 medium diced green pepper
1 cup of button or
cremini mushrooms
3 Tbs olive oil
1/2 tsp salt,
pepper to taste
1/2 tsp oregano

Preheat grill on high for 15 minutes. Mix all ingredients together evenly in a large bowl. When grill is heated, carefully place a large piece of aluminum foil on the grates or use a grill pan with holes in it (if you use a grill pan with holes, keep it on the grill while the grill heats up). Pour vegetables onto the foil/ grill pan. Make an even layer and cook 8 minutes with the top down, stirring every few minutes until the vegetables char up nicely.

*You can also use eggplant, zucchini, yellow squash and red peppers, just dont use the foil or pan, they will grill and mark up well directly on the grates, make sure to spray the grates with non stick spray first.

Yield: Serves 4-6

Spicy Kidney Bean Shaved Brussel Sprout Avocado Salad (gluten free)

1 can of drained and washed kidney beans,
1 medium avocado peeled and diced medium, 3 Tbs smal diced green bell pepper, 4 medium sizes brussel sprouts grated on a box grater, 1/4 cup thinly sliced celery, 1 Tbs each chopped parsley and scallions
dressing: 1/4 cup of Louisiana brand or Franks brand hot sauce whisked together with 1 tsp sugar, 3 Tbs apple cider vinegar, 2 Tbs vegetable oil, salt and pepper to taste, 1/4 tsp dried oregano and 1/2 tsp garlic powder

Place all of the ingredients in a large bowl and carefully mix together. Allow it all to marinate 30 minutes in the fridge. Enjoy cold.   *Yield:* Serves 3-4

Sesame Crusted Pickle Fried Beets with Green Goddess Dressing

1 recipe of the Green Goddess Dressing from this book
2 medium sized beets, peeled and cut into 1/8 inch circles
2 cups plain flour, 2 cups panko bread crumbs, 1 cup water
1/4 cup sesame seeds, toasted or raw, 1/2 tsp dried basil, 1/4 tsp salt
1/3 cup rice wine vinegar or red wine vinegar
1/4 inch vegetable or canola oil to fry in a large non stick skillet

Heat 3 inches of water to a boil. Add in the beet slices and cook them 7 minutes. You want them tender but not mushy. Taste to make sure the texture is right. Drain and cool. Toss them in the vinegar and let them marinate in it for 15 minutes. In a flat glass dish, add in the panko bread crumbs, salt, basil and sesame seeds. Mix well. In a bowl, place 1 cup of the flour. In another bowl, whisk together the remaining cup of flour with the 1 cup of water (this will act as your egg to help the coating stick to the beets). Drain the beets from the vinegar and dip them into the plain flour first, then into the flour/water mix and finally into the bread crumb mixture. Coat them completely. Heat the oil in the non stick pan for 3 minutes on high. Dip a beet into the oil. If bubbles form, they are ready to fry. Cook each side about 2 minutes or until golden. Drain on a cooke rack that has been placed on top of a foil lined cookie sheet (this way you can heat them again later and they will stay crispy without burning on the bottom because they will be elevated). Sprinkle with a little salt and serve topped with the Green Goddess dressing. Enjoy.

Yield: Serves 2-4

Herb Stuffing

4 cups of a good quality white bread cut into small cubes and left out
overnight to harden up a bit
3 stalks celery minced
1 medium onion minced
2 Tbs chopped fresh dill
1/2 tsp dried oregano
1/2 tsp chopped fresh sage
2 cups water with 2 Tbs of Better Than Bouillon No Chicken Base
or Roasted Garlic Base dissolved into it
2 Tbs Earth Balance buttery spread
1 tsp garlic powder
salt and pepper to taste

   Heat the water, bouillon base, butter, garlic powder and oregano. When
boiling, turn off the heat and add the rest of the ingredients. Stir well to mix
and serve hot.

Yield: Serves 6-10

Cheesy Garlic Bread Sticks

1 ball of homemade dough from this book, risen (the dough recipe makes 2
balls of dough, but you will only use 1 here)
3 cloves of garlic, rough chopped
2 Tbs extra virgin olive oil
1/4 tsp salt
3 Tbs of Follow Your Heart brand vegan shredded parmesan cheese
1/4 cup of shredded Daiya brand Farmhouse Cheddar Block (you will
need to shred it yourself)
a few pinches of black pepper and dried basil

   Remove the risen dough from the bowl that it rose in but do not knead it
again. Place it on a floured cutting board and press onto a rectangle shape,
about 12 x 7 inches. Place it on a foil covered sheet pan that has been
sprayed with a little non stick spray. Cover it and let it rise for about an
hour and a half. Once risen, cut bread stick shapes about 3/4 of the way
down into the dough, but not all the way through (this will keep bubbles
from forming during baking). Heat the oven to 440 degrees. Mix the oil,
garlic and salt together and spread over the dough, pushing it in gently
with your fingers. Spread the cheeses, black pepper and basil over the top.
Bake for about 14 minutes or until golden. You can brown it under the
broiler if needed for 1 minute. Remove from oven and brush the edges
with a little more olive oil. Sprinkle with a little more salt. Cut it into
bread sticks and enjoy warm.

Yield: Serves 3-4

Smoked Paprika Pickled Beets (gluten free)

3 medium beets, peeled, sliced into 1/8 inch half moons, boiled 8 minutes or until just softened and completely cooled, 1/2 cup apple cider vinegar, 3/4 cup water, 3/4 tsp smoked paprika, 8 black peppercorns, 1 tsp salt and 1/3 cup sugar

Bring the vinegar, water, sugar and salt to a boil. Remove from heat and whisk in the peppercorns and the smoked paprika until mixed very well. Cool this mixture. Place the cooked cooled beets in a glass jar that has a tight fitting lid. Pour the vinegar brine mixture over them until covered. Place the lid on top and let sit about a day in the fridge until pickled. Enjoy. These will last about a month in the fridge.

Yield: Serves 6-8

Marinated Spinach, Mango, Mushroom and Kidney Bean Salad (gluten free

3/4 cup carrots, peeled and cut into thin slices on a bias angle
1 cup kidney beans, cooked and drained
5 cups baby spinach, raw
3/4 cup button or cremini mushrooms, quartered
1/3 cup small diced green peppers
1 ripe mango, peeled and medium diced , 1/2 cup zucchini, medium diced
marinade:
1/3 plus 2 Tbs cup red wine vinegar, 1 clove minced garli, pinch of salt
1/2 tsp minced fresh peeled ginger, 1 Tbs vegetable or olive oil
a few cracks of fresh black pepper, 2 Tbs sugar or pure maple syrup

Heat about 5 inches of water to a boil in a large pot. Drop in the carrots and mushrooms. Cook them 2 minutes and then add in the spinach and zucchini. Stir and cook 1 more minute. Drain and cool it in cold water. Once cool, drain it and gently squeeze all of the water from the spinach. **For the marinade,** simply whisk all of the marinade ingredients together. Mix the rest of the vegetables, beans and mango in a large bowl with the spinach mixture. Pour the marinade over the top, mix well and chill in the fridge 2 hours. Enjoy.

Yield: Serves 3-4

Baby Artichoke Tartlets

filling:

1 cup vegan mayo (I like soy free Vegenaise, but any will work)
1/2 container Tofutti vegan plain cream cheese
1/2 cup nutritional yeast
juice of half lemon
1/2 teaspoon salt
1 jar marinated artichokes drained

dough:

1 1/2 cup King Arthur flour
4 Tbs Earth Balance Vegan Soy Free Butter Spread
1/2 teaspoon salt
1/2 cup water

Place all the filling ingredients in a food processor until smooth.

Boil 3 cups of water and drop in a 1 1/2 cups of flat leaf baby spinach. Blanch 30 seconds, drain and cool, squeeze out excess water. Place in food processor with the dip for another 10 seconds.

For the dough, Mix together the flour and salt in a bowl. Add the butter and cut into the flour with a pastry cutter until small balls form. Add the water and mix gently until a dough forms. If too dry, add more water, if too wet, add flour. Fold the dough over on itself 8 times to create layers. Flour a cutting board roll out flat to about 1/8 inch thick and use a biscuit cutter to cut circles. Place each circle into a sprayed mini muffin tin. Press into tin. Spoon filling into each tartlet dough. Fill 3/4 way to the top of the dough.

Preheat oven to 400 and bake 12-15 minutes until browned and bubbling. Cool a few minutes and serve.

Yield: Serves 6-10

— 33 —

Bloody Mary (gluten free)

the juice from 1 wedge of lemon or lime
1/4 cup vodka
1/2 cup tomato juice
2 or 3 shakes of Tabasco sauce or more to taste
2 tsp grated horseradish
2 dashes of vegan worcestershire sauce
1 pinch of celery salt
1 pinch of black pepper
1/3 cup crushed ice or small ice cubes

   Place all of the ingredients together in a shaker and shake until mixed well. Pour into a glass and enjoy with a celery stalk and olives and baby pickles skewered on a tooth pick. You can add a little more horseradish, lime/ lemon juice or Tobasco sauce if you like it a little more tangy or spicy.

Yield: Makes 1 bloody mary

Avocado White Bean Hummus (gluten free)

2 cans of cooked cannellini
or navy beans, washed
and drained, 1/3 cup tahini
1 ripe avocado, peeled with the
pit removed
lemon juice from 2 fresh
lemons
1/2 tsp salt or to taste
a few Tbs of water
1 clove fresh garlic

   Place all of the ingredients into a food processor and process until smooth. Add more water if it seems dry. Taste it and see if it needs more flavor. If it does, add a little more lemon juice, salt or tahini. Enjoy.

Yield: Serves 4-8

Creamy Parmesan Pesto Salad Dressing (gluten free)

1/2 a batch of my Pesto recipe from this book
1 Tbs of Follow Your Heart brand parmesan shreds rough chopped with a knife
3/4 cup Follow Your Heart brand Vegenaise mayo (I like the soy free one)
1 Tbs red wine vinegar, pinch of salt, 1/2 tsp garlic powder, plain rice milk

   Place all of the ingredients in a bowl but not the rice milk. Slowly add in the rice milk a little at a time until you get the thickness you desire for pouring the dressing over a salad. Enjoy.

Yield: Serves 4-6

Homemade Cornbread

Goes great with my From Scratch Baked Beans, my Simple BBQ Baked Pinto Beans or my Chili recipe.

1.5 cups yellow cornmeal
1.5 cups King Arthur Flour
1 tsp baking powder
1 tsp baking soda
pinch of salt
1/4 cup sugar + 2 Tbs sugar
1/4 cup canola or vegetable oil + 2 Tbs canola or vegetable oil
1.5 cups plain club soda
2 Tbs of finely ground flax seed meal dissolved in 5 Tbs of hot water

Preheat the oven to 400 degrees. Spray an 9x9 inch pan, pyrex dish or 9 inch cast iron skillet with non stick spray. In a large bowl mix the cornmeal, flour, salt, baking powder, baking soda and sugar. Mix the rest of the ingredients in a measuring cup and add to the flour mixture. Whisk well and pour into the baking pan. Bake for 20-25 minutes or until golden and firm in the center. You can use the broiler to brown the top until beautifully golden. Once you remove it from the oven, brush the top with a little Earth Balance butter. Serve each piece topped with Earth Balance vegan butter.

Yield: Serves 4-6

Parmesan Crusted Avocado Fries or Coconut Crusted Avocado

These are so crisp, rich and buttery. I like to serve them with my Ranch
Dressing recipe from this book and some hot sauce. To make these coconut avocado,
simple replace the parmesan with 4 Tbs sweetened flaked coconut.

3 ripe avocados that have had the flesh carefully scooped out, pits removed and
sliced into 1/4 inch thick pieces long ways
2 cups panko bread crumbs mixed together with 3 Tbs of chopped Follow Your Heart
brand vegan parmesan cheese, 1/2 tsp salt, 1 tsp garlic powder and 1/2 tsp each
dried basil and dried oregano and placed in a flat glass sided baking dish
1 cup of flour placed in bowl
another 1 cup of flour whisked together with 1 cup of water until smooth
1/4 inch vegetable oil in a large non stick pan

Carefully coat the avocado slices in the plain flour. Next, dip them into the flour/
water mixture (this will act as the egg to make the panko stick to the slices). Finally,
dip them into the panko mixture and coat them completely. Heat the oil on high
for 3 minutes on the stove. Dip an avocado slice into the oil, if bubbles form around
it, they are ready to cook. Cook until golden on both sides, about 2 or 3 minutes
per side. Drain them on a cookie cooling rack placed on top of a sheet pan lined
with foil, this way you can crisp them again in the oven later without burning the
bottoms.

Indian Chickpea Broccoli Pakora Fritters (gluten free)

1 cup chickpea flour (available at health food stores and Indian markets)
1 cup freshly opened plain club soda/seltzer water
1/2 teaspoon salt
1/2 teaspoon garlic powder
2 cups medium cut broccoli florets with about an inch of the stem in tact
enough canola or vegetable oil to fill a non stick fry pan a 1/2 inch

Whisk together in a large bowl the chickpea flour, salt, garlic powder and
club soda. Set aside.

 Heat the non stick pan with the oil in it over medium high heat for about 3
minutes. Test to see if it is ready to fry by flicking some of the batter into it.
If it sizzles, it is ready. Dip the florets into the chickpea batter and then
immediately into the oil. Cook for 2 minutes, then flip broccoli and cook
another 2 minutes until golden. Drain on a cookie cooling rack on top of a
foil lined cookie sheet. These can be reheated and recrisped on the rack as
well thrown into the oven for a few minutes.

You can also use cauliflower for this recipe, it works wonderful as well.

Yield: Serves 4-8

Pommes Frites or "Fast Food Style French Fries" (gluten free)

These inolve a few simple steps to get a nice big plate of perfectly golden, crispy fries.

2 large russet potatoes, peeled, with the sides cut off of them so they look like a large rectangle
2 inches of canola or vegetable oil
salt to taste
3 cups cold water

Cut each of the peeled potatoes lengthwise into about 4 or 5 long, flat rectangles about 1/8 of an inch thick, and then cut each of those rectangles into long matchsticks. They will be about 4 or 5 inches long and about 1/8 of an inch thick. When they are all cut, soak them in cold water for an hour. Drain the potatoes and dry them completely on paper towels. Make sure no water is on them at all or they will make the oil pop and hiss. Heat your oil to 300 degrees over medium high heat in a large non stick skillet. Drop in your fries. Cook them 6 minutes. Drain them on paper towels again (this is called blanching, they will not be cooked all the way here yet) and then raise the oil heat to 400 degrees. Add the fries back in once the oil has reached 400 degrees and this time cook them until golden, about 5 minutes or so. Drain them and sprinkle them with salt, and pepper, if you like pepper on your fries. Enjoy.

Yield: Serves 2-3

Garlic Sauteed Vegetables (gluten free)

3/4 cup each broccoli and cauliflower cut into bite size pieces, 1/2 cup quartered button mushrooms, 1/3 cup each asparagus cut into 1 inch pieces, red bell pepper and zucchini cut into bite size cubes, 3 cloves of rough chopped fresh garlic, 1 cup of raw baby spinach, 1 Tbs olive oil, 1/4 to 1/2 tsp salt and pepper

Heat a large non stick skillet for 3 minutes on high. Add in the olive oil and the broccoli, cauliflower, garlic and mushrooms with a pinch of salt and pepper. Allow them to sit in a flat layer for 30 seconds untouched. Stir them and cook another minute. Add in the zucchini and asparagus. Cook 2 more minutes. Add in the spinach and salt and pepper to taste. Cook 1 more minute. Enjoy. *Yield:* Serves 2-3

Italian Beans, Kale and Potato Soup (Minaste) (gluten Free)

This goes great with my Avocado BLT.

1 small can of tomato paste, 4 cups water, 1 bunch kale chopped
2 stalks celery medium diced, 3 cloves chopped garlic
2 peeled carrots cut into medium chunks, 1 onion diced into medium chunks
1 baking potato peeled and chopped into medium chunks, 1 can drained
kidney beans, 1/2 tsp red wine vinegar, 3/4 tsp salt. 1/2 tsp dried oregano
1/2 tsp dried basil, a few pinches dried red pepper flakes

Bring 1/4 cup water to a boil in a large soup pot. Add the carrots, onions, celery, garlic, potatoes and kale. Add a pinch of salt. Stir well for 4 minutes (I prefer this water saute method to avoid an oily film on top of the soup). Add the tomato paste, beans, water, dried herbs, vinegar and remaining salt. Stir all together well. Bring to a boil then cook over medium heat 15 minutes or until thickened and the potatoes are fully cooked. I like topping it with Follow Your Heart brand vegan parmesan cheese.
Yield: Serves 4-6

Spicy Smoked Paprika Garlic Cabbage
and Mushrooms (gluten free)

Cabbage and other cruciferous vegetables such as kale and brussel sprouts are among the healhiest to eat. Studies have shown them to have possible cancer fighting qualities to them, so eat as many as you can. This is even better topped with a little Tofutti brand sour cream.

3 cups of green cabbage medium diced
2 cups button mushrooms sliced
1 medium red onion medium diced
4 cloves fresh garlic chopped
1 tsp olive oil
1 tsp smoked paprika (make sure it is smoked and not plain or spicy)
1/4 tsp cayenne pepper (add more if you want it spicier)
1/2 tsp salt and a few pinches of black pepper
1 Tbs Earth Balance brand buttery spread

Heat a large non stick pan for 3 minutes on high. Add in the olive oil and then the cabbage, mushrooms, salt, black pepper and onions. Push them into an even layer and let it sit 3 minutes before stirring. Add in the garlic. Stir and cook another 5 minutes. Add in the paprika, Earth Balance, cayenne pepper and more salt if needed. This is great with a few pan seared Beyond Meat brand Italian or Bratwurst sausages.

Yield: Serves 3-5

Kale, Strawberry, Avocado, Olive and Black Bean Red Leaf Lettuce Salad

4 cups red leaf lettuce, washed and chopped
3 cups of kale that has been stemmed and chopped and then dropped in boiling water 3 minutes, drained
1/4 cup sliced cucumber
1/4 cup sliced red radish
12 of your favorite seedless
 olives, rough chopped
1/4 cup peeled and thinly sliced carrots
1 medium beet that has been peeled,
sliced into 1/8 inch thick half moons
and boiled 8 minutes, then cooled
1 medium avocado, peeled and diced
6 strawberries sliced
1/2 cup cooked black beans
3/4 cup extra firm tofu, diced and
 tossed with 1 Tbs
of soy sauce, 1/2 Tbs of sesame oil and 1/2 Tbs of sesame seeds
1 large roma tomato, diced

   Simply lay the chopped lettuce in a large salad bowl and arrange the ingredients on top like in the picture.

Yield: Serves 3-5

Orange Citrus Couscous with Chickpeas and Vegetables

   This is simple and has a great orange flavor and is full of vitamins from all of the vegetables.

1 cup plain couscous
3/4 cup water
3/4 cup orange juice
1/3 cup each small diced red bell peppers, fresh or frozen green peas, zucchini, red onion and carrots
3 Tbs chopped fresh parsley
1/2 cup cooked chickpeas

   Place the orange juice, water and a pinch of salt into a pot and bring to a boil. Place the couscous, beans and vegetables in a large bowl. Pour the hot orange juice mixture over the couscous. Cover the couscous with plastic wrap or a bowl for 5 minutes. Remove plastic or plate, add the parsley and fluff the couscous with a fork. Enjoy.

Yield: Serves 3-4

Falafel and Spinach Feta Salad with Tahini Dressing (gluten free)

1 recipe of the Falafel from this book that has been prepared and kept warm, 1/2 cup Follow Your Heart brand crumbled feta, 2 cups fresh baby spinach chopped, 1 cup chopped iceberg lettuce or baby greens salad mix, 1 large tomato cut into bite size pieces, 1/2 cup of cucumbers sliced thinly into half moons, 1/3 cup thinly sliced onions. 1/3 cup of kalamata olives or Sicilian olives
for the dressing: whisk 1/2 cup tahini with 1/4 cup of water, 1 tsp chopped parsley, 1/2 tsp garlic powder, 2 Tbs lemon juice, 1 Tbs olive oil, salt and pepper to taste, 1 tsp sugar

Simply mix the spinach and iceberg and lay them on a platter. Top them with the chopped vegetables, feta and falafel and then top with the dressing. *Yield:* Serves 2-3

Greek Feta Cucumber Salad (gluten free)

1/2 of a container of Follow Your Heart brand vegan feta crumbles
1 cup half moon sliced English cucumbers, 1/3 cup kalamata olives
1/3 cup thinly sliced white or red onion, 1/2 cup grape tomatoes cut in half
3/4 cup raw baby spinach cut into thin strips
for the dressing:
3 Tbs red wine vinegar, 1 Tbs olive oil
1/2 tsp sugar and 1/4 tsp dried oregano
pinch of salt and a pinch of dried red pepper flakes
1 tsp chopped fresh basil, 1/2 tsp chopped fresh chives
  For the dressing, mix the dressing ingredients together. Pour them over the rest of the ingredients in a large bowl. Mix well. Serve chilled.

Yield: Serves 3-5

Kale, Sun Dried Tomato, Mushroom and Marinated Artichoke Stuffed Bread

1 ball of homemade dough from
this book, risen
1 stemmed bunch of kale chopped
3 Tbs oil cured sun dried tomatoes
(the kind in a jar, not a bag)
1/2 cup marinated artichokes,
drained and roughly chopped
1 cup button mushrooms, sliced
2 cloves minced garlic,
salt, pepper, dried oregano to taste
1 tsp red wine vinegar,
1 tsp extra virgin olive oil

Heat a large pot of water. When boiling, add in the chopped kale. Cook 3 minutes, drain and cool completely. Make sure you squeeze all of the water out of the cooled, cooked kale. Set aside.

Heat a large non stick pan for 2 minutes over high heat, then add the olive oil, mushrooms and garlic. Cook 2 minutes then add the artichokes and sun dried tomatoes. Cook another minute then add the kale, vinegar, a few pinches of salt, pepper and oregano. Taste to make sure the flavor is good, if it is bland, add more salt or another small splash of vinegar. Cool this completely.

Remove the risen dough from the rising bowl. Do NOT re knead it, simple lay it on a floured cutting board from risen and gently push it into a rectangle shape. Take a rolling pin and finish rolling it into a large rectangle, about 14 by 10. Lay the cooled filling on the edge of the dough closest to you, long side ways. Roll the dough up and over the filling until you have a long log shape. Place on a cookie sheet that has been lined with foil, spray some non stick spray on the foil and place the stuffed dough on top. Cover with a towel and let it rise an hour.

Preheat the oven to 440 degrees. Brush the dough with a little olive oil and bake for 20 minutes or until golden. Pull it out of the oven and brush with a little more olive oil. Slice and serve warm.

Yield: Serves 4-6

Balsamic Grilled Cauliflower Steaks Topped With Green Goddess Dressing (gluten free)

1 large head of cauliflower cut across into 5 or 6 steaks (make sure to leave the bottom part of each steak on so that it stays in 1 piece when grilled)
1 recipe of the Green Goddess Dressing from this book
for the marinade:
whisk together 1/2 cup balsamic vinegar, 1/3 cup olive oil, 1/2 tsp garlic powder, 1/2 tsp dried red pepper flakes, 1/4 tsp dried basil, 1/2 tsp salt and 1 Tbs sugar

   Place the steaks in a large flat dish and pour the marinade over them. Let them marinate 1 hour. Heat a grill for 15 minutes on high, then spray with non stick spray and then grill each side of the steaks for 3 or 4 minutes. Remove from the grill and serve warm topped with the Green Goddess. Enjoy.

Yield: Serves 3-4

Miso Tahini Sauce

1/4 cup tahini
1 Tbs white or yellow miso
1 Tbs maple syrup, 1/2 Tbs soy sauce, 1 tsp rice vinegar
1 tsp grated fresh ginger
4 Tbs water or more to thin it out a little

Simply whisk all of the ingredients together. Enjoy.

Light and Crispy Vegetable Tempura

Club soda is the secret to a light crispy tempura. Do not make unless you have some on hand.

2 cups plain flour
1/2 cup cornstarch, 1/2 tsp salt, 1/2 tsp garlic powder
2 cups freshly opened plain club soda
vegetables of your choice, I find asparagus, carrots or peeled sweet potatoes cut into thin rounds or cauliflower florets work best
1/2 inch vegtable oil in a large skillet

Mix the flour with salt, cornstarch and garlic powder. Add club soda and whisk very fast until a pancake type batter forms.

Heat oil in a non stick frying pan for 3 minutes on medium high heat. Test if it is hot enough by flicking some batter into it, if bubbles form around it, it is ready to fry.

Dip each vegetable into the batter a few at a time and quickly but carefully place into the hot oil. Do not overcrowd pan, cook in batches if necessary. Cook each side until golden brown (3-4 minutes per side). Flip and cook the other side. Drain on a cookie cooling rack placed on a cookie sheet lined with foil. You can also cook ahead and reheat on the cookie rack/sheet set up. This will keep it from getting soggy when reheating. Serve with sweet and sour sauce, soy or teriyaki sauce.

Yield: Serves 6-8

Jalapeno Cheddar and Scallion Corn Muffins

1.5 cups yellow cornmeal
1.5 cups King Arthur brand flour
1 tsp baking powder
1 tsp baking soda
pinch of salt
1/4 cup sugar + 2 Tbs sugar
1/4 cup canola or vegetable oil + 2 Tbs canola or vegetable oil
1.5 cups plain club soda
2 Tbs of finely ground flax seed meal dissolved in 5 Tbs of hot water
1 cup of Daiya brand Farmhouse Block Cheddar, shredded yourself
1 small jalapeno pepper, minced, seeds removed first
1/3 cup sliced scallions

Preheat the oven to 400 degrees. Spray a muffin tin with non stick spray. In a large bowl mix the cornmeal, flour, salt, baking powder, jalapeno, cheddar, baking soda and sugar. Mix the rest of the ingredients in a measuring cup and add to the flour mixture. Whisk well and pour into the muffin tin, filling each one about 3/4 of the way full. Bake for 20-25 minutes or until golden and firm in the center. You can use the broiler to brown the top until beautifully golden. Once you remove them from the oven, brush the top with a little Earth Balance vegan butter. Serve each one spit open and warm, with Earth Balance vegan butter spread inside.

Yield: Makes about 14 muffins — 46 —

Spicy Korean Fire Noodles

3 cups of cooked ramen noodle discs, kept warm (available in Asian markets in the noodle isle) **for the sauce:** whisk together 1 tsp Better Than Bouillon brand Roasted Garlic Base or No Chicken Base, 2 Tbs water, 1 tsp dark soy sauce, 1 Tbs nutritional yeast, 1 Tbs hot chili paste (more if you want them spicier), 1 tsp rice vinegar, 2 Tbs minced scallions, 1 Tbs vegan oyster sauce, 1 Tbs sesame oil, 1/2 Tbs smoked paprika and 1 Tbs vegetable oil

Mix the sauce with the cooked noodles. Garnish with fresh scallions. *Yield:* Serves 2-3

Panzanella Salad

2 cups worth of the Crunchy Garlic Herb Crouton recipe from page 94, 3 medium size vine ripened tomatoes diced into medium size pieces, tossed with a pinch salt and placed in a colander with a bowl under it for 20 minutes to catch the juices, 1 cup English cucumbers cut unto 1/8 inch thin half moons, 1/3 cup thinly sliced onions, salt and pepper to taste, 1/4 cup chopped fresh basil
for the dressing: whisk together 1/3 cup red wine vinegar, 1/2 tsp dijon mustard, 3 Tbs olive oil, salt and pepper to taste and the juice from the strained tomatoes

Toss all of the ingredients together in a large bowl and serve chilled. *Yield:* Serves 3-4

Maple Tamari Tofu, Asparagus, Beet and Avocado Salad

4 cups chopped iceberg lettuce or mixed greens salad mix
1 medium beet that has been peeled, cut into 1/4 inch half moons and boiled 7 minutes and then cooled in ice water
1 medium bunch of asparagus with the hard bottoms cut off, dropped in boiling water for 1 minute and then cooled in ice water
1/4 cup carrots, peeled and cut into matchsticks
1 avocado, peeled and cut into half moons
1/2 cup cucumbers cut into half moons, 1/4 cup onions cut into half moons
3/4 block of extra firm tofu that has been frozen, thawed and had all of the water completely squeezed from the block with your hands, then cut it into cubes, 1 medium tomato, diced
2 Tbs tamari or soy sauce whisked together with 2 Tbs maple syrup and 1 tsp toasted sesame oil

Toss the thawed, drained and cubed tofu with the tamari/maple syrup and sesame oil mixture. Now, simply arrange the ingredients on top of the greens.

Yield: Serves 4-5

Zucchini Bread Muffins

Great as a side for chili or any soup since they are not overly sweet,
or even as a dessert with a little So Delicious brand Coco Whip on top.
You can also bake this as a loaf if you want in 2 different 9 inch loaf pans,
they will just take a little longer. I like to crack these open and spread some
Earth Balance brand buttery spread on them.

2 cups King Arthur brand flour
1/2 cup sugar and 1/2 cup brown sugar
1 tsp each baking powder and baking soda
1 tsp cinnamon, a pinch of salt
3/4 cup zucchini, grated and then squeeze all of the water out that you can
1 Tbs finely ground flax seed whisked together with 4 Tbs warm water
1/3 cup vegetable oil plus 2 Tbs vegetable oil and 1 tsp apple cider vinegar
1.5 cups freshly opened plain club soda plus 3 Tbs more of club soda

Spray a silicone non stick 12 muffin pan (I find the silicone ones easiest to
work with, the muffins pop right out when done) with non stick spray or line
an aluminum muffin tin with cupcake liners. Let the flax/water mixture sit 3
minutes in a large bowl and then add in the oil and apple cider vinegar.
Whisk together. In a different bowl, mix the flour, the 2 sugars, salt,
cinnamon, baking powder and baking soda. Add this into the flax and oil
bowl along with the zucchini. Whisk in the club soda. When you have a thick
and smooth batter, fill each tin or silicone half full with the batter. Heat the
oven to 375 degrees and then add in the muffins. Bake about 24 minutes or
until golden. Do not open the oven until at least 20 minutes, so that they will
not fall in the middle. I like to put them under the broiler for 2 more minutes
before taking out of the oven to brown the tops up nicely. Enjoy warm.

Yield: Makes 12 to 14 muffins

Chinese Mixed Vegetables in White Garlic Sauce

1 cup of broccolini or Chinese broccoli cut into 1 inch pieces, 1/3 cup each peeled sliced carrots and sliced button mushrooms, 1 cup cauliflower florets cut into bite size pieces, 1 cup bok choy cut into bite size pieces, 3 cloves garlic roughly chopped, 1/2 tsp minced fresh ginger, 1 tsp sesame oil **for the sauce:** 1 cup water whisked together with 1 Tbs Better Than Bouillon brand Roasted Garlic Base, 1/4 tsp garlic powder, 1 tsp soy sauce, 1 tsp sesame oil, 1 tsp sugar, 1 tsp rice vinegar, 1 Tbs vegan oyster sauce and 1.5 Tbs cornstarch

Heat a large non stick skillet for 3 minutes on high. Add in the tsp of sesame oil and then the garlic, ginger and all of the vegetables. Keep them in a flat layer for 1 minute to get some color on them. Stir them and cook another 3 minutes. stirring often. Whisk the sauce and pour it over the vegetables. When it thickens and glazes all of the vegetables, it is ready to serve. This is a delicious side dish or a light meal over rice. *Yield:* Serves 2-3

Mushroom Barley Soup with Butternut Squash

1 cup cooked barley, 3 cups sliced button or cremini mushrooms
1 cup of peeled butternut squash, diced small
3/4 cup peeled carrots cut into half moons, 3 stalks of celery cut into half moons, 1 small onion, diced, 1/4 tsp chopped fresh sage
1 Tbs fresh chopped dill, 5 cups of water with 3 Tbs of Better Than Bouillon brand No Chicken base or Roasted Garli Base and 2 Tbs of nutritional yeast whisked into it, salt and pepper to taste
Bring 1/4 cup of water to a boil in a large pot, add in the mushrooms, butternut squash, carrots, celery, onions, sage and dill (this water saute method cuts down on the fat and keeps a greasy film from forming on top of your soup). Stir around for 5 minutes. Add the water/bouillon mixture and the barley. Bring to a low boil for 3 minutes or until the squash is soft, season with salt and pepper. Serve hot.

Yield: Serves 3-4

Beet Avocado Salad with Lemon Pepper Chive Aioli (gluten free)

1 large ripe avocado, peeled, pit removed and sliced into 1/4 inch thick half moons
1 large beet, peeled and sliced into 1/4 inch thick half moons
pinch of salt
for the aioli:
1/4 cup vegan mayo whisked together with 1 tsp fresh chopped chives, a few small drops of red wine vinegar, 1/2 tsp lemon pepper seasoning and 2 Tbs of water

Bring 3 inches of water to a boil. Add in the beets. Cook them 8 minutes. Drain them and then cool them. Arrange them with the avocado slices and beets. Top with a little salt and pepper and then the sauce. Enjoy.

Yield: Serves 2-3

Hot and Sour Tofu, Cabbage and Eggplant Soup

1 block of tofu that has been frozen, thawed and had all the water squeezed from the block between your hands and cut into 1 inch matchsticks, 1 tsp each minced fresh garlic and ginger, 3 cups shredded green cabbage, 1 cup button mushrooms thinly sliced, 1 cup peeled carrots cut into 1 inch matchsticks, 2 cups Japanese eggplant cut into 1 inch strips, 1 Tbs sesame oil and 1/2 cup bamboo shoots **for the broth:** 5 cups water whisked together with 1.5 Tbs Better Than Bouillon brand roasted garlic base, 3 Tbs vegan oyster sauce, 2 Tbs rice vinegar, 1.5 Tbs sugar, 3 Tbs cornstarch, 2 Tbs hot chili garlic paste and 1 Tbs soy sauce

Heat a large non stick pan or pot for 3 minutes on high. Add in the sesame oil and the garlic, ginger, carrots, tofu, cabbage, eggplant, bamboo shoots and mushrooms. Add a pinch of salt. Cook it all together for 5 minutes, stirring often. Add in the whisked broth and stir for about one minute on high heat until thickened and cook one more minute. *Yield:* Serves 3-4

Potato Latkes

1.5 pounds russet potatoes,
1 small yellow onion, minced,
2 Tbs fresh parsley, minced, vegetble oil to fry,
1/4 cup flour, 1/2 tsp garlic powder, 1/2 tsp baking powder,
1/2 tsp salt or to taste, 1/2 tsp freshly ground black pepper

Peel and grate the potatoes. Set them in a bowl with a little salt. Squeeze out all of the water from the grated potatoes that you can. Drain out the water and add in the rest of the ingredients. Heat a large non stick pan with a thin layer of oil in it for 3 minutes. Add in 2 Tbs of the mixture and flatten it into a round shape, about 3 or 4 will fit in the pan at a time. Cook each side until golden, about 4 minutes per side. Drain and sprinkle with a little salt. Top with Tofutti brand sour cream or apple sauce and enjoy. You can warm these again on a cookie cooling rack that has been placed on a foil lined sheet pan in the oven for a few minutes at 375 degrees. Warming them this way will crisp up the top and bottom of the latkes witout burning the bottoms since they are elevated. *Yield:* Serves 3-6

Kalamata Olive and Artichoke Caper Bruschetta

3 medium tomatoes small diced, 1/4 tsp minced garlic, 1/2 tsp red wine vinegar, pinch of salt, 1/3 cup rough chopped marinated artichokes, 2 Tbs finely chopped onion, 5 finely sliced fresh basil leaves, 1 Tbs capers, 10 pitted rough chopped pitted kalamata olives

Mix all of the ingredients together and enjoy over grilled crostini bread, grilled tofu or over angel hair pasta. Add some Follow Your Heart brand shredded parmesan as a topping if desired.

Yield: Serves 3-4

Navy Bean Corn Chowder

2 cans of navy beans, drained and washed
1-2 cups plain rice milk
1.5 Tbs Better Than Bouillon brand No Chicken Base or Roasted Garlic Base
salt and pepper to taste
1/2 cup chopped onion, 1 tsp dried basil
1/4 cup chopped celery, 2 cloves minced garlic
1 cup of peeled, medium diced potato
1/4 cup small diced red bell pepper
1 cup plain canned corn, drained and rinsed
3 Tbs Earth Balance Soy Free Buttery Spread

Bring a few inches of water to a boil. Add in the peeled, diced potatoes and cook for 6 minutes. Drain and cool, set aside. In a blender or food processor, add in the beans, the No Chicken base and the dried basil. Start the blender or food processor and add in enough rice milk until you get a consistency a little bit thinner than pancake batter. Set aside.

In a large pot, heat the Earth Balance butter until melted and then add in the onions, celery, garlic, red peppers and cooked potatoes. Season with salt and pepper and stir around for about 3 minutes. Next, add in the white bean mixture from the blender/processor and then the corn. Stir until mixed well and cook over medium heat another 5 minutes. Stir in another Tbs of Earth Balance buttery spread and season with more salt and pepper if needed, enjoy warm.

Yield: Serves 4-6

Pork and Japanese Eggplant Gyoza Dumplings or Steamed Dumplings

for the dough: 1 1/2 cups of King Arthur brand flour, 1/2 tsp salt and 1/2 cup hot water
for the filling: 2 links of Beyond Meat brand Bratwurst with the skin removed by running them under warm water, 1/3 cup minced Japanese eggplant , 1/2 tsp each minced fresh ginger and garlic, 1 tsp soy sauce, 1 Tbs minced fresh scallions

 For the filling, heat a large non stick pan for 3 minutes on high. On one side of the pan, throw on the peeled sausages and on the other half, 1 tsp sesame oil, the garlic, ginger and eggplant. Break up the sausage and brown for 3 minutes, while stirring the eggplant, garlic and ginger at the same time. Now, stir it all together then add the scallions and soy sauce. Stir well. Remove from the pan and drain the grease off of the sausage mixture on a paper towel lined plate, dab a paper towel on top as well to remove the excess oil, then cool it. **For the dough,** add the hot water to the flour/salt mixure and knead until a smooth dough forms. Add a little more water if needed. Wrap it in plastic and let it chill in the freezer 25 minutes. On a lightly floured board, roll the dough very thin with a rolling pin. You can also use a pasta rolling machine and roll the dough to the second to last filling to flatten the dough as well. Take a wine glass and cut out circles. You can bunch the leftover dough up and roll out again for more circles. Brush around the edges of the circles with a small amount of water. Place a circle of dough in your hand and add about a 1/2 a tsp of the filling in the middle of each circle. Take one side of the circle and have it meet with the other side, pinching as they touch, so that it looks like a canolli. Now, make tiny folds, one at a time, on first the right side of the pinch, so that 3 tiny folds have been made, and then pinch it at the end. Repeat with the left side of the pinch. This takes some practice. If it seems too difficult, you can just seal them with a fork until you master the technique. **For steamed dumplings,** simply place them in a steamer on top of parchment paper that has been cut in a circle and had several small holes cut into it and steam 8 minutes and serve. **For gyoza,** heat a large non stick pan that has a lid for 2 minutes on high. Add in 1 Tbs vegetable oil and place each dumpling into the oil, with each dumpling standing on their flat bottom side in the oil. Turn the heat to medium. Cover the pan with the lid and cook about 2 minutes. Remove the lid and make sure the bottoms are browning but not burnt. Once they are golden on the bottom, add in about 5 Tbs of water and place the lid back on. Turn the heat back to high and let the water steam finish cooking the dumplings until the water is evaporated. Serve dipped in hot chili oil and or soy sauce.

Yield: Makes about 24 dumplings

Pasta Dough

This works well if you have a pasta rolling machine to make homemade ravioli, manicotti or fettuccine with the cutter attachment. I fill my ravioli with tofu ricotta or a pesto vegan beef filling. The semolina flour provides a gorgeous golden yellow color to the pasta without the use of eggs. I believe this to be the original way pasta was made in the old days, simple and delicious. Fresh pasta has a velvety texture and cooks in about 2 minutes, very quickly. Do not overcook.

3 cups semolina flour, 1 cup of very hot water
a pinch of salt, 1 Tbs olive oil

Mix the semolina flour with the salt. Place in a large mixing bowl. Mix the very hot water (this is important to make the dough stick together properly) with the olive oil and then pour into the flour. Knead quickly. If it seems way too dry add a little more water. When it comes together in a smooth ball, wrap in plastic wrap and refrigerate 2 hours before use.
Yield: Serving sizes depend on what you make

Chinese Flaky Scallion Pancakes

2 cups King Arthur brand flour
3/4 cup very hot water
1/2 tsp salt
sesame oil
vegetable oil for cooking
1.5 cups sliced scallions

Place the flour and salt in a large bowl. Mix in the hot water and stir with a wooden spoon until a loose dough forms. Transfer to a floured cutting board and knead into a smooth dough. Wrap in plastic wrap for 2 hours in the fridge. Divide the dough into 3 pieces. Roll each piece into a very thin, large rectangle, about 10 inches long by 6 inches wide. Heat 1 Tbs vegetable oil and 1 Tbs sesame oil for 1 minute. Add in 2 Tbs of flour, whisk well. Brush 1/3 of this on each pancake and then add 1/2 cup scallions, evenly distributed on the dough and top with a little salt. Roll the dough lengthwise into a long cigar shape, making sure to tuck the scallions into the roll so that they do not get pushed out. Once you have a long roll, shape this into a cinnamon roll shape, so that it looks like a coiled up snake. Place a little flour on this and roll into a thin 6 to 7 inch flat pancake (this entire rolling process creates layers in the finished product). Heat a large non stick pan filled with 2 Tbs of vegetable oil for 3 minutes. Cook each side about 3 to 4 minutes or until golden. Serve with soy sauce mixed with a little rice wine vinegar. *Yield:* Makes 3 pancakes

German Pretzel Buns

1 ball of dough recipe of the Basic Dough recipe from this book, risen (the dough recipe from the book makes 2 balls, but you will only use 1 here), coarse sea salt, water, 1/2 cup baking soda

Rip pieces of dough off of the risen ball of dough about the size of a one and a half golf balls. Roll them into balls with flat bottoms. Let them sit, covered with a warm towel for 25 minutes. Heat about 3 inches of water in a large non stick pan with the baking soda in the water. Heat your oven to 425 degrees. When the water is boiling, add in 5 buns at a time. Cook each side 1 minute and then flip them and cook another minute. Drain them and cook the rest of the buns in the water. Slash a cross pattern in the top of each bun and sprinkle with a tiny bit of salt. Place on a non stick sprayed parchment lined sheet pan and bake them for about 15 minutes or until golden. Remove from the oven and brush them with a little melted Earth Balance buttery spread. Enjoy. *Yield:* Makes about 10 buns

Crispy Fried Artichokes with Rosemary Balsamic Aioli

1.5 cups of canned and quartered non marinated artichokes
2 cups of flour, 1 cup water, 3 cups of panko bread crumbs, 1/2 tsp garlic powder
1/2 tsp salt, 1/2 tsp dried basil, 1 Tbs of Go Veggie brand vegan parmesan cheese
1/2 inch of vegetable oil in a large non stick skillet

for the aioli:

1/2 cup Vegenaise brand vegan mayo, 1 tsp balsamic vinegar
a pinch of two of fresh rosemary, minced, 2 to 4 Tbs of water, a pinch of salt

For the aioli sauce, whisk the ingredients together, adding a little water at a time, until you have a not too thick but not too thin sauce. Set aside. **For the artichokes**, mix the panko bread crumbs, salt, garlic powder, dried basil and parmesan and place them in a flat pan or glass dish with sides. In another flat dish, place 1 cup of the flour. In a bowl, whisk together the other 1 cup of flour with the 1 cup of water until it looks like a thin pancake batter (this will act as the egg so that the bread crumbs will stick). Working from left to right, dip the artichokes into the flour until coated, then the flour/water mixture and then into the bread crumb mixture until they are coated in the bread crumbs. Heat the oil over medium high heat for 3 or 4 minutes. Dip an artichoke in, if bubbles form, they are ready to cook. Cook each side of the artichokes about 2 minutes or until golden. Remove from the oil, drain and season with a pinch of salt. Serve warm with the aioli dip. If you make these in advance, you can re heat them and make them crispy again on a cookie cooling rack that has been placed on top of a foil lined cookie sheet in the oven at 375 for 10 minutes. This way, since they are elevated, the bottoms will not burn.

Yield: Serves 4-6

Watermelon Feta Salad with Mint Vinaigrette

1 pack of Violife brand feta cut into half inch cubes, 3 cups of peeled seedless watermelon cut into 1/2 inch cubes **for the vinaigrette:** blend in a blender 2 Tbs fresh mint, a pinch of salt, 1 tsp sugar, 3 Tbs vegetable oil, 1 Tbs water and 3 Tbs apple cider vinegar (add a tiny bit more water if it seems too thick)

Simply toss all of the ingredients together gently and serve chilled.

Yield: Serves 3-5

Garlic Sauteed Eggplant, Broccoli, Cauliflower and Kidney Beans (gluten free)

A ton of vitamins, minerals and fiber in this dish, along with great flavor.

1 cup each of broccoli, eggplant and cauliflower cut into bite size pieces, 1/3 cup thinly sliced leeks, 3 cloves rough chopped garlic, 1/2 cup asparagus cut into 1 inch pieces, 1.5 cups raw baby spinach, 3/4 cup cooked kidney beans, 1.5 tsp olive oil, 1/2 tsp salt and some black pepper to taste

Heat a large non stick pan for 3 minutes on high. Add in the olive oil and then all of the ingredients but not the spinach or beans. Push it all into a flat layer and let it sit for 1 minute not disturbed in order to get some nice color on the vegetables. After a minute, stir it and let it sit in a flat layer again for another minute. Now, add in the spinach and beans and stir well. Cook it all together 1 more minute until the spinach is wilted. Enjoy.

Yield: Serves 2-3

Potato, Mushroom and Broccoli Hash (gluten free)

3 large red potatoes cut into 1/2 inch squares
1/2 yellow onion medium diced, 1 medium green pepper large diced
1 cup broccoli and 1 cup sliced mushrooms both cut into bite sized pieces, blanched in boiling water one minute, then drained and cooled
2 Tbs extra virgin olive oil, 1 tsp salt, 1 tsp garlic powder
1/2 tsp dried oregano, 1 tsp chili powder, a few pinches of black pepper

Preheat oven to 385 degrees. Line a cookie sheet with foil, then parchment. In a large bowl, mix together the potatoes, onions, peppers, salt, garlic powder, black pepper, oregano, chili powder and olive oil. Coat well. Place on cookie sheet and bake until potatoes are getting browned, about 30 to 35 minutes. Remove from the oven and add the pre blanched broccoli and mushrooms. Stir well and add a pinch more of salt. Cook another 10 minutes in oven. Serve hot with ketchup or sriracha.

Yield: Serves 6-8

Spicy Mushroom and Onion Tofu Sambal Buns

1 risen ball of dough from the Basic Dough recipe from this book (the dough recipe makes 2 balls of dough, but you will only use 1 here), 2 Tbs toasted sesame seeds for topping **for the filling:** 1/2 tsp each rough chopped garlic and fresh ginger, 1 cup onion diced small, 2 cups of button mushrooms sliced thin, 1/2 tsp soy sauce, 1 tsp Sambal hot chili paste, a pinch of salt, 1 tsp sesame oil, 1 Tbs sliced scallions, 1/4 a recipe of the pan seared chewy tofu from this book, cut roughly into bite size chunks, 2 Tbs sweet chili sauce

Heat a large non stick pan for 2 minutes on high. Add in the oil and then the mushrooms and onions. Spread them flat and allow them to develop some color for a minute. Add a pinch of salt. Stir and allow to sit another minute. Stir and allow to sit 1 more minute. Add in the tofu, garlic and ginger. Cook it all together 2 more minutes. Add in the scallions, sweet chili sauce, Sambal and soy sauce. Stir well. Cool this mixture completely. Take your ball risen dough and cut it into about 12 to 14 golf ball sized pieces, but do not re knead the dough. Place them on a well floured board and push or roll each one into about a 4 inch circle. Place about 1.5 Tbs of the filling in the middle of each circle. Fold the edges up around the filling, sealing them at the bottom by pinching the dough together. Place them seam side down in a non stick sprayed non stick pan, make sure they are just barely touching one another (they will rise into each other and become extra soft). Allow them to rise, covered, for an hour. Brush the tops with a tiny bit of water and sprinkle the sesame seeds on top of each roll evenly. Heat the oven to 425 degrees and bake for about 17 minutes or until golden. You can brown them even more under the broiler for 1 minute, just watch them so they do not burn. Brush with a little sesame oil after they come out of the oven. Serve with my Beef and Broccoli. *Yield:* Serves 3-5

Vegan Egg Pasta Dough

1.5 cups King Arthur brand flour
2 Tbs Follow Your Heart brand
Vegan Egg powder, 1/4 tsp salt
1 tsp olive oil (if making Asian noodles,
use 1 tsp of sesame oil and no olive oil)
1/2-3/4 cup hot water

Mix the flour and salt in a large bowl. In a measuring cup, add in the Vegan Egg, olive oil and hot water. Mix well. Pour this into the flour in the bowl. Pull it all together into a dough ball with your hands. If it seems too dry, add a little more water, small amounts at a time. Knead the dough until smooth. Place in plastic wrap and keep in the fridge for 30 minutes. Roll this out with a pasta machine in the same manner as my semolina pasta dough recipe. *Yield:* Serves 2 to 4 people

Potato, Spinach and Mushroom Gratin Cassoulet

3 medium sized russet potatoes, peeled and sliced into 1/8 inch discs
3/4 cup button or cremini mushrooms, sliced
2 cups baby spinach, uncooked
1 clove garlic, minced
1/2 tsp dried oregano
1 tsp olive oil

sauce:
1 cup plain rice milk
1 cup water
2 Tbs Earth Balance soy
free buttery spread
1 tsp lemon juice
1 tsp salt or to taste
2 Tbs Go Veggie brand
vegan parmesan
1/3 cup flour
1 tsp garlic powder
1/2 package of Daiya
brand shredded
cheddar cheese
4 Tbs nutritional yeast

Boil a large pot of water. Place the sliced peeled potatoes in for 5 minutes, drain and cool completely, set aside.

Heat a non stick saute pan for 3 minutes, add the olive oil, mushrooms, garlic, oregano and a pinch of salt. Saute 2 minutes then add the spinach. Cook until the spinach is wilted. Set aside.

For the sauce, place all of the sauce ingredients, besides the cheese, in a sauce pan. Bring to a low boil, whisking constantly until it starts to thicken, this takes about 2 minutes. Add in the cheese and whisk constantly until it is melted into the sauce. Taste for flavor, it should be rich and smooth.

Heat the oven to 400 degrees. Spray an 8x8 glass baking dish with non stick spray. Mix the potatoes, spinach, mushrooms and sauce together, then place into the baking dish. Cover with foil and bake 45 minutes, uncover, sprinkle a little more vegan parmesan cheese on top and bake another 15 minutes. You can broil it for the last minute to brown it up nicely. Serve hot.

Yield: Serves 4-6

Creamy Polenta (gluten free)

2 cups of plain rice milk mixed with 1 cup of water
4 Tbs of Earth Balance buttery spread, 1 cup instant polenta
4 Tbs of Follow Your Heart brand
vegan parmesan cheese shreds
1 tsp salt and some pepper to taste, 1/2 tsp each dried basil and garlic powder

Bring the rice milk/water, dried basil, garlic powder and salt to a boil in a large pot. Slowly add in the polenta, whisking constantly. Turn the heat to medium. In about 2 minutes it will thicken. Be careful not to let the bubbling polenta burn you. Remove from heat and add in the butter and cheese. Stir well and add more salt if needed and some pepper. I like to serve this topped with my Savory Meatball recipe and homemade tomato sauce.   *Yield:* Serves 3-4

Italian Sweet and Sour Eggplant (gluten free)

This makes a quick and easy side dish for any meal in place of a traditional leafy green salad.

1 Tbs olive oil
1 medium red pepper medium diced, 1 small red onion medium diced
1/4 cup celery cut thin on an angle, 4 Tbs red wine vinegar mixed
together with 1 tsp olive oil and 3 Tbs sugar and
a pinch of salt, 1 medium eggplant cut into bite size chunks

Heat a large non stick pan on high for 3 minutes. Add in the Tbs of olive oil, then the eggplant, celery, onions and peppers. Cook 4 minutes or until the eggplant is softened. Stir often and then add in the red wine vinegar mixture. Cook 30 more seconds. Enjoy.

Yield: Serves 3-5

Kidney Bean and Leek Black Bean Kale Chili

This has so much flavor as well as being high in fiber and vitamins.

2.5 cups of your favorite homemade or store bought tomato sauce mixed with 2 Tbs ketchup, 1 Tbs of Louisiana brand or Franks brand hot sauce, 1 tsp liquid smoke and 1 tsp soy sauce
1 cup water
3/4 cup each cooked and drained black beans and kidney beans
1/2 cup small diced onions
1/3 cup small diced celery
1/3 cup small diced peeled carrots
1/2 cup green peppers diced small
2 cups of shredded stemmed kale
1/2 cup washed leeks sliced in thin half moons
1 tsp vegetable oil
3/4 a pack of Impossible brand ground
salt and pepper to taste
2 cloves minced garlic
2 Tbs fresh minced cilantro
spice mix: 1 Tbs chili powder, 1 tsp garlic powder, a few pinches of cayenne pepper (depending on how how you want it), 1 tsp smoked paprika, 1/2 tsp dried oregano and 1 tsp cumin powder

  Heat a large non stick skillet or Dutch oven for 2 minutes on high. Add in the oil and then the onions, garlic, celery, carrots, peppers and leeks. Stir 2 minutes. Add a pinch of salt and then the Impossible ground. Break it up with a spatula and cook 2 minutes. Add in the kale. Cook 2 more minutes and then add in the rest of the ingredients including the spice mix. Stir well and simmer 20 minutes on medium, stirring often. Add more water if too thick. Taste for flavor. Add salt, garlic powder or more hot sauce if needed or desired. Top with some Tofutti brand sour cream and shredded So Delicious brand cheddar jack if you want. Enjoy with my Homemade Corn Bread or Zucchini Muffin recipes from this book.

Yield: Serves 3-4

Spiced Green Pea and Potato Samosas

dough:
2 cups King Arthur brand flour mixed with 1 tsp salt
5 Tbs vegetable oil
1/2 to 3/4 cup water

filing:
1 large russet potato, peeled and rough chopped into chunks
1 tsp garam masala powder
1/2 tsp cumin powder
1/2 tsp garlic powder
1/4 cup chopped cilantro
1/2 tsp salt
a few pinches of cayenne pepper and black pepper to taste
2 Tbs Tofutti brand sour cream
1/3 cup thawed green peas or fresh cooked green peas

3/4 of an inch of vegetable oil in a non stick pan to fry them in

  For the dough, place the flour and salt in a large bowl. Add in the oil. Mix it with your fingers and then start adding in the water, a little at a time, until a dough forms, make sure it is not too dry. Knead it a minute and then wrap in plastic and place in the fridge. **For the filling,** boil the potato chunks for 12 minutes or until soft. Drain and mash with all of the ingredients. Taste for flavor. Add more salt if needed. Cool it down completely. Divide the dough into 6 equal sized pieces on a floured board. Roll each one into about an 8 inch thin circle. Cut each circle in half with a pizza cutter. Fold one side towards the center of the half circle and then the other side in as well, over the other folded in half, so it looks like an ice cream cone. Pinch a little so that it is sealed at the fold. Open the top part which is not sealed with your fingers and add in the filling, leaving enough room at the top to fold the dough over the filling at the opening. Push it down in there as far as you can. Fold it over and seal the top dough over the filling. Repeat with all the samosas. Heat the oil for 3 minutes on high. Dip a samosa in, if bubbles form, they are ready to fry. Cook about 6 at a time until each side is golden, about 3 minutes per side. Drain. Enjoy these dipped in a little tamarind sauce.

Yield: Makes 12 samosas

Rich and Creamy Potato Salad (gluten free)

3 russet potatoes peeled,
medium size diced
3 stalks celery minced
1/2 onion minced
2 Tbs chopped fresh
 dill, 4 Tbs
sweet relish, 1/2 tsp
garlic powder
4 Tbs vegan mayo
1 Tbs yellow mustard
1/2-1 tsp salt or to taste
few pinches black pepper

Bring a pot of water to a boil, add the diced potatoes. Cook until just soft, about 6-10 minutes. When soft, drain and cool completely on a sheet pan, do not cool them in cold water, let them air dry completely. This creates a delicious texture to the potatoes and is the secret to this potato salad. When cooled, add all of the ingredients in a large bowl. Stir carefully, if dry, add more vegan mayo and serve chilled. I like to mash this all together gently with a potato masher or a fork, very lightly, not to a mush, just until a few of the potatoes mash a bit. Stir again. This makes the potato salad extra creamy.

Yield: Serves 4-8

Sesame Five Spice Asian Roasted Red Potatoes (gluten free)

These make a nice side for any Asian style entree in place of rice for something a little different and equally as delicious.

4 cups of unpeeled medium diced red potatoes
3 Tbs of toasted sesame oil
1 teaspoon garlic powder
1 teaspoon salt
1 teaspoon Chinese five spice powder
1 Tbs toasted sesame seeds and 1 Tbs chopped scallions for garnish

Heat the oven to 400 degrees. In a large bowl, toss the potatoes, oil, garlic powder, five spice powder and salt together until mixed well. Pour them onto a large sheet pan that is lined with foil and topped with parchment paper. Roast them in the oven for about 35 minutes or until golden and softened but not mushy. Stir half way through the baking process. Remove from the oven and serve them topped with the toasted sesame seeds and scallions.

Yield: Serves 3-4

Homemade Crispy Chinese Scallion Oil Noodles

This recipe requires a hand cranked pasta machine. These have a great flavor.

for the noodles: mix 1 1/2 cups water with 1/2 tsp of salt and 1/2 cup of very hot water and knead until smooth **for the scallion oil and sauce:** 1 cup of green scallions tops cut into 1 inch pieces and then cut into matchsticks, 1/3 cup vegetable oil, 3 Tbs soy sauce, 2 Tbs dark soy sauce and 1 Tbs sugar

For the sauce, heat the vegetable oil for 3 minutes on medium high. Add in the scallions and cook until they start to brown, about 4 minutes. Remove the scallions and drain. Cool the oil off of the heat for 3 minutes and add in the soy sauces and sugar. Heat again and whisk until bubbling. Set aside. Chill the noodle dough 20 minutes in the freezer wrapped in plastic. Divide the dough into 4 equal sized pieces. Place the manual pasta machine on the widest setting. Flatten each piece as flat as you can get them with a rolling pin. Roll each piece, one at a time, through the widest setting on the pasta machine. Go to the next level thinner level on the machine and roll them through. Repeat this process with each sheet of dough until you get to the 3rd to last setting on your machine. Take the spaghetti cutter on the machine and run each flattened sheet through, one at a time. Flour the cut sheets well so that they do not stick. When each are cut into noodles, cook them for 1 minute in boiling water and then drain. Mix them with the scallion oil/soy sauce mixture. Taste, add more soy sauce if needed. Top with some of the fried scallions and a few fresh ones. Enjoy. *Yield:* Serves 3-4

Nordic Root Vegetable Soup

3/4 pearled barley, 3/4 cup leeks sliced into thin half moons (use only the white thick bottom part of the leek for this), 1/3 cup thin sliced celery, 1/3 cup diced yellow onion, 3/4 cup peeled and medium diced celeriac root (you can use turnips if you can not find celeriac root), 3/4 cup peeled parsnips cut into half moons
2 cloves garlic rough chopped, 1 tsp fresh thyme minced
2 cups fresh baby spinach rough chopped
2 Tbs Earth Balance brand buttery spread
4 cups of water whisked together with 2 Tbs of Better Than Bouillon brand Roasted Garlic Base or No Chicken Base and 2 Tbs nutritional yeast, salt and pepper to taste

Heat a large Dutch oven or a large heavy bottomed pot for 3 minutes on high. Add in the Earth Balance and then add in the onions, leeks, parsnips, celeriac root, celery, garlic, thyme and a pinch of salt and pepper. Stir around for 3 minutes and then add in the barley and the broth/water mixture. Bring to a boil and simmer on a low boil for 15 minutes or until the barley is cooked. Stir in the chopped baby spinach and cook 1 more minute. Enjoy. Yield: Serves 3-4

Sesame Seed Braided Golden Bread

one ball of dough from this book, risen (the dough
recipe from this book makes two balls of dough but
you will only use one ball here)
1 Tbs sesame seeds, a little water to brush the bread with

Remove the risen dough carefully from the bowl it has risen in.
Do not punch it down or knead it again. Take a sharp knife
and cut the ball of risen dough into 3 equal sized pieces. On a
lightly floured board, roll each piece out with your hands into
three 14 inches ropes. Place the ropes next to each other about
a half inch apart. Fold each rope over the middle rope,
alternating the left and right rope. Always fold each rope over
the center rope, forming a braid. It is similar to braiding hair.
When you reach the end, lightly pinch the top and bottom ends
together. Place the braid on a foil lined sheet pan that has been
brushed with a little olive oil. Cover the dough with a moist
towel or a large bread dough cover or even just a box. Let it rise
for 2 hours. Preheat the oven to 425 degrees. Brush the bread
with a little water to help the seeds stick and then sprinkle the
top with the sesame seeds. Bake 15-20 minutes or until golden
brown. Let cool 5 minutes and enjoy.

Yield: Serves 3-5

Simple Vegetable Stock (gluten free)

This works great for any soup or to use for rice, instead of cooking it in
plain water, for extra flavor. If you are using this for Pho or an Asian soup,
you can add in some fresh, peeled and sliced ginger and replace the salt
with soy sauce.

12 cups of water, 4 medium carrrots, roughly chopped
2 bay leaves, 8 button mushrooms cut in half, 10 whole black peppercorns
5 celery stalks, rough chopped
2 medium onions, peeled and roughly chopped
1/2 bunch of scallions, left whole, 1 tsp salt
4 cloves garlic, chopped in half, 1 tsp garlic powder, 2 Tbs nutritional yeast

Simply place all of the ingredients into a large pot. Bring to a boil and boil
for 20 minutes. Drain out all of the vegetables, bay leaves and peppercorns
and save the broth. Enjoy.

Yield: Makes about 9 cups of broth once cooked down.

Sesame Ginger Grilled Leeks

2 large leeks with the green tops cut off and the the the bottom roots cut off
marinade: whisk together 1/3 cup soy sauce, 2 Tbs sesame oil, 2 Tbs water, 1 tsp sugar, 1/4 tsp garlic powder, 1 tsp rice vinegar and 1 tsp minced fresh ginger

  Bring a large pot of water to a boil. Cut the leeks into about 5 inch pieces but keep them whole. Boil them about 10 minutes. Drain them, squeeeze them dry, cool them and cut them in half from top to bottom. Marinate them in the marinade for 15 minutes while you heat the grill. Grill them flat side down about 3 minutes and then flip and grill the other side 3 minutes. Enjoy. Yield: Makes about 8 leek halves

Fried Farfalle Bowtie Pasta with Avocado Basil Aioli

36 large store bought farfalle bowtie pastas, cooked 6 minutes until al dente and then cooled in cold water or you can make homemade farfalle , but only cook that in the water 2 minutes before cooling and coating (I used my homemade farfalle or the fpicture)
1 1/2 cups panko bread crumbs mixed with 1/2 tsp each salt, garlic powder, Go Veggie brand vegan parmesan and dried basil
1 1/2 cups plain flour
3/4 cup water
for the aioli:
1/3 of a medium sized peeled avocado mixed with 1/2 cup Vegenaise brand vegan mayo, 1 tsp lemon juice, a pinch of salt, 1/2 a clove of garlic, 3 fresh basil leaves and 3 Tbs of water blended in a blender until smooth, you can add a little more water if too thick

  In a bowl, place 3/4 cup of the flour. In another bowl, whisk the other 3/4 cup flour with 3/4 cup water (this will act as the egg to make the bread crumbs stick to the pasta) and in a final flat glass sided dish, place the panko mixture in a flat, even layer. Dip each piece of the cooked pasta into the plain flour first, then the flour/water mixture and lastly into the panko mixture. Coat each piece well with the panko. Heat about 1/2 an inch of vegetable oil in a large non stick skillet for 3 minutes on high. Dip a piece of the coated pasta into it, if bubbles form, they are ready to cook. Cook each side until golden brown. Drain them on a cookie cooling rack that has been placed on a foil lined cookie sheet (this way you can crisp and heat them again later in the oven if you are not eating them immediately without burning the bottom since they will be elevated). Serve them with the aioli dipping sauce.

*If you make these withe homemade pasta, use my Homemade Farfalle pasta recipe from this book.

Yield: Serves 4-5

Silky Smooth Butternut Squash Bisque

I serve this with my Pesto Bread Stick recipe from this book with some Follow Your Heart Brand soft block Mozzarella shredded myself and melted on top of the bread sticks. They are great for dipping into this deliciously elegant soup.

1 medium butternut squash, peeled and cut into small cubes
1/2 a medium onion, diced
2 cloves of garlic, minced
1 tsp fresh chopped dill
1 Tbs Better Than Bouillon
brand No Chicken base or Roasted Garlic Base
1 can coconut milk
1/4 cup water or rice milk
3 Tbs Soy Free Earth
Balance Buttery Spread
1 tsp sugar
salt and pepper to taste
1/2 tsp garlic powder

Heat a large pot with water. When boiling, add in the butternut cubes. As these cook (they take about 15 minutes) heat a pan with 2 Tbs of the Earth Balance Buttery Spread, add in the garlic and onions. Cook about 3 minutes until just browned. Add in the fresh dill. Set aside.

Drain the squash, place it in a tall pot and add in the rest of the butter, salt and pepper, coconut milk, water or the rice milk, onions, garlic, dill, garlic powder, the No Chicken base and sugar. Take a hand blender and puree until silky smooth. If it is bland, add more dill, salt, sugar, pepper or garlic powder. If you have no hand blender, use a normal blender. Garnish with toasted green salted pumpkin seeds and scallions. Serve hot.

Yield: Serves 3-5

Carrot Raisin Salad (gluten free)

4 cups peeled and shredded carrots
1 cup of raisins
1/3 cup Vegenaise brand vegan mayo
2 Tbs sugar
pinch of salt
1 tsp fresh lemon juice

Simply mix all of the ingredients together and chill in the fridge. Enjoy.

Yield: Serves 4-8

Dill Pickle Rotini Pasta Salad

1 cooked and cooled box of Ronzoni brand Smart Taste rotini pasta (this pasta tastes like regular white pasta but has more fiber), 1 cup of dill pickles cut into half inch cubes, 1 Tbs fresh dill, 1/2 cup of So Delicious brand cheddar jack shreds or 5 slices of Follow Your Heart brand American slices that you shred yourself **for the dressing:** whisk together 1/2 cup soy free Veganaise brand mayo, 2 Tbs Tofutti brand sour cream. 2 Tbs apple cider vinegar, 1/2 tsp salt or to taste, 1 Tbs fresh lemon juice, 1/4 tsp black pepper and 2 Tbs water

   Simply mix the whisked dressing with the rest of the ingredients and chill in the fridge. Add more salt or vinegar if needed or more mayo of you want it creamier. If the pickles are organic, you can stir a little dill pickle juice into the pasta salad too, since the organic brine has no chemicals inside of it. Enjoy. *Yield:* Serves 3-6

Wonton Soup

1 recipe of the Szechuan Dumplings from this book (page 74), prepared but uncooked and without the sauce **for the broth:** 18 cups of water, 3 stalks of celery rough chopped, 10 cremini mushrooms or button mushrooms cut in half, 4 dried shitake mushrooms, 1 onion cut in half and peeled, 1/4 tsp salt, 1 tsp soy sauce, 8 individual stalks of scallions, 1 tsp Better Than Bouillon brand Roasted Garlic Base and 2 Tbs vegan oyster sauce

   Bring the broth ingredients to a boil in a large pot. Allow it all to simmer on a medium boil for about 40 minutes. Drain out the vegetables out with a strainer but keep the broth. Press the vegetables in the strainer with another large bowl to extract all of the liquid from them. Add the broth back to the pan and taste. If it seems too salty, add a little water to it. It should be rich and flavorful. Bring the broth back to a boil and drop in your uncooked dumplings. Let them boil about 3 minutes and then serve the soup topped with a few fresh sliced scallions and sliced baby bok choy. *Yield:* Serves 3-4

Beet, Kale and Cabbage Borscht

3 medium beets, peeled and shredded (a food processor works well for this or you can cut the peeled beet into thin matchsticks) 1 bunch of kale with stems removed, chopped roughly, 2 ribs of celery cut into half moons, 2 medium carrots, peeled and cut into half moons, 2 medium red potatoes, peeled and cut into medium chunks, 1 Tbs chopped fresh dill 1 medium onion, diced small, 2 cups of diced green cabbage 2 cloves garlic, minced, 3 Tbs tomato paste, 1 tsp red wine vinegar, 4 cups water with 2 Tbs of Better Than Bouillon brand No Chicken Base or Roasted Garlic Base whisked into it and salt and pepper to taste, 1 tsp olive oil, Tofutti brand vegan sour cream

   In a large, non stick pot, heat the olive oil for 2 minutes on high heat. Add in the onions, potatoes, beets, celery, garlic, carrots and cabbage. Saute, stirring often, for 8 minutes. Add a little salt and pepper. Add in the water/bouillon mixture, kale, tomato paste, dill and vinegar. Simmer on medium heat for 15 minutes until the kale is cooked and the potatoes are tender. Serve hot topped with a little of the sour cream and more chopped fresh dill. Enjoy. *Yield:* Serves 3-5

Spicy Sausage Kale, Spinach and Mushrooms (gluten free)

1 bunch of kale, stems removed and chopped medium fine, 3 cups raw baby spinach, 1 cup sliced button mushrooms, 2 cloves rough chopped garlic, 1/4 tsp dried red pepper flakes, 1/2 tsp salt, 1 tsp red wine vinegar and 2 links of Beyond Meat brand spicy Italian sausages cut into half moons

Heat a large non stick pan on high for 3 minutes. Add in 1 tsp of olive oil and then the mushrooms, kale, sausage and garlic. Let them sit in a flat layer for 1 minute and then add in the spinach. Cook it all together 3 minutes and add in the salt, vinegar and red pepper flakes. Cook 30 more seconds. Serve warm.

Yield: Serves 3-4

Smoky Oyster Mushroom and Scallion Cream Cheese Fried Wontons

24 eggless wonton wrappers or you can use the dough from my Gyoza recipe rolled out and cut into squares to fill and shape however you like
1 container of Tofutti brand vegan cream cheese, softened
2 Tbs minced scallions, 1/2 cup raw oyster mushrooms chopped
1/2 tsp toasted sesame oil, 1 tsp minced garlic, 1/2 tsp liquid smoke
salt and pepper to taste, vegetable oil or canola oil to fry

Heat a non stick pan for 3 minutes over high heat. Add in the sesame oil, mushrooms and garlic. Saute for 3 minutes. Add the liquid smoke and a pinch of salt to taste. Cool the mushrooms (drain off any excess liquid), chop them finely and add them to the cream cheese and the scallions. Mix until uniform. Add salt and pepper to taste. Lay out the wrappers in a diamond shape with the tips facing you. Add about a Tbs of the filling in the middle of each wonton. Brush the edges of the wontons with water and then fold the edge nearest to you over the filling into triangle shapes. Pinch the edges shut tightly with your fingers. It may take a little more water on your fingers to get them sealed tight. Heat about a half inch of canola or vegetable oil in a non stick pan for about 3 minutes. Add in the filled wontons, about 7 at a time. Cook each side for about 2 minutes until golden. Drain and serve hot.

Yield: Serves 4-6

Creamy Smoky Black Bean Butternut Soup

2 cans of black beans drained and washed,
1.5 cups of water, 3 Tbs chopped scallions, 1/2 tsp soy sauce,
1 Tbs Better Than Bouillon brand No Chicken Base, 2 Tbs of your favorite salsa,
salt to taste, 3/4 cup peeled and small diced butternut squash, 1 medium onion
diced, 2 minced garlic cloves, 1/3 cup small diced red bell pepper, 1/3 cup small
diced celery, 2 Tbs Tofutti brand sour cream, a few chopped scallions and
avocado for an optional garnish
spice mix: 1/2 tsp smoked paprika, 1 tsp ground cumin, 1 tsp garlic powder,
1/4 tsp dried oregano and 1/2 tsp chili powder, cayenne pepper to
taste depending on how spicy you want it

  Place only 1 can of the black beans in a blender with the 3 Tbs scallions, soy
sauce, the salsa, the Better Than Bouillon base, a pinch of salt and the water.
Blend until smooth. Set aside. Heat 1/4 cup of water in a large pan until
boiling. Add in the celery, onions, butternut, red peppers and garlic (this
water saute keeps the fat amount down plus does not leave a film at the top of
the soup). Stir around for 3 minutes with a pinch of salt added. Add in the
black beans, the spices and the blended black beans as well. Cook on medium
for about 10 minutes on medium. Stir often. Add in the sour cream and cook
another minute. Top with the optional chopped scallions and avocado.

Yield: Serves 3-4

Homemade From Scratch Sofrito Smoky Pinto Beans

for the sofrito: 1 medium white onion, peeled and rough chopped
6 cloves garlic, peeled, 1 large green pepper, seeded and rough chopped
1 ají dulce pepper (you can use a small red bell pepper if you can not find one, or a
half of a seeded jalapeno pepper if you want it a little spicy), 1 bunch cilantro, cleaned

  Simply place all of these ingredients into a food processor and pulse until mixed but
not soupy. You want it slightly thick. Add in a little water if needed to get it mixing.
You will use about 3 Tbs of the sofrito, you can freeze the rest for later use.

for the beans:
1 pound of dried pinto beans, washed and soaked in 10 cups of water overnight or 8
hours, 1 cup plain tomato sauce
spice mix: 1 tsp each dried cumin, garlic powder and 1/2 tsp each smoked paprika,
salt, dried oregano and chili powder
1/2 Tbs Better Than Bouillon brand No Chicken Base or Roasted Garlic Base

  Drain the soaked beans and cover them about 4 inches over the top of them with
water in a large pot. Bring it to a boil and boil about 1 hour or until the beans are
tender. In a saute pan, add in a tsp of olive oil. Bring it to a high heat for 2 mintes
and add in 3 Tbs of the sofrito. Cook for 3 minutes, stirring often. Keep about 1 inch
of the cooking water over the top of the cooked beans and add in the sofrito, tomato
sauce, the No Chicken Base and spices. You can add more water if it seems too thick.
Taste for flavor. If it needs more salt or spices, add them now. Enjoy. Yield: Serves 5-7

Stuffed Twice Baked Broccoli and Cheddar Potatoes (gluten free)

6 large russet potatoes
3/4 cup Daiya brand cheddar cheese Farm House Block, shredded (you will need to shred it yourself)
6 Tbs vegan mayo
half a bunch chopped scallions
1/2 tsp garlic powder
1 tsp salt
(to your liking)
1/2 tsp black pepper
1.5 cups steamed and cooled broccoli florets

Cover potatoes individually with foil and bake at 450 until soft, about 45 minutes to an hour or microwave until cooked.

When cooked, remove from foil carefully and cut in half length wise. Carefully scoop out the flesh into a large bowl, making sure to leave enough room in the potato skin to refill and making sure it is a sturdy vessel to hold the filling. In other words, don't scoop too close to the potato skin. When all are scooped, add the rest of the ingredients into the bowl (except for the empty potato vessels). Mash well with a potato masher. If it is too dry, add a little rice milk. Taste for salt and flavor. It should be rich and delicious. Adjust seasoning if needed.

Preheat oven to 400 degrees. Scoop the filling evenly into 6-8 of the potato halves. Discard or eat the remaining potato halves. Bake for 20 minutes or until browned and a slight crust is formed on top in a non stick spray sprayed casserole dish. You can place them under the broiler the last 2 minutes to brown them up perfectly.

Yield: Serves 4-8

Crostini
Grilled
Bread

Crostini is basically just grilled bread with whatever toppings you like. I prefer them with topped with my Pesto, Bruschetta or my Sun Dried Tomato Basil Dip recipes.

day old leftover bread, sliced thinly into however many pieces you can cut it into (my Golden Sesame Braided Loaf is great), 1 clove of garlic, olive oil for brushing each slice

Heat a grill for about 10 minutes on high. Brush each slice with a little olive oil. Grill each side for 1 to 2 minutes. As soon as they come off of the grill, rub each one with a clove of fresh garlic and top with your topping or toppings. Enjoy.

Yield: Depends on the amount of bread you have left

Barley Black Bean Vegetable Salad in Smoked Paprika Maple Dijon Dressing

2.5 cups water mixed with 1 Tbs Better Than Bouillon brand No Chicken
Base or their Roasted Garlic Base, 1/3 cup finely chopped onions
3 Tbs oil cured sun dried tomatoes (make sure they are the ones packed in oil in a jar) chopped finely, 2 Tbs capers
1/3 cup peeled and small diced carrots, 1/3 cup finely diced green peppers
1/3 cup finely diced celery, 3/4 cup cooked black beans, 1 cup pearl barley
for the dressing:
3 Tbs dijon mustard
1 tsp smoked paprika
2 Tbs olive oil
1 tsp red wine vinegar
2 Tbs maple syrup
2 Tbs water
1 tsp each minced parsley and chives
salt and pepper to taste

For the dressing, simple whisk the dressing ingredients together and set aside.
Bring a pot of the water and bouillon base to a boil. Add in the barley and cook on low heat, covered for 15 minutes. Cool it completely and then mix this with the vegetables, beans and dressing. Enjoy cold.

Yield: Serves 4-6

Garlic Butter Grilled Cabbage Wedges (gluten free)

3/4 cup Earth Balance brand buttery spread melted with 3 cloves of minced garlic on the stove top together for 1 minute with 1/4 tsp salt and a pinch of black pepper
1 small full green cabbage cut in half and then each half cut into quarters with a little of the stem left on each quarter so they stay held together

Place the melted garlic butter in a blender and blend until the garlic is completely infused into the buttery spread. Place the 8 quarters of cabbage in a steamer and steam for 5- 6 minutes until softened but not mushy. Heat a grill on high for 10 minutes. Brush each side of the cabbage quarters with the garlic butter. Grill each side about 3 minutes, brushing with a little of the remaining garlic butter while grilling. Enjoy. *Yield:* Serves 3-4

Vinegar Cherry Pepper, Sicilian Olive, Red Radish, Kidney Bean and Toasted Green Pumpkin Seed Salad (gluten free)

4 cups baby romaine lettuce mix, 1/2 cup pitted Sicilian olives
1/2 cup peeled and sliced into 1/8 inch half moon raw beets, boiled
7 minutes and cooled
1/2 cup small Italian vinegar marinated cherry peppers
3 red radishes, sliced thin, 1/4 cup sliced cucumbers
1/2 cup chopped fresh broccoli, dropped in boiling water for 1 minute,
then drained and cooled, 1 medium roma tomato, chopped
1/4 cup carrots, peeled and cut into matchsticks
2 Tbs salted green pumpkin seeds, 1/2 cup cooked red kidney beans

 Simply lay down the salad greens in a large salad bowl and arrange your ingredients however you like.

Yield: Serves 4-5

Creamed Corn

2 cups canned corn, drained and washed, 2 Tbs sugar
1/4 cup melted Earth Balance brand buttery spread
salt and pepper to taste, 2 Tbs plain flour, 1 1/4 cup plain rice milk

  Heat the melted butter in a large pot. Add in the corn, stir to coat and then add in the flour. Coat the corn in the flour and then add the rest of the ingredients. Stir together well. Heat until thickened. Enjoy warm.

Yield: Serves 6-8

Coconut Milk Steamed Rice (gluten free)

 This is a personal favorite, simple and delicious. I like to serve this with the vegetable tempura recipe from this book and a crispy iceberg salad.

2 cups white jasmine rice
2 cups coconut milk
2.5 cups water
1/2 cup sugar
pinch of salt

 Whisk together the coconut milk, water, sugar and salt in a large pot. Bring to a boil. Add rice, stir and cover pot and turn heat to medium low. Cook 25 to 35 minutes until the liquid is absorbed. Leave top on after cooking for 10 more minutes. I like to stir in some cooked black beans to this rice right when it is finished cooking.

Yield: Serves 4-6

Ranch Dressing (gluten free)

1 cup of Soy Free Vegenaise brand vegan mayo
1 Tbs red wine vinegar or apple cider vinegar
1/4 tsp garlic powder, 3 Tbs water, 1 tsp fresh chopped dill
2 Tbs finely chopped scallions, pinch of salt

 Simply whisk all of the ingredients together. If it seems too thick, add a little more water. Goes great with my Buffalo Tofu recipe or over any salad.

Yield: Serves 8-10

Italian Beans and Greens Soup

This simple, hearty soup goes well with vegan cold cut sandwiches on a soft Italian roll or a bowl of brown rice topped with my Gomasio sesame topping from this book.

1 bunch of kale, stemmed, chopped and boiled 6 minutes, drained and cooled
1 medium onion diced small
3 cloves garlic minced
2 cans cannellini beans, washed and drained
2 Tbs nutritional yeast
3 Tbs Better Than Bouillon No Chicken Base dissolved in 5 cups water
salt to taste
a few pinches dried red pepper flakes if you like it spicy

Squeeze all the excess water out of the kale. Heat 1/4 cup water in a large soup pot, when hot, add the garlic and onions. Saute for 2 minutes (I prefer this water saute method because it does not leave a film of oil on top of the finished soup). Next, add the rest of ingredients and stir well. Simmer 10 minutes. Adjust seasoning with salt if needed. Serve hot.

Yield: Serves 4-8

Homemade Szechuan Dumplings

for the dough: 1 1/2 cups of King Arthur brand flour, 1/2 tsp salt and 1/2 cup hot water
for the filling: mix 1/2 cup of Impossible brand ground with 1 tsp soy sauce, 1 Tbs minced scallions and 1/2 tsp each minced fresh ginger and fresh garlic
for the sauce: mix 1.5 Tbs of hot chili oil with 1 Tbs minced scallions, 1.5 Tbs soy sauce and 1/2 tsp rice vinegar

For the dough, add the hot water to the flour/salt mixure and knead until a smooth dough forms. Add a little more water if needed. Wrap it in plastic and let it chill in the freezer 25 minutes. On a lightly floured board, roll the dough very thin with a rolling pin. You can also use a pasta rolling machine to flatten the dough to the second to last setting. Take a pizza cutter and cut out square shapes about 2 by 2 inches. You can bunch the leftover dough up and roll out again for more squares. Brush around the edges of the squares with a small amount of water. Add about a 1/2 a tsp of the filling in the middle of each square. Touch the top and bottom opposite corners together. Squeeze the sides together, sealing them, so that you have a triangle shaped dumpling. Push your finger up gently into the bottom of the filling, making a small dent in the filling, and then bring the 2 bottom corners of the dumpling together. It will look like a tortellini. Repeat until all are filled and boil them for about 2 minutes in water until they float. Drain and toss in the sauce. *Yield:* 34 dumplings

Nacho Cheese Sauce

1 1/2 cups water, 3/4 cup nutritional yeast
1 teaspoon garlic powder, 1 1/2 cups plain rice milk
1 teaspoon lemon juice, 3 Tbs Follow Your Heart brand shredded parmesan
1/3 cup flour, 1/2 to 1 tsp salt
2 Tbs Earth Balance brand butery spread , 1 package Daiya brand shredded cheddar

Mix all ingredients except the cheese and heat over medium heat until butter is melted into the mixture, whisking every few seconds. Add one package of cheddar cheese shreds and the parmesan and whisk all until the cheese is completely melted, take about 3 minutes. Add a little more salt or nutritional yeast if needed and serve over nachos or macaroni.

Yield: Seves 8-10

Onion Naan Bread

Make the sponge dough recipe, **as follows:**

Mix 1.5 cups of King Arthur Flour with 1 tsp of active dry yeast that has been dissolved in 1.25 cups of water. Cover and set aside 8 hours. It will have risen after this time. This is called a sponge.

After 8 hours, add to this 1 large minced onion and 1 teaspoon of yeast that has been dissolved in 2 tablespoons of water and one teaspoon canola oil. Let stand 5 minutes, then add another 1.5 cups of flour that has been mixed with a teaspoon of salt and a teaspoon of baking powder. Knead well, adding extra flour if too wet. When you get a uniform ball, let rise for 1 hour covered.

Place ball onto a floured surface. Cut into 2 equal size pieces but be sure not to deflate them too much or they will be hard to roll out.

Heat a long flat electric griddle. Roll each piece out to about 12 inches long and 3 inches wide. Spray the griddle and place 2 naan at a time on the griddle. Cook about 4 minutes per side or until browned on both sides. *If you have no electric griddle, just heat a large non stick pan for a few minutes on medium and split the 12 inch naan doughs in half into 6 inch long pieces and cook 2 at a time in the non stick pan for a few minutes per side until browned and cooked.

Yield: Serves 6-10

Spinach Artichoke Dip (gluten free)

 Great for dipping veggies into or topping my Mushroom Scallion Crusted Eggplant or Tofu Cutlets into or my Pumpkin Seed Crusted Vegan Chicken Cutlets into, all from this book.

1 cup vegan mayo (I like soy free Vegenaise, but any will work)
1/2 container Tofutti vegan plain cream cheese
1/2 cup nutritional yeast
1 Tbs lemon juice
1/2 teaspoon salt
2 jars marinated artichokes drained

 Place all ingredients in a food processor, process one minute.

 Boil 3 cups of water and drop in 3 cups of fresh flat leaf baby spinach. Blanch 30 seconds, drain and cool, squeeze out excess water. This is a very important step, squeezing the water from the spinach, or the dip will be watery. Place the cooked spinach in food processor with the dip for process for another 10 seconds.

 Spoon spread into a sprayed 9x9 inch casserole dish. Bake at 375 degrees 15-20 minutes or until bubbly.

Yield: Serves 6-8

Spinach Pasta Dough

You can use this dough for homemade ravioli, tortellini, spaghetti, agnolotti, fettuccine, linguine etc as long as you have a hand crank manual pasta machine.

1.5 cups semolina flour, 1/2 cup very hot water, 1 Tbs olive oil, 1.5 cups raw baby spinach, 1/2 tsp salt

Bring a pot of water to a boil. Drop in the spinach for 1 minute. Drain, cool and completely squeeze all of the liquid out of the cooked spinach. Place the spinach in a blender with the hot water until blended and the water is green. Place the semolina flour and salt in a bowl. Add in the oil and the spinach water mixture. Knead very fast. If it seems too dry, add a little more water. Knead until smooth. Store wrapped tightly in plastic or a plastic bag in the fridge until ready to roll into whatever shape you like.

Yield: Serves 3-4

Sun Dried Tomato Basil Dip (gluten free)

Strictly use the oil cured sun dried tomatoes, for any recipe involving sun dried tomatoes. They come in a jar packed in oil.

1 container Tofutti brand plain cream cheese
3 Tbs vegan mayo, 1/3 cup nutritional yeast
1 tsp lemon juice
5 leaves basil rough chopped
1/2 teaspoon salt
3 Tbs drained oil
cured sun dried tomatoes (the kind packed in oil, not the bagged ones)

Place all ingredients in a food processor for one minute. Serve cold.

Yield: Serves 6-8

Duchess Potatoes (gluten free)

2 lbs russet potatoes, peeled and cut into 1/2 inch chunks
2 Tbs Earth Balance brand buttery spread
2 Tbs Tofutti brand sour cream
1 tsp fresh minced chives
1/2 tsp salt, pepper to taste
1/2 tsp garlic powder

Boil the potatoes for 9 minutes or until fork tender. Drain them well and mix with the other ingredients. Mash this mix with a potato masher until it looks like mashed potatoes. Taste for salt, add more if needed. Place this mixture into a piping bag with a fluted tip (if you have no bag or tip, just spoon them into a plastic zip bag with a bottom corner cut off to make a homemade piping bag). On a parchment lined cookie sheet, pipe each one into a 2 inch wide and about 1.5 inch high mound, moving the bag around in a circle as you pipe. Bake for 15 minutes in a 420 degree oven and then place them under the broiler for 2 minutes until browned on top. Enjoy.

Yield: Makes about 10-12 potatoes

Antipasto Salad

1 cup chopped cauliflower
1/2 cup peeled and sliced carrots
3/4 cup marinated artichokes
1/2 cup lupini beans
1/2 cup pepperoncini
1 package of Yves brand vegan salami
3/4 cup Violife or Follow Your Heart brand Mozzarella, cut into cubes
1/2 cup of your favorite olives

Bring 2 inches of water to a boil. Drop in the cauliflower and carrots. Cook for 3 minutes and then drain and cool. Toss them in a little bit of red wine vinegar, salt, and red pepper flakes. Arrange your antipasto plate however you like. You can also use roasted red peppers, marinated mushrooms, crostini, vegetables or anything you like for this dish.

Yield: Serves 4-6

Baked Steak Fries (gluten free)

These go great with veggie burgers, jumbo vegan hot dogs or a vegan crispy chicken fillet sandwich.

4 medium sized russet potatoes cut in half, then each half into 3 wedges that can lay down steady on the skin side
3 Tbs canola, vegetable or olive oil
1 tsp garlic powder
1 tsp chili powder
1 tsp salt

Prehat oven to 385 degrees. Line a cookie sheet with foil, then parchment paper, and then top with a pan length cookie cooling rack (this prevents the bottoms from burning and the parchment paper stops the oil that drips during baking from burning). Mix all ingredients together well with gloved hands. Place each potato laying on its skin side on the cookie rack/sheet pan concoction. Bake for 35-45 minutes until the potatoes are soft. You can also top these with the nacho cheese sauce recipe for cheese fries.

Yield: Serves 6-8

Japanese Ginger Dressing

I designed this recipe to mimick the dressing that comes on salads at many Japanese restaurants. It is very simple and tasty.

1 cup peeled and rough chopped carrots
1.5 Tbs fresh grated ginger
3/4 cup vegetable oil
5 Tbs water
1/3 cup minced white onion
1/4 cup soy sauce
1 to 2 Tbs sugar (use 2 if you like it a little sweeter)
1 clove peeled garlic
1/2 cup rice vinegar
1/2 tsp salt or to taste

   Simply place all of the ingredients in a blender and blend until slightly chunky or silky smooth, however you prefer. Restaurants usually serve it slightly chunky, but I like mine smooth. Enjoy over a crispy and simple Iceberg lettuce salad.

Yield: Serves 6-8

Balsamic Tofu, Broccoli, Kidney Bean, Mango and Monterey Jack Mixed Greens Salad

4 cups of mixed salad greens
1/2 cup sliced cucumbers
3/4 cup cooked kidney beans
1 small beet, peeled, cubed and boiled 8 minutes and cooled
1 large tomato, diced
1 ripe mango, peeled and cubed
1/2 block of extra firm tofu, cubed and tossed in 1 teaspoon olive oil that has been mixed with 1 Tbs balsamic vinegar, 1/2 tsp soy sauce, a pinch of black pepper and 1/4 tsp dried basil
1/4 cup peeled carrots cut into matchsticks
1/2 cup Daiya brand Monterey Jack, chopped however you like
1/2 cup broccoli, chopped, dropped in boiling water for 30 seconds, drained and cooled

   Place the salad greens in the bottom of a large bowl and topped with the rest of the ingredients. Enjoy.

Yield: Serves 3-5

Basic Dough for Bread, Pizza, Rolls, Focaccia

This dough is great for pizza, stromboli, garlic rolls, focaccia, fried dough, stuffed bread etc. This recipe makes 2 balls of dough. It takes a few hours for the starter to mature but the end results are far better than a standard dough recipe. King Arthur Flour provides the best results.

Mix 2.5 cups of King Arthur Flour, sifted, with 1 tsp of active dry yeast that has been dissolved in 2 cups of water. Cover and set aside 8 hours. It will have risen after this time. This is called a sponge.

After 8 hours, dissolve 1 teaspoon of yeast into 3 tablespoons of water mixed in with 1/2 tablespoon extra virgin olive oil. Pour this into the sponge and squeeze all together with your hands.

Mix 2.5 more cups of sifted flour with a half teaspoon of salt. Do NOT forget to add the salt. Add this to the sponge/oil /yeast mixture. Knead well. If it is too wet, add more flour. When it comes together into a nice uniform dough ball, split in half and place each ball into a seperate floured bowl. Cover. Allow to rise 1 hour, then punch down, re knead and let it rise one more hour before use. They can sit in the fridge 2 to 4 days. I find a slow rise in the fridge gives a better texture as well.

Yield: Makes 2 balls of dough

Basil Pesto (gluten free)

I use toasted green
 pumpkin
 seeds instead
 of pine nuts
 due to a nut allergy.

3 cups fresh basil leaves
3 Tbs salted green
pumpkin seeds
1 tsp salt
1 clove garlic
2 Tbs nutritional yeast
extra virgin olive oil

Place all of the ingredients in the food processor besides the olive oil. Start the processor and slowly add in the olive oil until it forms into a pesto. Taste it, if it is is bland, add more nutritional yeast or a little more salt. Enjoy.

Yield: Serves 3-5

Spicy Chipotle Dressed Green Beans (gluten free)

3 cups fresh green beans snipped and cleaned
1/2 cup of chipotle
vinaigrette, the full **recipe follows:**
1 small can chipotle peppers
1/2 cup red wine vinegar
1/2 cup sugar
pinch of salt
1/4 cup canola oil
1 clove garlic
1/4 cup water

*You will only use half of this chipotle sauce, save the other half for a marinade or dressing.

Put all ingredients except the green beans in a food processor and process until smooth. Bring a large pot of water to a boil, add the green beans. Cook until just tender, about 5 minutes. Drain well and toss with 1/2 cup of the chipotle vinaigrette and a pinch or two of salt.

Yield: Serves 4-6

Beyond Simple Low Fat Vegetable Soup (gluten free)

3 cups of your favorite vegan tomato sauce (I like a tomato basil flavored one)
1.5 cups water
1 Tbs ketchup
1 tsp garlic powder
1/2 tsp red wine vinegar
1 tsp salt
1/2 cup thinly sliced asparagus
1 medium onion diced small
1 green pepper diced small
2 carrots diced small
1 zucchini diced small
1 cup frozen peas

Bring all the ingredients except for the zucchini and peas to a slow boil in a large pot, stirring often. Turn down to medium heat, simmer 10 minutes, do not overcook the vegetables. Add the zucchini and peas, simmer 2 more minutes and it's done. If it is too thick for your liking, add more water.

*You can add cooked alphabet noodle pasta to this to make alphabet soup, just add a little more water to the soup because the pasta will eat up a lot of the liquid, add 3/4 cup of cooked pasta at most.

Yield: Serves 6-8

Fire Roasted Tomato Salsa

2 containers of grape tomatoes, cut in half
1 tsp olive oil
2 Tbs each fresh cilantro and fresh scallions
minced jalapeno to taste (depending on how spicy you like it)
1 to 2 Tbs lime juice
a few pinches of salt
2 Tbs minced red onion
1 clove minced garlic
1/3 cup plain tomato sauce

Heat the oven to 400 degrees. Mix the tomatoes with the olive oil and a few pinches of salt and pepper. Roast the tomatoes on a parchment paper lined sheet pan for 12 to 15 minutes. Remove, cool and then pulse in a food processor until chopped but not pureed. Place them in a large bowl with the rest of the ingredients. Stir in a little lime juice at a time until you get the flavor you desire. Add salt and pepper if needed. Enjoy.

Yield: Serves 3-4

Butter Lettuce and Bacon Cobb Salad with Creamy Black Pepper and Chive Dressing

There are a few different types of vegan bacon you can use for this on the market, you can also use any type of vegan cheese you like, you can buy some shredded and some you can shred them yourself. Daiya brand havarti jack flavor or monterey jack flavors work great. The homemade crouton recipe from this book is very delicious, but if you need to save time, you can use some store bought vegan ones.

4 cups butter lettuce, chopped
3/4 a block of extra firm silken tofu (make sure it is silken tofu and that it is the kind that comes in a cardboard box, it has a hard boiled egg type texture) cut into medium size cubes
1/2 tsp black salt (it has an egg flavor, available in spice stores and health food stores)
1/2 a pack of Lightlife brand Bacon, pulled apart and each side brushed with a little vegetable oil, cooked 10 minutes at 400 degrees on a parchment paper lined cookie sheet until crisp, flip half way through
1 avocado, peeled and medium diced
1 large tomato, diced, 3 Tbs Kalamata olives, pitted
1/2 cup So Delicious brand Cheddar Jack Cheese
1/2 cup cucumber, peeled and cut into half moons
1/4 cup onions cut into half moons
1/2 cup cooked kidney beans or chickpeas
1 recipe of my Crunchy Garlic Herb Crouton recipe from this book (optional)

For the dressing, whisk together 3/4 cup Soy Free Vegenaise with 1/2 tsp salt, 1/2 tsp black pepper, 1 Tbs fresh chopped chives, 1 tsp red wine vinegar and 1/4-1/2 cup water until you have a medium thick dressing, add more water if it is too thick. Chill it in the fridge. Make sure the bacon has crisped in the oven. Let the bacon cool and crumble it with you hands. Set aside. Carefully toss the tofu in 1 tsp oil and the black salt. You can add more black salt if you want more of an egg flavor. Place the lettuce in the bottom of a large bowl and top with all of the ingredients and as much dressing as you like.

Yield: Serves 3-4

Buttered Sage Baked Spaghetti Squash (gluten free)

Spaghetti squash is a delicious winter squash. It has the look of spaghetti strands after baked, is high in fiber and has a nice mellow flavor.

1 large spaghetti squash, carefully sliced in half lengthwise with the seeds dug out with a spoon
3 Tbs Soy Free Earth Balance vegan butter
1/4 tsp garlic powder
1/2 tsp chopped fresh sage
salt and pepper to taste

Preheat oven to 385 degrees. Place a half inch of water in a glass casserole dish. Lay each half of the squash face down in the water/casserole dish. Bake for about 35-50 minutes until completely soft to the touch. Remove from oven and let cool for a few minutes. Hold the squash with a hand towel and with a fork, scrape the inside of the squash from top to bottom into a bowl. It will look like spaghetti. When both halves are done, add the remaining ingredients. Stir together. Taste taste it and serve hot.

Yield: Serves 4-8

Simple White or Brown Rice in a Rice Cooker (gluten free)

This is a basic water to rice ratio for cooking white or brown rice for side dishes or to serve beneath stir fries or stews etc. A rice cooker is a great investment, they are only about $30 dollars for a digital one. Make sure to pick one up that has a white and brown rice button as well as a "warm" button, which is great to keep soups, stews or the rice hot for as long as needed. As a rule of thumb, 2 cups of uncooked rice will serve about 4 or 5 people. I use jasmine rice for most dishes, it has the best flavor, but for Indian dishes, use basmati rice, it has a great nutty and fragrant flavor.

for white rice: Simply always add 1/2 cup more water than rice, for instance, for 1 cup of white rice, use 1 1/2 cups of water, or for 2 cups of white rice, use 2 1/2 cups of water, etc. **for brown rice:** Double the amount of water to brown rice plus about 3 Tbs of water, for instance, use 1 cup of brown rice to 2 cups of water plus 3 Tbs of water, etc. Brown rice takes longer to cook and requires more liquid. Always add a few pinches of salt to white or brown rice before cooking. I like short grain brown rice the best, it has a great flavor and texture.

Spicy Olive Oil Grilled Eggplant (gluten free)

2 long Japanese eggplant, each one quartered and then cut in half so that each piece is about 6 inches long, 1/2 tsp salt, a pinch of black pepper, 1 tsp red pepper flakes, 1/3 cup olive oil

Heat a grill on high for 15 minutes. Mix all of the ingredients together and grill each side about 3 minutes. Enjoy. *Yield*: Serves 3-4

Caramelized Onion Green Beans (gluten free)

4 cups of fresh snipped green beans
1 large red onion, peeled and chopped in half and then sliced into half moons, 1/2 Tbs extra virgin olive oil, 1/2 tsp garlic powder
salt and pepper to taste

Heat a non stick pan over medium heat for 2 minutes until hot. Add the olive oil next and then the onions. Let the onions sit 30 seconds before stirring, this helps them brown. Add a pinch of salt and then stir around for a few minutes until browned. Remove from heat and set aside. Bring 6 cups of water to a boil. Add the green beans and boil about 4 minutes or until tender, not soggy. Drain and mix with the onions, salt, pepper, garlic powder and a Tbs of olive oil. Mix.
Yield: Serves 4-8

Buffalo Balsamic Tofu Salad Topper (gluten free)

1 block of extra firm tofu that has been frozen, thawed and had all of the water sqeezed out of the thawed block (this leaves you with a delicious, chewy tofu block) and cut into small cubes, 2 Tbs balsamic vinegar
1/3 cup Franks Red Hot brand hot sauce, 1/4 tsp garlic powder and a pinch of salt

Simply toss all of the ingredients together and serve over any salad. *Yield:* Serves 2-3

Hearts of Palm Avocado Ceviche (gluten free)

2 cans of hearts of palm, drained, washed and cut into small bite size pieces, 2 roma tomatoes, seeded and diced small, 1/3 cup each small diced red onion and fresh cilantro, juice of 1.5 limes, 1 small fresh sliver of habanero pepper minced (use more if you want it spicier), 1 avocado peeled and diced small, 1 small clove of garlic minced, a few pinches of salt and pepper, 2 Tbs olive oil

Simply mix all of the ingredients together and allow it to chill in the fridge at least 30 minutes. *Yield:* Serves 3-5

Chipotle Grilled Vegetables (gluten free)

1/2 a recipe of the chipotle marinade from this book
1 eggplant, sliced lengthwise into 1/4 inch thick slices
2 red and 2 green peppers with the flat sides cut off to grill
2 large zucchini, sliced lengthwise into 1/4 inch thick slices

Toss the vegetables in the marinade and marinate for 30 minutes. Heat the grill for 15 minutes. Spray with non stick spray and lay the vegetables on the grates. Grill each side for about 4 minutes. Spoon a little of the marinade over the finished vegetables and serve warm.

Yield: Serves 3-5

Rich and Creamy Tahini Goddess Dressing

1/2 cup tahini
2 Tbs olive oil
1/4 cup toasted sesame oil
1.5 Tbs red wine vinegar
1/3 to 1/2 cup water
2 Tbs chopped scallions
1 Tbs lemon juice
1 Tbs soy sauce
2 garlic cloves
1 tsp toasted sesame seeds
1/2 tsp salt
pinch of black pepper

Place all ingredients in a blender but not the water. Turn on the blender and slowly add water, a little at a time, unil you reach the desired thickness. You can add more vinegar if you want a stronger flavor. Enjoy over any salad.

Yield: Serves 4-6

Classic Broccoli Cheddar Soup

3 large russet potatoes, peeled and medium diced
some plain rice milk
2 Tbs Soy Free Earth Balance Buttery Spread
1 Tbs Better Than Bouillon brand No Chicken Base
1 tsp garlic powder
1.5 cups broccoli florets, chopped small and dropped in boiling water for 30 seconds, then drained and cooled
2 Tbs nutritional yeast
1 Daiya brand Farmhouse Cheddar block, shred it up yourself
salt and pepper to taste
1 Tbs fresh dill

Place the potatoes in boiling water for about 10 minutes or until softened. Drain them and add them into a food processor or blender. Add in the bouillon base, the garlic powder, nutritional yeast, salt and pepper. Turn on the machine and slowly add in the plain rice milk until you get a medium thin pancake type consistency. Transfer this back to the cooking pot. Take a whisk and add the shredded cheese into the potato mixture. Heat over medium, whisking constantly until the cheese has melted. Add in the dill, Earth Balance and the broccoli florets. Cook 1 more minute. Taste for flavor. If bland, add more salt, garlic powder, bouillon or nutritional yeast. Enjoy this hot.

Yield: Serves 3-4

Pear, Golden Raisin and Cabbage Vinaigrette Slaw (gluten free)

This is perfect for a warm summer day.

4 cups shredded green cabbage
2 medium sized pears with the
4 sides cut off, cut into thin slices
2 Tbs sugar, 1 Tbs olive oil or vegetable oil
5 Tbs red wine vinegar or apple cider vinegar
juice of 1 lime
1 medium carrot peeled
and shredded
1 medium red onion sliced
into thin half moons
1/2 tsp salt
1/3 cup golden raisins

Simply mix all of the ingredients together and let sit 3 hours in the fridge before serving. Enjoy.

Yield: Serves 4-5

Cold Sesame Noodle Salad

one box of Dreamfields
brand linguine, cooked
3 Tbs toasted sesame seeds
1/2 cup soy sauce
1/4 cup sesame oil
1/4 cup canola oil
3 Tbs rice wine vinegar
1 teaspoon sriracha
1/3 cup sugar
1 bunch chopped
scallions
one red pepper diced small
one green pepper
diced small

Make the dressing by placing the soy sauce, vinegar, sriracha, sugar, sesame oil, canola oil and half of the chopped scallions in a food processor. Process 30 seconds.

In a separate bowl mix the cooked noodles, the rest of the scallions, sesame seeds and peppers. Pour the dressing over the top and mix well. Taste to make sure it is as spicy as you like, if not, add more sriracha and if you like it more salty, add more soy sauce. Garnish with sesame seeds and scallions. Chill in fridge 2 hrs and serve cold.

Yield: Serves 4-6

Simple Indian Smoked Paprika Onion Chutney (gluten free)

You will see this on the table at your local Indian restaurant. This makes a delicious condiment for any Indian dish. I like it on top of my Butter Chicken recipe, Tandoori Curry or just on plain steamed basmati rice. It is a little spicy and very delicious.

1 cup small diced onion soaked in ice water for 10 minutes
2 Tbs plain tomato puree
1/2 tsp cumin
pinch of salt
pinch or two or cayenne pepper (depending on desired spice level)
1/4 tsp smoked paprika

Drain the onions and then mix them with the rest of the ingredients. Chill in the fridge in an airtight container.

Yield: Serves 6-8

Spicy Italian Pickled Vegetables (gluten free)

1 cup cauliflower cut into bite size pieces, 1/2 cup peeled carrots cut into 1/8 inch thick discs, 1/3 cup medium diced red bell peppers, a few fresh basil leaves **for the pickling solution:** 1/4 cup red wine vinegar, 1/4 cup apple cider vinegar, 3/4 cup water, 1 tsp salt, 1/3 cup sugar, 1/2 tsp dried red pepper flakes and 1/4 tsp dried oregano

Bring the pickling solution to a boil and cook 30 seconds, whisking often. Completly cool it down. Heat 5 inches of water to a boil. Drop in the carrots, cauliflower and red bell peppers. Boil for 2 minutes. Drain and then cool them. Place the cooked vegetables in a glass jar (that has a lid) along with the fresh basil leaves. Pour the cooled pickling solution over them and place the top on the jar. Let sit at least 24 hours in the fridge. These will last about a month if kept in the fridge.
Yield: Serves 4-5

Creamy Tomato Basil Soup (gluten free)

2 jars of your favorite vegan tomato basil sauce or 4 cups of homemade tomato basil sauce, 1 can plain coconut milk
1/2 cup plain rice milk, 1/2 tsp balsamic vinegar, 1/2 tsp salt
10 leaves fresh basil sliced thin
1.5 Tbs sugar, 1/2 tsp garlic powder

Simply mix all of the ingredients together in a large soup pot with a whisk over medium heat until hot. Serve with my vegan grilled cheese recipe from this book.

Yield: Serves 4-6

Banana, Sunflower Butter, Kale and Avocado Smoothie (gluten free)

This makes a quick, healthy, very tasty and easy breakfast. Packed with nutrition. Double or tripple the ingredients for more than 1 smoothie if desired.

1 banana peeled, 1/2 cup fresh kale, 1/4 of a peeled ripe avocado, 1 Tbs sunflower butter or peanut butter
1/4 to 1/2 cup rice milk, depending on how thick you want it

Place all ingredients in a blender and blend until smooth. Enjoy.

Yield: Makes 1 smoothie

Chickpea Spinach and Cucumber Mango Salad (gluten free)

This makes a nice summer salad or works as a great side to any of the Indian entrees from this book.

1 can of chickpeas, drained and washed, 3 cups of raw baby spinach, 1 ripe mango, peeled and medium diced, 1/3 cup small diced red pepper, 1 cup of English cucumbers cut unto 1/4 inch thick half moons, 1/2 cup cauliflower cut into bite size pieces, 1/2 cup peeded carrots cut into 1/8 inch thick half moons
for the dressing: whisk together 1/3 cup apple cider vinegar, a pinch of salt, 2 Tbs olive oil, 1 Tbs sugar, 1/4 tsp dried basil and 1/2 a clove minced garlic

Heat a large pot of water to a boil. Drop in the carrots and cauliflower. Cook them 2 minutes and then scoop them out with a slotted spoon and cool them in cold water. Drop the spinach into the boiling water and cook 1 minute. Drain, cool and completely squeeze all of the water out of it. Place all of the ingredients in a large bowl and pour the marinade over the top. Mix well and serve chilled. *Yield:* Serves 3-4

Crispy Crunchy Garlic Steak Fries

3 medium sized russet potatoes, 2 cups plain flour
3 cups panko bread crumbs, 1/2 Tbs garlic powder
1-2 tsp salt, 1/2 tsp black pepper
vegetable or canola oil (about 1 inch deep in a non stick skillet or saute pan)

Mix the panko bread crumbs, salt, garlic powder and black pepper together in a flat glass casserole dish and set aside. Cut the potatoes in half lengthwise and then cut each half into 4 wedges, lengthwise, so that each potato gives you 8 wedges. In one bowl, place one cup of flour. Dip the wedges into the flour until they are all coated. In a different bowl, mix one cup of flour with one cup of water and whisk until smooth. Dip the flour coated wedges into this mixture, about 6 at a time. Finally, shake them off a bit and coat them in the panko bread crumb mix until covered and place them on a plate. Repeat this until all of the potatoes are coated. Heat 1 inch of the oil in a non stick skillet or saute pan over medium heat for a few minutes. When you can dip the tip a fry into the oil and bubbles gently form around it, they are ready to cook. Carefully place about 8 wedges at a time, on their sides, into the oil. Cook one side until golden, then flip and cook the other side. Drain on a cookie rack placed on a cookie sheet lined with foil. Season each fry with a little salt as soon as you take them out of the oil. Repeat until all of the fries are done. You can reheat these on the cookie rack sheet pan set up as well. These go great dipped in my Ranch Dressing recipe.

Yield: Serves 4-6

Garlic Sauteed Savory Bok Choy and Asparagus

1 lb of bok choy or baby bok choy, washed and dried with about an inch of the bottom of the stalk chopped off and discarded (cut the stalks in half if they are very large), 12 stalks of asparagus with the hard bottoms chopped off and discarded, cut in half from top to bottom, 1 tsp each rough chopped garlic and peeled fresh ginger, 2 tsp soy sauce, 1 tsp Better Than Bouillon brand Roasted Garlic Base mixed with 2 Tbs water, 1 tsp sesame oil

Heat a non stick pan for 2 minutes on high. Add in the sesame oil, garlic, ginger and bok choy. Lay it all in a flat layer. Cook 20 seconds and stir. Cook for about 2 more minutes, stirring often. Add the asparagus. Cook 1 more minute. Add in the soy sauce and water/bouillon mixture. Cover the pan and let it finish cooking for 1 more minute. Enjoy. *Yield:* Serves 3-4

Parsnip Cauliflower Mushroom Bake (gluten free)

3 cups of cremini mushrooms cut into thin slices
1/2 tsp minced fresh thyme and 1 tsp rough chopped garlic, 1/4 tsp dried oregano
1 cup peeled parsnips chopped into 1/4 inch chunks
1 cup cauliflower cut into small florets, 1/3 cup thin sliced leeks (use only the white part of the leeks), 1/2 tsp garlic powder, 1/4 to 1/2 tsp salt and a few cracks of fresh black pepper, 2 Tbs each Tofutti brand sour cream and Earth Balance brand buttery spread, 2 Tbs Follow Your Heart brand parmesan shreds
3 slices of Field Roast brand original flavor Chao Cheese shredded yourself

Boil the parsnips for 8 minutes and then add in the cauliflower and leeks. Cook 3 more minutes. Drain, cool in cold water, drain again and place them all in a food processor with the salt, pepper, parmesan, garlic powder, Tofutti and Earth Balance. Process until smooth and then spoon this into a non stick sprayed 9 inch glass baking dish into an even layer. Heat a large non stick pan for 3 minutes on high and add in 1 tsp of olive oil and then the mushrooms, garlic and a pinch of salt. Cook each side about 2 minutes and then add in the oregano and thyme. Place the mushrooms on rop in rows and spread on the Chao shredded cheese. Cover and bake at 400 degrees for 20 minutes. Enjoy. Yield: Serves 3-4

Crispy Vegetable Spring Rolls

12 frozen spring roll wrappers, thawed, removed from package and covered with a wet towel
2 cups cabbage, finely shredded
1/2 cup carrots, finely shredded
2 Tbs chopped fresh basil
4 Tbs water
canola or vegetable oil

Mix the cabbage, carrots and basil together. Lay a spring roll wrapper on a cutting board with one corner facing you. Place about 2 to 3 Tbs of the filling about an inch above the corner facing you. Roll that corner over the filling and then pull the covered filling in towards you tightly. Push the 2 corners to your left and right over the filling and then roll it all into a tight tube. Before you roll it all the way up, use a pastry brush and brush the water on the inside edges of the wrapper (this helps the rolls stay sealed). Repeat until you have filled all the rolls. Heat 1/4 inch of oil in a non stick pan for 3 minutes over medium high heat. Dip a corner of a spring roll in, if bubbles form around the roll, it is ready to fry. Cook 3 or 4 at a time about 3 minutes per side until golden brown. Serve with sweet chili sauce, hoisin sauce or soy sauce

Yield: Serves 3-5

Spicy Sweet Chili Mayo

1/2 cup vegan mayo
1/2 tsp tahini
1/4 tsp lemon juice
1/2 - 1 tsp Sriracha, depending on desired spice level
1.5 Tbs sweet chili sauce
pinch of garlic powder

Simply whisk all of the ingredients together. Serve this over rice topped with black sesame seeds, over grilled vegetables or to dip sushi into.

Yield: Serves 4-6

Crunchy Garlic Herb Croutons

3 cups of leftover bread cut into 1/2 inch cubes (my Focaccia or Garlic Basil Roll recipes from this book work great for this)
2 Tbs extra virgin olive oil
1/2 tsp each dried basil, oregano, garlic powder and salt
1/4 tsp black pepper

Preheat the oven to 400 degrees. Line a cookie sheet with foil. Toss all of the ingredients together. Place them in an even layer on the sheet pan and bake about 10 to 12 minutes or until browned and crisped. Cool them and use over any salad.

Yield: Serves 3-6

Southern Style Pimento Cheese

This is a southern classic that is used for sandwiches or for a dip.

2 cups worth of Daiya Farmhouse Block Cheddar, shredded (you will need to shred it yourself, be sure to use the block and not the pre shredded, it tastes different)
1 container of Tofutti brand cream cheese, softened
2 to 3 Tbs of Vegenaise brand mayo
1/2 a cup of jarred pimentos, drained and cut into small cubes
1/4 tsp each garlic powder and onion powder
a few pinches of salt and pepper
1/4 tsp minced fresh jalapeno with the seeds removed

Place all of the ingredients in a large bowl. With an electric hand mixer, beat the mixture until smooth. If you need it a little more creamy and a bit chunky, add more mayo. Adjust salt if needed. Enjoy cold.

Yield: Serves 3-5

Crunchy Onion Rings

3 large onions cut into 1/4 inch circles and then pushed apart into several rings

3 cups panko bread crumbs mixed with 1 tsp salt, 1/2 tsp black pepper and 1 tsp garlic powder

3 cups flour

1.5 cups water

1/2 inch of vegetable in a large non stick saute pan for frying

Put 1.5 cups of flour in a large bowl. In another bowl, mix the other 1.5 cups of flour with the 1.5 cups of water, whisk it well (this will act as the egg to make the bread crumbs stick to the onions). In a large flat casserole dish, place the panko bread crumb mixture. Working from left to right, dip the onion rounds, a few at a time, into the flour, then the flour/water mixture (coat well with this mixture) and finally into the bread crumbs. Make sure they are all the way coated in the bread crumbs. Heat the oil filled saute pan over medium high heat for 4 minutes. Dip an onion ring in, if bubbles form, it is ready to fry. Working in batches, about 8 at a time, cook the onion rings for about 2 minutes per side until both sides are golden. Drain on a foil lined cookie sheet that has a cookie cooking rack placed on top of the foil (this way you can reheat them later without burning the bottoms and they will crisp up nicely again). Sprinkle with a little salt once out of the oil and try them with my Spicy Mustard Cholula Dip from my Crunchy Fried Dill Pickle recipe.

Yield: Serves 4-8

Easy Tofu Scramble or Cheddar Jack Scramble (gluten free)

Makes a great side for pancakes.

1 block firm tofu (not extra firm) crumbled very well between your hands
3 Tbs nutritional yeast
1 teaspoon Indian black salt (sold in spice stores and Indian markets, gives food an egg type flavor, it is very good)
1/4 teaspoon black pepper
1/2 teaspoon garlic powder
1 Tbs water
1tsp salt
1/2 cup So Delicious brand cheddar jack shredded vegan cheese (optional)

 Mash all together well with your hands. Place in a microwave safe bowl, cover in plastic and heat on high for 1 minute. For a cheddar jack scramble, simply stir 1/2 cup of So Delicious brand cheddar jack shredded vegan cheese into the eggs before placing in the microwave.

Yield: Serves 3-5

Extra Crunchy Fried Green Tomatoes with Sour Cream and Onion Fresh Chive Topping

3 large green tomatoes, cut
into 1/8 inch thick slices
3 cups of panko bread
crumbs mixed
with 1/2 cup yellow
cornmeal,
1 tsp garlic powder,
1 tsp salt, 1/2 tsp
dried thyme and
1/2 tsp black pepper
3 cups flour
2 cups water
1 recipe of the Sour Cream
and Onion Dip recipe from this book
2 Tbs fresh chopped chives
1/2 inch of vegetable oil in a large non stick pan

   Take 1 cup of the flour and place it in a bowl. Take the other 2 cups of flour and mix them with the 2 cups of water. Whisk well (this will act as your egg to make the bread crumbs stick). Coat your green tomato slices in the flour, then dip each one into the water/flour mixture. Shake off the extra liquid and then coat the slices in the panko/cornmeal mix. Make sure they are fully coated. Heat the oil for about 3 minutes on high. Dip one of the coated tomatoes in the oil, if it bubbles, they are ready to fry. Cook about 8 at a time for 2-4 minutes per side until golden. Drain them on a foil lined cookie sheet that has a cookie cooling rack placed on top (this way you can heat them again later without burning the bottom since they will be elevated). Sprinkle with a little more salt. Top with the Sour Cream and Onion Dip and fresh chives.
Yield: Serves 4-6

Simple Garlic Sauteed Vegetables (gluten free)

1/4 cup red bell peppers cut into bite size pieces
1 cup broccoli florets cut into bite size pieces
3/4 cup sliced button or cremini mushrooms
1/3 cup asparagus cut into 1 inch pieces
3 cloves garlic, rough chopped
1 Tbs olive oil
salt and pepper to taste

   Heat a non stick pan for 3 minutes on high. Add in the olive oil, broccoli, mushrooms and peppers and then the garlic. Add a little salt and pepper. Let them sit a minute in an even layer and then stir or flip the pan. Cook another 2 minutes, stirring once in a while. Add in the asparagus. Cook 1 minute more and then add in a Tbs of water to finish off the broccoli with the steam. Cook another minute until broccoli is crisp but tender. Season with salt and pepper. Serve hot. — 97 — *Yield*: Serves 3-4

Fresh Herb and Butter Long Grain Brown Rice (gluten free)

This is a fresh and delicious whole grain dish. Go to a department store and pick up a $30 digital rice cooker. They are very simple to use.

2 cups long grain brown rice
3 cups of water, 1tsp salt
4 Tbs chopped fresh dill
3 Tbs chopped fresh basil
1 bunch of green onions, rough chopped
1 tsp garlic powder
5 Tbs Earth Balance soy free buttery spread

Place the rice, a pinch of salt and the water in a rice cooker. Hit the "brown rice" button. When cooked, transfer the cooked rice to a large bowl and add the rest of the salt and ingredients. Taste to make sure the flavor is great, if not, add more salt, garlic powder or butter. Fluff with a fork and serve hot. This is also good with toasted slivered almonds tossed into it.

Yield: Serves 6-8

Simple Steamed Bulgur Wheat

Bulgur wheat is high in fiber and B vitamins and has a very nice texture and flavor in this recipe. This makes a great side to any meal or salad if you want a tasty alternative to rice or pasta.

1 cup bulgur wheat
2 cups water
1 Tbs Better Than Bouillon brand No Chicken Base
pinch of salt

Heat the water, salt and the No Chicken Base to a boil. Add in the bulgur wheat, stir and cover. Turn the heat to low and simmer 15 minutes. Enjoy.

Yield: Serves 3-4

Fried Okra

Okra is a vegetable you either love or hate. This recipe is for the okra fans out there.

2 cups fresh okra with the tops and bottoms cut off
1 cup flour mixed with 1/4 cup yellow cornmeal, 1/4 cup chickpea flour, 1/2 tsp salt, 1/2 tsp garlic powder and a few pinches of black pepper
1 1/4 cup freshly opened plain club soda (make sure it is fresh and still bubbly)
1/2 inch of vegetable oil in a large non stick pan

Whisk the flour/cornmeal mixture together with the club soda. Heat the oil on high for 3 minutes. Flick a little batter into the oil. If bubbles form, it is ready to fry. Dip the okra into the flour/cornmeal batter and then carefully drop the coated okra pieces into the oil. Cook it in 2 batches. Cook each side a few minutes until golden. Drain on a foil lined sheet pan with a cookie cooling rack placed on top (this way you can crisp them again in the oven later without burning the bottoms). Sprinkle with a little salt. Enjoy.

Yield: Serves 4-6

Sun Dried Tomato Vinaigrette (gluten free)

1/2 cup of oil cured sun dried tomatoes, drained (make sure they are the kind that are packed in oil, these have the best flavor)
4 leaves of fresh basil
1/4 tsp salt
1/2 tsp sugar
3 Tbs olive oil
1/4-1/2 cup water
1 Tbs red wine vinegar
1/2 clove fresh garlic

Place all of the ingredients into a blender besides the water. Blend and add in a little water at a time until you get a smooth dressing. If it seems too thick you can add more water. This is delicious over any salad.

Yield: Serves 3-6

From Scratch Baked Beans (gluten free if you omit the soy sauce)

You can chop and pan saute up some Lightlife brand jumbo vegan hot dogs to add to these too once baked for beans and franks if you want.

plenty of water
1 lb dry navy beans
or great northern beans
1 medium onion
 chopped
1 cup ketchup
1/2 cup brown
 sugar
1/3 cup molasses
1 teaspoon
 garlic powder
1/8 cup maple syrup
1 Tbs yellow mustard
1 1/2 teaspoons salt
black pepper to taste
1 bay leaf
1 Tbs soy sauce
1 teaspoon liquid smoke

Soak the beans, covered in water about 3 inches over the top of the beans, in a large bowl for 8 hours. Drain them and cover them in water again in a large pot. Bring them to a boil, boil for an hour (scoop off any foam that may form on the top) and drain them but keep the cooking liquid (the beans will not be fully cooked, they will finish cooking in the oven). In a large oven safe pot with a lid or a Dutch oven, combine the beans, 1.5 cups cooking liquid, onion, ketchup, brown sugar, molasses, maple syrup, salt, mustard, pepper, bay leaf, liquid smoke, garlic powder and soy sauce. Mix well. Cover and bake at 300 degrees for 3 to 4 hours or until the beans are very tender and sauce has thickened to desired consistency. Stir occasionally and add more of the reserved bean cooking liquid if needed during cooking time, do not let them dry out. Remove the bay leaf, season again with salt and pepper if needed and enjoy.

Yield: Serves 8-12

Crispy Potato Parmesan Roses (gluten free)

6 medium red potatoes sliced thin on a mandolin
or vegetable slicer but not paper thin, 1/4 tsp minced thyme
3 Tbs melted Earth
Balance brand buttery spread, 3 Tbs
finely chopped Follow Your Heart
brand parmesan
3/4 tsp salt, 1/4 tsp minced rosemary
1/4 tsp black pepper
1 tsp garlic powder

Yield: Makes 10-12 roses

Toss all ingredients together. Take a silicone muffin tin and spray it with non stick spray. Stack each tin with about 13 coated potato slices, face down, being sure to alternate the direction of each slice to help form the rose shape. Bake at 400 degrees for about 45 minutes until browned on top. Poke with a toothpick to be sure they are done and soft in the middle. If not, bake 5 to 10 more minutes until soft in the middle. Let cool 5 minutes uncovered out of the oven and top with my Basil Aioli recipe from this book if desired.

Two Tomato, Artichoke and Pepperoncini Pasta Salad

1 container of Barilla brand White Fiber Spaghetti or Dreamfields brand Spaghetti (both have extra fiber but taste like regular white pasta)
5 medium sized pepperoncini peppers (they come in a jar, marinated) with the tops cut off, cut into thin strips
2 medium sized tomatoes cut into thin strips (remove seeds)
1/4 cup oil cured sun dried tomatoes, cut into strips (make sure you use the ones that that come in a jar packed in oil)
2 small jars of marinatd artichokes that are quartered, drained
1 Tbs extra virgin olive oil
3 cloves garlic, minced
4 cups raw baby spinach
1/2 tsp salt
pepper to taste
3 Tbs red wine vinegar or white wine vinegar
1/2 tsp garlic powder

Cook the spaghetti for about 6 minutes. Drain and cool it. Heat a large non stick pan for 2 minutes on high, then add in a half Tbs of the oil, the garlic, artichokes, tomatoes, sun dried tomatoes and a pinch of salt and pepper. Cook 1 minute and then add in the spinach. Cook 1 more minute until the spinach is wilted. Cool this and then mix it with the cooled spaghetti and the rest of the ingredients. Taste, if it needs more salt or vinegar, add it now.

Yield: Serves 4-6

Garlic Broccoli or Garlic Broccoli Rabe (gluten free)

4 cups broccoli crowns cut into florets (I like to keep a long stem on them, you get more vitamins from it this way) or
1 large bunch of raw broccoli rabe with the woody bottoms cut off (boil the broccoli rabe for 1 1/2 minutes, drain and cool before sauteeing if using it)
4 cloves garlic chopped into thin slivers
2 Tbs extra virgin olive oil
a few pinches of salt to taste
a few pinches dried red pepper flakes to taste

Heat a large saute pan over medium high heat 3 minutes, then add the olive oil, garlic and broccoli. Stir around a few minutes then add salt and red pepper flakes. When broccoli seems tender, remove from the heat and enjoy warm.

Yield: Serves 4-6

Tuscan White Bean Kale Soup

Creamy, rich and delicious.

2 cans of cannellini beans, drained and washed
4 cups water whisked together with 3 Tbs of
Better Than Bouillon brand No Chicken Base
or Roasted Garlic Base, 1 tsp garlic powder and
3 Tbs nutritional yeast
3/4 cup peeled and small diced carrots
1/2 cup each small diced onions and celery
1/2 cup washed leeks cut into thin half
moons, 3 cloves minced garlic
1 tsp minced fresh thyme, 1 bay leaf
1 medium to large bunch of kale, stems
removed and rough chopped
2 Tbs Earth Balance brand buttery spread

Heat 1 tsp of olive oil on high in a large pot for 2 minutes. Add in the onions, celery, carrots, garlic and leeks. Saute 3 minutes and then add in the kale. Stir for another 2 minutes and add in the water mixture, thyme, bay leaf and the beans. Bring to a boil for 12 minutes. Remove from the heat, and with a ladle, spoon 1/2 of the soup into a blender, making sure it is mostly beans, leeks and broth. Do not get the much kale or the bay leaf into the blender. Blend until smooth and slightly thick. Add more soup liquid if needed to get the beans smooth. Add this blended mix back into the soup and add in the Earth Balance. Cook 4 more minutes, remove the bay leaf and enjoy.

Yield: Serves 3-4

Garlic Buttered Mushrooms Oreganata (gluten free)

Oregano and mushrooms are a classic combination, paired with garlic, this makes an absolutely gorgeous side dish. I serve them with a bowl of Angel Hair pasta and some crusty Italian bread.

4 cups of Button or Cremini mushrooms, cut into quarters
4 cloves of garlic, peeled and minced, salt and pepper to taste
1/2 tsp dried oregano or 1/2 tsp fresh oregano, chopped
2 Tbs Earth Balance brand Soy Free Buttery Spread
1 tsp extra virgin olive oil

Heat a large non stick pan for 2 minutes over high heat. Next, add in the olive oil and garlic. Saute 30 seconds, then add in the mushrooms, salt and pepper. Make sure all of the mushrooms are flat in the pan and do not stir them for 2 minutes. After 2 minutes, flip the pan or stir the mushrooms. Flatten them out again and let them cook about another 4 minutes. Finally, finish them off with the buttery spread, a little more salt and the oregano. Serve hot.

Yield: Serves 3-5

Godlen Coconut Curry Baby Bok Choy Rice Noodles

1/2 a pack of wide rice noodles (available at Asian markets), 2 cups sliced baby bok choy **the cooking liquid:** whisk together 1 can coconut milk, 2 cups water, 1 Tbs green curry paste, 1 tsp sesame oil, 1 Tbs Better Than Bouillon brand Roasted Garlic Base, 3 Tbs sugar, 1 tsp soy sauce, 1 tsp turmeric powder and 1 tsp hot chili paste

Bring the cooking liquid to a boil with the bok choy in a large flat non stick pan. Cook 1 minute. Add in the rice noodles, flipping them with a pair of tongs constantly for about 5 minutes. If they are still a little undercooked, add a little more water and cook a little longer. Serve topped with fresh chopped basil. *Yield:* Serves 3-4

Japanese Vegetable Fritters with Coriander Wasabi Lime Sauce (gluten free)

for the fritters: 1 cup shredded zucchini, 1 cup peeled shredded carrots, 2 Tbs chopped scallions, 1/4 cup red bell pepper cut into thin half inch strips, 1/4 cup asparagus cut into thin slices on an angle, 1/2 tsp garlic powder, 3 Tbs chickpea flour, 1 Tbs gluten free soy sauce, pinch of salt and pepper, 2 Tbs Follow Your Heart brand Vegan Egg whisked with 1/4 cup water   **for the sauce:** stir together 4 Tbs of Tofutti brand sour cream with 1/2 tsp fresh lime, a pinch of salt, 1 tsp minced cilantro and 1/4 tsp wasabi powder

Mix all of the fritter ingredients in a large bowl with your hands. Heat a large non stick pan for 3 minutes on high. Add in about 3 Tbs vegetable oil. Form the wet batter into about 2 inch flat patties (cook about 5 fritters at a time) and cook each side about 3 minutes until golden. Drain on a paper towel. Add a little more oil to the pan and cook the remaining fritters. Serve with the dipping sauce. *Yield:* Makes about 8-10 fritters

Garlic Mushroom and Oil Cured Sun Dried Tomato Sauteed Kale (gluten free)

1 large bunch of kale, stems removed and rough chopped, 2 cloves minced garlic 1 cup sliced button mushrooms, 1 tsp red wine vinegar
salt, pepper and red pepper flakes to taste, 1 tsp extra virgin olive oil
3 Tbs oil cured sun dried tomatoes (use the ones in a jar packed in oil)

Bring a large pot of water to a boil. Add in the stemmed kale and boil 3 minutes. Drain, cool and then squeeze all of the water out of the kale. Heat a non stick saute pan for 2 minutes on high heat. Add in the olive oil, then the mushrooms and garlic, salt and pepper. Cook 3 minutes, add in the kale, sun dried tomatoes, red wine vinegar and red pepper flakes. Cook 2 more minutes. Season with salt and pepper if needed. Serve hot.
Yield: Serves 2-4

Garlic Pan Seared Cabbage, Mushrooms and Brussel Sprouts (gluten free)

Here is a very healthy recipe for a cruciferous cavalcade of delicious vegetables. Cruciferous vegetables, such as cauliflower, cabbages, brussel sprouts, kale and broccoli are shown in studies to possibly have some cancer fighting properties to them. They really are the powerhouse of the vegetable kingdom. They are also a great source of vitamins and fiber, and if prepared correctly, taste amazing. Here is a great example.

3 cups of cabbage, chopped into 1 inch diced pieces
2 cups brussel sprouts, quartered
2 cups quartered button or cremini mushrooms
1/2 Tbs extra virgin olive oil
3 cloves minced fresh garlic
salt and pepper to taste

Get a large non stick pan very hot (for about 3 minutes ove a high heat). Add in the olive oil and all of the vegetables besides the garlic. Flatten them out in the pan and let them sit for about a minute, do not stir them around yet. This will get a charred caramelization to start forming on the vegetables. Add in the minced garlic and salt and pepper to taste. Now, stir or flip the vegetables in the pan and let the unbrowned side of the vegetables sit another 2 minutes. Flip the pan or stir them one more time and let them sit another 3 minutes until the brussel sprouts are cooked and all are a bit browned. Season with more salt and pepper if needed.

Yield: Serves 3-4

Classic Cole Slaw

3 cups shredded green cabbage
1 cup shredded red cabbage
1/2 cup peeled shredded carrots
dressing:
1/2 cup Vegenaise
brand vegan mayo
1/2 tsp celery powder
1/2 tsp garlic powder
2 Tbs apple cider vinegar
2 Tbs sugar
1 tsp dijon mustard
salt and pepper to taste

For the dressing, whisk the dressing ingredients together. Pour this into the cabbage mixture. Mix well and store in the fridge for an hour or until chilled.

Yield: Serves 4-6

Fast Food Style Hash Browns (gluten free)

2 medium russet potatoes, peeled and each cut into 2 segments, 1 Tbs Follow Your Heart brand Vegan Egg powder whisked with 1/4 cup water, 1/2 tsp salt, black pepper to taste

Bring a pot of water to a boil and add in the potatoes. Boil until just fork tender but not mushy, about 10 minutes. When tender, drain but do not run water on them. Let them air cool in the freezer on a plate for 10 minutes. When cool, grate them on a grater and mix with the Vegan Egg mixture, salt and pepper. Form into 4 flat hash brown patty shapes, about 4 inches by 2 inches. Place on parchment paper on a plate in the freezer for 15 minutes. Place about 1/4 inch of vegetable oil in a non stick pan and heat for 3 minutes on high. Add in the patties and cook each side until golden. Drain, sprinkle with a little salt and enjoy. *Yield:* Makes 4 patties

Green Bean Casserole

4 cups al dente cooked green beans (cooked about 4 minutes in boiling water) chopped into 1/2 inch pieces, 1/2 cup minced mushrooms, 1 cup plain rice milk, 2 Tbs soy free Earth Balance brand buttery spread, 2 Tbs nutritional yeast, 3 Tbs plain flour, 1 Tbs Better Than Bouillon brand Roasted Garlic Base, 1/2 tsp salt, pepper to taste, 2 cups store bought fried onion topping (most are vegan, double check to be sure)

Heat the butter in a sauce pan, add the mushrooms, cook 3 minutes. Add the flour, stir in, cook 30 seconds then add the rest of the ingredients except the green beans. Whisk a minute or two until thickened. Pour this over the cooked green beans, mix well, and pour this into a non stick spray sprayed 8 by 8 inch glass baking dish. Bake 15 minutes. Spread the onions on top and bake at 375 degrees for 10 more minutes. *Yield*: Serves 4-6

Simple Salt and Pepper Butter Blanched Broccoli (gluten free)

3 cups of broccoli florets cut into bite size pieces
salt and pepper to taste
2 Tbs of Earth Balance buttery spread

Bring about 5 incches of water to a boil. Drop in the broccoli florets and cook for 45 seconds. Drain them and toss them in the Earth Balance, salt and pepper. Enjoy.
Yield: Serves 3-4

Grilled Avocado with Lemon Lime Cilantro Sour Cream (gluten free)

3 ripe avocados, cut in half, seeded
spice mix: a pinch of cayenne,
1/2 tsp each smoked paprika, chili
powder and garlic powder mixed
with 1/4 tsp sugar and 1/4 tsp salt
1/2 cup Tofutti brand sour cream
1/2 tsp each lime and lemon juice
1/2 a clove minced garlic
1 Tbs minced cilantro, 1 tsp minced
scallions, a pinch of salt and pepper

   Heat a grill on high for 15 minutes. Mix the sour cream, lime juice, salt, pepper, cilantro and garlic. Keep chilled. Spray the heated grill with non stick spray. Sprinkle your 6 avocado halves with some of the spice mix. Lay the halves face down on the grill and grill for 1.5 minutes and then turn a quarter of a turn and grill 1 minute more (this will create beautiful grill marks). Remove from heat and top them with the lime cilantro sour cream. Enjoy.

Yield: Serves 3-4

Simple Sesame Soy and Ginger Roasted Vegetables

   These go great with my Sesame Hoisin Grilled Tofu recipe and some steamed brown rice topped with my Spicy Sweet Chili Mayo recipe and black sesame seeds.

1 cup Japanese eggplant sliced on a bias
1 red bell pepper cut into long strips
1 cup broccoli florets cut into bite size pieces
1 large carrot, peeled and sliced into thick 3 inch matchsticks
1 cup button mushrooms quartered
1 bunch of asparagus with the tough bottoms cut off
1/2 cup medium size diced onion
1/2 tsp fresh ginger mixed with 2 Tbs sesame oil, 1/2 Tbs soy sauce and 1 tsp minced garlic

   Heat the oven to 400 degrees. Line a large sheet pan with foil. Place it in the oven, empty, for 5 minutes to heat it up. Mix the vegetables with the oil/soy sauce mixture. Add a pinch of salt or two. Pour onto the hot pan, carefully, and roast them for 15 minutes or until browned.

Yield: Serves 3-5

Grilled Spicy Street Corn (gluten free)

8 ears of fresh corn, shucked and brushed with a little olive oil and salt
for the topping:
2 Tbs fresh chopped cilantro
2 Tbs chopped scallions
1 cup vegan mayo (I like Vegenaise brand)
1/2 tsp chili powder, 1/2 tsp smoked paprika
1/2 tsp salt
a few pinches of cayenne pepper, depending on how spicy you want it
1/2 Tbs fresh lime juice
1/2 tsp garlic powder
6 Tbs Follow Your Heart brand feta or parmesan shreds (do not mix this
into the topping, add it on top of the corn at the end)

Mix all of the topping ingredients together. Heat a grill for 12 minutes on
high. Cook the corn about 3 minutes per side until it is slightly charred for
about 10 minutes total. Remove from the heat and brush each ear of corn
liberally with a layer of the topping. Sprinkle with more salt and pepper,
cilantro, scallions, cheese and a a few red pepper flakes if you like. Serve hot.

Yield: Serves 3-5

Chinese Style Garlic Green Beans

These remind me of the green beans you would get at a Chinese buffet. They taste great.

4 cups green beans with the ends snipped and discarded, 1Tbs rough chopped garlic, 1 Tbs vegetable oil **for the sauce:** whisk together 2 Tbs soy sauce, 2 Tbs vegan oyster sauce, 1 Tbs sugar, 1 tsp sesame oil, 3 Tbs water and 1 tsp cornstarch

Bring 5 inches of water to a boil. Add in the green beans and boil 3 minutes. Drain well and cool. Heat a large non stick pan for 3 minutes on high. Add in the oil and garlic. Cook 30 seconds and then add in the green beans. Cook about 3 more minutes, stirring often. Add in the sauce and stir until thickened. You can add some spicy garlic chili paste to the sauce if you want them to be spicy. Enjoy. *Yield:* Serves 3-4

Hasselback Potatoes (gluten free)

10 medium sized red or Yukon Gold potatoes
3 Tbs Extra Virgin Olive Oil mixed with 1/2 tsp salt, 1/2 tsp garlic powder, 1/2 tsp chopped fresh chives and a few pinches of black pepper

To make the potato slits, place a potato in the middle of two chopsticks, a chopstick on each side of the potato. With a knife, cut width wise several slits in the potato all the way down to the chopsticks. The potato should look fanned, make the slits as close to each other as possible. The chopsticks will keep you from cutting the potatoes to the point where they would fall apart. Repeat this process with all of the potatoes. Heat the oven to 450. On a parchment paper lined sheet pan topped with a cookie cooling rack, place the fanned potatoes on top of the rack (this will keep the bottoms of the potatoes from burning while baking). Brush a little of the olive oil/herb topping on the potatoes. Bake for 30 minutes. Remove potatoes from oven, brush the remaining filling into the slits of the now softened potatoes. Bake for another 15 to 20 minutes or until soft and crisped. Sprinkle with a little more salt, fresh chives and serve w my Sour Cream and Onion Dip recipe from this book.

Yield: Serves 4-6

Hearts Of Palm Mozzarella Sticks

1 14 oz can of whole hearts of palm cut in half lengthwise
1 cup of flour whisked together with 1 cup of water.
1 cup of flour in a flat casserole dish
2 cups of panko bread crumbs in a flat casserole dish mixed with 1 tsp salt, 2 Tbs nutritional yeast, 1 tsp garlic powder, 1 tsp dried oregano and 1tsp dried basil
vegetable oil to fry
marinara sauce for dipping

Take the cut lengthwise hearts of palm and coat them in the flour, then into the flour/water mixture, and lastly, into the seasoned bread crumbs.

Heat a 1/2 inch of vegetable oil over medium high heat for 3 minutes. Dip one of the coated heart of palm sticks into the oil, if bubbles form around it, it is ready to cook. Drop each one into the oil and cook each side until golden. Remove from oil and sprinkle with salt. Serve hot with marinara dipping sauce.

Yield: Serves 4-6

Bacon and Cheddar Crispy Potato Skins

10 medium sized red potatoes or 5 medium sizes russet potatoes
1 Tbs olive oil, 1/2 a block Daiya brand Farmhouse Block Cheddar shredded
1/4 tsp garlic powder
5 strips of Lightlife
brand bacon, cut
into small cubes
(if you have another
favorite vegan bacon,
you can use
that as well) that have
been crisped up a little in
a non stick pan in a
little olive oil
salt and pepper to taste
Tofutti brand sour cream
(optional topping)
sliced scallions to top

Cut 4 thin, equal sides off of the potatoes (you can use the rest of the potato for mashed potatoes, latkes or potato salad). Toss these in the olive oil, salt, pepper and garlic powder. Heat the oven to 400 degrees. Place the potato skins on a parchment paper lined sheet pan. Bake them for about 20 minutes or until softened and crispy. Cool them a bit and scoop out a little of the inside potato flesh. Sprinkle on a little of the cheese and then the crisped bacon cubes. Place them under the broiler until the cheese melts. Remove from the oven and sprinkle with a little salt and a little sour cream if you are using it. Enjoy.

Yield: Serves 3-4

Homemade Parmesan Focaccia topped with Garlic and Fresh Basil

This is great as a side or sliced down the middle for vegan avocado blt's.

One ball of homemade dough recipe from this book, risen in a bowl (the homemade dough recipe makes 2 balls but you will only use one here).

Remove dough from bowl onto a lightly floured surface. Do not re knead it, just gently form in into a rectangle shape. Place onto a foil lined cookie sheet that has a little olive oil brushed onto it.

In a separate bowl mix 3 Tbs extra virgin olive oil with 3 cloves rough sliced garlic, salt, 6 chopped basil leaves and 1 Tbs grated Go Veggie brand vegan parmesan cheese or Follow Your Heart brand parmesan. Place on top of dough and push down into the dough with your fingertips. Let this rise 2 hours, covered.

Preheat oven to 425 degrees. Make shallow cuts into the focaccia dough with a pizza cutter into the sizes you want each piece before baking, this helps avoid bubbles. Top with a few more sprinkles of salt and the vegan parmesan cheese. Bake 15 minutes or until golden brown.

Yield: Serves 4-8

Hummus (gluten free)

2 cans drained chickpeas
juice of 2 lemons
1 clove garlic
1 teaspoon salt
1/4 cup toasted sesame tahini
1 Tbs olive oil
1/8 to 1/2 cup water to thin

Place all in food processor. If too thick, add more water. Process until smooth. If you want a sharper flavor, add more tahini, lemon juice and salt.

Serve with raw cut up english cucumbers, red peppers, blanched cooled broccoli, celery sticks, peeled julienned carrots, whole grain pita toasts etc.

You can also add ingredients such as fresh dill, chipotle peppers, roasted red peppers, roasted garlic, artichokes etc for a different flavor.

Yield: Serves 8-10

Grilled Chicken Caesar Bowtie Pasta Salad

1 box of farfalle pasta, cooked, drained and cooled
4 patties of Delight Soy brand or Maywah brand vegan Chicken Steaks or
1 block of extra firm tofu that has been frozen, thawed and had the water completely squeezed out of it (this creates a chewy texture for the tofu)
1/2 cup of Follow Your Heart brand vegan shredded parmesan cheese
1/2 cup kalamata olives, sliced in half
3/4 cup grape tomatoes, sliced in half, 2 Tbs chopped fresh parsley
1 recipe of the Caesar dressing recipe from the Caesar Salad recipe from this book
3 Tbs soy free Vegenaise brand mayo
1 Tbs red wine vinegar
1 cup romaine lettuce, chopped
salt and pepper to taste

Marinat the chicken patties or the tofu in a little Italian dressing for a few minutes. Heat a grill for 15 minutes on high, spray the grates with a little non stick spray and grill each side of the chicken or tofu 3 minutes per side. Cool them and dice or slice into strips. Mix all of the ingredients together and season with salt and pepper and a little more vinegar if needed. Garnish with a little more cheese and fresh chopped parsley.

Yield: Serves 4-8

Hush Puppies

If you live in the South, or ever have, you know how good hush puppies are.

1 1/2 cups yellow cornmeal
1/2 cup plain flour
1 tsp sugar
1 tsp salt
1/2 tsp baking powder
1 medium onion minced
1/2 tsp garlic powder
1 Tbs canola oil
1 cup plain club soda

Combine all ingredients and stir until you have a thick batter. You can add a little more club soda if it seems way too thick and dry. Heat an inch of canola or vegetable oil over medium heat in a non stick frying pan until you can flick a little batter into the oil and bubbles form around it, it is ready to fry. Drop in a large spoon full at a time, cook about 10 at a time at most, cooking each side until golden brown. Drain on a paper towel and sprinkle with a little more salt. Serve with tartar sauce, which is simply 1/2 cup vegan mayo mixed with 2 Tbs sweet relish, a teaspoon of fresh dill and a pinch of salt whisked together.

Yield: Serves 6-8

Cheddar Chive Biscuits

2 cups King Arthur brand flour, sifted
8 Tbs vegetable shortening, 1 Tbs chopped chives
1/3 cup Daiya brand Farmhouse Block cheddar shredded yourself
1 tsp each salt, garlic powder and 1 Tbs baking powder
1/2 cup plus 2 Tbs freshly opened plain club soda mixed with 1 tsp apple cider vinegar

Place the flour, garlic powder, salt, pepper, cheese, baking powder and baking soda in a bowl. Add in the shortening and using a pastry cutter or a fork, cut the shortening into the flour until many small beads or flour are formed in the dough. Add in the club soda/vinegar mixture. Gently fold it in with a rubber spatula or flat wooden spoon. Do not over knead it. Fold it over on itself about 8 times to help form layers. Gently roll it on a lightly floured board into half inch thickness. Cut out circle shapes about 2 or 3 inches wide. Heat the oven to 450 degrees. Place the biscuits, with the edges slightly touching one another. Bake them about 18 minutes until browned on top. Brush the tops with a little melted Earth Balance brand buttery spread right out of the oven. Enjoy. *Yield:* Makes 6 to 8 biscuits

Spicy Sausage Breakfast Patties (gluten free)

3 links of Beyond Meat brand Hot Italian sausages with the skin peeled off by running them under warm water, 1/4 tsp fresh minced sage

Mix the ground sausage with the minced sage. Form into 6 or 7 patties that are about 2 inches wide. Heat a non stick pan for 3 minutes on high and add the patties in. Cook 2 minutes per side until browned. Great with my pancakes or on a biscuit. *Yield:* Makes 6 or 7 patties

Italian Three Bean Salad (gluten free)

1 can chickpeas
1 can red kidney beans
1 can cannellini beans
3 stalks small diced celery
1 small red onion small diced
6 leaves fresh basil chopped
1 small zucchini small diced

dressing:

1/2 cup red wine vinegar
1 Tbs balsamic vinegar
a few pinches of salt
1 teaspoon garlic powder
1/4 cup extra virgin olive oil
3 Tbs sugar

Whisk the dressing ingredients together. Drain and rinse the beans. Place in a bowl with the rest of the ingredients and dressing. Mix well and serve chilled.

Yield: Serves 6-8

Tuscan Kale with Sauteed Garlic Mushrooms, Cauliflower and Kalamata Olives (gluten free)

2 bunches of Lacinato Kale (also known as black kale or dino kale)
3 cloves minced garlic
1 cup cauliflower cut into bite size chunks
1.5 cups button mushrooms, quartered
1/4 cup pitted kalamata olives, cut in half
1 Tbs red wine vinegar
1/2 tsp salt
black pepper to taste or red pepper flakes if you want it spicy
1 tsp olive oil

Heat 5 inches of water to a boil. Rough chop the kale. Place it in the boiling water until soft, about 4 minutes. Drain and squeeze all of the water out. Heat a large non stick pan for 3 minutes on high. Add in the olive oil, then the garlic, mushrooms and cauliflower. Let them sit a minute to get some color, then stir them. Add a little salt. Cook 2 more minutes, then add in the cooked kale, olives, vinegar, salt and pepper. Cook 3 more minutes. Serve warm.

Yield: Serves 3-4

Steamed Asparagus with Creamy Saffron Aioli

1 head of asparagus with the hard bottoms cut off (about 1.5 inches cut off of the bottom)
for the aioli: whisk together 1/2 cup Vegenaise brand vegan mayo with 1 pinch of saffron.
1 tsp red wine vinegar, pinch of salt, 1 Tbs water and 1 tsp minced parsley until smooth

Steam the asparagus for 2 minutes or drop it in boiling water for 1 minute if you have no
steamer. Drain it and toss in a little salt and pepper. Put it on a plate and spoon the sauce
over the top. Enjoy. *Yield:* Served 2-3

Jalapeno Havarti Shell Macaroni & Cheese

1 box of small or medium shell pasta, cooked 6 minutes and cooled (I like
Barilla brand White Fiber shells since it has extra fiber and a white flour texture)
sauce:
2 cups plain rice milk
1.5 cups water, 1 Tbs lemon juice, 1 tsp garlic powder, 1 tsp salt
1/2 cup nutritional yeast, 4 Tbs Earth Balance Soy Free Buttery Spread
1/3 cup flour, 1 block of Daiya brand Jalapeno Havarti Farmhouse block,
shredded (you will need to shred it yourself)

Mix all of the sauce ingredients in a large pan but NOT the cheese yet.
Whisk well over medium heat until it just starts to bubble. Add in the
shredded cheese. Whisk constantly until the cheese is melted and the sauce
has thickened. Taste it, if it seems bland, add more salt, lemon juice or
nutritional yeast. Heat the oven to 375 degrees. Spray a 9x13 inch glass
baking dish with non stick spray. Pour the cooked shell pasta into the cheese
sauce. Mix well and place this into the baking dish evenly. Cover with foil or
a top and bake for 40 minutes. Remove the top and bake for 6 more minutes.
Enjoy.

Yield: Serves 6-8

Thyme Maple Buttered Roasted Carrots (gluten free)

These make a nice holiday side dish.

2 1/2 cups of peeled carrots cut on an angle into 1/4 inch thick slices
1 Tbs olive oil
1/2 tsp salt, 1/4 tsp black pepper
1/2 tsp fresh chopped thyme and 1/4 tsp dried basil
2 Tbs Earth Balance brand buttery spread
2 Tbs maple syrup
1 Tbs brown sugar

Heat the oven to 400 degrees. Mix the carrot slices with the olive oil, salt, pepper, thyme and dried basil. Place them on a parchment paper lined cookie sheet and roast for 25 minutes or until softened and browned a little. While they cook, place the Earth Balance, maple syrup and brown sugar in a small pot with a pinch of salt. Melt it all together for 1 minute on medium heat. When the carrots come out of the oven, place them in a bowl and toss them with the melted mixture. Enjoy.

Yield: Serves 3-4

Layered Taco Dip (gluten free if soy sauce is left out of the refried bean recipe)

double recipe of the guacamole from this book
1 recipe of refried beans from this book
1 cup of your favorite salsa
1 container of Tofutti brand vegan sour cream
1/4 cup chopped green onions
1 cup of iceberg lettuce, shredded
1 cup of So Delicious brand shredded jack cheese or 1 cup of shredded Field Roast brand Chao cheese (you will need to shred the Chao yourself)
1/4 cup sliced olives

Take a 9 x 9 inch glass casserole dish and spread the refried beans on the bottom. Next, place the guacamole in a ziploc bag and the sour cream in another ziploc. Snip the edges off, creating a pastry bag. Squeeze the guacamole from the bag onto the beans in a zig zag pattern. Take a spoon and carefully and evenly spread the guacamole over the beans. Take the sour cream and pipe it over the guacamole now, spreading it carefully and evenly over the guacamole. Spoon the salsa over the sour cream and spread with the spoon into an even layer. Now sprinkle the lettuce on top, then the cheese, olives and scallions. Keep refrigirated until ready to serve.

Yield: Serves 4-6

Savory Italian Fennel Seed Tiralli

A savory Italian wreath shaped snack cracker. Simple, addictive and delicious.

2 cups of King Arthur brand flour, 1 Tbs whole fennel seeds, 1 tsp salt, 1/2 cup white wine, 1/4 cup olive oil

Place the flour, salt and fennel seeds in a large bowl. Mix the oil and wine together and pour the mix into the flour. Knead until a dough forms for about 2 minutes. Cut it into 5 equal pieces and roll each piece into about a 16 inch rope. Take the end of the rope and connect it about 3 inches down the rope, forming the shape of a small oval wreath, overlapping the end of the rope to where you connected it to. Press down a little and cut the wreath shape off with a knife. Repeat until you have several wreath shapes cut from all of the ropes of dough. Bring 6 inches of water to a boil. Boil 10 tiralli at a time for 3 minutes and drain on a kitchen towel. Repeat until all are boiled. Heat the oven to 375 degrees and bake them on a foil and parchment paper lined cookie sheet about 40 minutes or until golden and hardened. Allow them to cool and enjoy as a snack or with pasta. They are also great dipped in my Hummus recipe.

Yield: Makes about 30 tiralli

Lemon Pepper Tofu Avocado Mixed Greens Salad (gluten free)

5 cups of mixed baby salad greens
1 cucumber, sliced into rounds
2 ripe tomatoes, diced
1.5 large avocados, peeled and diced
1 carrot cut into matchsticks
1/2 cup cannellini beans, drained and rinsed
1 block of extra firm tofu that has been frozen, thawed and completely squeezed dry (this freezing process creates a nice chewy texture, delicious)
1 Tbs lemon pepper seasoning
1 tsp of truffle oil or olive oil

Cut the tofu into bite size squares. Pour the oil and lemon pepper onto the tofu and toss carefully. Set the tofu aside. Mix the salad ingredients (not the tofu yet) in a large bowl. Keep a little of each ingredient for the top garnish. Place the lemon pepper tofu on top, in the middle of the greens, and arrange the salad. This is great topped with goddess dressing.

Yield: Serves 3-5

Vegetable Steamed Dumplings or Gyoza/Potsicksers

for the wrappers: 1.5 cups King Arthur brand flour, 1/2 tsp salt and 1/2 cup very hot water **for filling**: 1 cup of cabbage chopped finely, 1/3 cup peeled small diced carrots, 1/2 cup minced mushrooms, 1/3 cup small diced onion, 1 tsp each minced fresh garlic and ginger, 1.5 tsp soy sauce,1 tsp sesame oil

 For the wrapper dough, place the flour and salt in a large bowl. Add in the hot water and knead quickly for a few minutes until a smooth dough forms. Add a tiny bit more water if it seems too dry. Wrap in plastic and chill in the fridge 20 minutes. **For the filling**, heat a large non stick skillet on high for 3 minutes. Add in the sesame oil and then add the rest of the filling ingredients but not the soy sauce. Sautee it all together for 4 minutes. Stir often. Add in the soy sauce, stir and cool it completely. On a lightly floured board, roll the dough very thin with a rolling pin. You can also use a pasta rolling machine and roll the dough to the second to last filling to flatten the dough as well. Take a wine glass and cut out circles. You can bunch the leftover dough up and roll out again for more circles. Brush around the edges of the circles with a small amount of water. Place a circle of dough in your hand and add about a 1/2 a tsp of the filling in the middle of each circle. Take one side of the circle and have it meet with the other side, pinching as they touch, so that it looks like a canolli. Now, make tiny folds, one at a time, on first the right side of the pinch, so that 3 tiny folds have been made, and then pinch it at the end. Repeat with the left side of the pinch. This takes some practice. If it seems too difficult, you can just seal them with a fork until you master the technique. **For steamed dumplings**, simply place them in a steamer on top of parchment paper that has been cut in a circle and had several small holes cut into it and steam 8 minutes and serve. **For gyoza**, heat a large non stick pan that has a lid for 2 minutes on high. Add in 1 Tbs vegetable oil and place each dumpling into the oil, with each dumpling sitting on the flat bottom in the oil. Turn the heat to medium. Cover the pan with the lid and cook about 2 minutes. Remove the lid and make sure the bottoms are browning but not burnt. Once they are golden on the bottom, add in about 5 Tbs of water and place the lid back on. Turn the heat back to high and let the water steam finish cooking the dumplings until the water is evaporated. Serve dipped in hot chili oil and or soy sauce. *Yield:* Makes about 24 dumplings

Mama Ciolli's Fried Dough

This is a favorite from my youth up until this very day.

1 ball of the basic dough recipe from this book, risen
canola oil or vegetable oil

Heat an inch of oil in a pot on medium high. When you can drop a small piece of dough in and it bubbles, it is ready to fry (after about 4 minutes). Tear one inch chunks off of the risen dough and drop carefully into the oil, about 6 at a time. Cook both sides until golden, drain and sprinkle with salt or roll in powdered sugar while still hot if you prefer your fried dough sweet.

Yield: Serves 6-8

Sun Dried Tomato Pesto

2 cups fresh basil leaves, 1 cup fresh baby spinach, 4 Tbs nutritional yeast
1 Tbs Follow Your Heart brand parmesan shreds, 1/2 tsp salt
1/3 cup oil cured sun dried tomatoes (make sure they are the ones in a jar packed in oil and not the ones from a bag)
1/3 cup toasted and salted green pumpkin seeds, 1/3 cup olive oil

Place all of the ingredients but the olive oil in a food processor. Turn it on and add in the oil in a slowly add in the oil until a pesto forms. Add a little water if too thick. Enjoy on any cooked pasta.

Pasta Fagioli/Pasta Fazool/Minestrone

2.5 cups of your favorite homemade or store bought tomato sauce

3 stalks celery, diced small

1 small onion, diced small, 2 cloves minced garlic

3/4 cup peeled carrots, diced small

1 small green pepper, diced small

3 cups of uncooked baby spinach or 1 bunch of stemmed and chopped kale that has been boiled for 3 minutes and drained

1 1/2 cups of water whisked together with 1 Tbs Better Than Bouillon brand No Chicken Base or Roasted Garlic Base

1 can of cooked red kidney beans or 1 can of cooked white cannellini beans, drained and rinsed

2 cups of cooked ditalini pasta or cooked baby farfalle pasta, cooled

1 tsp each dried oregano, basil and garlic powder

1 tsp balsamic vinegar or red wine vinegar

1/2 tsp salt plus salt and pepper to taste

In a large pot, heat the 1/4 cup of water (this water saute method cuts down on the fat plus leaves no greasy film on top of your soup). Add in the carrots, celery, onions, garlic, peppers and cooked kale or spinach. Stir around for 5 minutes and then add in the beans, tomato sauce, vinegar, the water/bouillon mixture, salt, pepper, oregano, basil and garlic powder. Cook over medium heat for 10 minutes or until the carrots are soft. Just before serving, add in the cooked pasta (this will keep the pasta from getting soggy). If it seems too thick, add a little more water. Add salt and pepper if needed.

Yield: Serves 3-4

Mushroom Dill Rice (gluten free)

2 cups leftover cold brown or white rice
3 cups sliced button mushrooms
1 cup chopped oyster mushrooms
1 large onion medium diced
2 Tbs fresh dill
1 tsp salt or to taste
1 tsp extra virgin olive oil
2 Tbs Earth Balance Vegan Butter
3 cloves minced garlic

 Heat a large non stick pan for 3 minutes on medium high heat, then add the
oil, garlic, a pinch of salt, mushrooms and onions. Saute 5 minutes. Add the
vegan butter, saute another 30 seconds then add the rice, dill and salt. Break
the cold rice up well with a spatula and cook until the rice is hot.

Yield: Serves 4-6

Garlic Bread

 Mix 1/2 cup of melted Earth Balance brand buttery spread with 3 cloves of
minced fresh garlic, 2 Tbs of Follow Your Heart brand parmesan, 1/4 tsp
salt and 1 tsp chopped fresh parsley. Split a baguette in half length wise and
brush this onto both halves. Bake at 400 degrees for 10 minutes and place it
under the broiler for the last minute to brown up nicely. Enjoy.

Yield: Serves 3-5

Oil Cured Sun Dried Tomato, Cannellini Bean, Red Grape and Pan Seared Tofu Baby Greens Salad (gluten free)

Be sure to use sun dried tomatoes that are in a jar packed in oil and not the bagged, dried ones. The ones in the jar are much more tender and delicious. The grapes add a beautiful depth to this simple salad.

4 cups baby salad greens
3/4 cup red grapes, cut in half
1 recipe of pan seared tofu from this book, tossed in a little balsamic vinegar and salt added at the end of cooking the tofu
1/2 cup drained and rinsed cannellini beans
3 Tbs of oil cured sun dried tomatoes, julienne cut
1/4 cup of your favorite olives
1/2 cup peeled and sliced cucumbers
1/4 cup peeled and thin sliced carrots

Place the baby greens at the bottom of a large salad bowl. Arrange the rest of the ingredients on top the salad greens and enjoy.

Yield: Serves 2-4

Olive Oil and Garlic Green Beans (gluten free)

3 cups snipped
green beans
2 Tbs olive oil
1 teaspoon salt
1/4 teaspoon
black pepper
4 cloves of
garlic minced

Bring 5 cups of water to a boil. Drop in green beans until just softened, about 5 to 6 minutes. In a separate small non stick pan, heat the olive oil, drop in the garlic until barely browned. Drain the green beans and toss in the olive oil/garlic mixture. Add the salt and pepper to taste.

Yield: Serves 4-8

Smoky Southern Style Collard Greens

4 bunches of collard greens with the stems removed and discarded, chop the remaining leaves into bite sized pieces
1 medium onion, diced
3 cloves minced garlic
1 tsp vegetable oil
4 cups of water whisked together with 1.5 Tbs Better Than Bouillon brand Roasted Garlic Base, 2 tsp apple cider vinegar, 1 tsp smoked paprika, 2 tsp liquid smoke, 1 tsp sugar and a few pinches of salt and fresh cracked black pepper

Heat a very large pot for 2 minutes on high. Add in the oil, garlic and onions. Cook 3 minutes and add in the chopped collards. Stir this all together and cook 2 minutes and add in the liquid. Stir and cook this all together about 45 minutes or until very tender and most of the liquid has evaporated, stirring often. Taste for flavor. If you want more of a vinegar taste, add a little more vinegar. Enjoy with my Corn Bread recipe and my From Scratch Baked Beans.

Yield: Serves 4-5

Olive Oil and Garlic Roasted Cremini and Button Mushrooms (gluten free)

2 cups whole white button mushrooms (if the mushrooms are larger than average, cut them in half)
2 cups whole cremini mushrooms (if the mushrooms are larger than average, cut them in half)
2 cloves garlic, rough chopped
1/2 tsp garlic powder
1 tsp salt
1/2 tsp black pepper
1/2 tsp dried oregano
1 Tbs extra virgin olive oil

   Preheat the oven to 400 degrees. Line a sheet pan with foil and then parchment paper. Spray it with non stick spray. Mix all of the ingredients in a large bowl. Place the mushroom mix on the sheet pan and bake for 20-25 minutes or until cooked and slightly browned. Seaon again with salt and pepper if needed. Serve warm.

Yield: Serves 4-6

Whole Wheat Wreath Bread

   This has a hearty whole grain flavor and is full of fiber and B vitamins. You can also use this dough recipe for any of the bread, pizza or bagel recipes in this book. I admit that I enjoy the white flour doughs a little better but everyone has their own tastes and this is a great recipe.

1 1/4 cup cups whole wheat flour, 1 1/4 cup King Arthur white flour
1 1/4 cup water
1 tsp ycast, 1 tsp olive oil, pinch of salt

   Mix 1 1/4 cup of the white flour with 1 cup of water that has been 1/2 tsp of the yeast mixed into it. Let this sit 8 hours. This is a starter or sometimes called a sponge. After it has sat 8 hours, mix the whole wheat flour with the salt, do not forget the salt. Mix the olive oil and the rest of the yeast into the starter/sponge mixture and then add in the rest of the flour and salt. Mix well, if it is too wet, add more flour. Knead it together until it forms a nice dough. Cover it and let it rise for 2 hours. When risen, remove from the bowl but do not punch it down, place it on a lightly floured board. Split it into 2 long pieces. Roll each one about 18 inches long. Braid them together as if you were braiding hair and then form this into a circle or wreath shape. Cover it and let it rise for 2 hours on a foil and parchment lined sheet pan. Heat the oven to 440 degrees. Brush the dough with a little olive oil and bake it for about 15 minutes. Once golden, remove from the oven and brush with a little more oil. Enjoy warm.

Yield: Serves 3-4

Olive Oil Roasted Brussel Sprouts (gluten free)

5 cups medium sized brussel sprouts
3 Tbs extra virgin olive oil mixed with 1 teaspoon garlic powder, 1/2
tsp black pepper and 1 teaspoon salt

 Preheat oven to 375 degrees. Line a large casserole dish with tin foil sprayed
with non stick spray. Mix the brussel sprouts with the olive oil mixture.
Pour onto the foil in the casserole dish and then cover the brussel sprouts
with foil. Place in the oven for 45-55 minutes or until the brussel sprouts are
soft and browned.

Yield: Serves 6-8

Classic Macaroni Salad

1 box of your favorite elbow macaroni (I like Dreamfields brand or Ronzoni
brand Smart Taste elbows, they are high in fiber but taste like traditional
white pasta)
1/3 cup each small diced celery, white onions, red bell peppers and carrots
(peel the carrots first)
1/4 cup minced sweet gherkin pickles or sweet relish
for the dressing:
whisk together 1/2 cup Vegenaise vegan mayo with 1/4 cup Tofutti brand
vegan sour cream, 1 tsp yellow mustard, 1 Tbs sugar, 1 Tbs red wine vingar,
1 Tbs chopped fresh dill, 1/2 tsp salt, 1/2 tsp garlic powder and 1/4 tsp
black pepper

 Cook the macaroni for about 7 minutes or until cooked but not mushy.
Cool the macaroni in cold water, drain completely and mix with the rest of
the ingredients. Add salt and pepper if needed. Enjoy chilled.

Yield: Serves 4-6

Pesto Bread Sticks

1 ball of homemade dough, risen, recipe is in this book
1 recipe of homemade pesto from this book

Carefully remove the dough from the bowl. Do not re- knead it. Put a little flour on a large cutting board and gently press the dough into a large rectangle shape, about 12 inches across and 6 inches vertically, about 1/2 inch thick. Line a sheet pan with foil, brush a little olive oil on the foil and place the rectangle shaped dough on the foil lined pan. Cover with another sheet pan that is placed upside down on top of the first sheet pan (to leave space for the bread to rise). Let rise for 1.5 hours. Uncover and using a pizza cutter, cut bread stick shapes like the ones in the picture. Do not cut all the way to the bottom of the dough, just halfway down (this prevents huge air bubble pockets from forming while baking). Spread the pesto evenly and gently across the dough and then sprinkle the pesto with a few shakes of Go Veggie brand vegan parmesan cheese. Place into a 420 degree pre heated oven for 15 minutes until golden on the bottom.

*These are also very tasty if you take a soft block of Follow Your Heart brand vegan mozzarella cheese (make sure it is the soft block and not the hard one, the soft melts best) and shred it and place the shreds on top of the pesto topped dough with a little salt and dried oregano before baking. That is how I prepared them in the picture.

Yield: Serves 3-4

Poor Man's Caviar (Simple Spicy Black Bean and Corn Salad) (gluten free)

This is great as a side salad or to dip some buttery vegan Club and Ritz style crackers or tortilla chips into. If you use tortilla chips, small dice up a large avocado and add it into the salad.

2 cans corn drained and washed
2 cans black beans drained and washed
1/2 bunch chopped scallions
1/2 bunch chopped cilantro
1 small onion small diced
1 small green and red pepper small diced
3 stalks celery small diced
1/4 cup apple cider vinegar
1 Tbs chili powder
1 teaspoon garlic powder
1 Tbs Sriracha, 1/4 cup organic sugar
1 Tbs olive oil, 1 tsp salt

Place all ingredients in a bowl. Mix well, serve chilled.

Yield: Serves 6-8

Chinese Vegetable Pancakes

for the pancakes: 1 cup shredded green cabbage, 1/2 cup peeled shredded carrots, 4 Tbs thin sliced scallions, 1/2 tsp garlic powder, 1/4 tsp salt, 1 tsp soy sauce, 6 Tbs plain flour, 1 Tbs Follow Your Heart brand Vegan Egg powder whisked together with 1/4 cup water **for the sauce:** whisk together 3 Tbs Vegenaise brand mayo with 1 tsp sugar, 1/4 tsp soy sauce, 1/2 Tbs water and 1/4 tsp rice vinegar until smooth

Mix all of the pancake ingredients together with your hands in a bowl. Shape the mixture into 4 very thin patties, about 3 to 4 inches across each. Heat 1/4 of an inch of vegetable oil in a large non stick skillet for 3 minutes on high. Turn the heat to medium and cook each pancake about 3 minutes per side or until golden. Drain, chop into quarters and top with the sauce. *Yield:* Serves 3-4

Potato Leek Soup

3 large russet potatoes, peeled and medium diced
1.5 cups leeks, washed and sliced thin
1 Tbs fresh dill, 1-3 cups plain rice milk
1 tsp salt, 4 Tbs Earth Balance soy free buttery spread
1/2 tsp black pepper
1 Tbs Better Than Bouillon No Chicken Base or Roasted Garlic Base

Cover the potatoes with water and bring the potatoes to a boil. When soft (10 to12 minutes), drain and blend with a hand blender or in a blender with the No Chicken Base, salt, black pepper, a little more butter and some of the rice milk. Add the rice milk to the blender a little at a time until you get a smooth consistency. Set aside.

In a large pot, melt the butter, then add the leeks, pepper and a few pinches of salt. Saute 5 minutes, until browned, then add the potato mixture and freh dill. Cook 5 minutes, stirring often. If it seems too thick, add more rice milk. If it seems too bland, add more salt, butter or the No Chicken Base. Serve topped with freshly chopped scallions, chives or vegan bacon bits.

Yield: Serves 2-4

Black Bean, Spinach, Avocado Kale Salad

3/4 a bunch of kale, stems removed and rough chopped, 3 cups raw baby spinach, 1 can drained and washed black beans, 1 avocado peeled and medium diced, 2 tomatoes medium diced, 1/4 of a jalapeno minced, 1/3 cup small diced celery
for the marinade: whisk together 1/4 cup apple cider vinegar mixed with 2 Tbs olive oil, 2 Tbs sugar and 1/4 tsp salt

Bring a large pot of water to a boil. Add in the kale and cook 3 minutes. Add in the spinach and cook 1 more minute. Drain, cool and completely squeeze all of the water out of the greens. Stir all of the ingredients together and chill in the fridge. *Yield:* Serves 3-4

Grilled Broccoli Stalks with Creamy Dijon Caper Sauce (gluten free)

3 individual heads of broccoli, extra virgin olive oil
salt and pepper to taste
sauce:
2 Tbs Dijon mustard, 1 tsp minced shallots
1 tsp chopped parsley, 4 Tbs Soy Free Vegenaise brand vegan
mayo, 1 tsp red wine vinegar
1/4 tsp salt, 1/4 tsp garlic powder
1 Tbs capers, minced
water to thin

Whisk all of the sauce ingredients together, slowly add in the water until you get a medium thin sauce. Taste, adjust seasonings if needed. Trim the hard bottoms off of the broccoli but leave the edible part of the stalk fairly long. Cut each individual head of broccoli into 3 or 4 large, long pieces. Bring about 5 inches of water to a boil. Drop the broccoli into the water for 1 minute. Drain and cool completely. Heat a grill on high for 15 minutes. Toss the broccoli in a little olive oil, salt and pepper. Spray the grill grates well with non stick spray and lay the broccoli onto the grates. Grill about 2 or 3 minutes per side. Remove from grill and spoon the sauce over top. Enjoy.

Yield: Serves 4-6

Vietnamese Avocado Smoothie (gluten free)

These are deliciously sweet, rich and refreshing.

1 medium haas avocado, peeled with the
pit removed
1/2 cup crushed ice cubes 1/3 cup Natures Charm
brand condensed sweetened coconut milk
1/4 to 1/2 cup rice milk

Place all of the ingredients into a blender. Add a little more rice milk if it is too thick to blend, but you want it pretty thick, so add in a little more at a time. Pour into a glass and top with a little of the condensed coconut milk if desired. Enjoy cold.

Yield: Makes 1 smoothie

Indian Chickpea Tamarind and Mushroom Kale Avocado Salad (gluten free)

1 can of chickpeas drained and rinsed, 1/3 each cup small zucchini and red bell pepper, 1/2 cup each sliced button mushrooms and bite size cut cauliflower, 1 avocado medium diced, 2 cups of stemmed chopped kale
for the dressing: whisk together 1.5 Tbs tamarind sauce (not the paste) with 3 Tbs rice vinegar, 3 Tbs vegetable oil, 1 tsp sugar and a pinch of salt

Heat a large pot of water 3 inches deep to a boil. Add in the chopped kale. Cook it 3 minutes on a boil. Add in the mushrooms and cauliflower after 3 minutes. Cook them 2 more minutes with the kale. Drain it, cool it and squeeze all of the water out of the kale and mushrooms the best you can without breaking up the cauliflower too much. Mix this with the zucchini, bell peppers, avocado and chickpeas. Toss gently in the dressing. Add a little salt and pepper if needed. Enjoy. *Yield:* Serves 3-5

Roasted Vegetables (gluten free)

Preheat oven to 400 degrees. Line a cookie sheet with aluminum foil and then parchment paper. Spray with non stick spray.

2 cups quartered brussel sprouts, 1 head chopped cauliflower
2 cups whole button mushrooms, 1 cup large sliced carrots, 1 diced red bell pepper

Mix all the vegetables with 3 Tbs olive oil, 1 tsp dried oregano, 1 tsp garlic powder and 1/2 tsp salt. Pour onto cookie sheet and roast in over 20-25 minutes or until browned.

Yield: Serves 4-8

Rustic Truffle Oiled Olive Bread

1 ball of risen dough from the basic dough recipe from this book (the
dough recipe makes 2 balls of dough, you will only use 1 ball here)
1/4 cup of kalamata olives, rough chopped
1/4 cup green pitted spicy Sicilian green olives or oil packed non spicy green
olives, rough chopped
truffle oil for brushing

 Take your risen ball of dough and flatten it on a floured cutting board a bit.
Do not knead it again though. Cut the dough into 3 equal pieces. Flatten
them out a bit until each piece is about 10 inches long and 2 inches wide
and evenly distribute the olives on each piece. Press the olives into the
dough. Roll each piece into a long sausage shape, about 12 inches long.
Place the three dough logs next to each other and cross one of the logs over
the middle piece, and then the other over the middle piece, making sure the
piece that is in the middle is always getting folded over with the other dough
logs until you have one large, braided loaf. Cover and let this rise for 2
hours on a parchment paper topped foil lined cookie sheet. Preheat the
oven to 450 degrees. When the dough has risen, brush it with a little truffle
oil and bake for 18 minutes or until golden. Brush with a little more truffle
oil once out of the oven and enjoy.

Yield: Serves 3-4

Garlic Butter Basil Pan Seared Potatoes

3 medium red potatoes cut into a little smaller than 1/2 inch cubes, 2 Tbs thinly sliced basil, salt and pepper to taste, 3 Tbs Earth Balance brand buttery spread, 2 cloves minced garlic

Heat a large non stick pan for 3 minutes on high (make sure it is non stick or the potatoes will stick). Add in 1 Tbs of the Earth Balance and then the potatoes in a flat even layer. Add in a little salt and pepper. Let them sit in a flat layer for 2 minutes so they begin to become golden. Turn the potatoes with tongs and brown the other sides for 3 minutes. Stir them and cook about 2 more minutes or until softened. Add in the rest of the Earth Balance, the garlic and basil. Cook about 1 more minute. Taste for salt and pepper. Enjoy.

Yield: Serves 3-4

Sicilian Olive and Truffle Oil Roasted Garlic Lemon Spaghetti

1 box of Barilla brand white fiber spaghetti
1 cup of oil marinated green Italian olives, chop them in half lengthwise (not oil cured olives)
3 Tbs lemon juice
1 tsp red wine vinegar
1/2 cup chopped Italian
flat leaf parsley
6 cloves garlic, chopped
4 Tbs truffle oil
salt and pepper to taste

Bring the truffle oil to a high heat and add in the chopped garlic. Cook 15 seconds to just barely brown the garlic. Remove from heat. Cook the spaghetti 6 minutes, drain it and toss the spaghetti with the garlic oil and rest of the ingredients. Taste to make sure it is salty and lemony enough, if it is bland, add more lemon juice or salt.

Yield: Serves 3-6

Fresh Ramen Noodles

1.5 cups King Arthur brand flour, 1/2 tsp salt, 1/2 cup very hot water with 1/2 tsp baking soda whisked into it

A manual pasta machine is needed to make these. Mix the baking soda water with the flour and salt. Knead into a smooth dough for about 2 minutes. Place the manual pasta machine on the widest setting and divide the dough into 3 equal size pieces. Flatten each piece as flat as you can get them with a rolling pin. Roll each piece, one at a time, through the widest setting on the pasta machine. Go to the next level thinner level on the machine and roll them through. Repeat this process with each sheet of dough until you get to the 3 rd to last setting on your machine. Take the spaghetti cutter on the machine and run each flattened sheet through, one at a time. Flour the cut sheets well so that they do not stick. When each are cut into noodles, cook them for 1 minute in boiling water and then drain. You can simply toss the cooked noodles in a little soy sauce, sesame oil, chopped scallions and hot chili paste or you can add them to soup broth. Enjoy. *Yield:* Serves 3

Simple Bruschetta Topping

2 containers of grape tomatoes, 1/2 tsp red wine vinegar, 1/2 tsp salt
4 fresh basil leaves, 1/2 a clove of garlic

Place all of the ingredients in a food processor and pulse 5 or 6 times until you get a chunky bruschetta topping. Chill and serve over grilled vegetarian chicken, tofu or baguette bread cut into rounds and toasted in the oven a few minutes until crisp with a little olive oil and salt brushed on them pre baking. *Yield*: Serves 6-8

Balsamic Watermelon, Cucumber and Arugula Salad (gluten free)

You can use baby spinach if you do not enjoy the flavor of arugula.

3 cups seedless watermelon, peeled and cut into half inch chunks
1 cup of seedless cucumber cut into 1/4 inch half moons
2 Tbs fresh basil, julienne cut, 2 cups fresh arugula
a few pinches of salt and pepper
1/2 cup cherry tomatoes cut in half
1/3 cup thin sliced celery
1/2 recipe of the Balsamic Reduction from this book

Place all of the ingredients in a large bowl and gently toss them. Chill in the fridge and enjoy on a warm summer day.

Yield: Serves 3-4

Simple Caesar Salad

dressing:

1/2 cup plain hummus
(homemade or store bought)
2 tsp Dijon mustard
1 Tbsp lemon juice, or to taste
3 tsp capers, minced
1/2 tsp fresh minced garlic
salt and pepper to taste
1 Tbsp olive oil
water to thin

salad:

5 cups romaine lettuce, cleaned and chopped into bite size pieces

1/4 cup of kalamata olives or green Sicilian olives

1/2 cup of the homemade crouton recipe from this book or your favorite
vegan store bought croutons

1/3 cup of shredded Follow Your Heart brand vegan parmesan cheese

For the dressing, simply mix all of the ingredients together in a large
bowl. Add some water, a little at a time, whisking constantly until you
get a smooth dressing. Taste for flavor, it should be rich and tangy.
Adjust the seasoning if needed. In a large bowl, place your chopped
romaine, the croutons, olives and a few pinches of the shredded
parmesan. Pour a little dressing in and toss with tongs. If it seems dry,
add more dressing. Present this on a plate or in a large bowl and top it
with a few more olives and the shredded parmesan. Enjoy.

Yield: Serves 4-8

Watermelon Red Pepper Vinaigrette (gluten free)

1 cup seedless watermelon
cut into small chunks
1/3 cup diced red bell pepper
4 leaves chopped fresh basil
1 Tbs chopped fresh chives
1 clove fresh garlic
pinch of salt
3 Tbs red wine vinegar
3 Tbs vegetable oil or olive oil
1 Tbs sugar

Simply place all of the ingredients in a blender and blend until smooth.
Goes great over any salad.

Yield: Serves 4-5

Simple Cheese Grits (gluten free)

3/4 cup instant grits
2 cups of water mixed with 1 cup of plain unsweetened rice milk
1 tsp salt
1/2 tsp garlic powder
black pepper to taste
1 cup of So Delicious brand cheddar jack shredded cheese
2 Tbs Earth Balance soy free buttery spread
1 Tbs nutritional yeast

  Bring the water to a boil. Stir in the grits, salt, pepper and garlic powder. Turn the heat to low and with a whisk, whisk until thickened. Keep a constant eye on it, sometimes they cook faster, sometimes slower but keep whisking. When thickened, add in the butter, cheese, nutritional yeast and more salt and pepper if needed. You can top these with fresh chives if you like.

Yield: Serves 4-6

Borlotti Beans with Fresh Thyme and Rosemary

1 pound of dried Borlotti beans that have been covered in water for about 8 hours
4 Tbs tomato paste
2 sprigs of fresh thyme
1/2 tsp chopped fresh sage
1/2 tsp fresh rosemary, minced
1 tsp olive oil
1 medium onion, diced small
3 cloves of garlic, minced
1/2 cup celery, diced small
1 Tbs of Better Than Bouillon brand No Chicken Base
salt and pepper to taste
1 bay leaf

  Drain the beans and place them in a large pot. Cover with water, about 4 inches over the top of the beans and add in the thyme and bay leaf. Bring to a boil and cook the beans for about 45 minutes or until soft but not mushy. Add more water if needed. While the beans cook, heat the olive oil in a non stick saute pan for 2 minutes. Add in the celery, onions and garlic. Cook for 4 minutes. When the beans are soft, add these sautéed vegetables and the rest of the ingredients into the beans. Whisk well and cook another 10 minutes. Add in the fresh sage and rosemary and remove the bay leaf and thyme sprigs. Taste and add more salt and pepper if needed. Serve with my Creamy Polenta recipe from this book.

Yield: Serves 6-10

Simple Chicken Gravy

This goes great over mashed potatoes or the mushroom crusted eggplant cutlet recipe from this book.

1 cup water
2 cups plain rice milk
1/3 cups flour
1 Tbs nutritional yeast
2 Tbs Better Than Bouillon No Chicken Base
1/2 tsp garlic powder
1/8 tsp black pepper
3 Tbs Earth Balance soy free buttery spread
1 Tbs Gravy Master
(available in the seasoning isle at most grocery stores).

Heat a non stick pan over medium heat, melt the butter. Add the flour into the butter and stir around with a wooden spoon for a few seconds, then add the remaining ingredients. Whisk for a few minutes until thickened. Enjoy.

Yield: Serves 6-8

Deviled Yukon Gold Potatoes (gluten free)

20 small Yukon Gold potatoes (about the size of an egg)
4 or 5 Tbs Vegenaise brand vegan mayo
1/2 tsp black salt (this will give the filling an egg type flavor, make sure to use it, you can find it in the spice section at health food stores)
2 Tbs sweet relish
1/2 tsp turmeric powder
1/2 tsp garlic powder
1/2 tsp salt or to taste, black pepper to taste
1 Tbs yellow mustard
paprika for the topping

Boil the potatoes whole for about 12 minutes or until soft but not mushy. Remove from the hot water and cool them in cold water. Lay them flat and cut them in half from right to left so that you have 2 long flat halves. Take a spoon and carve out the middle of the potatoes, leaving about an 1/8 of an inch of potato flesh inside the potato (you will fill it with the filling later). Place the scooped out potato insides and the rest of the ingredients besides the paprika into a large bowl. Mash them with a potato masher or fork until smooth. Taste for flavor, if it needs more salt, add it now, if too dry, add a little more mayo. Take a pastry bag with a fluted tip and place the mashed ingredients inside. Pipe this into the hollowed out potato skins. Sprinkle with a little paprika. Enjoy these chilled.

Yield: Makes about 25 deviled potatoes

Corn, Cherry, Asparagus and Avocado Salad (gluten free)

3 cups of mixed baby salad greens

1/2 a bunch of asparagus with the hard woody bottoms trimmed off

1 avocado, peeled and sliced

1 carrot, peeled and sliced

1 cup of broccoli chopped into bite size pieces

1 medium beet, peeled and sliced into half moons

1/4 cup cherries, pitted and sliced

1 medium tomato, diced

10 pitted kalamata olives sliced in half

1/2 cup sliced cucumbers

2 ears of fresh corn, cut off the cob

1/2 cup cooked black beans

Place the salad greens at the bottom of a large salad bowl. Bring 6 inches of water to a boil. Add in the corn, cook 2 minutes. Drain, cool and set aside but keep the water for boiling. Add the broccoli and asparagus into the boiling water. Cook them 2 minutes, drain and cool them. Add in the sliced beets next and cook them in the boiling water for 7 minutes, drain and cool. Arrange all of your toppings in a beautiful manner on the salad greens like in the picture. Enjoy with your favorite dressing.

Yield: Serves 4-6

Simple Fresh Summer Rolls with Sweet Chili Hoisin Dipping Sauce

These are a nice, light alternative to fried spring rolls, great for summer. I serve them as a side to the Mock Duck Thai Curry recipe from this book. Delicious. My nut free peanut sauce recipe works as a great dip for these too.

2 cups cooked rice noodles, cooled (available at most grocery stores or Asian markets)
1/4 cup chopped fresh basil
1/4 cup chopped fresh scallions
1/2 cup shredded peeled carrots
8 rice wrappers (available at Asian markets and some grocery stores)

sauce:
1/3 cup hoisin sauce
3 Tbs sweet chili sauce
1 Tbs sugar
2 Tbs water

Mix the cooked, cooled noodles with the basil, scallions and shredded carrots. Set aside.

Fill a large, wide bowl with warm water. Dip each rice wrapper, one at a time, into the water for 5 seconds. Only do 2 total for each wrapping session. Place the dipped rice wrapper on a large cutting board or clean counter, flat. Add a handfull of the noodle filling in the middle of the wrapper. Fold the sides over the noodles and then the bottom over the noodles, rolling into a tight thick cigar shape. Assemble the rest of the rolls accordingly.

For the sauce, simply whisk all of the sauce ingredients together. If is seems too thick, add a little more water. If it seems too thin, add a little more hoisin sauce.

*If you like, you can add sliced tofu, vegan chopped chicken or marinated tempeh to these for an entree style dish.

Yield: Serves 6-8

Crisp and Golden Fluffy Dinner Rolls

1 ball of dough from the Basic
Dough recipe from this book on page
81 (that recipe makes 2 balls of
dough, but you will only use 1 here)
a little olive oil for brushing

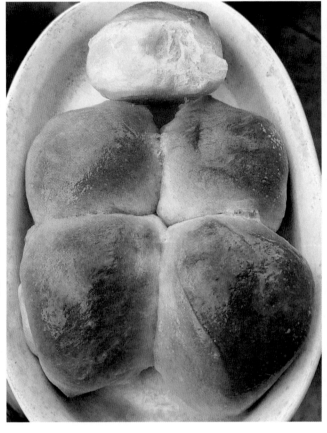

Line a 9 or 10 inch pan with
parchment paper cut into a circle to fit
inside the pan. Spray the inside sides
of the pan with non stick spray. Take
the risen ball of dough, do not punch
it back down, and pinch off golf ball
size pieces and pinch them into round
balls. Place them in the pan. Allow
them to touch each other so that they
rise into each other, this makes them
very soft. Once your pan is full of balls
of dough (should make about 16 rolls).
Cover and let rise 2 hours. Preheat the
oven to 440 degrees. Brush the tops of
the rolls with a little olive oil and bake
about 15 minutes. Place them under
the broiler for the last minute to get
them extra golden. Remove from the
oven and brush the tops with a little
more olive oil. These are great hot
with a little Earth Balance brand
buttery spread on them.

Yield: Makes 14-16 rolls

Simple Guacamole (gluten free)

Guacamole should be simple with just a few ingredients, so that the
buttery ripe avocado can be the star of the show.

2 ripe avocados
juice of 1/2 to 1 lime
1/2 teaspoon garlic powder or
1 clove minced fresh garlic
1/2 teaspoon salt

Cut the avocados in half and remove the pit. Scoop the flesh into a bowl
with the rest of the ingredients. Mash them all together, taste and add
more lime or salt if needed. Enjoy cold.

Yield: Serves 3-5

Simple Salt and Black Pepper Blanched Vegetables (gluten free)

I try to eat a variation of this daily, especially one with a green vegetable and cruciferous vegetables such as broccoli, cauliflower etc. You can add any vegetables you like. Try to cut the vegetables into similar sizes so they cook evenly. Try to eat 5 different vegetables a day for more supple skin, hair and energy, and to minimize health problems!

1 cup medium sized chopped broccoli
1 cup medium sized chopped cauliflower
1/2 cup large diced zucchini
3/4 cup quartered mushrooms
1/2 a red pepper medium diced
6 stalks asparagus chopped
1 medium sized carrot, peeled and sliced thin
salt and pepper

Bring 3 cups water to a boil. Drop all of the vegetables in the water for no more than 90 seconds. Drain, mix with a tsp of olive oil or a tsp of Earth Balance brand buttery spread and a few pinches of salt and black pepper. Serve immediately.

Yield: Serves 4-6

Simple Southwestern Kale, Sweet Potato, Pinto Bean, Mushroom and Rice Soup

3/4 cup cooked, cooled rice (cooked barley can also be used here)
3/4 cup cooked pinto beans
1 bunch of kale, stems removed, leaves chopped and boiled 4 minutes, then cooled and squeezed dry
1 medium sweet potato, peeled and diced small
1 carrot cut into half moons
1/2 a medium white onion, diced small
2 stalks of celery, sliced into half moons
1 clove minced garlic
4 cups of water with 2.5 Tbs of Better Than Boullion No Chicken Base or Roasted Garlic Base whisked into it

spice mix:
1 tsp garlic powder, 1/2 tsp dried oregano, 1/2 Tbs chili powder, 1/2 tsp red pepper flakes, salt and pepper to taste

Mix the spices together and set aside. In a large, wide pot, bring 1/4 cup water to a boil (I prefer this water saute method for soups because it will not leave you with an oily film on top of your soup). Add in all of your vegetables but not the beans and rice. Add in a pinch of salt and stir around 4 minutes. Add in the rice, beans, spice mix and the broth mixture. Simmer 10 minutes until the sweet potatoes are cooked. You can add hot sauce or more red pepper flakes if you like it spicier. This goes great with my homemade biscuit recipe, split open the flaky layers and top them with Earth Balance buttery spread.
Yield: Serves 3-5

Asian Baby Corn and Cucumber Cherry Salad

1/3 cup of pitted fresh cherries (you can cut 4 squared sides off of each cherry and discard the pit, it is easier this way)
1/3 cup baby corn cut into chunks
1/3 cup seedless cucumbers sliced into
1/4 inch thick pieces on an angle
1/3 cup thinly sliced white onion
2 Tbs rice wine vinegar, 1 tsp vegetable oil, 2 Tbs sweet chili sauce
1 Tbs sugar
1 tsp hot chili paste, a few chopped chives

Mix all of the ingredients together and serve chilled.

Smoky Mozzarella Creamy Penne Pasta Salad With Olives and Roasted Red Peppers

You can use gluten free pasta for this recipe as well. If you are not a fan of olives, you can leave them out or you can substitute capers for the olives. If you want to make the dish completely soy free, just leave out the soy sauce.

1 box of Dreamfields brand Penne Pasta, cooked 8 minutes, cooled
1/4 cup chopped celery
1/4 cup chopped scallions
1 Tbs chopped fresh basil
1/4 cup diced roasted red peppers
3 Tbs nutritional yeast
1 Tbs chopped parsley
1 Tbs red wine vinegar
1/2 cup Soy Free Vegenaise brand mayo
1/2 of a hard block of Follow Your Heart brand Mozzarella, cubed small
1/3 cup Daiya brand Monterey Jack cubed small
1 Tbs soy sauce
2 tsp liquid smoke
1/2 Tbs olive oil
1 tsp garlic powder
1/2-1 tsp salt
1/4 cup chopped green olives or kalamata olives

Place the mozzarella cubes in a bowl and toss them in the soy sauce, olive oil and liquid smoke. Let them marinate 30 minutes in the fridge. Once marinated, drain and toss all of the ingredients together. Add more mayo, vinegar or salt if needed. Chill in the fridge and serve.

Yield: Serves 6-8

Smoky Red Beans and Rice

A classic dish with a smoky kick that is savory and delicious.

2 cups jasmine rice
2.5 cups water
2 Tbs Better Than Bouillon No Chicken Base or No Chicken Base
1/2 tsp salt
1/2 tsp garlic powder
1 tsp chili powder
1/2 tsp liquid smoke, 1 tsp smoked paprika
2 cups cooked small red beans
1 large onion diced small
1 Tbs olive oil

Place the rice, liquid smoke, bouillon, water, salt, garlic powder and chili powder and smoked paprika in a rice cooker. Stir together well, make sure the bouillon is dissolved. Cook, then cool completely on a sheet pan.

In a large non stick pan, heat the olive oil for 2 minutes, add the onions. Saute 2 minutes then add the cold rice. Break up with a spatula until rice is warm. Add the beans and salt and pepper to taste. Top with scallions and hot sauce if desired.

Yield: Serves 4-6

Nut Free Peanut Sauce

This will work for any recipe that calls for a peanut sauce and is just as tasty. It is also great as a dip for my Summer Roll recipe or tossed with soba noodles.

1/2 cup plain Sun Butter brand sunflower butter
1 Tbs soy sauce
2 Tbs hoisin sauce
3 Tbs chopped scallions
1 clove of garlic, peeled
1 Tbs tahini
2 Tbs chopped cilantro
2 Tbs rice wine vinegar
1 Tbs Sriracha or hot chili oil (more or less depending on the spice level desired)
2 Tbs sugar
1 to 2 cups water

Simply place all of the ingredients besides the water into a blender. Turn it on and add in the water slowly until it reaches your desired thickness. Enjoy.

Yield: Serves 3-4

Soba Noodle Salad in Spicy Sunflower Butter "Peanut" Sauce Dressing

This is a recipe designed for people who are allergic to nuts. The sunflower "peanut sauce" dressing is every bit as rich and satisfying as a traditional peanut sauce. This is great served chilled.

sauce:

1/2 cup of Sun Butter brand smooth sunflower butter
2 Tbs hoisin sauce
1 Tbs soy sauce
2 Tbs rice wine vinegar
1 Tbs each of chopped cilantro and green onions
2 cloves garlic
1 Tbs Sriracha (you can add more if you like it spicier or leave it out if you do not want any spice)
1 tsp fresh grated ginger
1 Tbs sesame oil
3 Tbs sugar
pinch of salt
2 Tbs tahini
water to thin

for the salad:

4 cups of cooked and cooled soba noodles
1/2 cup each of julienne cut red bell peppers, green peppers, carrots, fresh scallions, baby bok choy and zucchini

Mix all of the sauce ingredients besides the water in a food processor. Start the machine and slowly add in some water, enough until you achieve a medium thick sauce. Taste it for flavor. It should be rich, tangy, slightly sweet, a hint salty and spicy. You can add in more hoisin, sugar, salt, Sriracha or vinegar if you feel it needs more flavor.

In a large bowl, toss the soba noodles with the julienne cut vegetables and the sauce. Taste for flavor, adjusting by adding in more hoisin, Sriracha, sugar or vinegar if it seems to be needed. Serve chilled. This looks impressive when served in a large hollowed out cabbage leaf.

Yield: Serves 3-5

Jalapeno Poppers

8 medium size jalapenos cut in half lengthwise with the seeds removed and the stems removed
1 container of Tofutti brand cream cheese, softened and mixed with 1 Tbs of minced scallions, 1/4 cup shredded Follow Your Heart brand vegan parmesan, 1/4 tsp salt and 1/2 tsp garlic powder
2 cups flour
1 cup water
1.5 cups of panko bread crumbs mixed with 1 tsp garlic powder, 1/2 tsp salt and 1/2 tsp dried oregano
1 inch of vegetable oil in a non stick pan

   Place 1 cup of flour in a large bowl. In another bowl, whisk the other 1 cup of flour with the 1 cup of flour (this wll act as the egg to help the bread crumbs stick to the jalapenos). In a flat glass sided dish, add in the bread crumb mixture. Fill the jalapeno halves with the cream cheese mixture to the tops of the jalapenos (if you place the mixture in a plastic bag and cut the tip off of the end, it will be easier to fill the jalapenos this way). Freeze the filled jalapenos for 1 hour. When frozen, dip each one into the flour, then the flour/water mixture and finally into the bread crumbs. Coat them completely. Heat the oil on high for 3 or 4 minutes and then dip a coated jalapeno into the oil, if bubbles form, they are ready to fry. Cook them about 3 minutes per side or until golden. Drain and enjoy.

Yield: Makes 16 poppers   — 146 —

Spinach, Mozzarella and Tomato Basil Caprese Salad (gluten free)

1 soft block of Follow Your Heart brand Mozzarella (if you want, you can use the hard block of their mozzarella cheese, but the soft block has more of a fresh mozzarella texture) cut into thirds width wise and cut into 1 inch squares
4 Roma tomatoes, sliced thin
1 cup raw baby spinach
4 leaves of fresh basil, cut into thin strips
1 Tbs extra virgin olive oil
1/2 recipe of the balsamic reduction dressing from this book
salt and pepper to taste

  Lay the spinach down on a plate or platter. Arrange the tomatoes and the cheese on top of the spinach, overlapping each other, like in the picture. Drizzle the olive oil and some of the balsamic reduction dressing over the top. Sprinkle with the fresh basil and a little salt and pepper. Serve chilled.

Yield: Serves 4-6

Spaghetti al Limone

1 box of Ronzoni brand Smart Taste spaghetti (this type has extra fiber but tastes like regular white pasta) or 1 box of your favorite spaghetti, juice of 1 large lemon, 3/4 cup of the hot cooking water that you will cook the spaghetti in, 1/2 a container of Follow Your Heart brand shredded parmesan, 3 Tbs Earth Balance brand buttery spread, 3 cloves fresh garlic rough chopped, salt and pepper to taste, lemon zest, fresh chopped basil or parsley for garnish

Cook the spaghetti for 7 minutes. As it cooks, heat the buttery spread, olive oil and chopped garlic in a pot and slightly brown the garlic on high for about 1 minute. Set aside. Drain the pasta but keep 3/4 cup of the hot pasta water set aside. Place the spaghetti back into the cooking pot and add in the garlic/oil/butter spread mixture as well as the lemon juice and the 3/4 cup pasta water. Cook this over medium heat for 1 minute, tossing with tongs until the noodles are coated. Add in a little more water if it looks too dry. Add in half of the parmesan and toss with the tongs. Add salt and pepper as needed. Serve topped with the rest of the parmesan and the lemon zest, basil or parsley. Enjoy. *Yield:* Serves 3-4

Split Pea Basil Soup (gluten free if you omit the soy sauce)

2 cups dried split peas, 6 cups water, 3/4 cup diced carrots, 1/2 Tbs soy sauce
3/4 cup diced celery, 1 diced medium onion, 1/2 cup diced red bell
pepper, 6 leaves fresh basil chopped, 1 tsp dried basil, 1 tsp garlic powder

Bring the 6 cups of water to a boil. Add the split peas and cook about 35 minutes or until soft. Once soft, drain and reserve a little of the cooking liquid. Blend the split peas with a little of the cooking liquid in a blender or with a hand blender. You want a thin pancake batter consistency. If it seems too thick, add more water or cooking liquid. Transfer the blended split peas back to a cooking pot and add the rest of the ingredients. Simmer over a medium heat about 20 minutes or until the carrots are cooked. If it is bland, add more garlic powder, salt or soy sauce. This soup will thicken in the fridge, just add more water or some vegetable stock to reheat and thin it out.

Yield: Serves 4-8

Tabouli Salad

1.5 cups bulgur wheat, 3 cups water, juice of 2 lemons
2 bunches of parsley finely chopped, 1 medium red onion diced small
3 Tbs extra virgin olive oil, 1/2 tsp salt or to taste
1 English seedless cucumber diced small
1 container of grape tomatoes chopped roughly in a food processor
8 leaves fresh mint chopped, 1/2 a bunch of chopped scallions

 Bring the water and salt to a boil. Add bulgur wheat. Stir, bring to a medium heat and cover, cooking 12 to 15 minutes. Cool completely after cooked. Place in a large bowl and fluff with a fork. Add the rest of ingredients and some salt and pepper to taste. Serve chilled. This goes well with a hummus platter with toasted pita points, olives, stuffed grape leaves and fresh vegetables or my Kafta Kebab recipe.

Yield: Serves 8-10

Italian Lentil Soup
(gluten free if you omit the soy sauce)

1.5 cups dry green lentils, 4 cups water, 1 tsp soy sauce, 1/2 tsp dried basil
1 cup diced carrots, 1/2 cup diced celery, 1 cup tomato sauce, pinch of oregano
1 medium onion diced 1 green pepper diced, 2 cloves garlic minced
1/2-1 tsp salt or to taste 1 tsp balsamic vinegar 1 tsp garlic powder

 Add the lentils to 4 cups of boiling water and cook 20 minutes, then add the rest of the ingredients to the lentils. Simmer over medium heat for 10 -15 more minutes. If it is bland, add more garlic powder, salt or tomato sauce.

Yield: Serves 4-8

Tofu or White Bean or Chicken Noodle Soup

2 cups raw baby spinach (optional)
8 cups water mixed with 3 Tbs Better Than Bouillon brand No
Chicken Base or Roasted Garlic Base and 2 Tbs nutritional yeast whisked together
2 carrots peeled and sliced into half moons
1 onion small diced
3 stalks celery medium diced, salt and pepper
1 Tbs chopped fresh dill
1/2 teaspoon fresh sage
1 cup cooked and cooled angel hair pasta or vegan egg noodles
1 cup diced Maywah brand or Delight Soy brand vegan chicken or 1 block
extra firm tofu small diced or 1 cup of cooked and drained cannellini
beans

Bring 1/4 cup water to a boil in large soup pan. Add the carrots, celery,
spinach, onions, fresh dill, sage and a few pinches of salt and pepper. Stir all
for 2 minutes (I prefer this water saute method for soups because it does not
leave a greasy film on the top of your soup like an oil saute will do). Add the
white beans, chicken or tofu and stir together. Add the water/no chicken
base/nutritional yeast mixture and salt. Bring to a boil. Once boiling,
remove from heat add in the cooked noodles. Add 2 cups baby spinach too if
desired and stir until wilted.

Yield: Serves 3-5

Kappamaki Cucumber Rolls (gluten free)

These require a sushi mat. They make a regreshingly delicious side dish or light entree. If you prefer, you can substitute peeled sliced avocado for the cucumber.

1 English cucumber, cut in quarters, then halved with the seeds sliced out from left to right and then each quarter cut into about three 8 inch strips, 3 Nori sheets that have been folded in half and cut in half so that you now have 6 nori sheets, 1 Tbs rice vinegar, 1 cup of white sushi rice, a pinch of salt, 1.5 cups of water and a small 4 inch square of dried kombu (kombu is optional), soy sauce for dipping

Cook the rice in a rice cooker with the 1.5 cups of water, pinch of salt and the optional kombu. Remove the kombu when the rice is cooked and stir in the vinegar. Bring it to room temperature. Lay 1 nori half on the sushi mat about an inch from the bottom of the mat, wider side of the nori facing you. Wet your fingers a bit and take about 3 to 4 Tbs of the rice and push it onto the nori, leaving about 1 inch of nori bare at the top and 1/4 inch bare at the bottom of the wide ends of the nori. Place a cucumber strip about 1 inch up away from you onto the rice. Using the mat, roll the bottom of the nori and rice up and over the cucumber, pulling the mat in and sushi roll up and in tight towards you as you roll. When you get to the end, wet the bare top end of the nori with just a little water to seal it as you roll. You will have 1 large log now. Repeat this process with the rest of the ingredients. With a wet sharp knife, slice each log into 6 pieces. Enjoy.
Yield: Serves 2-3

Cooked Kale, Cauliflower, Mango and Papaya Black Bean Salad (gluten free)

1 bunch of kale that has been stemmed and rough chopped

1 cup cauliflower chopped into bite size chunks, 3/4 cup peeled, seeded and medium diced papaya, 1 mango, peeled, pitted and medium diced

1 medium tomato, medium diced 1/4 cup small diced onion

1/2 cup cooked black beans dressing:, 1/2 cup red wine vinegar

1 Tbs olive oil, 2 Tbs sugar, pinch of salt, 1/2 tsp dried basil

Bring 4 inches of water to a boil. Add in the chopped kale. Boil 4 minutes, add in the cauliflower and cook another minute. Drain and cool in cold water. Drain again and squeeze the water out of the kale. Whisk the dressing ingredients together and mix with the rest of the ingredients. — 151 — Yield: Serves 3-4

Rosemary Ginger Roasted Parsnips and Carrots (gluten free)

1 cup of peeled parsnips and carrots cut into 1/4 inch thick 2 inch long mathticks tossed together with 1 tsp minced ginger, 1/2 tsp salt, 1/2 tsp fresh minced rosemary, 2 Tbs olive oil, 1 tsp rice wine vinegar, a few cracks of black pepper and 1 tsp minced fresh garlic

Heat the oven to 425 degrees. Line a sheet pan with parchment paper. Place it in the oven with nothing on it for 10 minites. Open the oven and pour all of the mixed ingredients onto the hot sheet pan. Roast until browned and softened but not mushy, about 15 to 20 minutes.

Yield: Serves 3-4

Balsamic Reduction Dressing (gluten free)

1 1/2 cups balsamic vinegar, 1/4 cup sugar, pinch of salt

Heat the vinegar, salt and sugar over high heat until boiling. Turn heat down to medium and simmer on a low boil for 10 minutes. Take off heat and allow to completely cool. Makes a great salad dressing, marinade or dip for strawberries.

Yield: Serves 8-10

Balsamic Reduction Tomato Basil Salad (gluten free)

6 medium vine ripened tomatoes, top cut off and quartered
1 medium red onion sliced into half moons, a pinch of salt
6 fresh basil leaves julienne cut, 1 cup balsamic vinegar, 1/4 cup sugar

Make the reduction first, heat the vinegar, salt and sugar over high heat until boiling. Turn heat down to medium and simmer on a low boil for 10 minutes. Take off heat and allow to completely cool. If you place it in the freezer, it will cool faster. As it cools it will thicken. This also makes a great marinade or salad dressing. Put the chopped vegetables into bowl, pour the cooled reduction over the top and carefully stir to coat from the bottom, make sure not to damage the tomatoes. Serve chilled. Great summer dish.

Yield: Serves 6-8

Basil Roasted Red Potatoes (gluten free)

These are a wonderful easy side dish.

6 medium size red potatoes cut into
 large dices
 2 Tbs extra virgin olive oil
1-2 teaspoons salt (to your liking)
1/2 teaspoon black pepper
2 Tbs fresh basil or 1/2 Tbs dry basil
1/2 Tbs garlic powder

 Preheat oven to 400 degrees. Line a cookie sheet with foil, then
parchment paper. Mix all ingredients. Pour onto cookie sheet and bake for
30-40 minutes until browned a bit. Stir halfway through baking process.

Yield: Serves 4-8

Beyond Simple Fruit Salad (gluten free)

1 medium pineapple, peeled and cored (just cut the peeled sides off is the
easiest way to core it) medium diced
1 cup seedless red or green grapes
15 sliced strawberries
1 ripe canteloupe, peeled and seeded, medium diced
1 ripe honeydew melon, peeled and seeded, medium diced
4 kiwi, peeled and sliced into half moons

 Simply and gently mix all ingredients in a large bowl. Serve chilled.

Yield: Serves 4-6

Buffalo Brussel Sprouts

2 cups of brussel sprouts, cut in half length wise
1 cup flour mixed with 1/2 cup cornstarch, 1/2 tsp salt and 1 tsp garlic
powder
1 inch of canola or vegetable oil in a non stick pan
Buffalo sauce:
1/2 cup Earth Balance Soy Free Buttery Spread melted together with 1/2
cup Franks Red Hot Sauce

 Soak the cut brussel sprouts in 3 cups of water for a minute. Now, toss them
in the flour/cornstarch mixture. Heat the oil for 4 minutes over medium
high heat. Fry the brussel sprouts for about 4 minutes until crisp and
browned. Drain on paper towels and toss them in the Buffalo sauce. Enjoy.

Yield: Serves 3-6

Candied Pecan Sweet Potato Casserole (gluten free)

1 recipe maple buttered mashed sweet potatoes (from this book)
2 cups pecan halves
3 Tbs sugar
3Tbs maple syrup
1/2 tsp ground cinnamon
pinch of salt

 Place the mashed sweet potatoes in a 8x8 or 9x9 inch glass casserole dish
sprayed with non stick spray.

 Candy the pecans by toasting them in a non stick pan over medium heat for
about 4 mins, then add the sugar, salt, cinnamon and maple syrup. Stir well
to coat and allow to cool in the non stick pan. When cooled, preheat the
oven to 375 degrees and top the sweet potatoes with the pecans. Bake 20
minutes. This is a great thanksgiving dish.

Yield: Serves 4-6

Cheddar and Bacon Loaded Baked Potatoes

4 Russet potatoes wrapped in foil
Tofutti brand Sour Cream

So Delicious brand shredded cheddar jack cheese or Follow Your Heart
brand shredded vegan parmesan cheese
cube 8 strips of Lightlife brand bacon and put the cubes in a non stick skillet
over high heat in a little oil until crisp or use Bacos (they are vegan)

chopped chives or scallions

salt and pepper to taste
Earth Balance soy free buttery spread

 Preheat the oven to 450 degrees. Bake the foil wrapped potatoes for about an
hour or until soft. Remove the foil, split the potatoes in half with a knife and
load them with as many and as much of the toppings that you like.

Yield: Serves 2-4

Chipotle Vinaigrette Marinade (gluten free)

1 small can chipotle peppers
1/2 cup sugar, pinch of salt, 1/2 cup red wine vinegar
1 clove garlic, 1/4 cup water, 1/4 cup canola oil

Put all in food processor until smooth.

Yield: Marinates 10-12 pieces of tofu or vegetables or vegan chicken

Smoked Paprika Avocado and Golden Raisin Salad (gluten free)

3 cups chopped iceberg lettuce
1/3 cup each: sliced cucumbers,
red bell peppers, asparagus,
broccoli florets chopped small,
cooked black beans, golden
raisins, fresh tomatoes, thin
sliced white mushrooms and
peeled carrots cut into
matchsticks
1 avocado peeled, sliced thin
1/2 tsp smoked paprika

Heat 3 inches of water to a boil. Add in the chopped asparagus and broccoli florets. Cook them about 30 seconds and then drain them and cool them in cold water. Lay the iceberg lettuce at the bottom of the salad bowl. Sprinkle the smoked paprika on top of the avocado slices and arrange the salad like the picture. Enjoy with any dressing.

Yield: Serces 3-4

Cinnamon Buttered Baked Acorn Squash (gluten free)

2 acorn squash
Earth Balance Soy Free Buttery Spread
cinnamon
salt and pepper

Cut the acorn squash in half lengthwise. Scoop out the seeds. Place each half face down in a casserole dish filled with about 1/4 inch of water. Bake in a 400 degree pre heated oven for about 25-30 minutes or until soft. Remove from oven and season the insides with the butter, salt, pepper and a little cinnamon.

Yield: Sberves 2-4

Cucumber Tomato Salad (gluten free)

2 English cucumbers cut in half then into bias cut half moons
1 red onion sliced into half moons
1 pint of grape tomatoes cut in half
2 Tbs chopped fresh dill
1/4 cup red wine vinegar
2 Tbs olive oil
1/4 cup sugar
pinch of salt
1 Tbs chopped fresh dill

Whisk together the vinegar, dill, oil, sugar and salt. Place the remaining ingredients into a mixing bowl and mix with dressing. Serve chilled

Yield: Serves 3-5

Easy Refried Pinto or Black Beans (gluten free if you omit the soy sauce)

2 cans drained and washed pinto beans or 2 cans drained and washed black beans
1/2 cup can of your favorite salsa
1 teaspoon salt
1 Tbs chili powder
1 teaspoon garlic powder
1/2 teaspoon ground cumin
1/4 cup water
1/2 teaspoon soy sauce

Blend all ingredients in a food processor. Taste to see if it needs more salt or spices. If too dry looking, add more salsa or water. Heat in microwave or in the oven in a sprayed casserole dish at 350 degrees covered for 20 minutes. These are great with my wild mushroom fajita and my Spanish rice recipes from this book.

Yield: Serves 4-8

Easy Spanish Rice in Rice Cooker

2 cups jasmine white rice
2.5 cups water with1.5 Tbs Better Than Bouillon No Chicken Base whisked
into it until dissolved
1/2 tsp salt
1 Tbs chili powder
1 tsp garlic powder
1 tsp dried oregano
1 Tbs vegetable oil
1/2 tsp cayenne pepper (optional, if you like it a little spicy)

Add all ingredients to the rice cooker. Stir well and turn on the rice cooker.
Takes about 30 minutes to cook. Serve with refried beans, fajitas, tacos,
nachos, chipotle grilled chicken etc.

Yield: Serves 6-8

French Onion Soup

3 large onions cut into half moons
2 Tbs of Better Than Bouillon brand No Beef Base and 1 Tbs No Chicken
Base dissolved with a whisk into 6 cups of water
2 Tbs Earth Balance Soy Free Butter
a few pinches of salt and pepper to taste
fresh chopped chives to garnish

Heat a large pot over medium high heat for 3 minutes, then add the butter
and onions. Let the onions sit 20 seconds before stirring. You want a nice
brown color to them. Add a pinch or salt and pepper and saute until
browned. If they seem to dry out before browning, add a Tbs or two of
water. When browned, add the water/bouillon base mixture. Bring to a boil
and it is done. Taste to make sure it is rich and delicious, if not, add more
base or salt. You can top this soup with a piece of sliced baguette bread that
has been toasted in the oven with a piece of Vegan Gourmet provolone or
Field Roast brand Chao cheese melted on top.

Yield: Serves 4-6

Fresh Cranberry Sauce (gluten free)

1 bag of fresh cranberries, about 3 cups
1 cup of water
pinch of salt, 1
cup sugar (you can use less sugar if you like it less sweet)

    Place all of the ingredients into a pot. Bring to a boil and reduce to medium heat. Cook 5 minutes, remove from the heat and mash with a potato masher or puree smooth with a hand blender. *Yield:* Serves 4-6

Garlic Sauteed Kale (gluten free)

2 bunches kale, stemmed, rough chopped boiled 5 minutes then drained,with the water squeezed out
2 cloves garlic minced
1 tsp extra virgin olive oil
1 teaspoon red wine vinegar
1/2 teaspoon salt

Heat olive oil in a saute pan, add garlic, cook until slightly browned. Add the rest of the ingredients and cook 3 minutes, stirring constantly.

Yield: Serves 4-6

Baba Ganoush (gluten free)

A delicious roasted and rich eggplant dip, great for pita, crackers or for a raw vegetable platter.

2 medium Italian eggplants
1/4 cup tahini, 1/4 cup olive oil, 1 tsp salt
1/2 tsp cumin, 2 Tbs lemon juice, 1/4 tsp smoked paprika
3 Tbs flat leaf parsley, 2 small garlic cloves

    Heat the oven to 400 degrees. Cut the eggplant in half lengthwise. Brush the cut open sides with a little olive oil and place them face down on a parchment paper lined cookie sheet. Roast about 30 minutes or until completely soft. Remove from oven, salt the eggplant flesh with a little salt and place the eggplant face down in a colander for 5 minutes until any extra liquid drains out of them. Scoop out the flesh and place it in the food processor with the remaining ingredients, but not the olive oil. Start the food processor and slowly add the olive oil until the completely smooth. Taste, if it needs more salt or lemon, add it now. Enjoy.

Yield: Serves 4-5

Gomasio (gluten free)

Gomasio is a toasted sesame seed condiment that goes great over cooked brown rice or any whole grain.

1/2 cup raw sesame seeds
1/2 tsp sea salt

   Heat a non stick pan for a minute over medium and then add in the sesame seeds. Stir them around until golden. Remove from the pan, cool them and with a mortar and pestle or in a small food processor, mix them with the salt and either pulse the food processor for a second or two or grind them a bit with the mortat and pestle. You don't want it to be a dust, just some of the seeds broken open to release the delicious sesame flavor.

Yield: Serves 10-15

Green Goddess Dressing (gluten free)

1/2 cup plain rice milk
2 tsp apple cider vinegar
1/4 cup tahini
1 Tbs lemon juice
2 tsp Dijon mustard
1 tsp capers
1 tsp sugar
1 clove garlic
1/4-1/2 tsp salt
1/4 tsp black pepper
1/4 cup fresh parsley, chopped
4 Tbs fresh basil, chopped
3 Tbs fresh chives, chopped

   Simply place all of the ingredients in a food processor or blender until smooth. Add more water if too thick. Serve over your favorite salad.

Yield: Serves 4-6

Homemade French Dressing (gluten free)

1 cup sugar
1 cup ketchup
1 cup vegetable oil
2 cloves garlic
1/2 cup white vinegar
1 tsp celery seed
1/4 tsp liquid smoke
pinch of salt, 1/2 cup of water

Place all ingredients in a blender or food processor until smooth.
Add a little more water if it is too thick. Refrigirate.

Yield: Serves 10-15

Homemade Red Wine Vinaigrette (gluten free)

3/4 cup red wine vinegar
1/2 cup canola or vegetable oil
1/2 teaspoon each dried basil, dried oregano
4 Tbs sugar
1/2 tsp salt

Blend all ingredients with a hand blender or place in a jar and shake well
before each use.

Yield: Serves 8-10

Basil Aioli Dipping Sauce (gluten free)

This is great over my White Bean Asparagus Cakes, my Pommes Frittes,
my Mushroom Crusted Eggplant Cutlets, my Thick Cut Baked Potato
Chips or as a dip for raw vegetables or over a salad. Creamy and delicious.

1/2 cup soy free Vegenaise brand vegan mayo
1.5 teaspoons of red wine vinegar, a pinch of salt
3 to 4 Tbs water, 4 minced fresh basil leaves

Simply whisk the ingredients together until thinned just a little and smooth,
serve cold.

Yield: Serves 3-4

Homemade Thousand Island Dressing (gluten free)

1 cup vegan mayo
1/3 cup ketchup
pinch of salt
1/4 cup chopped sweet relish
1/3 cup water

Whisk all together, serve chilled.

Yield: Serves 4-6

Lemon Buttered Pastina

As a child, I would ask my mother to make me pastina, often. It is a very satisfying pasta and very simple to prepare. I love you mom.

1 cup of uncooked DeCecco brand Acini di Pepe Pastina (this is the best pastina on the market, hands down)
3.5 cups of water
1 Tbs lemon juice
3 Tbs Earth Balance soy free buttery spread
1/2-1 tsp of salt, more or less if you like
2 Tbs chopped fresh chives (optional)

Bring the water to a boil. Add the pastina, stir often and cook for 9 minutes. If there is any water left, drain it out, then add the pastina back to the pot. Add the rest of the ingredients, stir well and enjoy. Top with chopped fresh chives if you are using them.

Yield: Serves 2-4

Lemon Poppy Seed Dressing (gluten free)

1/3 cup sugar
1/2 cup lemon juice
1 Tbs diced onion
1 tsp Dijon mustard
1/2 tsp salt
2/3 cup canola or vegetable oil
1 Tbs poppy seeds

 Place the sugar, lemon juice, salt, onions and Dijon mustard into a blender.
Turn it on and slowly add in the oil. When thickened, add in the poppy seeds
and pulse for one second just to mix them into the dressing. Chill it and enjoy
over salad.

Yield: Serves 8-10

Mango Black Bean Salsa (gluten free)

 This goes great over marinated grilled tofu or grilled Delight Soy or
Maywah brand vegan chicken steaks.

2 ripe mangoes, peeled and medium diced
2 Tbs yellow or red onion, minced
2 Tbs chopped scallions
1/2 cup chopped grape tomatoes
1/2 cup canned black beans, drained and rinsed
1/4 cup diced english cucumber, skin on
1.5 Tbs lime or lemon juice
few pinches of salt
1 tsp vegetable oil
2 Tbs sugar

 Mix all of the ingredients together in a large bowl and refrigerate until
chilled.

Yield: Serves 3-5

Mango Vinaigrette (gluten free)

1 large ripe mango that has been peeled and had the edible flesh around the pit cut off
1/4 cup vegetable or avocado oil
1/2 tsp salt
1/8 cup apple cider vinegar
1 or 2 Tbs sugar
1/2 clove fresh garlic
1/2 Tbs chopped fresh parsley

   Place the mango flesh, oil, salt, vinegar, garlic, parsley and sugar into a small blender or food processor. Blend or process until smooth. If it seems too thick, thin it with a little bit of water and blend it again. Taste for flavor, season again if needed.

Yield: Serves 2-4

Maple Buttered Mashed Sweet Potatoes (gluten free)

3 large sweet potatoes peeled and cut into medium chunks
6 Tbs Earth Balance Soy Free Vegan Butter Spread
3 Tbs maple syrup
3 Tbs sugar
1 teaspoon garlic powder
1 teaspoon salt
1/2 teaspoon black pepper

 Bring a large pot of water to a boil and add the chopped peeled sweet potatoes and cook until soft, 12-14 minutes. Drain well and add them back to the emptied cooking pot. Add the rest of the ingredients and mash with a masher. If too thick, thin with some plain rice milk.

Yield: Serves 4-6

Balsamic Grilled Cauliflower Lemon Pepper Avovado Salad

4 cups of your favorite salad greens, 1/3 cup white button mushrooms sliced paper thin, 1/3 cup red grapes cut in half, 1 pitted avocado sliced in half with a few pinches of lemon pepper seasoning spinkled on top, 1/3 cup chopped broccolini that has been dropped in boiling water 30 seconds and then drained and cooled, 1/4 cup of your favorite cooked beans, 1/3 cup each sliced cucumber and diced tomato, a few of the Pickled Beets from this book, a head of cauliflower sliced into 1/3 inch steaks with part of the stem kept in tact marinated for 20 minutes in a mixture of 1/3 cup balsamic vinegar, 1 Tbs olive oil, 1 tsp sugar & a pinch of salt

Heat a grill for 12 minutes on high. Spray the grates with non stick spray and grill the lemon pepper avocado about 3 minutes and the marinated cauliflower for 3 minutes per side. Arrange the salad like the picture and enjoy with your favorite dressing. *Yield:* Serves 3-4

Mushroom Gravy

1 tsp minced garlic , 1 cup cremini mushrooms sliced
3 Tbs Earth Balance brand Soy Free buttery spread, 1/3 cup small diced leeks 1 1/2 cups plain rice milk whisked together with 1 cup of water, 1.5 Tbs of Better Than Bouillon brand Roasted Garlic Base and 1 Tbs nutritional yeast 6 Tbs white flour, salt and pepper to taste, 1 tsp Gravy Master (available in the spice isle of grocery store)

Melt the buttery spread in a thick bottomed pot. Add in the mushrooms, leeks, garlic and a pinch of salt. Cook for 3 minutes, then stir in the flour. When it is all mixed together, add in the rest of the ingredients. Whisk over a medium heat until thickened. Season with salt and pepper. You can serve it like this or you can blend it up for people who do not like visible mushrooms.

Yield: Serves 3-6

Olive Tapenade (gluten free)

1 cup pitted Kalamata olives, 1 cup pitted green Italian olives
1 Tbs capers, 1/4 of a small red onion, rough chopped, 1 tsp extra virgin olive oil, 1 clove of garlic, 2 Tbs flat leaf Italian parsley, rough chopped

Place all of the ingredients in a food processor and pulse until chopped but not too fine. Chill in the fridge until ready to use. Enjoy.

Yield: Serves 4-8

Pumpkin Seed Pesto Rice (gluten free)

So simple, so delicious.

4 cups of cooked,
warm
jasmine rice
1 Pesto recipe from this book
toasted salted green pumpkin
seeds and chopped scallions
for garnish
2 Tbs nutritional yeast
salt and pepper to taste

Simply mix the pesto with the warm cooked rice, nutritional yeast and salt and pepper to taste. Top with a few pumpkin seeds and chopped fresh scallions. You can stir cooked beans into this for extra fiber, it tastes great.

Yield: Serves 3-5

Roasted Cauliflower and Kale (gluten free)

This is a great way to get cruciferous vegetables into your diet, which studies suggest have cancer fighting qualities to them. Kale is also a great source of calcium and iron.

1 head cauliflower chopped into medium sized florets
1 head of kale, stemmed, chopped and boiled 4 minutes, then drained, cooled and squeezed dry.
2 cloves garlic chopped roughly
3 Tbs extra virgin olive oil
1 tsp salt or to taste

Preheat the oven to 400 degrees. Mix the cauliflower, salt, garlic and olive oil in a bowl. Pour onto a foil lined cookie sheet sprayed with non stick spray. Roast in the oven for 20 minutes, remove, pour into a bowl and mix it with the kale and a little more salt. Place back on the sheet pan and back into the oven for another 10 minutes.

Yield: Serves 4-6

Saffron Yellow Rice

This makes a great side dish to Mexican or Indian food. I would suggest getting a rice cooker, they cook rice perfect every time and are very simple to use.

2 cups jasmine rice
3 pinches of saffron
1/2 teaspoon salt
2 Tbs Better Than Bouillon brand No Chicken Base or Roasted Garlic Base dissolved in 2 3/4 cups water
2 Tbs Earth Balance Vegan Butter spread

Place all into a rice cooker, stir well and turn on. Add the butter after cooked and fluff with fork. Serve warm. I like it with chipotle grilled chicken with avocado salsa, refried beans and vegetables or Indian curry. If you make Indian food, basmati rice works very well instead of jasmine.

Yield: Serves 6-10

Savory Sausage Ball Cookies

I would eat these every Christmas eve growing up. This is a veganized version, rich and delicious. They taste as close to the real pork sausage version as I remember, minus the cholesterol and saturated fat.

1 Tbs olive oil
1 1/2 cups Bisquick
4 links of Beyond Meat Bratwurst brand sausages with the skins removed, mash the skinless links together with your hands
1.5 cups shredded Daiya Farmhouse Block cheddar (you will need to shred it yourself)
salt and pepper to taste

Mix all of the ingredients together with your hands. Preheat the oven to 375 degrees. Roll the sausage mix into balls about 3/4 the size of a golf ball. Place them all on a foil and parchment paper lined sheet pan. Bake about 12-15 minutes. Enjoy.

Yield: Makes about 20-30 sausage balls

Sesame Stick, Chocolate Chip, Cashew, Dried Cherry and Toasted Pumpkin Seed Snack Mix

This is great to snack on anytime. Pumpkin seeds are high in iron.

3 cups salted sesame sticks
1 bag of Guittard brand dark chocolate chips
1 cup dried cherries
1.5 cups salted roasted cashews, whole or half pieces
1 cup of toasted salted green pumpkin seeds

Simply mix all of the ingredients together in a large bowl. Store in an airtight container. Enjoy.

Yield: Serves 8-10

Simple BBQ Baked Beans (gluten free)

2 cans small white beans, pinto beans or navy beans, drained and washed
1 cup ketchup
2 Tbs molasses
3 Tbs brown sugar
1/2 tsp salt
1 teaspoon liquid smoke
1 tsp sriracha
1 tsp yellow mustard
1 Tbs apple cider vinegar

Mix all ingredients besides the beans with a whisk, then stir in the beans. Preheat oven to 385 degrees, spray a casserole dish with non stick spray, add bean mixture and bake covered for 30 minutes.

Yield: Serves 4-6

Simple BBQ Sauce (gluten free if you omit the soy sauce)

1 cup ketchup
1 Tbs red wine vinegar
pinch of salt
1 teaspoon liquid smoke
3 Tbs brown sugar
2 Tbs molasses
1 tsp yellow mustard
1/2 tsp garlic powder
1/2 tsp soy sauce

Whisk all together over medium heat for 10 minutes over medium heat in a pot on the stove.

Yield: Serves 4-6

Simple Garlic Roasted Asparagus (gluten free)

2 bunches of asparagus with the hard bottoms sliced off
2 cloves minced garlic
a few pinches each of salt and pepper
1.5 Tbs extra virgin olive oil

Preheat oven to 385 degrees. Line a cookie sheet with foil, then parchment paper. Mix all of the ingredients in a bowl and place evenly on the cookie sheet. Bake 10-12 minutes or until tender.

This is also good drizzled with balsamic reduction sauce when plated.

Yield: Serves 3-5

Simple Garlic Sauteed Spinach (gluten free)

This is great plain, in a tofu scramble, a toasted vegan cheese panini melt or mixed into your favorite pasta.

8 cups fresh baby spinach leaves
3 cloves minced garlic
1/2 tsp salt
red pepper flakes to taste (optional, if you like it spicy)
1 tsp extra virgin olive oil

Heat a large saute pan over medium high heat for 2 minutes, add the oil, then the garlic. Cook 20 seconds then add the rest of the ingredients. The spinach will seem like a lot but it wilts
down quickly. Stir it all around until the spinach is cooked, check the seasoning and serve warm.

Yield: Serves 3-4

Simple Herb Garlic Compound Butter (gluten free)

3 cloves peeled garlic
1 tsp chopped fresh dill
1 tsp chopped fresh chives
1/2 cup soy free Earth Balance brand buttery spread, softened (left on the counter a few hours)
pinch of salt

Take 2 Tbs of olive oil, chop up the garlic and slightly brown it in the oil for a minute over medium high heat. Pour off the oil, add the garlic and the rest of the ingredients into the buttery spread. Mix and chill. Goes great over grilled vegetables, pasta, grilled tofu, vegan chicken etc. A little dab per person will do nicely.

Yield: Varies depending on how you are using it

Simple Olive Oil and Herb Dip For Bread (gluten free)

1/2 cup extra virgin olive oil
1/2 tsp garlic powder
a few pinches of dried red pepper flakes
2 Tbs balsamic vinegar
1/2 tsp dried basil
1/2 tsp dried oregano
1/2 tsp salt

Mix all together with a fork, that's it. The balsamic will stay separated, that's ok, just dip the bread more!

Yield: Serves 3-5

Smashed Baked Crispy Red Potatoes (gluten free)

18 small sized red potatoes peeled, 2 Tbs olive oil, 1 tsp salt, 1/2 tsp black pepper, 1/2 tsp garlic powder, 1 tsp fresh basil, 1 tsp fresh chopped chives

Heat a large pot of water, bring to a boil. Cook the whole potatoes for about 15 to 18 minutes or until just slightly soft. Drain and gently smash them flat with a potato masher but do not mash too hard or break them up. Mix them gently with the rest of the ingredients. Heat the oven to 400 degrees. Bake them on a parchment paper lined sheet pan for 15 minutes or until crisp and browned. Sprinkle with more salt if needed. These are great topped with my Sour Cream and Onion Dip from this book. Enjoy.

Yield: Serves 4-6

Sour Cream and Onion Dip (gluten free)

This is a delicious dip for ruffled style potato chips.

1 container of Tofutti brand
vegan sour cream
1 tsp fresh dill,
chopped
1 tsp fresh scallions,
chopped finely
1/2 tsp finely chopped
fresh chives
a few pinches of salt,
pepper and garlic powder
1/2 tsp apple cider vinegar

Simply whisk or stir all of the
ingredients together well. Serve chilled.

Yield: Serves 3-5

Spanish Steamed Bulgur Wheat

This makes a delicious side dish and alternative to rice and is very high in fiber and vitamins.

1.5 cups cups bulgur wheat
3 cups water
1 teaspoon each salt, chili powder, garlic powder and ground cumin
2 Tbs Better Than Bouillon brand No Chicken Base or Roasted Garlic Base

Bring the spices, water, salt and bouillon paste to a boil in a pot, add bulgur wheat, stir and turn on medium low heat. Cover and cook 12-15 minutes. Let sit covered 5 minutes after cooking and then fluff with a fork, serve hot.

Yield: Serves 4-6

Spicy Asian Baked Black Beans

This recipe is very tasty served over steamed jasmine rice with the vegetable tempura recipe from this book.

2 cans of cooked black beans, drained and rinsed
1/2 cup sweet chile sauce (available in Asian markets)
1/4 cup hoisin sauce
1/2 of a red onion minced
sliced scallions for garnish

Mix all of the ingredients together, besides the scallions, in a large bowl. Heat the oven to 400 degrees. Spray a medium sized glass casserole dish with non stick spray. Add in the bean/sauce/onion mixture and cover with foil. Bake 25 minutes. Serve hot topped with the fresh chopped scallions.

Yield: Serves 6-8

Sweet and Sour Sauce

1 Tbs cornstarch
2 Tbs water
2/3 cup pineapple juice
1/3 cup rice vinegar
1/3 cup sugar
4 Tbs ketchup
1 Tbs soy sauce

Whisk together the cornstarch and water, set aside. Heat the rest of the ingredients over medium heat, when hot, add the whisked cornstarch/water mixture (this is called a slurry). Let it all cook together until thickened.

Yield: Serves 3-5

Thyme and Olive Oil Roasted Beet Root (gluten free)

4 medium sized beets, peeled
and cut into 1/4 inch
thick circles
2 Tbs extra virgin olive oil
1/2 tsp fresh chopped thyme
1 Tbs fresh lemon juice
1 tsp salt
black pepper to taste
1 tsp garlic powder

Heat the oven to 375. Line a sheet pan with parchment paper. Whisk together the oil, lemon juice, garlic powder, thyme, salt and pepper. Toss it with the beets in a large bowl. Spread evenly on the sheet pan. Bake for 40 to 50 minutes or until fork tender. Enjoy.

Yield: Serves 4-6

Toasted Whole Grain Pita Points

These are great dipped in hummus with a fresh vegetable tray, grape leaves and mixed olives.

6 whole grain pita pockets cut into triangles by cutting in half, then each half into 4 triangles
2 Tbs olive oil
1/2 teaspoon salt
1/2 teaspoon each dried oregano, garlic powder and basil

Preheat oven to 375 degrees. Mix all ingredients carefully in a bowl. Place on a cookie sheet that has been lined with foil and then parchment paper. Bake 10-13 minutes. They will crisp more as they cool.

Yield: Serves 4-6

Tofu Ricotta (gluten free)

1 block firm tofu
1 teaspoon salt
1/2 cup nutritional yeast
3 leaves fresh basil
juice of half a lemon
1/2 teaspoon garlic powder

Press all of the water out of the tofu by gently squeezing it.

Place all ingredients in a food processor and process until smooth.

This can be used to make 12 stuffed shells, about 18 homemade ravioli or a lasagna layered with noodles, Gardein brand beefless crumbles mixed with pesto and topped with tomato sauce and Follow Your Heart brand shredded monterey jack cheese, covered and baked at 375 degrees for 50 minutes.

Yield: Serves 4-6

Chickpea, Tomato and Artichoke Salad (gluten free)

2 cans of chickpeas, washed and drained
3 small jars of drained marinated artichokes
6 fresh basil leaves rolled up and sliced thin
1 pint of grape tomatoes cut in half
3 stalks celery diced small
1 medium onion diced small
1/2 cup lemon juice
1/4 cup vegetable or olive oil
2 Tbs Red Wine Vinegar
1 tsp salt
1/3 cup sugar

Whisk together the lemon juice, vinegar, salt, sugar and vegetable oil. Place the rest of the ingredients in a large bowl and pour the lemon dressing over the top, stir carefully. Serve chilled.

Yield: Serves 3-5

Chive and Cheddar Perogies

Well worth the effort. Crisp and buttery on the outside, creamy and rich on the inside.

for the dough:
2 cups King Arthur brand flour
4 Tbs vegetable oil
1/2 tsp salt
1/2 to 3/4 cup water

for the filling:
1/2 a recipe of the Roasted Garlic Mashed Potato recipe from this book, cooked, cooled and mixed with 1 tsp chopped fresh chives and 1/2 a cup of Daiya brand Farmhouse Block cheddar cheese that you have shredded yourself

   For the dough, mix the salt, oil and flour well with your hands. Add in the water, a little at a time as you knead it, until a smooth dough forms. You may end up not using it all or having to add a little if the dough seems dry. Place in a plastic bag and chill it in the freezer 30 minutes. Flour a large cutting board and roll the dough thin but not paper thin. Cut out 3 inch circles and place 1 Tbs of the filling in the middle of each circle. Fold them into half moons over the filling and seal with a fork or use an empanada press to seal and shape the edges. Gather the leftover dough, knead and roll it flat again. Heat 3 inches of water in a large non stick pan. When boiling, drop in 6 perogies at a time and cook until they float, about 3 minutes. Remove from the water and repeat with the remaining ones. Once all are boiled, heat a large non stick saute pan for 1 minute and add in 1 Tbs of Earth Balance buttery spread. Add about 6 perogies at a time and brown each side in the butter about 3 minutes. Repeat this process with the butter again with the remaining perogies. Remove from pan and top with Tofutti brand sour cream. Enjoy.

Yield: Makes about 16 perogies

Entrees

Crispy Cauliflower Pakora Sandwich with Mint Mango Curry Mayo and Smoky Onion Chutney on Homemade Naan Bread

1 recipe of the Homemade Onion Naan recipe from this book, cooked and warm
1 recipe of the Pakora Batter from my Broccoli Pakora Fritter recipe minus the broccoli from page 37
1 prepared recipe of the Smoked Paprika Indian Onion Chutney from page 89
3 cauliflower steaks cut from a cauliflower across the width of the cauliflower about 1/4 inch thick with a tiny part of the stalk kept on so that the steak stays in 1 large piece, marinated in a mixture or 1/2 cup tamarind sauce (not paste) and 1 Tbs Rogan Josh Indian Curry for 20 minutes (both available at Indian markets)
shredded raw baby spinach
1/2 inch vegetable oil to fry
for the sauce: mix together 1/2 cup Vegenaise brand vegan mayo with 1 tsp minced mint, 1/2 tsp curry powder and 2 Tbs mango chutney or mango jelly

   Heat the oil on high for 3 minutes. Flick a little of the pakora batter into the oil. If bubbles form, it is ready to fry. Remove the cauliflower from the marinade and dip each one until coated in the pakora batter. Place each one in the oil, 2 at a time, and fry each side about 3 minutes on medium high until golden. When they are cooked, cut a few pieces of naan, each about the size of the cauliflower steak. Place some of the curry mayo on each piece of naan as well as the onion chutney and spinach. Place the cooked cauliflower steak on top and assemble the sandwich. Enjoy.

Yield: Makes 4 sandwiches

Kofta Kebabs with Garlic Tahini Sauce (gluten free)

1 pack of Impossible brand ground mixed well with 1/2 tsp ground cumin, 1/2 tsp ground sumac (optional), 1/2 tsp allspice, 1/2 tsp salt, 1 Tbs each fresh minced parsley and fresh mint, 1 tsp minced garlic, 1/3 cup minced onions and 1/4 tsp cayenne pepper **for the sauce:** whisk together 1/4 cup tahini with 1 tsp lemon juice, 1/2 tsp ground cumin, a pinch of salt, 1 clove minced garlic and a few Tbs of water until thinned a bit but still creamy

Divide the Impossible mixture into 4 large balls. Take a kebab and form one of the balls into a large cylinder. Poke a kebab through the center and form the cylinder into about a 6 inch log running the length of the kebab so it sort of looks like a corn dog but a little thinner with equal amounts of kebab stick sticking out of each end. Repeat with the remaining kebabs. Heat a grill on high for 15 minutes and cook each kebab about 2 minutes per side.

Yield: Makes 4 Kebabs

Brunswick Stew

4 Tbs Earth Balance buttery spread, 3 cloves minced garlic
1 large yellow onion, diced small, 1 tsp of gravy master (find in the spice isle)
1 15 oz can of fire roasted diced tomatoes or plain diced tomatoes, with the juice
4 cups water whisked together with 2 Tbs Better Than Bouillon brand No Chicken Base
1 1/2 cups of the BBQ sauce recipe from this book or your favorite BBQ sauce
2 Tbs vegan worcestershire sauce, 1 Tbs brown sugar
1/4 tsp cayenne pepper, 2 yukon gold
potatoes, peeled and medium diced
1 tsp liquid smoke, 4 links Beyond Meat brand bratwurst
sausage with skin removed (running it under cold water makes this easier)
1 cup of drained canned corn, 1 cup canned or frozen lima beans
1 tsp garlic powder, salt and pepper to taste

Heat a large non stick pan over medium high heat for 2 minutes. Add in a little vegetable oil and add in the peeled sausage. Cook for 4 minutes, breaking it up with a spatula until browned and resembling ground beef. Set aside. In a large pot, melt the butter over medium heat. Add in the onions and garlic. Cook for 3 minutes, then add in the sausage, potatoes, a little salt and pepper and then the rest of the ingredients. Stir well and cook for 15 minutes. Enjoy with my Flaky Chinese Scallion Pancakes or my Homemade Zucchini Muffin recipe.

Yield: Serves 4-6

Japanese Tofu Katsu with Tonkatsu Sauce

2 blocks of extra firm tofu that have been frozen, thawed and had all of the water completely squeezed out of the blocks between your hands (this process creates an extra chewy and delicious tofu) and then cut each block into 8 equal squares
2 cups flour
1 cup water
2 cups panko bread crumbs mixed with 1 tsp salt and 1 tsp garlic powder
for the sauce:
1 Tbs Earth Balance buttery spread, melted
1/4 cup ketchup
1 Tbs vegetarian worcestershire sauce
1 tsp soy sauce, 1 Tbs hoisin sauce
1/4 tsp garlic powder
1/2 tsp rice wine vinegar

For the sauce, simply whisk the sauce ingredients together and set aside. Take a bowl and place 1 cup of flour into it. Take another bowl and place in the other 1 cup of flour and whisk it together with 1 cup of water (this will act as your egg to keep the bread crumbs sticking to the tofu) and in a final flat dish with sides, place in the panko mixture. Working from left to right, dip the tofu, 1 piece at a time, into the flour until coated, then the flour/water mix and lastly into the bread crumbs, coating each piece of tofu completely. Heat a large non stick pan with a half inch of vegetable oil on high for 3 minutes. Dip in a piece of the coated tofu, if bubbles form, it is ready to fry. Cook about 6 at a time for a few minutes a side until golden on each side. Drain them on a cookie cooling rack that is placed on top of a foil lined cookie sheet (this way you can heat them again later if needed in the oven without burning the bottoms). Top with the sauce and enjoy.

Yield: Serves 3-4

Avocado Salsa Topped Chipotle Grilled Chicken or Tofu (gluten free)

5 Maywah brand or Delight Soy brand Vegan Chicken Steaks or 1 block of extra firm tofu, frozen, thawed and then squeeze all of the water out of the thawed block, leaving you with an extra chewy tofu block. Cut in into 6 large triangles.

1/2 recipe chipotle vinaigrette dressing

salsa:

2 ripe avocados pitted, peeled and diced small
1/2 minced sweet red pepper
1 Tbs chopped fresh cilantro
1/2-1 Tbs lime juice
1/4-1/2 tsp salt
2 Tbs minced red onion
1 clove minced garlic
2 Tbs sliced scallions

Preheat a grill for 15 minutes . Marinate the vegan chicken steaks or tofu in the chipotle vinaigrette for 15 minutes. Grill each side of the chicken or tofu 3 minutes. Make the salsa by mixing all of the salsa ingredients . Add more salt, some garlic powder or lime juice if needed.

chipotle marinade recipe:

1 small can chipotle peppers
1/2 cup red wine vinegar
1/2 cup sugar
pinch of salt
1/4 cup canola oil
1 clove garlic
1/4 cup water

Place the marinade ingredients in a blender and blend until smooth. Use half of the marinade for the tofu or chicken and save the rest for my Chipotle Green Bean recipe of for a marinade for grilled vegetables etc.

Yield: Serves 3-5

Flaky Jamaican Beef Patties

for the dough:
3 cups of King Arthur flour, 1/2 cup vegetable shortening
1 teaspoon turmeric powder, 1 teaspoon salt
1/2 cup Earth Balance brand buttery spread, chilled
3/4 cup of water mixed with 1 teaspoon apple cider vinegar

for the filling:
1 pack of Beyond Meat Beefless Ground or 1 pack of Impossible Ground
1 medium onion, minced, 2 cloves garlic minced
1/2 to 1 teaspoon salt, 1/2 teaspoon garlic powder, 1/2 teaspoon soy sauce
pinch of cayenne pepper or a few drops of hot sauce, depending on spice level you like
1 teaspoon olive oil, 1 teaspoon allspice

  For the dough, mix the flour, turmeric powder and salt together in a large bowl. Place the
butter and shortening into this and cut them into the dough with a pastry cutter or a fork
until little beads are formed in the flour. Add in the water and vinegar slowly while mixing
with your hand until a dough forms. Make sure it is not too dry or too wet. Fold the dough
over on itself a few times to form layers and then put in the fridge wrapped in plastic for an
hour. **For the filling,** heat a large non stick pan for 2 minutes. Add in the oil, garlic and
onions. Cook 2 minutes. Add in the beefless ground. Cook 5 minutes and then add in the
rest of the filling ingredients. Stir and then cool completely. On a floured board, roll out
your dough into a 1/8 inch thick giant circle. Cut out 3 or 4 inch circle shapes with a glass
cup or biscuit cutter. Fill one side of each circle with about 2 Tbs of the filling. Brush the
edges with a little water to help them stay sealed when you fold them. Fold the dough over
the filling, forming a half moon. Crimp the edges with a fork to seal them. Repeat this
process until all of the dough is used up, you will have to roll out the leftover dough scraps
to make more circles out of the dough for the pockets. Heat the oven to 400 degrees. Place
the filled pockets on a parchment paper lined sheet pan. Brush them with a little olive oil
and bake about 15 to 20 minutes or until golden. Enjoy.

Yield: Makes about 15 to 18 patties — 182 —

Homemade Farfalle Pasta

1 recipe of the Homemade Pasta Dough recipe from this book (use the one made with semolina and not my Vegan Egg Pasta Dough recipe for this one) or you can use my Spinach Pasta Dough recipe as well

Roll your pasta dough as flat as you can get it with a rolling pin and then roll it out on your pasta machine to the second to last setting. Flour a large cutting board with a little semolina flour. With a pizza cutter, cut the dough into about 1.5 inch squares. Pinch at the top and bottom the of each square as if you are making a bowtie or butterfly shape. Squeeze where the top and bottom meet in the middle so that it will hold the shape when cooked. Repeat with all of the pasta. Cook in boiling water for about 2 to 3 minutes and toss in some Earth Balance brand buttery spread and lemon or with my Homemade Tomato Sauce recipe or you can use them after they are cooked and drained for my Fried Farfalle recipe.   *Yield:* Serves 4-5

Baked Leek Oyster Mushroom Creamy Ziti

1 box Ronzoni brand ziti rigati pasta cooked and cooled
2 cups homemade or your favorite tomato sauce
3/4 cup soy free vegan mayo, 1.5 tsp salt, olive oil
2 Tbs lemon juice, 1/2 cup nutritional yeast
1 small jar or marinated artichokes drained
1/2 cup cleaned and chopped leeks, 1 container Tofutti brand cream cheese
2 cups raw oyster mushrooms, 2 cloves minced garlic

Preheat oven to 375 degrees. Spray a 9x13 inch casserole dish with non stick spray. Set aside. In a food processor mix the cream cheese, mayo, leeks, artichokes, salt, lemon juice and nutritional yeast. Process until smooth.

Heat a non stick pan for 3 minutes, then add in a teaspoon of olive oil, the garlic, mushrooms and a pinch of salt, pepper and dried oregano. Sautee for 3 minutes, then mix the food processor contents into the pasta, add the mushrooms and stir well, coating the pasta and mushrooms evenly. Place this into the casserole dish, spreading evenly. Top with the tomato sauce and bake uncovered for 35-40 minutes. Remove from oven and stir it all together in the casserole dish, making a lovely rich pink sauce. Top with Go Veggie brand vegan parmesan cheese.

Yield: Serves 6-8

Hamburger, Kale and Mushroom Calzone

1 ball of the homemade dough recipe from this book, risen (the dough
recipe makes 2 balls of dough, you will only use 1 ball of dough here)
1 pack of Beyond Meat Beefless Ground or Impossible Ground
2 cups of cremini or white button mushrooms, sliced thin
1/2 tsp garlic powder, 1/2 recipe of the Tofu Ricotta recipe from this book
1/2 tsp dried oregano
1 head of kale, stems removed and discarded, chopped roughly
2 cloves garlic, minced, 1/2 tsp red wine vinegar
6 slices of Field Roast brand Original flavor Chao cheese, shredded yourself
1/3 cup small diced yellow or white onion

Brown the beef in a non stick pan on high heat with the minced garlic
and a little olive oil. Break it up with a spatula until cooked. Set aside.
Heat 4 inches of water to a boil and add in the chopped kale leaves. Boil
4 minutes. Drain, cool and squeeze out all the excess water. Heat the non
stick pan for 3 minutes on high and then add in a little olive oil and the
onions and mushrooms. Add in a little salt and cook for 4 minutes or until
the mushroom liquid is evaporated. Add in the cooked kale, vinegar, the
garlic powder, oregano, beef and salt and pepper to taste. Divide the
risen dough (do not re knead the dough) into 3 equal pieces and roll each
one into about an 8 inch circle on a floured cutting board. Equally place
3 Tbs of the ricotta and the filling into the middle of each calzone and
then place the cheese evenly on top of the fillings. Fold the dough over
the filling and cheese and seal the edges together with a fork. Let them
rise, covered, 30 minutes on top of a cookie sheet that has been lined with
foil and parchment paper. Heat the oven to 440 degrees. Brush the
calzones with a little olive oil and cut 3 small 1 inch slits in the top of each
calzone. Bake for about 14 minutes or until browned. Broil the last
minute to get them golden brown on top. Serve warm with a little of your
favorite tomato sauce.

Bangers and Mash with Sauteed Onion Brown Gravy

A tasty English classic.

1 recipe of
Roasted Garlic
Mashed
Potatoes from
this book
4 links of
Beyond Meat
brand Bratwurst
links

for the gravy:

1/2 cup plain
rice milk
1/2 cup water
1/2 tsp garlic powder
1/4 cup onions cut into half moons
2 1/2 Tbs flour
1 Tbs nutritional yeast
1 Tbs Better than Bouillon brand no chicken base or no beef base
1 tsp Gravy Master liquid (available in the spice or soup isle of any grocery store)
2 Tbs Earth Balance soy free buttery spread
salt and pepper to taste

Prepare the mashed potatoes, set aside, covering with a top or plastic wrap to keep warm. For the gravy, heat the Earth Balance spread in a pot over medium heat. Once melted, add in the onions. Cook for 5 minutes, stirring frequently. Add in the flour, stir in for one minute then add in the rest of the gravy ingredients. Whisk together and heat until thickened, about 3 minutes, whisking constantly. Add salt and pepper to taste. Set aside, covered. Cook the sausages or bratwurst in a non stick pan with a little bit of non stick spray for about 7 minutes, turning every minute or so until browned and slightly crisp. Once cooked, serve them on top of the mashed potatoes and top it off with some of the onion gravy. You can garnish it with a few steamed green peas or chopped scallions.

Yield: Serves 3-4

Spicy Beef and Broccoli

1 cup of seitan, store bought
or homemade, torn into flat
bite size pieces
2 cups of broccoli cut
into bite size pieces
3 cloves of garlic
thinly sliced
1 small thin dried spicy red
chili pepper cut into
thin circles
1 Tbs sesame oil
for the sauce: whisk together
1/3 cup soy sauce,
1/2 cup water, 1/2 tsp
Better Than Bouillon brand Roasted Garlic
Base, 2 Tbs hoisin sauce, 1 tsp rice
vinegar, 1 Tbs sugar, 2 Tbs vegan oyster sauce and 1 Tbs cornstarch

Heat a large non stick pan for 3 minutes on high. Add in the sesame oil and then the broccoli, seitan, garlic and dried chili peppers. Saute it all together, stirring often, for 4 minutes. Whisk the sauce ingredients again and add it into the pan. Stir it all together until thickened. Serve hot over steamed rice.

Yield: Serves 2

Grilled Sweet and Sour Sesame Pineapple Tofu Skewers

2 blocks of extra firm tofu that have been frozen, thawed and had all of the water squeezed out of them (this process creates an extra chewy and delicious texture for the tofu) and then cut into 1 inch chunks
1 medium green pepper cut into 1/2 inch squares
1 medium red pepper cut into 1/2 inch squares
2 cups of fresh pineapple cut into 1 inch chunks
1 cup red onion cut into 1/2 inch pieces
1 recipe of my homemade Sweet and Sour Sauce recipe from this book or your favorite store bought one mixed with 1 Tbs toasted sesame oil and 2 Tbs hoisin sauce
skewers

Soak the skewers in water and heat a grill on high for 15 minutes. Make the skewers by placing on a chunk of tofu, then a red pepper, then pineapple, then the onion, then green pepper. Repeat until you have an inch of skewer at the top and bottom of each skewer. Brush all of the finished filled skewers with the sauce and spray the grill with a lot of non stick spray. Save a little of the sauce to brush over the skewers while griling. Grill each side 3 minutes or until charred. Enjoy. This goes great with my Coocnut Milk Steamed Rice recipe from this book.

Yield: Makes 12 to 14 skewers

Biscuits and Sausage Gravy

biscuits:
2 cups King Arthur
brand flour, sifted
1/2 Tbs baking powder
1/2 teaspoon salt
8 Tbs vegan shortening
1 1/4 cup freshly opened
club soda mixed w/1tsp apple cider
vinegar

gravy:
2.5 cups plain rice milk
2 Tbs nutritional yeast
1/3 cup plus 2 Tbs flour
1 Tbs fresh dill
1/2 tsp salt

1 tsp Better Than Bouillon brand No Chicken Base or Roasted Garlic Base
2 links of Beyond Meat brand Italian Sausage, skin removed
2 Tbs Earth Balance Soy Free vegan butter spread

Preheat oven to 450 degrees. Mix flour with salt and baking powder and
soda in a large bowl. Put the shortening into the bowl and cut it into the
flour with a pastry cutter until it looks like pea sized balls in the flour. Add
the club soda/vinegar mixture into the flour. Gently mix and knead it by
folding the dough over itself over and over. If the dough seems too dry, add
more club soda before folding it over on itself. This is a very important step, it
creates layers and makes a fluffy, better biscuit. If the dough seems too wet,
add more flour. Do not over mix the dough or the biscuits will be tough.
When mixed into a nice dough, flatten the dough out to about 1/2 inch thick.
Cut into biscuits with a biscuit cutter. Refold the leftover dough and cut more
biscuits. Place each biscuit into a non stick cake pan sprayed with non stick
spray. Make sure the biscuits are touching each other, this makes them bake
softer and more tender. Bake for 18 miutes or until risen and browned
on top. Remove from the oven and brush with a little melted Earth Balance
buttery spread.

gravy: Heat a non stick pan with 1 Tbs Earth Balance vegan butter. Add
the sausage and cook until browned. Set aside.
In a medium size pot, add the rice milk, nutritional yeast, No Chicken Base,
flour, salt, dill and remaining Tbs of vegan butter and bring to a medium
high heat. Using a whisk, whisk until it starts to thicken, 3 to 5 minutes. Add
the sausage. Add more salt if bland.

Yield: Serves 4-6

Homemade Scallion and Cheese Omelette Avocado Bagel Sandwich

4 of my homemade bagels from this book, cooked, warm and cut in half
a double batch of my American Cheese Omelette recipe from this book, cooked in
a large 12 inch non stick skillet and kept warm with a Tbs of fresh scallions mixed
into the omelette batter before cooking it
fresh avocado slices, salt and pepper to taste, optional hot sauce or ketchup

Simply cut the omelette into 4 equal size pieces, place each one on the bottom of
each bagel half and top with the avocado, a little salt and pepper and the optional
hot sauce or ketchup.   Yield: Makes 4 bagels

Sun Dried Tomato Pesto Baked Penne

3 Tbs Vegenaise brand vegan mayo
1 box of Ronzoni brand Smart Taste penne cook 6 minutes and cooled in cold water
1/3 cup nutritional yeast
1 Tbs lemon juice
5 slices of Field Roast brand Chao cheese original flavor that you have shredded
yourself
3 Tbs Follow Your Heart brand parmesan shreds
for the pesto:
2 cups fresh basil leaves, 1 cup fresh baby spinach, 4 Tbs nutrional yeast
1 Tbs Follow Your Heart brand parmesan shreds, 1/2 salt
1/3 cup oil cured sun dried tomatoes (make sure they are the ones in a jar packed in oil
and not the ones from a bag), 1/3 cup olive oil
1/3 cup toasted and salted green pumpkin seeds

For the pesto, place all of the pesto ingredients but the olive oil in a food processor.
Turn it on and add in the oil in a slow stream until a pesto forms. Add a little water if it
seems too thick. In a large bowl, mix all of the ingredients well with the pesto but not the
Chao cheese yet. Heat the oven to 375 degrees and spray a 9x9 inch glass baking dish
with non stick spray. Add in the pasta and pesto mixtire in an even layer. Top with the
shredded Chao cheese and a few pinches of dried oregano and cover. Bake for 25
minutes covered until the cheese is melted. Enioy.

Yield: Serves 4-5

Lemon Butter Chive Pan Seared Hearts Of Palm (gluten free)

6 stalks of canned hearts of palm with each stalk cut into 4 scallop sized pieces (24 pieces total), salt and pepper to taste, juice of half a lemon, 4 Tbs Earth Balance brand buttery spread, a few chopped fresh chives

Sprinkle each side of the hearts of palm with a little salt and pepper. Heat a large non stick pan on high for 2 minutes. Add in 2 Tbs of the buttery spread. When it melts, add in the hearts of palm. Watch them carefully until they are browned on the bottom. Flip them and brown the other sides of them. When browned on both sides, add in the rest of the buttery spread and lemon juice until the buttery spread melts. Serve them topped with the the lemon butter sauce and the chopped chives. *Yield:* Serves 3-4

Feta Spinach Topped Balsamic Grilled Tofu (gluten free)

2 blocks of extra firm tofu that have been frozen, thawed and had all of the water squeezed out of the thawed blocks between your palms (this process gives you an extra chewy block of tofu) and then each block cut into 4 large squares, 1 tsp lemon juice 1/2 a recipe of the Balsamic Vinaigrette from this book, 10 cups of raw baby spinach 1/2 a container of Follow Your Heart brand vegan feta cheese, 1 tsp minced garlic salt and pepper to taste

Place the tofu squares into a flat high sided glass dish and pour the balsamic marinade over the top. Flip them to coat both sides. Let them marinate 1 hour in the fridge. Heat a large non stick skillet for 2 minutes. Add in 1 tsp of olive oil and the garlic. Cook 30 seconds and add in the spinach and a pinch of salt. Cook 3 minutes until wilted. Cool it completely and squeeze out any excess water. Mix with the feta, lemon juice and a pinch of salt and pepper if needed. Heat a grill for 10 minutes on high. Spray the grates with non stick spray and add the tofu. Cook each side for 3 minutes. After you flip it the first time, add about 2 Tbs of the spinach feta mix on top of each piece of tofu. Put the top down on the grill and cook 3 more minutes. You can place this under the broiler to brown the feta a little more if desired. Enjoy with my Tabouli recipe. *Yield:* Serves 4-5

Bang Bang Chewy Tofu and Mushrooms

This is so delicious and addictive.

1 block of tofu that has been frozen, thawed and had all of the water squeezed from the block (this creates an extra chewy tofu) and torn into bite size chunks
1 cup of medium to large size button mushrooms quartered
2 cups plain flour
2 cups panko bread crumbs mixed with 1/2 tsp each garlic powder and salt
chopped scallions and black sesame seeds for garnish
for the sauce:
1/2 cup Vegenaise brand vegan mayo (I like the soy free version) whisked together with 1 tsp Sriracha, 1/4 cup sweet chili sauce and 1 tsp pure maple syrup

Make the sauce and set aside. Take 1 cup of the flour and place it in a large bowl. Take the other cup of flour and whisk it together with 1 cup of water until smooth (this will act as the egg to make the bread crumbs stick). In a flat glass sided dish, place the bread crumb mixture. Working from left to right, coat the tofu and mushrooms in the flour, then the flour/water mixture and then into the bread crumb mixture. Coat them completely in the bread crumbs. Heat a large non stick skillet with 1/2 inch vegetable oil for 3 minutes on high. Dip in a coated mushroom, if bubbles form, they are ready to fry. Cook each side of the tofu and mushrooms until golden. Remove from oil and serve them with the sauce drizzled over the top. Enjoy.

Yield: Serves 4-5

Caper, Mushroom and Olive Pizza Puttanesca

1 ball of homemade dough from this book, risen (the recipe makes 2 balls of dough but you will only use 1 here)
2 Tbs capers, 1/2 cup kalamata olives rough chopped
1/4 cup green spicy Sicilian olives, rough chopped
1 medium onion, cut into half moons, 2 cloves of minced garlic
1 soft block (not the hard block, the soft block melts better) of Follow Your Heart brand Mozzarella, shred it yourself
1/2 cup of your favorite homemade or store bought tomato sauce
olive oil, salt and pepper to taste, 1.5 cups of button mushrooms sliced
fresh chopped basil, fresh chopped oregano, Follow Your Heart
brand vegan parmesan and garlic powder to top

   Place the dough onto a floured cutting board. Push the dough into a circle but do not re knead the dough. Roll the dough into a circle on the floured cutting board. Place into a 14 inch olive oiled or non stick sprayed non stick round deep dish pizza pan. Cover it and let it rise an hour. While it rises, heat a large non stick saute pan over high heat for 3 minutes. When heated, add in the olive oil, mushrooms, garlic and onions. Saute them for 4 minutes. Add in the capers, olives and a pinch of salt and pepper. Stir and cool. When the dough is risen, heat the oven to 440 degrees. Spread the tomato sauce on the pizza, then add the mushroom/olive mixture evenly. Top with the vegan mozzarella. Sprinkle a little salt, dried oregano and garlic powder on top. Place in the oven and bake for 15 to 18 minutes. If the cheese needs more melting, place it under the broiler for a minute. Pull it out of the oven when the crust is golden. Brush the crust with a little olive oil. Sprinkle the pizza with a little salt, garlic powder, the fresh oregano and fresh basil. Let it cool 6 to 8 minutes, then slice and enjoy.

Yield: Serves 3-4

Shepherds Pie

This is a tasty meal for a cold winter night with a salad and my Cheese Biscuit recipe from this book.

1/2 a recipe of my Garlic Mashed Potato recipe from this book, prepared and warm
1 pack of Impossible Beefless Ground, thawed
2 Tbs plain flour
1 Tbs Earth Balance buttery spread
1/2 cup small diced onion, 1/3 cup small diced carrots and 1/3 cup thawed or fresh green peas, 2 cloves minced garlic
1/2 tsp dried oregano, 1/4 tsp salt
1 cup of water whisked together with 1 Tbs of Better Than Bouillon brand Roasted Garlic Base whisked with 1 Tbs tomato paste

Place a large non stick pan over high heat for 3 minutes. Add in the buttery spread, then the onions, garlic, carrots and a pinch of salt. Cook 3 minutes and add in the Impossible meat. Break it up with a spatula and cook 3 minutes and then add in the oregano, salt, peas and flour. Stir a minute and then add in the roasted garlic base stock and salt. Stir and cook until thickened a bit. Spray a 9x9 inch sided glass baking dish with non stick spray and spoon in this mixture. Top it with the mashed potatoes and make swirly lines in them with a fork as you spread them evenly over the Impossible mixture. Bake at 400 degrees for 20 minutes. Place under the broiler for the last minute to brown the top a little more. Enjoy.

Yield: Serves 3-4

Buttery Cracker Crusted Tofu Cutlets with Nacho Cheese Sauce

2 blocks of tofu that have been frozen, thawed and had all of the water squeezed out of the blocks of tofu between your hands (this process creates extra chewy tofu) and cut into 6 rectangles per block (do this by cutting each block in half from top to bottom and then cut each half into 3 even rectangles)
3 cups of plain Ritz brand or other buttery type vegan crackers that have been crushed into small pieces (not too fine though)
2 cups flour
1/2 tsp garlic powder
a few pinches of salt
vegetable oil to fry
1/2 recipe of the nacho cheese recipe from this book, kept warm

Take 1 cup of the flour and dip the tofu into the flour. In another bowl, w hisk the other 1 cup of flour with 1 cup of water. Dip the floured tofu into this, about 3 at a time, and lastly, in a flat casserole dish, place the cracker crumbs that have been mixed with the garlic powder and a little salt and drop the tofu into this and coat each piece completely with the cracker crumbs. Heat 1/4 of an inch of oil in a large non stick pan over high heat for 3 minutes. Add in the tofu, about 6 at a time. Cook each side about 2 minutes or until golden. Drain and serve topped with the nacho cheese sauce. Enjoy.

Yield: Serves 3-5

Caramelized Onion and Pesto Sausage Pizza

1 ball of dough from the 2 dough balls created by the basic dough recipe in this book, risen

pesto:

3 cups fresh basil leaves
1/4 cup toasted salted green pumpkin seeds
1 clove garlic, 1/2 tsp salt
4 Tbs nutritional yeast
3 Tbs extra virgin olive oil
3 Tbs water

toppings:

1 onion sliced in half moons
2 links of Beyond Meat brand Italian sausages that have had the skin removed by placing under running water and peeling it off, broken up and browned in a non stick pan with a little salt and pepper
1 soft block of Follow Your Heart Mozzarella, shred it yourself (make sure it is the soft block and not the hard block, the soft block melts better)
pinches of oregano, garlic powder and salt

Place all pesto ingredients in food processor, blend until smooth. Add water if too thick, add more salt and nutritional yeast if it is not flavorful enough. Set aside. Heat half inch of water in a medium pan, add onions. Place on medium high heat until water evaporates, add 1/8 cup more water and repeat. Salt the onions and cool.

Place risen dough on a floured surface. Do not re knead the dough, simply push on the center and sides until flattened. Use a rolling pin to shape into a round pizza. Place dough into a sprayed pizza tin. I prefer a deep dish dark 14 inch pizza tin. Cover and let rise 1 hour. Preheat oven to 430 degrees. When risen, spread pesto to cover the pizza, next add the onions, then the sausage and top it with the cheese. Pour some oregano, garlic powder and a few pinches of salt on top. Spray the cheese and crust with a non stick vegetable spray. This helps the vegan cheese melt better. Place in the oven 15 to 20 minutes or until crust starts to brown. When cooked, put the pizza under the broiler 2- 3 minutes to melt the vegan cheese all the way. Remove from oven and cool 6 to 8 minutes before slicing. Top with Go Veggie brand vegan parmesan cheese or Follow Your Heart brand vegan parmesan cheese. If the sausage is a little greasy, dab with a paper towel. Enjoy.

Yield: Serves 3-4

Chinese Eggplant and Tofu in Garlic Sauce

This is such a simple and tasty recipe. It goes great with my Homemade Biang Biang noodle recipe from this book or steamed brown rice or jasmine rice.

2 long Chinese/Japanese eggplant, cut in half length wise and then cut into 1/2 inch chunks on an angled bias
1 recipe my Chewy Pan Seared Tofu from this book, cut into 1 inch long by 1/4 inch wide thick matchsticks instead of torn into chunks before you sautee them for the Pan Seared Tofu recipe
1 tsp fresh grated ginger
1 Tbs sesame oil
for the sauce:
1/4 a cup soy sauce
1/2 tsp of minced garlic
2 Tbs sugar
1 Tbs rice wine vinegar
1/2 cup water
1.5 Tbs cornstarch
2 Tbs vegan oyster sauce
1 tsp sesame oil

For the sauce, whisk all of the sauce ingredients together and set aside. Steam the eggplant chunks for 5 minutes in a steamer. Heat a large non stick pan on high for 3 minutes. Add in the sesame oil and then the steamed eggplant and ginger. Stir it around for 3 or 4 minutes until the eggplant is browned and softened. Add in the tofu and then whisk the sauce and pour it into the tofu and eggplant. Stir until the sauce is thickened. Serve with my homemade Biang Biang Noodle recipe or over steamed rice.
Yield: Serves 2-3

Chicken or Eggplant Parmesan

1 large eggplant, peeled and cut into thin fillets lengthwise or 5 Delight
Soy brand vegan chicken patties or
a block of frozen tofu, thawed and
squeezed out extra firm tofu
until it is completely dry
3 cups panko bread crumbs
3 cups plain flour
1 teaspooon each - garlic
powder & dried oregano
1/2 Tbs salt
1/4 cup nutritional yeast
1 soft block of Mozzarella style
Follow Your Heart brand cheese,
shred it yourself or you can shred
1 pack of Fied Roast brand Chao
slices, Go Veggie brand vegan parmesan cheese

Put 1 1/2 cups of the flour in a large bowl, put the other 1 1/2 cups flour in
a bowl mixed and whisked with 1 1/2 cups water until it resembles a medium
thin pancake batter. In a third flat casserole dish, mix the bread crumbs,
oregano, garlic powder, nutritional yeast and salt. Working from left to right,
dip the veggie chicken or eggplant into the flour, then the pancake flour
mixture, and lastly the bread crumbs. Use your left hand to dip into the flour
and the pancake flour mixture and your right hand to cover the eggplant,
tofu or veggie chicken in the bread crumbs. When all are breaded, heat a non
stick pan with a half inch vegetable or canola oil until hot (if you throw a
bread crumb in and bubbles from around it, it is ready to fry). Cook each
side until golden. For eggplant parmesan, put a layer of your favorite
homemade or store bought sauce in the bottom of a sprayed 9x9 inch pan.
Layer the eggplant to cover the bottom, add more sauce on top along with
half of the shredded cheese and a few shakes of the parmesan cheese, then
layer on the rest of the eggplant. Top with the remaining tomato sauce and
remaining cheese along with a few pinches of salt, parmesan, garlic powder
and oregano. Bake covered with foil for 40 minutes at 375°.

For vegan chicken or tofu parmesan, simply put the breaded cooked chicken
cutlets or tofu cutlets in a large glass casserole dish sprayed with non stick
spray. Cover each cutlet with tomato sauce, a few shakes of the parmesan
and then some of the shredded cheese along with a pinch of salt, oregano
and garlic powder. Bake at 375° covered with foil for 12 minutes or until
the cheese is melted. You can finish off the melting by removing the foil and
putting the the chicken or eggplant under the broiler for a few minutes.

Yield: Serves 4-8

Butternut Squash and Caramelized Leek Ravioli in Sage Butter Sauce

1 recipe or the homemade pasta dough recipe from this book (the one made with semolina flour)
1/2 of a medium size butternut squash, seeds removed and baked face down in a 1/2 inch of water in a glass baking dish at 375 about 35 minutes or until soft
1/2 cup of cleaned leeks cut into thin half moons, 1/2 tsp salt, 1 Tbs nutritional yeast
1 Tbs Tofutti brand cream cheese, 4 Tbs Earth Balance brand buttery spread
1 tsp minced fresh sage, 1 tsp minced garlic

For the filling, make sure the squash is cooled and scoop out the flesh into a food processor. Heat a non stick pan for 3 minutes and add in 1 Tbs of the Earth Balance buttery spread and then the leeks with a few pinches or salt and pepper. Cook, stirring often for about 4 minutes until golden. Cool and add this to the squash in the food processor with the leeks, nutritional yeast, Tofutti and the 1/2 tsp salt. Process until somewhat smooth but not too smooth. Divide your pasta dough into 3 equal sized balls. Roll one of the balls as flat as possible with a rolling pin. Run the flattened dough through the pasta machine on the first setting, cutting it with a pizza cutter to make it a long, even rectangle after the first pass through the machine. Next, run it through on the number 3 setting. Cut this long piece of flattened dough in half and run each half through the pasta machine on the second to last setting. Flour the cutting board a little and then lay the 2 flattened pasta sheets next to each other. Place about a Tbs of the filling on one of the sheets, in rows of two, you can fit about 8 fillings per sheet. Now take the other flattened piece of dough and place it on top of the squash topped piece of dough. Carefully push the dough around the filling, removing all air bubbles. Take a pastry wheel or pizza cutter and cut the filled areas into ravioli squares or rectangles. Repeat this process with the remaining balls of dough. This will make about 24 ravioli. Boil the fresh ravioli for 2 minutes, drain and toss in a little olive oil. In a large non stick skillet, add in the 4 Tbs of Earth Balance and the garlic and turn on high until melted. Add in the fresh sage and then the cooked ravioli and a few pinches of salt and pepper. Toss. Enjoy.

Yield: Serves 3-4   — 196 —

Alfredo Style Linguine or Fettuccine

1 box of fettuccine or linguine pasta, cooked, or homemade fettuccine **for the sauce:** 4.5 cups of chopped cauliflower that has been boiled for 3 minutes and then cooled, 1 clove garlic, 1- 2 cups of plain rice milk, 4 Tbs Go Veggie brand vegan parmesan cheese, 1/2 cup nutritional yeast, 1 tsp salt, 1 Tbs lemon juice, 4 Tbs vegan butter, 1 tsp garlic powder, 2 Tbs vegan mayo

Place all of the sauce ingredients in a blender except for the rice milk. Turn on the blender and slowly add in enough of the plain rice milk until it is as thick as alfredo sauce. This will take a few minutes in the blender, you want it to be silky smooth. It should be rich and creamy and slightly thick. Taste it, if it is bland, add more salt, nutritional yeast or lemon juice. Heat the sauce a large non stick saute pan. When bubbling, add in the cooked pasta. Heat the pasta and taste again for a rich, creamy flavor. Add more butter if needed. Top with Follow Your Heart brand vegan parmesan cheese shreds.

Yield: Serves 4

Chicken Tenders or Tofu Tenders

2 cups of panko bread crumbs mixed with 1 tsp salt, 1 tsp garlic powder, 1/2 tsp black pepper and 1 tsp dried oregano
18-20 Maywah brand or Delight Soy brand plain vegan chicken nuggets
if using tofu, freeze 2 blocks of extra firm tofu, thaw them and squeeze every bit of water out of the blocks, then tear each block into about 12 chunks (this creates a very chewy tofu texture, like chicken)
2 cups flour, 1 cup water, half inch of vegetable oil
your favorite BBQ Sauce (there is a good recipe in this book) or ketchup

Place the panko bread crumb mixture in a flat casserole dish. Take 1 cup of the flour and place it in a bowl. Take the other cup of flour and whisk it in a bowl with the 1 cup of water (this will act as the egg for the bread crumbs to stick). Take the tofu or chicken nuggets and dip each one in the flour, then in the water/flour mixture and lastly into the panko bread crumb mixture. Make sure to coat the entire tofu chunk or chicken nugget. When they are all coated, heat the oil in a non stick pan for about 3 minutes over high heat. Dip a corner of a breaded nugget or tofu into the oil. If bubbles form around it, they are ready to fry. Gently add in about 12 breaded nuggets or tofu pieces at a time into the oil and cook each side for about 2 or 3 minutes or until browned on both sides. Drain them on a foil lined sheet pan topped with a cookie cooling rack (this will allow you to reheat them later without burning the bottoms while staying crispy). Sprinkle w a little salt and enjoy.

Yield: Serves 3-5

Creamy Sesame Beef and Vegetables over Brown Rice

2 cups worth of my homemade (recipe from this book) or store bought seitan, torn into
bite size chunks
3 cups of hot cooked brown rice (a rice cooker recipe with exact rice cooker measurements is
in this book if you are using a rice cooker, if not, go pick one up, digital ones are cheap and work
perfectly)
1/2 inch of vegetable oil in a non stick pan

for the sauce:
 1 cup vegan mayo
 1 Tbs sugar
 1/2 tsp garlic powder
 1 Tbs toasted
 sesame seeds
 1 tsp rice wine
 vinegar
 1 tsp soy sauce
 1/2 tsp toasted
 sesame oil
 2-4 Tbs water

for the breading:
 1 cup flour
 1/2 cup cornstarch
 1/2 tsp salt
 1/2 tsp garlic powder

for the vegetables:
 1 cup broccoli cut into bite size pieces
 1/4 cup peeled, thin sliced carrots cut on an angle
 1/4 cup mushrooms, quartered
 1/4 cup green or red bell peppers, cut into thin strips
 1/4 cup zucchini cut into thick matchsticks or medium diced

   Mix the breading ingredients in a large bowl. Coat the seitan in the mixture. Heat the oil
over medium high heat for 4 minutes, then add the coated seitan in 2 batches if needed.
Dip a piece in to make sure bubbles form around it, if they do not, heat the oil a little
longer Cook a few minutes per side until browned and crispy. Drain and set aside (I like to
drain them on a cookie cooling rack that is placed on a cookie sheet so that I can re-crisp
them later if needed). Heat about 4 inches of water to a boil in another pot. Add in the
vegetables and cook for 2 minutes, drain. Whisk the sauce ingredients together until you
have a medium thick sauce. Toss your cooked, hot seitan into the cream sauce. Place your
portion of seitan over some cooked rice topped with extra sesame seeds and place some the
cooked vegetables around the rice. You can top the vegetables with a little Sriracha or soy
sauce.

   Yield: Serves 3-4

Classic Beef Lasagna

8 homemade 9 inch pasta sheets , boiled 1 minute and cooled using the
homemade Pasta Dough recipe from this book or 8 no boil lasagna sheets
1 recipe tofu ricotta (from this book)
3 cups of your favorite homemade or store bought tomato sauce
2 cloves minced garlic, 1 small onion, diced small
1 package Gardein brand beefless crumbles, thawed or 2 cups of Beyond
Meat brand or Impossible brand Beefless Ground, cooked and drained
Go Veggie brand vegan Parmesan cheese
1 pack of Follow Your Heart brand soft block mozzarella, shredded yourself (be
sure it is the soft block since it is the only one that melts properly here)

  Heat a non stick pan for a minute over high heat, then add a little olive oil,
the onions and garlic. Saute 2 minutes, then add the beefless crumbles. Saute
another 2 minutes, then add a few pinches of salt, dried oregano, garlic
powder and a tsp of soy sauce. Stir well and remove from heat. Set aside.

  Take the oven ready lasagna noodles and spread the tofu ricotta evenly
over all 8 noodles. Spray a 9 inch pyrex with non stick spray. Put about 3/4
cup of the sauce on the bottom of the pyrex, spreading it evenly. Add half
the beef crumbles over the top of the sauce. Next, add 4 of the ricotta topped
lasagna noodles. If they overlap a little it is ok. Spread about a cup of sauce
over the ricotta noodles, then add a few sprinkles of the vegan Parmesan and
the rest of the beefless crumbles. Top with a third of the cheese shreds.
Top this with the remaining 4 ricotta topped noodles but make sure
the ricotta is face down, on top of the beef, sauce and cheese layer.
Top these noodles with the remainder of the sauce and then
rest of the cheese shreds. Cover with foil and bake in a preheated 385 degree
oven for 50 minutes. Remove the foil and turn the broiler on. Broil the top of
the lasagna until the cheese is bubbling. Top with Parmesan. This goes great
with my Garlic Parmesan Roll or Garlic Bread recipes. Slice and enjoy.
Yield: Serves 3-6

— 199 —

Classic Grilled Cheese Sandwich

Butter, cheese and golden, crispy toasted bread. Simple and delicious.

4 slices of high quality white or wheat sandwich bread
6 slices of Follow Your Heart brand American cheese slices
Soy Free Earth Balance Buttery Spread, softened a bit by leaving it out of the fridge for an hour or so

Vegan cheese often needs a kick start to get it melting. Lay your bread slices out and lay 1.5 pieces of the cheese on each slice of bread. Place the cheese topped bread slices on a plate and microwave them for about 30 seconds to get the melting started. Remove from microwave and then cool. Place the cheese sides of the sandwiches together and spread some Earth Balance on each side of the non cheese sides of the bread. Heat a non stick pan over medium heat for 2 minutes. Spray the pan with non stick spray. Cook each side of the sandwich for about 2 or 3 minutes or until golden. Slice them and serve with the Creamy Tomato Basil Soup recipe from this book.

*With this basic recipe, you can then add tomato to your sandwich, pre cooking, or add avocado, pesto, cooked drained spinach, different cheeses etc. Follow Your Heart makes good Pepper Jack and Gouda slices. The combination possibilities are endless.

Yield: Makes 2 sandwiches

Cacio e Pepe

This is a very simple dish, but the technique used creates a peppery and creamy rich pasta. I like using rigatoni pasta or linguine.

1 box of Barilla brand or Ronzoni brand rigatoni pasta, cooked until al dente, about 8 minutes or Dreamfields brand linguine, cooked 5 minutes
1 cup of the leftover pasta cooking water, kept hot, with 2 Tbs of nutritional yeast whisked into it
salt to taste
4 or 5 cracks of fresh black pepper
1 container of Follow Your Heart brand parmesan cheese, roughly chopped or 3/4 a container of Go Veggie brand vegan parmesan cheese

Once the pasta is cooked, drained and still hot, place it in a large bowl. Add in 1/3 cup of hot the cooking water/nutritional yeast mixture and about 3 Tbs of the parmesan cheese along with a crack of black pepper. Stir until the cheese is melted, and repeat this process 2 more times, adding the hot pasta water and cheese and pepper until you have a creamy, rich tasting pasta. Add salt to taste. Garnish with a little basil and more cheese. Serve hot.

Yield: Serves 4-6

Penne or Homemade Gnocchi Vodka Pasta

1 box Dreamfields brand penne pasta cooked 5 minutes and completely cooled (ice water cools it quick) or Barilla brand penne, cooked 7 minutes, drained and cooled or 1 recipe of my Homemade Gnocchi, cooked and cooled
2.5 cups of your favorite homemade or store bought vegan marinara sauce mixed with 1/2 cup of vodka
3 cloves minced garlic
1 tsp olive oil
3/4 cup vegan mayo blended in a blender with 1/2 cup nutritional yeast, 1 small jar of drained marinated artichokes, 1 Tbs lemon juice, 1 tsp garlic powder, 1 tsp salt, 2 Tbs Tofutti brand cream cheese and 1/4 cup plain rice milk
2 Tbs vegan butter

   Heat the olive oil in a large pan, then add the garlic, cook 20 seconds, then add the vodka/tomato sauce mixture. Add a few pinches of salt and pepper. Cook this for 5 minutes, stir it often, then add the cooked penne or gnocchi. Cook another minute and then add the vegan mayo mixture and butter. Stir all together until heated and you have a lovely pink vodka sauce. Season with more salt, another 2 Tbs of nutritional yeast (for a more cheesy flavor) and pepper if needed. Top with chopped fresh basil and Go Veggie brand vegan parmesan cheese or Follow Your Heart brand vegan parmesan. Chopped up Beyond Meat brand browned up sausage is great in this too.
Yield: Serves 4-8

Beef and Cheese Crunch Wraps

4 or 5 large flour burrito shells
4 or 5 corn tortillas, you can use 4 round tortilla chips per crunch wrap if you can not find tortillas
4 or 5 small flour soft taco shells
1 package of Beyond Meat Beefless Ground or Impossible Ground, cooked with a little salt, pepper and garlic powder until browned
1 container of Tofutti Sour Cream
1 recipe of my Nacho Cheese Sauce from this book
shredded lettuce and some chopped tomatoes
vegetable oil

   Place the large flour burrito shell on a cutting board. Place about 1/2 cup of the cooked Beefless Ground in the middle of the burrito. Pour a little of the nacho cheese sauce on top of the beef, then add the corn tortilla or the 4 tortilla chips. Spread a few Tbs of the sour cream on top of the corn tortilla or chips, then a little lettuce and tomatoes. Pour a little more nacho sauce on top and then place the smaller flour tortilla on top of the cheese. Bring the edges of the large flour tortilla over the smaller flour tortilla, folding it over while pinching the edges so it makes a hexagon shape once it is completely folded over the smaller flour tortilla. Place them face down, all of the ingredients should make about 5 or 6 crunch wraps. Heat a little oil in a large non stick pan for 2 minutes on high and them add in one crunch wrap at a time, folded side down until golden on the bottom, then flip and cook the the other side until golden. Cook the remaining wraps, enjoy.   — 203 —   *Yield:* Serves 4-6

.

Pesto Beef Agnolotti Pasta with Eggplant, Mushrooms, Kale and Sun Dried Tomatoes in Sage Butter Sauce

1/2 a pack of uncooked Beyond Meat brand or Impossible brand beefless ground
1/2 a recipe of the pesto recipe from this book, 1 bunch of kale, stemmed, rough chopped
1 cup sliced button mushrooms or cremini mushrooms
1 large tomato, medium diced, 3/4 cup small diced eggplant
4 Tbs of julienned oil cured sun dried tomatoes (make sure they are the oil packed ones, not
the ones in a bag), 1/2 recipe of the pasta dough from this book
1 small red bell pepper, julienned, 2 cloves minced garlic
3 large leaves of fresh basil, julienned, 1/2 tsp fresh sage
juice of half a large lemon, 1 tsp olive oil
4 Tbs of Earth Balance brand buttery spread

   Heat a pot of water to a boil, add in the chopped kale. Cook it for 3 minutes, then drain, cool
and set aside. Heat a non stick saute pan on high for 3 minutes. Add in the uncooked beefless
ground. Cook for 5 minutes until browned. Add a little salt and pepper. Cool it and then add in
the pesto. Mix well. Add more salt if needed. Set aside. On a lightly floured board, roll the dough
out as flat and as long as you can get it with a rolling pin. Cut it in half. Run each piece through
a pasta roller, on the first setting, then the third and then the second to last setting. Lay the sheets
next to each other. Place a tsp of the filling an inch from the bottom edge and repeat this, 1
tsp about a half inch apart, maybe 10 per sheet. Fold the edge over the mounds so that it looks
like 1 long roll. Press the edges around the mounds and cut along the top edge with a
fluted pastry wheel and then cut in between each one, leaving little pillows.
Repeat until they are all done. Heat a large pot of water to a boil and also heat a large,
non stick saute pan on high for 3 minutes. Add in the olive oil to the saute pan , then add in
the mushrooms, garlic and eggplant. Cook for 4 minutes, adding in a little salt and pepper.
Add in the tomatoes, kale, sage, basil and sun dried tomatoes. Cook for 3 minutes, while it cooks,
drop your pasta into the boiling water and cook 3 minutes. Drain the pasta and add it to the
vegetables in the saute pan and add in the butter, lemon juice and salt and pepper if needed.
Cook it all together another few seconds. Serve hot topped with shredded Follow Your Heart
brand vegan parmesan cheese.

Yield: Serves 3-4

Crunchy Southern Style Fried Chicken or Tofu

1 bag of thawed Maywah brand Chicken Legs (these are usually in the frozen section of Asian markets, some health food stores or can be ordered online, they look like drumsticks). Cut each one into 2 pieces from top to bottom, or, if you prefer tofu, you can use 3 blocks of extra firm tofu that have been frozen, thawed and had all of the water squeezed out of the block, this leaves you with a very chewy textured tofu.
1 cup of flour whisked together with 1 cup of water and 1 Tbs apple cider vinegar
2 cups of flour mixed with 1/2 cup cornstarch, 1 tsp salt, 1 tsp garlic powder, 1/2 tsp black pepper, 1 tsp paprika, 1/2 tsp dried thyme, 1/2 tsp celery salt, 1/2 cup plain corn flakes crushed up a bit or Pop Corners brand Sea Salt flavor chips crushed up a bit and 1/2 tsp dried oregano
oil for frying

If using tofu, tear each thawed, drained and squeezed dried block into 4 large chunks (12 total tofu chunks). Dip the chicken legs or tofu in the dried flour/cornstarch/crushed corn flake/herb mixture. Next, dip each piece into the flour/vinegar/water mixture and then back into the dried flour mixture. Make sure they are coated well. In a large non stick pan, heat an inch of vegetable oil over medium high heat for 3 minutes. When you can dip a coated chicken leg or coated tofu into the oil and bubbles form around it, it is ready to fry. Cook each side until browned and crisp, about 3-5 minutes a side. Drain on a large cookie cooling rack that has been placed on top of a foil lined sheet pan (you can reheat them later this way too without burning the bottom of the chicken or tofu). Sprinkle with a little more salt and enjoy with the Cole Slaw, Garlic Mashed Potato and Cheddar Chive Biscuit recipes from this book if you want.

Yield: Serves 4-6

Tofu Sushi Fashion Sandwich

1 cup of white sushi rice, a pinch of salt, 1.5 cups of water and a small 4 inch piece of kombu (kombu is optional), 1 Tbs rice vinegar, cooled, 2 sheets of nori seaweed cut in half so that you have 4 long rectangles, 1 peeled avocado, pitted and cut into very thin slices, 1 peeled carrot sliced very thin and marinaded in a mixture of 4 Tbs rice vinegar, 2 Tbs water and 1 tsp sugar for 8 hours, a few Tbs vegan mayo, 1 block of tofu that has been frozen, thawed and had all of the water completely squeezed out of it, a few shakes of dark soy sauce, 1 Tbs sesame oil, a few toasted sesame seeds

  Cook the rice in a rice cooker with the 1.5 cups of water, pinch of salt and the optional kombu. Remove the kombu when the rice is cooked and stir in the vinegar. Bring it to room temperature. Heat a non stick pan on high for 3 minutes. Cut the tofu into thin 2 inch long rectangles. Pour a few drops of the dark soy sauce on the tofu and then add the sesame oil to the pan. Cook each side of the tofu about 2 minutes and then cool completely. Take the nori rectangle, longer side facing you, wet your hands and place about 4 Tbs of the rice on the nori, pushing it down, covering one whole side of the nori. Sprinkle a few sesame seeds on it and then flip it over onto a sheet of plastic wrap so the rice is now face down. Now, take 2 Tbs of the rice with wet hands but only press it onto half of the bare nori. Spread 2 Tbs of the mayo on the bare part of the nori as well as the half with the rice. Place 3 pieces of the tofu, then a few carrots then a few avocado slices on top of the rice half. Cut the nori in half now with a sharp wet knife so that the bare side of the nori can be placed on top of the avocado, making a square. You can place plastic wrap over the whole square and form in into a more even square by using sushi mat over the plastic and gently pushing in on the sides. Take a sharp wet knife and cut the sushi from corner to corner, forming 4 triangle sandwiches. Repeat the process with the rest of the ingredients. Enjoy dipped in soy sauce or hoisin sauce. *Yield:* Serves 3-4

BBQ Tofu with Vegetables, Black Beans & Kidney Beans

1 recipe of the Pan Seared Chewy Tofu from this book
1/3 cup each cooked black beans and kidney beans, 1/2 cup quartered mushrooms, 1 cup chopped baby bok choy, 1/2 cup bite size chopped broccoli, 2 cloves rough chopped garlic, 1/3 cup small diced zucchini, 1/3 cup asparagus cut into 1 inch pieces, 1 tsp vegetable oil
sauce: 1/3 cup ketchup whisked together with 1/3 cup hoisin sauce, 1 Tbs molasses, 1 tsp apple cider vinegar, 1/2 tsp smoked paprika, 1 tsp sugar and a pinch of cayenne

  Heat a non stick skillet for 3 minutes on high. Add in the oil and the garlic, mushrooms, broccoli and baby bok choy. Saute 3 minutes, stirring often, and then add in the beans, zucchini, tofu and asparagus. Cook 2 more minutes, stirring often. Add in the sauce and cook 30 more seconds. Enjoy.

Yield: Serves 2

Grilled Polenta with Mushroom Marsala Sauce

for the polenta:

1 cup instant polenta

3 cups water

2 Tbs Earth Balance vegan buttery spread

3 Tbs Follow Your Heart brand vegan parmesan

1/2 Tbs salt

1 teaspoon garlic powder

1 teaspoon olive oil

for the sauce:

2 cups sliced button or cremini mushrooms

1 teaspoon dried oregano

2 cloves garlic minced

2.5 cups plain rice milk

1/3 cup flour

1 Tbs Better Than Bouillon No Chicken Base or Roasted Garlic Base

1/2 teaspoon salt

3 Tbs marsala cooking wine

2 Tbs Earth Balance vegan buttery spread

Bring the water, salt, garlic powder, vegan butter, pepper, olive oil and parmesan to a boil, whisking well. bring to a low heat and slowly add the polenta. Whisk fast or it will bubble and burn your arm. Cook 1 minute. Remove from heat and pour the mix into a non stick spray sprayed 9x13 inch pyrex glass casserole dish. Place in the freezer until polenta is cooled and firm (45 minutes or so). When completely cooled, take a cup and cut out circle shapes of polenta, I like them about 2 inches across. The leftover polenta scraps are a great whole grain snack. Heat a grill, spray well with non stick spray and grill each side 3-4 minutes. If you have no grill, pan sear each side until golden in a non stick pan with a little oil. Top with the sauce.

For the marsala sauce, in a bowl or measuring glass mix the rice milk, bouillon, flour, marsala, oregano and salt. Whisk well to mix. Set aside. Bring a sauce pan to a medium high heat for 2 minutes. Add the vegan butter, garlic and the mushrooms. Season with salt. Stir until the mushrooms are cooked and their liquid has evaporated. Add the liquid ingredients. Whisk well and cook until thickened. If too thick, add more water.

Yield: Serves 4-6

Kung Pao Tofu

This is spicy and delicious.

1 recipe of the Crispy Asian Style
Tofu Nuggets from page 288, cooked
3 red dried chilis cut into 1/4 inch pieces
(found in spice isle or produce isle)
1/3 cups peanuts, toasted in a dry
skillet for 2 minutes
1/3 cup each medium diced red bell
peppers, green bell peppers and zucchini
1 tsp each fresh grated ginger and garlic
1 Tbs sesame oil, 1/2 cup peeled sliced
carrots, 1 cup bite size cut broccoli florets
for the sauce:
2 Tbs dark soy sauce whisked with 2 Tbs regular soy sauce, 4 Tbs water, 1 tsp rice vinegar,
1 Tbs vegan oyster sauce, 1 Tbs hoisin sauce, 1 tsp cornstarch, 1 tsp sugar+1/4 tsp chili paste

Heat a large non stick pan for 3 minutes on high, then add in the oil, garlic, ginger, dried
red chili pieces, broccoli, carrots and bell peppers. Saute 4 minutes, stirring often. Add in
the tofu and zucchini and cook 1 more minute. Add in the whisked sauce and cook 1 more
minute until thickened and all is coated. Serve over steamed rice topped with the peanuts.

Yield: Serves 2-3

Spaghetti Alla Puttanesca

1 box of Dreamfields brand spaghetti, Barilla brand White Fiber spaghetti or Ronzoni Smart
Taste spaghetti (I like these brands because they
contain extra fiber but still have the same
texture as other pastas, you can use any
brand of pasta you like best though)
1/3 cup rough chopped pitted kalamata olives
1/3 cup roughly chopped capers
1/3 cup chopped fresh parsley
3 Tbs oil cured sun dried to tomatoes, rough
chopped (make sure they are the ones in the jar)
1 can of whole San Marzano tomatoes,
crushed with your hands with the juices
1 tsp balsamic vinegar
4 cloves garlic, rough chopped
1/2 tsp each salt and dried red pepper flakes
2 Tbs chopped fresh basil
1 Tbs olive oil, 3 Tbs of the pasta cooking water

Cook the spaghetti 6 minutes then drain and cool, set aside. Heat a large saute pan on
medium high for 3 minutes. Add in the oil and then the garlic. Cook a few seconds and then
add in the olives, sun dried tomatoes, salt and capers. Cook 1 minute and add in the hand
crushed tomatoes and their juices and the vinegar. Cook this all together 5 minutes. Add in
the cooked spaghetti, the 3 Tbs of pasta cooking water, the parsley and basil. Toss until the
spaghetti is coated. Add a little salt if needed. You can top this with a little Follow Your Heart
brand vegan parmesan if desired. Enjoy.

Yield: Serves 3-5

Homemade Artichoke Chicken Ravioli in Lemon Butter Sauce with Spinach and Broccoli

This recipe requires a manual crank pasta machine. Atlas makes a great one

1 recipe of pasta dough from this book
1 pack of Delight Soy brand or Maywah brand non breaded chicken patties
or non breaded nuggets
6 Tbs vegan mayo
1 small jar of marinated
artichoke hearts
1 tsp salt or to taste
2 cups broccoli florets,
cut small
3 cups raw baby spinach
juice of half a lemon
2 tsp fresh garlic
4 Tbs Earth Balance
brand buttery spread
salt and pepper to taste

Mix the chicken, artichokes, mayo and some salt in a food processor for 30 seconds. Taste, make sure it is rich and delicious. Set aside. Divide your pasta dough into 3 equal sized balls. Roll one of the balls as flat as possible with a rolling pin. Run the flattened dough through the pasta machine on the first setting, cutting it with a pizza cutter to make it a long, even rectangle after the first pass through the machine. Next, run it through on the number 3 setting. Cut this long piece of flattened dough in half and run each half through the pasta machine on the number 5 setting.

Flour the cutting board a little and then lay the 2 flattened pasta sheets next to each other. Place about a tablespoon of the chicken filling on one of the sheets, in rows of two, you can fit about 8 chicken fillings per sheet. Now take the other flattened piece of dough and place it on top of the chicken topped piece of dough. Carefully push the dough around the chicken filling, removing all air bubbles. Take a pastry wheel or pizza cutter and cut the filled areas into ravioli squares or rectangles. Repeat this process with the remaining balls of dough. This will make about 24 ravioli. Boil the fresh ravioli for 2 minutes, drain and toss in a little olive oil. Heat a large non stick pan for 3 minutes, add in a little olive oil, the garlic, broccoli and spinach. Cook 3 minutes and then add in the Earth Balance butter, your ravioli, salt, pepper and lemon juice. Cook 1 more minute and serve hot.

Yield: Serves 4-6

Homemade Tortellini

One legend says "Venus stays at an inn. Overcome by her beauty, the inkeeper spies on her through a keyhole, through which he can only see her navel. He is inspired to create a pasta in this shape". You can use my Tofu Ricotta filling for this, the filling for my Pesto Beef Cannelloni or the filling for my Artichoke Chicken Ravioli for these. They are great in lemon butter sauce or in broth.

1 recipe of the Homemade Pasta Dough from this book
filling of your choice, my Tofu Ricotta or Artichoke Chicken Ravioli fillings work great

Cut the dough into 4 equal pieces. On a floured surface, roll one of them thin enough with a rolling pin to go through the first setting on a manual pasta rolling machine. Run through the first setting, then the third, the fifth and then the second to last setting. Place this flattened dough back on a floured surface and cut out 1.5 inch circles out of the dough with a glass or cup. Place a little less than a tsp of filling in the center of each circle. Wet the edges of the dough and fold each circle into a half moon. With the flat edge facing you, push up into the center of the filling, folding the 2 corners of the half circle towards each other until the overlap, pressing them together, so that it looks like the picture. Repeat the process with the rest of the dough or for how ever many tortellini you want to make. Boil each one for 2 minutes if fresh. You can also freeze them when raw and bag them up. From frozen, they take 5 minutes to cook. Enjoy.

Yield: Depends on how many you would like to make

Homemade Egg Pappardelle Pasta with Garlic Spinach, Mushrooms & Asparagus in White Wine Butter Sauce

1.5 cups King Arthur flour
2 Tbs Follow Your Heart
brand Vegan Egg
1/2-3/4 cup hot water
1/2 tsp salt
1 tsp extra virgin olive oil
3 cups raw baby spinach
2 cups sliced button or
cremini mushrooms
3/4 cup asparagus stalks cut
into 3/4 inch long pieces
3 cloves fresh minced garlic
1/8 cup white wine
4 Tbs Earth Balance brand
Buttery Spread
1/2 tsp minced fresh sage
salt and pepper to taste

 Mix the flour and salt in a large bowl. In a measuring cup, add in the Vegan Egg, olive oil and hot water. Mix well. Pour this into the flour in the bowl. Pull it all together into a dough ball with your hands. If it seems too dry, add a little more water, small amounts at a time. Knead the dough until smooth. Place in plastic wrap and keep in the fridge for 30 minutes. With a rolling pin on a well floured board or counter, roll the dough into a long thin shape. Cut it into thirds. Take a hand cranked pasta machine and run them one at a time through the first setting, then the third and finally to the fifth setting or whichever setting is the second to last setting on your pasta machine. When all three sheets are done, flour them very well and roll into cigar shapes. With a sharp knife, cut across the cigar shaped tube into half inch portions (you should get 4 or 5 cuts per rolled up pasta tube). When all the pasta sheets are cut, unroll them into long noodles and toss them very well in flour.
Heat a pot full of boiling water as well as a large non stick saute pan. Heat the saute pan for 3 minutes on high heat and add a tsp olive oil, the garlic, mushrooms and asparagus. Saute 2 minutes, season with salt and pepper and add in the white wine and the spinach. Cook 2 minutes. Add your pasta into the boiling water and cook for 2 minutes. Drain it well. Add it into the saute pan with the vegetables and add the fresh sage and butter. When the butter is melted, taste for seasoning. If it needs salt and pepper, add it now. Plate and top with some Follow Your Heart brand vegan Parmesan Cheese. Enjoy.

Yield: Serves 3-4

Mee Siam

4 cups of cooked thin vermicelli rice noodles, 1 Tbs vegetable oil, 1/2 cup peeled carrots cut into thin matchsticks, 1 cooked recipe of the Pan Seared Chewy Tofu from this book, but cut into 1 inch strips before searing instead of torn into chunks, 1/3 cup thin sliced red bell pepper strips, 1/2 cup of green scallion tops cut into 3/4 inch pieces, 1/2 cup onions sliced into thin half moons, 3/4 cup bean sprouts, 1 tsp each rough chopped garlic and peeled ginger **for the sauce:** whisk together 3 Tbs sugar, 1 tsp dark soy sauce 3 Tbs tamarind sauce, 3 Tbs ketchup, 1 Tbs hot chili paste, 1 tsp sesame oil, 2 Tbs tau cheo ground bean paste (available in Asian markets), 1 tsp Better Than Bouillon brand roasted garlic base and 1.5 Tbs water

Heat a large non stick pan for 3 minutes on high. Add in the vegetable oil, then the carrots, red bell pepper, onions, ginger and garlic. Cook 2 minutes, stirring often. Throw in the prepared tofu and green scallion tops. Cook 1 more minute. Add in the whisked sauce and then the noodles. Stir until the noodles are coated and warm. Remove from heat and stir in the bean sprouts. Top with a few chopped shallots that you have crisped in some oil if desired. Enjoy. *Yield:* Serves 2-3

Sausage Rice

A rich and tasty one pot meal. I like to top it with sliced avocado, Tofutti brand sour cream and a few dashes of hot sauce.

3 links of Beyond Meat brand bratwurst or Italian sausages that have had the skin removed by running them under warm water and peeling it off
1/2 cup medium diced red onion
1/2 cup each medium diced red bell pepper and green bell pepper, 3 cloves garlic minced, 1 1/2 cups dry uncooked jasmine rice, 3 cups water whisked together with 2 Tbs of Better Than Bouillon brand No Chicken Base or Roasted Garlic Base and a pinch of salt, 1 Tbs tomato paste, 1 tsp chili powder, 1 tsp smoked paprika, 1/3 cup chopped vinegared cherry peppers, 1 Tbs Earth Balance brand buttery spread

Heat a large non stick skillet that has a cover for 3 minutes on high. Add in the Earth Balance and the peeled sausages. Break them up with a spatula for 3 minutes until browned a little and crumbled. Add in the red and green bell peppers (not the cherry peppers yet) and the onions and garlic. Cook 2 more minutes. Add in the dry rice and stir around a 30 seconds. Add in the smoked paprika, chili powder, the water/bouillon mixture and the tomato paste. Stir and bring it all to a boil and cover it. Turn to a low heat and simmer 15 minutes covered until the liquid is absorbed and the rice is cooked. Leave covered off of the heat 3 minutes and then stir in the cherry peppers. You can top it with fresh chopped scallions and Tofutti brand sour cream. *Yield:* Serves 3-4

Homemade Flaky Chicken Pot Pie

for the dough:

3 cups sifted King Arthur brand flour
1 tsp baking powder
1/2 teaspoon salt
7 Tbs vegetable shortening
1 1/4 cup water

for filling:

2 medium carrots peeled, medium diced and then steamed and cooled
1 cup of your favorite vegan chicken diced (I like Delight Soy brand brand patties or 3/4 cup Gardein Veggie Chicken strips, chopped), 1/2 cup thawed frozen peas, 1/2 cup diced zucchini raw, 1 cup cauliflower florets, steamed and cooled

for the gravy:

1 cup plain rice milk,1/2 cup water, 1 Tbs Better Than Boullion brand No Chicken Base, 2 Tbs nutritional yeast, a few pinches of salt, 1 tsp gravy master
1 Tbs fresh dill chopped
3 Tbs plain flour
1 Tbs vegan butter spread

Start with the dough, mix the flour, salt and baking powder together in a large bowl. Add the shortening and cut into the flour with a pastry cutter until small beads form. Add the water and gently mix until a dough forms. If too dry, add more water. Knead softly by folding the dough in half on top of itself over and over 8 times. Mix all of the filling ingredients, set aside in a large bowl. **Make the gravy** by placing all gravy ingredients in a medium sauce pan. Bring to a boil, whisking constantly. When it boils, turn on medium until thickened. Taste the gravy to make sure it is very flavorful since this is the base of the dish. Take the gravy and mix it with the vegetable/chicken mixture. Take a pie tin, spray with non stick spray. Preheat oven to 420 degrees. Take half the dough and roll into a circle on a floured board for the bottom of the pie. Push into the pie tin, then roll the other half for the top and set aside. Take the gravy/veggie/chicken mixture and pour into the bottom crust. Next take the top crust and place it over the mixture. Trim the ends with a knife if it hangs over too much. Now pinch the top and bottom dough together with your fingers forming a tight seal. Place the pie on a cookie sheet lined with foil and bake for 35 to 40 minutes or until the top is golden. Let cool 15 minutes then eat.

Yield: Serves 4-6

Moo Goo Gai Pan

A delicious Chinese take out dish made vegan.

1.5 blocks extra firm tofu that have been frozen, thawed and had the water squeezed out of the blocks of tofu between your palms (this process creates an extra chewy and delicious tofu)
1 cup chopped baby bok choy
1/2 cup peeled carrots cut into 1/8 inch thick slices
1/2 cup snap peas or snow peas
1 cup button mushrooms sliced
1/3 cup sliced water chestnuts
2 cloves minced garlic
1 Tbs sesame oil **for the sauce:**
1 cup water whisked together with 1 tsp soy sauce, 1 Tbs Better Than Bouillon brand Roasted Garlic Base, 1/4 tsp garlic powder, 1 tsp sesame oil, 1 tsp sugar, 1 tsp rice vinegar. 1 Tbs vegan oyster sauce and 1/4 cup cold water mixed with 1.5 Tbs cornstarch

Heat a large non stick skillet on high for 3 minutes. Add in the sesame oil and then the tofu, carrots, snap or snow peas and bok choy in a flat layer. Let it sit 1 minute and then stir around for 3 more minutes. Add in the water chesrnuts and garlic. Cook 1 minute and add in the water/bouillon base mixture. Cook 1 minute until thickened, stirring often. Enjoy with steamed brown or jasmine rice.

Yield: Serves 2-3

Tarragon Maple Dijon Black Bean, Tofu and Eggplant (gluten free)

1 cup eggplant, cut into diamond shaped chunks or cubes
1/4 cup onions, medium diced, 1/2 cup green pepper medium diced
1 clove of garlic, minced, 1 cup cooked and drained black beans
1 block of tofu that has been frozen, thawed and had all of the water squeezed out of the block between your hands (this gives the tofu an extra chewy texture)
1 tsp olive oil

for the sauce:
1/2 cup dijon mustard
1/4 cup maple syrup
1 tsp sugar
pinch of salt and pepper
1/4 tsp each garlic powder, fresh
tarragon and dried basil

Whisk all of the sauce ingredients together. Taste for flavor. If the dijon flavor is too strong, add a little more sugar. Set aside. Heat a large non stick pan for 2 minutes on high heat. Add in the oil and the tofu chunks. Cook them 2 minutes until browned. Add in the eggplant, onions, garlic and peppers. Add in a little more oil and a pinch of salt. Cook until the eggplant is soft and browned, about 3 minutes. Add in the beans and sauce and cook another 2 minutes. Enjoy.

Yield: Serves 3-4

Homemade From Scratch Sausage, Egg and Cheese Biscuits

biscuits:
2 cups King Arthur brand flour, sifted
1/2 Tbs baking powder
1/2 teaspoon salt
8 Tbs vegan shortening
1 1/4 cup freshly opened club soda mixed with 1 tsp apple cider vinegar

2 links of Beyond Meat brand spicy Italian sausages with the skin removed by running them under warm water, formed into 3 inch patties and browned in a non stick pan 2 minutes per side, 6 servings worth of the Vegan Egg by the Follow Your Heart brand, prepared and kept warm
Follow Your Heart brand American cheese slices

Preheat oven to 450 degrees. Mix flour with salt and baking powder and soda in a large bowl. Put the shortening into the bowl and cut it into the flour with a pastry cutter until it looks like pea sized balls in the flour. Add the club soda and vinegar mixture into the flour. Carefully mix and knead by folding the dough over itself over and over (add more club soda if the dough is too dry before folding). This is a very important step, it creates layers and makes a fluffy, better biscuit. If the dough seems too wet, add more flour. Do not over knead the dough or the biscuits will be tough. When mixed into a nice dough, flatten the dough out to about 1/2 inch thick. Cut into biscuits with a biscuit cutter. Refold the leftover dough and cut more biscuits. Place each biscuit into a non stick cake pan sprayed with non stick spray. Make sure the biscuits are touching each other, this makes them bake softer and more tender. Bake for about 18 minutes or until risen and browned on top. Remove from the oven and brush the tops with a little melted Earth Balance buttery spread.

Split your biscuit and layer it with the cooked sausage, the Vegan Egg and then the cheese. You can melt the cheese on top of the egg in the microwave for 20 seconds before placing it on the biscuit if you like it melted. I like it the best melted. *You can make baked cheese biscuits as well by adding 1/2 cup of So Delicious brand cheddar jack shredded cheese to the flour before preparing the biscuit recipe. These are a great side dish.

Yield: Serves 3-6

Homemade Spicy Gnocchi with Garlic Kale, Asparagus, Broccoli and Sausage

1 recipe of the Homemade Gnocchi recipe from this book, uncooked
1 medium bunch of kale, stems removed, chopped and boiled 3 minutes
then drained, squeezed dry and cooled, 1/2 cup medium diced zucchini
1 cup cremini mushrooms, sliced thin, 1/2 cup asparagus cut into 1 inch pieces
3 cloves garlic, rough chopped, 3/4 cup broccoli cut into small florets
3 Tbs Earth Balance buttery spread, 2 Tbs fresh lemon juice, red pepper flakes
1/2 tsp salt or to taste, 2 links of Beyond Meat brand Italian sausages
that have had the skin removed by running them under warm water and
peeling it off or 2 links of Field Roast brand Chipotle Sausage, cut in half
lengthwise and then cut into half moons on a bias angle

Heat 6 inches of water to a boil in a pot. Heat a large non stick pan for 2
minutes, add in a tsp of olive oil and add in the mushrooms, sausage, broccoli
and garlic. Cook 4 minutes, stirring often (if you use the peeled sausage, break
it up with a spatula while cooking it), with a pinch of salt. Add the gnocchi to the
pot of boiling water, stir them and cook them 2 minutes or until they float. Drain
them. Add the kale, asparagus and zucchini into the sausage/vegetable mix,
sautee for 1 more minute. Add in the butter, red pepper flakes, salt and lemon
juice. Taste for flavor, adjust seasoning if needed. Top with Follow Your Heart
brand vegan parmesan cheese. Enjoy.   *Yield:* Serves 3-4

Bruschetta Topped Pesto Grilled Tofu

1 recipe of the Basil Pesto and the Bruschetta Topping recipe from this book
2 blocks of extra firm tofu that have been frozen, thawed and had all
of the water squeezed completely out of the blocks between your palms (this
process creates an extra chewy tofu) and each block cut into 4 large squares

Place the tofu in a large flat dish and cover each side of each tofu squares
with pesto. A spoon makes it easier to spread the pesto. Heat a grill for 15
minutes on high. Spray it with non stick spray and grill each side of the tofu about 3
minutes. Remove from the grill and top with the bruschetta topping.   *Yield:* Serves 4

Homemade Jumbo Ricotta Beef Fresh Ravioli

This recipe requires a hand crank pasta machine.

1 recipe of Pasta Dough from this book (the semolina dough)
1 recipe Tofu Ricotta from this book
4 leaves fresh basil, sliced thin, 1 /2 a pack of Impossible brand ground

Brown the Impossible ground in a non stick skillet in a little olive oil with a pinch of salt and pepper. Cool and mix with the ricotta. Divide your pasta dough into 3 equal sized balls. Roll one of the balls as flat as possible with a rolling pin. Run the flattened dough through the pasta machine on the first setting, cutting it with a pizza cutter to make it a long, even rectangle after the first pass through the machine. Next, run it through on the number 3 setting. Cut this long piece of flattened dough in half and run each half through the pasta machine on the number 5 setting (or the second to last setting).

Flour the cutting board a little and then lay the 2 flattened pasta sheets next to each other. Place about a tablespoon of the ricotta beef mixture on one of the sheets, in rows of two, you can fit about 8 ricotta fillings per sheet. Now take the other flattened piece of dough and place it on top of the ricotta topped piece of dough. Carefully push the dough around the ricotta mounds, removing all air bubbles. Take a biscuit cutter or small cup and cut out round ravioli shapes around the mounds of pasta sheet topped ricotta. Repeat this process with the remaining balls of dough. This will make about 24 ravioli. Boil the fresh ravioli for 3 minutes, drain and then toss them in a little oil to prevent them from sticking together. Top the cooked ravioli with your favorite homemade or store bought marinara sauce and the fresh basil.

*You can fill these ravioli with any filling you prefer. You can also freeze them, but they will take about 5 minutes to cook if frozen.

Yield: Serves 3-5

Cauliflower Parmesan

1 head of cauliflower cut into 1/2 inch thick steaks by cutting across the whole cauliflower head from top to bottom creating about 3 or 4 steaks, 2 cups of panko bread crumbs mixed together with 1/2 tsp each of salt, dried oregano, dried basil and garlic powder, 2 cups flour, 1 cup water, 3 cups of your favorite homemade or store bought tomato sauce, 5 slices of Field Roast brand Chao slices, shredded yourself, 3 Tbs Follow Your Heart brand parmesan shreds, 1/2 inch of vegetable oil in a large non stick pan

Place 1 cup of flour in a flat dish. Take the other cup of flour and whisk it in a wide bowl with the cup of water until smooth (this will act as the egg to help the bread crumbs stick), and then place the seasoned panko bread crumbs in a large flat dish. Working from left to right, dip the cauliflower steaks, one at a time, into the flour, then the flour and water mixture and then into the bread crumbs. Coat each steak completely with the bread crumbs. Heat the oil for 3 minutes on high. Dip a coated steak in and see if bubbles form. If bubbles form, they are ready to fry. Cook 2 at a time, cooking each side about 3 minutes or until golden. Drain them and sprinkle with a pinch of salt. Spray a large glass baking dish with non stick spray. Place a thin layer of tomato sauce on the bottom and then arrange the cooked steaks inside and top each with some tomato sauce, parmesan and then the shredded cheese. Cover and bake in a 400 degree oven for 20 minutes. Uncover and make sure the cheese is melted. Enjoy. *Yield:* Serves 3-4

Saffron Raisin Cauliflower Bread Crumb Topped Penne

1 box of Ronzoni brand Smart Taste penne (this pasta has extra fiber but still tastes like regular white pasta), 3/4 cup of golden raisins, purple raisins or currants or a mix of them soaked in 1/2 cup of warm water that has a few strands saffron placed in it
1 cup of cauliflower cut into small florets, 1/2 cup small diced yellow or white onion
3 cloves garlic rough chopped, 2 Tbs lemon juice, 1 tsp salt, red pepper flakes to taste
3 Tbs Follow Your Heart brand vegan parmesan plus a little for topping
fresh basil for garnish, 2 Tbs olive oil **bread crumb topping:** 1 cup of panko bread crumbs
1/4 tsp dried oregano, 1 Tbs Earth Balance brand buttery spread, a few pinches of salt

Cook the penne about 7 minutes and then drain and cool completely. Heat a non stick skillet for 3 minutes and add in the Earth Balance and let it melt. Add in the bread crumbs, a pinch of salt and oregano. Stir around until they are browned. Set aside. Clean the pan and heat it again another 3 minutes and add in the olive oil. Add in the onions, cauliflower and garlic. Cook until browned, stirring often, about 5 minutes. Add in the cooked pasta, the raisins along with the water they are soaking in, the salt and the 3 Tbs of parmesan. Stir and taste, add more salt or lemon juice if needed. Serve topped with the toasted bread crumbs, basil, red pepper flakes and extra parmesan and top with some toasted pine nuts if desired.

Yield: Serves 3-4

Homemade Pesto Beef Cannelloni Baked in Artichoke Cream Sauce

This is my favorite pasta dish, rich and elegant. Homemade pasta tubes, stuffed, sauced and baked to absolute perfection.

1 pack of Beyond Meat brand Beefless Ground or Impossible ground that you have browned in a non stick pan and cooled

1 pesto recipe from this book, 1 pasta dough recipe from this book

the sauce:

3/4 cup soy free vegan mayo, 1/4 cup nutritional yeast
1 small jar of marinated artichokes, drained
1 clove garlic
juice of 1/2 lemon
1/2 tsp salt
1/2 cup water
1/2 container Tofutti cream cheese

Place the sauce ingredients in a food processor until smooth. It should be just able to pour but not too thin. Add water if too thick to pour.

Divide the dough in half, flatten it as much as you can with a rolling pin on a floured board. Roll the pasta dough out to the second to last setting on your pasta machine or kitchen aid attachment. You will have a very long sheet at this point. Cut it with a pizza cutter into 5x5 inch squares. Repeat with the remaining dough. You should end up with 10-15 pasta squares. Boil them in boiling water for one minute and drain, then cool in ice water. Fresh pasta cooks VERY fast.

Make the filling by mixing the cooked Impossible or Beyond Meat with one recipe of pesto and pinch of salt and a half tsp of garlic powder. Place the cooled drained pasta squares on a flat surface and spoon 2 Tbs of the beef filling onto the edge of each one and roll into a log. Preheat the oven to 375 degrees and spray a 9x13 inch casserole dish with non stick spray. Line the bottom of the dish with half of the cream sauce. Place the filled pasta tubes next to each other in the sauce. You should have about 10-15 cannelloni. Cover the pasta tubes with the remaining sauce. Bake until browned, about 20 minutes. Top with Go Veggie brand vegan parmesan cheese or Follow Your Heart brand parmesan shreds.

Yield: Serves 4-8

Homemade Sloppy Joes

The sauce is the key to a good homemade sloppy joe, this one is tangy with great flavor.

2 Tbs Earth Balance buttery spread
1 lb of Beyond Meat brand or Impossible brand groundless beef, thawed
1 medium green pepper, small diced
1 medium onion, medium diced
2 cloves minced garlic
your favorite whole grain or white vegan hamburger buns
for the sauce:
1 Tbsp tomato paste, 2/3 cup ketchup
1/3 cup water, 1 Tbs brown sugar
1 tsp yellow mustard, 1/2 tsp chili powder
1/2 tsp smoked paprika, 1/2 tsp garlic powder
1 tsp liquid smoke, salt and pepper to taste

For the sauce, whisk all of the sauce ingredients together and set aside. Heat a large non stick skillet for 2 minutes on high. Add in the onions and peppers and 1 Tbs of the buttery spread. Cook 2 minutes and add in the ground. Break it up with a spatula. Cook until browned, about 4 minutes. Add in the sauce and simmer on low for 10 to 12 minutes. Heat another non stick skillet over high heat for 2 minutes and add in the butter, melt it and add the buns in, face down, toasting them until golden. Remove from pan and load them up with the sloppy joe filling. Enjoy. *Yield:* Serves 3-4

Cornmeal Johnny Cakes

Whether you call them Johnny Cakes or Hoe Cakes, these traditional corn meal pancakes are sure to please. Top these with Earth Balance brand buttery spread and pure maple syrup.

1/2 cup yellow cornmeal mixed with 1 cup of King Arthur brand flour, a pinch of salt, 1 Tbs sugar
4 Tbs vegetable shortening
1/2 tsp each baking powder and baking soda
1 1/2 cups freshly opened plain club soda

Mix the flour, salt, sugar, cornmeal, baking powder and baking soda in a large bowl. Place the shortening in the bowl and using a pastry cutter, cut the shortening into the flour mix until tiny beeds form in the flour. You can use a fork if you have no pastry cutter. Add in the freshly opened club soda and whisk gently until just mixed. Heat a large electric skillet until warm and then spray with non stick spray. Place about 3 Tbs worth of batter per pancake on the skillet, you can fit about 6 pancakes on the skillet at a time. Cook each side until golden. Stack them up and enjoy warm.

Yield: Makes 8 Johnny Cakes

Italian Hoagie

1 loaf of fresh, chewy Italian bread
1 pack of Yves brand bologna or salami
1 pack of Smoked Tofurkey slices
1 pack of Field Roast Chao cheese
1/4 cup vinegar marinated sliced
cherry peppers or banana peppers
1/2 an onion sliced into half moons
1 cup of shredded lettuce
2 tomatoes cut into thin slices
1/4 cup sliced dill pickles
any vegan mayo you like
spicy brown mustard
a few shakes of Italian dressing (optional)

Simply slice the whole loaf of Italian bread lengthwise and layer the ingredients, making a delicious hoagie. You can slice it into 4-6 good sized pieces. This goes great with the beans and greens soup from this book and the potato salad or baked steak fries.

Yield: Serves 3-5

Bolognese Sauce

1 pack of Impossible brand ground,
browned in a pan
1/2 cup peeled carrots diced small
2 cloves fresh garlic minced
1/4 cup finely diced celery
1/4 cup finely diced onions
3 cups of your favorite homemade
or store bought tomato sauce
1/2 can of plain coconut milk
1 bay leaf
salt and pepper to taste
1/4 cup red wine
1 tsp balsamic vinegar
1/2 tsp each dried oregano,
garlic powder and dried basil

Heat a large saute pan or pot over medium heat for 2 minutes and then add in a 1/2 Tbs of olive oil. Add in the onions, celery, carrots and garlic. Saute 3 minutes and then add in the red wine. Cook 4 more minutes. Add in the rest of the ingredients. Stir until well mixed and cook for 10 minutes, stirring often. Taste for seasoning, add more salt and pepper if needed. Remove the bay leaf and serve over my cooked Gnocchi recipe, spaghetti, rotini or cooked bucatini pasta. Top with some Follow Your Heart brand vegan Parmesan Cheese.

Yield: Serves 3-4

Spanakopita Hand Pies

2 6 oz bags of fresh raw baby spinach
2 cloves minced garlic, 1/2 cup small diced yellow onion
1 container of Follow Your Heart brand feta crumbles
1 Tbs lemon juice, 1/2 tsp dried oregano
1 package of vegan filo dough
1/2 cup melted Earth Balance buttery spread

Heat a large non stick saute pan for 3 minutes on high. Add in a tsp of olive oil and add in the garlc and onion. Cook for 1 minute. Add the spinach and a pinch of salt. Cook about 2 minutes until the spinach is wilted. Cool and completely squeeze all of the water out of the spinach. Add in the feta, oregano, lemon juice and a pinch of salt. Taste for flavor. Add salt if needed. Cut the thawed filo dough sheets in half lengthwise into about 4 inch wide long strips (they will be about 4 inches wide and about 14 inches long). Carefully remove a sheet of the cut filo and brush it with some of the melted Earth Balance and place another sheet on top and repeat the brushing process with each of the sheets until it is 5 sheets thick. Brush the top of the 5th sheet as well. Place about 3 Tbs of the spinach feta mixture on the 4 inch wide edge closest to you and fold the filo over the filling forming a triangle. Repeat this triangle folding pattern back and forth until you get to the end of the sheet of filo and have a triangle shaped pie. Repeat this process with the remaining cut sheets of filo. Brush the tops with a little more melted Earth Balance. Heat the oven to 400 and bake them on a parchment lined cookie sheet, seam side down, until golden, about 13 minutes. Enjoy.

Yield: Makes about 8 to 10 hand pies

Italian Sausage and Cheese Baked Ziti

This goes great with the Meatball recipe from this book. If you prefer no sausage, some sauteed mushrooms and spinach are a tasty alternative to add into the cooked pasta before baking.

1 box of Barilla brand ziti, cooked al dente and completely cooled in cold ice water (to stop it from overcooking) and then drained or 1 box of Dreamfields brand penne, cooked and cooled
3 links of Beyond Meat brand Italian sausages, cut into half moons and pan seared in a non stick pan until crisped
2 cups of your favorite homemade or store bought tomato sauce
4 Tbs Follow Your Heart brand shredded parmesan
1 tsp each dried basil and dried oregano
2 cups water, 1/4 cup flour
3 Tbs Earth Balance brand buttery spread
1 tsp salt, 1 tsp garlic powder
1/2 cup nutritional yeast
1 tsp lemon juice
1 soft block of Follow Your Heart brand mozzarella shredded yourself or 8 slices of Field Roast brand Chao Cheese, original flavor

Mix the water, flour, nutritional yeast, lemon juice, salt, butter and garlic powder together in a pot over medium high heat. Whisk all together until thickened. Taste test it, it should have a rich cheesy flavor. If bland, add more salt, lemon juice or nutritional yeast. Set aside once thickened. Preheat the oven to 375 degrees. In a large bowl, mix the cooked ziti, the parmesan, the oregano, basil, the sausage and 1 cup of the tomato sauce. Add in the thickened nutritional yeast sauce. Taste for seasoning. Spray a 9x13 inch casserole or pyrex dish with non stick spray. Place the pasta mixture into the casserole dish, spread evenly with a spatula. Top this with the remaining tomato sauce and the shredded mozzarella cheeese or the Chao slices. Season the top with a little salt, garlic powder and dried oregano and basil. Cover the dish with foil that has been sprayed with a little non stick spray (to keep the cheese from sticking to the foil). Bake for 35 to 40 mins or until the cheese is melted. If the cheese needs more melting, place it under the broiler a minute. Goes great with garlic bread and a salad or blanched vegetables.

Yield: Serves 4-8

Hoisin Ginger Beef Stuffed Cabbage Rolls

1 medium cabbage with the bottom core cut off about half an inch flat across so that the cabbage is still held in tact **filling:** mix with your hands 1 pack of Impossible brand ground with 2 cloves minced garlic, 1 Tbs minced ginger, 1/2 tsp garlic powder, a pinch of salt, 2 Tbs hoisin sauce and 1/3 each small peeled and diced carrots, small diced red and green bell peppers, leeks and onions

Drop the whole cabbage in a large tall pot of boiling water for about 7 minutes. Remove from water and let cool a few minutes. Peel off the outer 4 leaves but save them. Peel off more leaves to use for stuffing. You should get about 14 good ones to use. Cut the white stemmy part off of the bottom of each cooked leaf a little so that they roll easier. Place equal amounts of the filling in a log shape at the edge of the leaves closest to you. Fold the bottom of the leaf over the filling and then pull the sides over the filling and roll it into a cigar shape. Repeat with all of the leaves and place them in a glass baking dish. Take about 1 cup of water and mix it with 1 Tbs of soy sauce and pour it around the rolls. Cover the rolls with the outer leaves you saved and then cover it all with foil. Bake at 375 degrees for about an hour. Enjoy with my Fried Rice recipe or my Savory Ramen Noodle recipe.   *Yield:* 14 rolls

Spicy Black Pepper Sweet and Sticky Asian Tofu Wings

1 inch of vegetable oil to fry, 3 cups flour, 1.5 cups water
2 blocks of extra firm tofu that have been frozen, thawed and all of the water squeezed out of the blocks between your palms and then torn into about 1.5 inch long pieces (this freezing process makes an extra chewy tofu)
2 cups panko bread crumbs mixed w/ 1 tsp black pepper, 1/2 tsp salt+1/2 tsp garlic powder
for the sauce: whisk together 3 Tbs soy sauce with 1 Tbs brown sugar, 2 Tbs maple syrup, 1 Tbs sriracha, 2 Tbs water, 1 Tbs sweet chili sauce, 1 Tbs chopped scallions & 2 Tbs hoisin

Place the panko mixture in a large flat glass sided dish. Place 1.5 cups of flour in a bowl and place the other 1.5 cups of flour in a bowl whisked together with the 1.5 cups of water until smooth (this will act as the egg so that the bread crumbs can stick to the tofu). Working from left to right, dip tofu pieces in the flour, then the water/flour mixture and then into the panko mix until the pieces are all coated. Heat a large non stick pan with the inch of oil for 3 minutes on high. Dip in a coated tofu piece. If bubbles form, they are ready to fry. Cook about 10 at a time until browned, flipping them after 2 minutes. Drain the tofu wings and place them in a large bowl, then pour in the sauce and stir/toss them until coated in the sauce. Serve hot topped with fresh slcallions and toasted sesame seeds.

Yield: Serves 4-5

Korean Spicy BBQ Tofu and Vegetables

1 block of extra firm tofu, frozen, then thawed out with all of the
excess water squeezed out of the block, then torn into bite size pieces (this
process makes the tofu extra chewy and delicious)
1 cup broccolini cut into 1 inch pieces, 1 cup sliced button or oyster mushrooms
1/4 cup small diced onion, 1 tsp each minced garlic and ginger
1/2 cup peeled carrots sliced on an angle
3 cups baby bok choy cut into bite size pieces
1 small green pepper medium diced
1/4 cup green beans cut into 1/2 inch pieces
2 tsp of sesame oil, scallions to garnish
for the sauce:
1/2 cup ketchup
1/2 cup hoisin sauce
2 Tbs sugar, 2 Tbs vegan oyster sauce
1 tsp hot chili paste (more or less, depending on how spicy you like it)
1 tsp rice wine vinegar, 1 tsp liquid smoke, 1/2 tsp sesame oil

For the sauce, whisk all of the sauce ingredients together and set aside.

Heat a non stick saute pan on high for 3 minutes, add 1 tsp of sesame
oil next and then the tofu. Cook it until it is browned a little (about 3 minutes)
and then add a little soy sauce and stir it around. Set the tofu aside and heat
the pan again for 2 minutes on high. Add in another tsp of sesame oil
and then the broccolini, bok choy, onions, ginger, garlic, mushrooms,
carrots, green peppers and green beans. Saute 3-4 minutes, stirring often.
Add in the cooked tofu. Saute 2 more minutes and add in the sauce. Cook 30
seconds, making sure the tofu and vegetables are coated evenly. Serve hot over
steamed rice or rice noodless. Garnish with scallions.

Yield: Serves 2-4

Egg Foo Young

for the egg: whisk together 1 cup of cold water with 4.5 Tbs of Follow Your Heart brand Vegan Egg, 1/4 tsp white pepper, 1 tsp sliced scallions and 1/2 tsp rice vinegar
for the flling: 2 small thinly sliced button mushrooms, 15 thawed green peas, 1/2 tsp minced garlic, 1/4 cup baby spinach cut into thin strips and 1 Tbs carrots julienne cut
for the gravy: whisk together 1 cup of water with 1.5 Tbs cornstarch, 1 Tbs hoisin sauce, 1 tsp Better Than Bouillon brand No Chicken Base or Roasted Garlic Base, 1/2 tsp sesame oil and 1/2 tsp sugar in a pan over medium heat until thickened

Heat a 6 or 8 inch non stick pan for 3 minutes on high. Add in 1 tsp sesame oil and add in the mushrooms, carrots and a pinch of salt. Cook 2 minutes and add in the garlic, spinach and peas. Cook 1 minute, spray the sides with non stick spray and add in the egg mixture. Spread it so the egg mixture is touching the bottom of the pan. Let it cook for 3 minutes and then flip the omelette in the pan and cook the other side 3 minutes. Serve sliced into triangles over steamed jasmine rice topped with the gravy. You can garnish it with fresh sliced scallions and sesame seeds if desired.
Yield: Serves 2

Kimchi and Scrambled Egg Fried Rice

2.5 cups of cooked and cooled jasmine rice
1/4 cup small diced medium onion
1 tsp each minced fresh garlic and ginger
1 recipe worth of Follow Your Heart brand Vegan Egg, prepared, cooked and set aside, 1/3 cup of broccoli cut into small florets, 3/4 of a block of tofu that has been frozen, thawed and had all of the water pressed out of the block, then cut into small cubes (this process makes the tofu extra chewy and delicious)
1/2 cup peeled and small diced carrot
1/4 cup thawed green peas or fresh peas, 1 tsp mushroom powder or garlic powder
1 Tbs sesame oil, 2 Tbs soy sauce, 1/3 cup vegan kimchi

Heat a non stick pan on high heat for 2 minutes. Add in the sesame oil and then the onions, garlic, ginger, tofu, broccoli and carrots. Cook 3 minutes. Add in the peas and cook for a minute and then add in the cooked, cooled rice. Break it up with a spatula and cook for 3 minutes. Add in the soy sauce, mushroom powder, kimchi and cooked vegan egg, mix well. Cook for another minute. Taste for flavor. If it needs more soy sauce, add it now. I like to serve this topped with some hoisin sauce, chopped scallions and hot chili oil.

Yield: Serves 2-3

Extra Crispy Chicken Fillet Sandwich

If you can not find Delight Soy brand or Maywah brand chicken, you can use Gardein brand or you can freeze a block of tofu, thaw it and squeeze all of the water out of the block between your hands. This process gives tofu a nice chewy texture. You can then slice it into large squares and bread it like the vegan chicken steaks.

1 pack Maywah or Delight Soy brand Vegan Chicken Steaks
2 cups of panko bread crumbs, 3 cups plain flour
1 teaspooon each - garlic powder, dried oregano and dried basil, 1 tsp salt
1 cup shredded iceberg lettuce, sliced pickles, vegan mayo

Put 1 1/2 cup of the flour in a large bowl, put the other 1 1/2 cups flour in a bowl mixed and whisked with 1 1/2 cups of water until it resembles a medium thin pancake batter. In a third flat casserole dish, mix the bread crumbs, garlic powder, oregano, basil and salt. Working from left to right, dip the veggie chicken into the flour, then the pancake flour mixture, and lastly the bread crumbs. If you use your left hand to dip into the flour and the pancake flour mixture and your right hand to cover the veggie chicken in the bread crumbs, this will avoid your hands from getting too messy. When all are breaded, heat a non stick pan with a half inch vegetable or canola oil until hot (if you throw a bread crumb in and bubbles from around it, it is ready to fry). Cook each side until golden. Drain on a cookie rack. Take your favorite roll, I prefer a regular old white or wheat vegan hamburger roll. Toast it in the oven or on a griddle for a minute then add the chicken fillet, shredded lettuce, lots of vegan mayo and 6 or 8 sliced pickles. This works great warm or as a picnic item.

Yield: Serves 4-6   — 227 —

Classic Double Cheeseburger

1 pack of Impossible brand ground formed into 4 bun size thin patties, 4 slices of Follow Your Heart brand American cheese, lettuce, tomato, pickles, onions, ketchup, vegan mayo, mustard and 2 of your favorite buns

Heat a large non stick pan that has a lid on high for 3 minutes. Add in 1 tsp of vegetable oil and then your patties. Season with a little salt and pepper. Cook one side 2 minutes. Flip them and top the 4 patties with the cheese. Cover the pan so the cheese melts. A drop or 2 of water added now into the hot pan will melt the cheese better. Cook for 2 more minutes. Toast your buns in a pan or in the oven. Stack 2 patties on each bun and top with the lettuce, tomato, pickles and condiments. Enjoy.

Yield: Makes 2 burgers

Spinach Florentine Artichoke Pizza

1 ball of the homemade dough recipe from this book, risen (the dough recipe makes 2 balls of dough but you will only use 1 here) 2 packs of 6 oz bags of raw baby spinach 3 cloves of minced garlic, 3/4 cup of jarred marinated artichokes roughly chopped your favorite homemade or store bought tomato sauce
1 block of Follow Your Heart brand soft block mozzarella grated yourself (make sure it is the soft block, it melts the best)

Remove the risen dough from the bowl and place on a large floured cutting board. Do not knead it again, push it into a rectangle as flat as possible and then roll it with a rolling pin into an 8x12 inch rectangle. Spray a 8x12 inch deep dish pan with non stick spray and place the dough inside. Cover and let it rise 1 hour. Heat a large non stick pan on high for 2 minutes. Add in 1 tsp of olive oil and then the garlic. Cook 20 seconds and add in the spinach, artichokes and a pinch of salt and pepper. Stir until the spinach is cooked down, about 2 minutes. Cool this mixure and squeeze any excess water from the spinach. Once the dough is risen, spread a thin layer of the tomato sauce over the pizza. Top it with the spinach artichoke mixture and then the shredded cheese and a few pinches of salt, dried oregano and salt. Bake in a 440 degree oven for 15 to 17 minutes. Place it under the broiler for an extra 2 or 3 minutes to finish melting the cheese and brown the crust. Remove from the oven and allow to cool 10 minutes before slicing to allow the cheese to set. Top with Follow Your Heart brand parmesan if desired. Enjoy.

Yield: Serves 2-3

Mushroom Scallion Crusted Tofu or Eggplant with Creamy Spinach Artichoke Dip

1 block of extra firm tofu that has been frozen, thawed and had all of the water squeezed out of the tofu block gently between your hands (this process makes the tofu extra chewy and delicious) or 1 medium eggplant, peeled and cut into 1/8 inch discs

2 cups of panko bread crumbs

1 teaspoon salt

8 white button mushrooms chopped fine

1 sliced bunch of scallions

1/2 teaspoon each garlic powder and dried oregano

3 cups all purpose flour

canola oil

1 recipe of the Spinach Artichoke Dip recipe from this book, baked and warm

Chop the tofu into 6 large triangles by slicing it twice down the sides and once diagonal in the center. If you are making eggplant cutlets, peel your eggplant and cut into 1/8 inch discs. Place chopped mushrooms, sliced scallions, salt, garlic powder, bread crumbs and oregano in a casserole dish, mix well. Set aside. Place 1 1/2 cups of the flour in a different flat casserole dish and take the other 1 1/2 cups flour and place in a bowl whisked together with 1 1/2 cups water until it is the consistency of pancake batter (this acts as a vegan version of the eggs that will help the bread crumb coating stick).

Working from left to right, dip the tofu or eggplant rounds into the flour first, covering completely, then the flour and water pancake consistency mix and lastly into the bread crumbs.

Heat a non stick pan with 1/4 inch canola oil. When hot (after about 3 minutes) add the tofu or eggplant and cook each side 3 minutes or until golden. Drain, sprinkle with a little salt and top with the artichoke dip. Enjoy.

Yield: Serves 4-6

Homemade Gnocchi

These are great cooked and topped with my Bolognese Sauce recipe from this book, or my Marinara or in my Vodka Pasta recipe. Just replace the cooked penne with the cooked gnocchi to make Gnocchi in Vodka Sauce. You can also just toss the cooked gnocchi in a little Earth Balance brand buttery spread, salt, lemon juice and a little fresh sage. You can line these with a gnocchi board if you have one or with a fork.

1.5 cups white flour plus a little for rolling
2 medium size russet potatoes cut into 1/2 inch thick circles, 1 tsp salt
1 tsp extra virgin olive oil

Bring 6 inches of water to a boil in a large pot. Add in the potatoes. Cook them for about 15 minutes until just fork tender. Drain them and let them air cool for a few minutes. Do not pour water on them. Place the flour, salt and olive oil in a large bowl. With a potato ricer, rice the potatoes into the bowl. Mix it all together with your hands, pushing it against the bottom of the bowl until you have a smooth dough ball. Place it in a plastic bag for 10 minutes. On a floured cutting board, take lemon sized pieces of the dough at a time and roll one at a time into a large rope about 18 inches long. With a sharp knife, cut about 1/4 inch pieces so they look like little pillows. When all of the ropes are cut into 1/4 inch pieces, roll them into little balls and roll each one down a fork with a little pressure, making the ridged design and your gnocchi a little longer. Cook these in boiling, salted water for about 3 minutes or until they float. Do not overcrowd the pot, cook about 25 at a time. You can freeze them before cooking if you want. If you freeze them, they will take about 6 minutes to cook.

Yield: Serves 6-10

Spicy Miso and Tofu Vegetable Ramen Bowl

6 cups of cooked vegan ramen noodles (you can find them dry in Asian markets, they come in flat discs) cooked, drained and cooled
6 cups of water whisked together with 2.5 Tbs Better Than Bouillon brand No Chicken Base, 1/2 Tbs of white or yellow miso paste, 2 tsp sriracha and 1 Tbs soy sauce (if you do not want it spicy, leave out the sriracha)
3/4 cup peeled carrots, cut into thick half moons or krinkle cut
1/2 cup white onion cut into half moons, 2 cups button mushrooms sliced
1 tsp minced fresh garlic, 1 tsp minced fresh ginger
1.5 cups broccoli cut into small florets, 1/4 cup chopped scallions
1 recipe of chewy pan seared tofu from this book, 1/4 cup sliced scallions

Take 3 large soup bowls and place even amounts of the scallions, broccoli florets, pan seared tofu and the noodles into each bowl. Set aside. In a large pot, heat a quarter inch of water. Once hot, add in the mushrooms, carrots, garlic, ginger and a pinch of salt. Stir around for 3 minutes. Add in your stock mixture of the water, bouillon, soy sauce and sriracha. Heat until right before boiling. Now, take your three bowls and ladle even amounts of this vegetable stock mixture over the filled bowls (the hot broth will cook the broccoli and heat the noodles). Garnish with scallions and a touch of sesame oil. Enjoy.

Yield: Makes 3 large bowls of soup

New England Style Lobster Roll

2 14-ounce can hearts of
palm, drained
1 Tbs Old Bay Seasoning
1 tsp lemon juice
1 Tbs sweet relish
1/2 cup vegan mayo
(I like soy free Vegenaise)
1/4 cup minced celery
1/4 cup minced onion
1 tsp fresh dill, chopped
salt and pepper to taste
6 vegan lobster roll buns or your favorite soft roll, you can even cut a vegan soft hot dog roll into a lobster roll bun shape
melted Earth Balance buttery spread

Cut the hearts of palm in half length wise and then into 1/8 inch half moons. Place them into a bowl and add in the mayo, Old Bay, dill, celery, onion, lemon juice, salt and pepper. Stir well and then taste it, make sure it is seasoned well, season a little more if needed. Take the buns and brush a little melted Earth Balance Buttery Spread on the edges and toast them face down (butter side down) on a warm griddle or non stick pan. Once toasted, scoop some of the filling inside, top with a few freshly sliced chives and more Old Bay if you like and enjoy.

Yield: Serves 3-6

Curried Onion and Egg Sandwich with Tamarind Tofu and Mango Chutney Mayo

2 Tbs of Earth Balance brand buttery spread, 1/2 cup fresh chopped baby spinach, a few fresh basil leaves, 1/3 cup sliced red pepper, thinly sliced cucumber
1 12 inch Banh Mi bread roll cut in half lengthwise and then into 2 six inch pieces, 1 cup of cold water whisked with 3 Tbs Follow Your Heart brand Vegan Egg, 1/3 cup thinly sliced yellow onion and 1 tsp curry powder
for the tofu: 1/2 a block of extra firm tofu that has been frozen, thawed and had all of the water squeezed out of the block between your palms (this process creates an extra chewy tofu) and cut into six 1/3 inch thick rectangles, 2 Tbs tamarind sauce (not paste) mixed with 1/2 tsp liquid smoke and 1 tsp rice vinegar
for the mayo: mix 3 Tbs Vegenaise brand mayo with 1 Tbs mango chutney

  Heat a large non stick skillet for 3 minutes on high. Brush the tofu slices with the tamarind mixture. Add the tofu into the pan and sear each side about 2 minutes on high. Set aside. Wipe out the pan and heat it 2 more minutes on high. Add in the 2 Tbs of Earth Balance brand buttery spread. Dip the bread face down into the onion/egg mixture, coating the one side, making sure to get onion on them well as the egg. Place them face down in the melted butter spread. Cook about 3 minutes, flip and cook 20 seconds more (this is similar to making french toast but only coating 1 side of the bread). Remove from the pan and spread some of the mayo on the egg and then add the tofu, basil, spinach, cucumber and red peppers. Top with the top half and enjoy.

Yield: Makes 2 sandwiches

Rich and Decadent Stromboli

for the filling:

1 Pack Yves brand Veggie Bologna, 1/2 pack Smoked Tofurkey Slices
4 Tablespoons vegan mayo
1 recipe Vegan Sun Dried Tomato Cream Cheese (recipe follows)
yellow mustard

sun dried tomato cream cheese:

half container plain Tofutti cream cheese

2 Tbs oil cured sun dried tomatoes

3 Tbs nutritional yeast

juice of half a lemon

3 leaves fresh basil, 1 tsp salt

Process the sun dried tomato cream cheese ingredients until smooth in a food processor. Make the basic dough recipe from this book and use one ball of risen dough for this recipe. Spoon sun dried tomato cream cheese into a ziploc bag, cut the tip off the bottom so that you can squeeze out the spread into the stromboli.

Place the risen dough on a floured surface. Do not re knead dough, push with floured hands into a large rectangle shape (15x10 inches roughly) Use a rolling pin to complete the shaping. On the end closest to you going lengthwise, spread yellow mustard all the way down. On top of this, overlap the vegetarian bologna. Squeeze the sun dried tomato dip from the ziploc bag tip down the length of the veggie bologna and then smooth with a spoon. Place the vegan mayo on top of this and spread evenly. Top it all with the Tofurkey slices. Next is to roll the stromboli, starting from the side closest to you, roll it into a large log shape. Place on a tin foil and parchment paper lined and non stick sprayed cookie sheet. Allow to rise one hour covered. Preheat oven to 425. Brush stromboli lightly with olive oil. Bake for 20 minutes. When golden brown, remove and allow to cool 10 minutes. Slice and serve with your favorite marinara sauce.

Yield: Serves 3-4

Spicy Korean Beef and Rice Bowl

1 package of Impossible brand ground, 1 tsp each fresh chopped garlic and peeled ginger, 1/2 cup fresh thin sliced scallions, 3 cups of cooked white or brown rice, 1 tsp vegetable oil **for the sauce:** whisk together 1 Tbs rice vinegar, 1 Tbs hot chili paste, 1 Tbs brown sugar, 1 Tbs soy sauce, 1 tsp dark soy sauce, 1 Tbs water & 1 Tbs sesame oil

Heat a large non stick skillet for 3 minutes on high. Add in the vegetable oil, garlic and ginger. Cook 20 seconds and add in the Impossible ground. Cook 3 minutes or until the ground has browned. Add in the scallions and the sauce. Cook 1 more minute. Serve over rice. Top with toasted sesame seeds and fresh sliced scallions. *Yield:* Serves 3-4

Homemade Moo Shu Tofu and Vegetables

These are fun to make and eat and are packed with unbelievable amounts of flavor.

for the Moo Shu wraps:

1-3/4 cups King Arthur brand flour, 3/4 cup very hot water, 1 tsp toasted sesame oil 1/4 tsp salt **for the filling:** 1 recipe of the Pan Seared Chewy Tofu recipe from this book, prepared, but cut into 1 inch matchsticks before pan searing instead of into chunks, 1.5 cups Napa cabbage, cut thin, 1/3 cup Japanese eggplant cut into matchsticks, 1/2 tsp each fresh minced ginger and fresh minced garlic 3/4 cup button mushrooms sliced thin, 1/3 cup onion cut into thin half moons 1/3 cup peeled carrots cut into matchsticks, 1/3 cup red bell pepper cut into thin strips, 1 tsp toasted sesame oil **for the sauce:** 1/3 cup hoisin sauce whisked together with 1/3 cup sweet chili sauce, 1/2 tsp rice wine vinegar and 1/2 tsp liquid smoke and set aside

For the wraps, mix the flour and salt in a large bowl. Pour in the hot water and the tsp of sesame oil. Mix quickly and knead into a smooth dough. Let it chill 20 minutes in the freezer and then pinch it into about 14 balls, about 1 inch a piece. Flatten them into 2 inch discs with your hands and then brush each one with a little tiny bit of sesame oil on the tops and then place the oiled side of each disc on top of another disc, leaving you with 7 double layer discs. Flour them and the cutting board they are on a little and roll them into 5 or 6 inch very flat circles with a rolling pin. Heat a skillet for 3 minutes on high and when hot, spray with a little non stick spray and cook the double layer discs, 1 at a time. Cook each side until browned a bit and when done, remove from pan and caferefully pull the cooked double layer disc apart, leaving you with 2 thin cooked discs. Repeat with the rest of the dough. Once peeled apart, place them on top of one another to keep warm. **For the filling,** heat a large non stick skillet for 3 minutes on high and add in the toasted sesame oil and the onions, garlic, ginger, carrots mushrooms, cabbage and red peppers. Cook for 3 minutes, stirring often, then add in tofu. Cook 1 minute more and then add in the sauce and warm through. Fill your Moo Shu wraps with some of the filling and enjoy topped with hot chili oil or more hoisin.

Yield: Serves 4-5

Pickled Beet, Scallion and Avocado Topped Dragon Rolls (gluten free)

This recipe requires a sushi mat.

1 cup of white sushi rice, a pinch of salt, 1.5 cups of water and a small 4 inch square of dried kombu (kombu is optional)
1 Tbs rice vinegar, 2 sheets of nori seaweed, cut in half so that you have 4 long rectangles, 1 peeled avocado, pitted and cut into very thin slices,
4 or 5 beets from my Pickled Beets recipe, sliced into thin strips, 8 scallion green tops cut into 4 inch long pieces, black sesame seeds for garnish, soy sauce for dipping, 1 recipe of the Spicy Sweet Chili Mayo from this book

Cook the rice in a rice cooker with the 1.5 cups of water, pinch of salt and the optional kombu. Remove the kombu when the rice is cooked and stir in the vinegar. Bring it to room temperature. Take the soy sauce, sesame oil, hot chili oil and water and mix it together in a bowl. Take the sushi mat and cover it in plastic wrap. Take a sheet of the half cut nori and place it on the plastic wrap with the long end facing you. Wet your hands a little and take about 3/4 of the cooled rice and place it on the nori, flatterning it out to fit the shape of the nori. Sprinkle a few black sesame seeds on the rice. Now, pick up the sheet and flip it over so that the rice is now at the bottom, on the plastic, about a half inch from the bottom of the sushi mat, long end facing you. Place about 3 scallion strips and and 3 strips of the pickled beet strips running the length of bottom of the seaweed from left to right, leaving about 1/4 of an inch of seaweed bare closest to you. Carefully take the sushi mat and roll it up over the filling, pulling it in tight as you roll. Do not roll the mat up into the rice, rather, use it to guide your roll. When you get to the end, unroll the mat and you will have 1 large sushi log. Take the avocado from 1 half of the avocado and fan it into about an 8 inch long shape and place your knife blade under it. Place it on top of the rice. Place some plastic wrap over the whole covered roll now, shape the avocado to the rice by gently pressing down on it. The plasic is also to make them easier to cut. Take a wet sharp knife and slice the log into 6 rolls. Repeat the process with the rest of the nori, filling and topping. Enjoy topped with the spicy mayo and dipped in soy sauce.

Yield: Serves 3-6   — 235 —

Chili Garlic Home Style Bean Curd

1 cup broccoli cut into bite size pieces, 1/3 cup each peeled sliced carrots and bite size diced green peppers, zucchini and sliced mushrooms, 1/3 cup asparagus cut into 1 inch pieces, 1 tsp minced garlic and peeled fresh ginger, 1 block of extra firm tofu that has been frozen, thawed and had all of the water completely squeezed from the block between your hands (this process creates an extra chewy tofu) cut into 1/4 inch thick triangles **sauce:** whisk 2 Tbs vegan oyster sauce, 1/8 cup dark soy sauce, 1/8 cup soy sauce, 1/2 cup water, 1 tsp rice vinegar, 1 tsp garlic chili paste, 1 Tbs each sesame oil, sugar, sweet chili sauce and 1.5 Tbs cornstarch

Heat a large non stick skillet on high for 3 minutes. Add in 1 tsp vegetable oil and lay your tofu triangles flat into the pan. Cook each side 2 minutes. Remove from pan and heat the pan another minute. Add in 1 Tbs of vegetagle oil and add in the ginger, garlic, mushrooms, broccoli, peppers and carrots. Cook, stirring often, for 3 minutes. Add in the zucchini and asparagus. Cook 2 minutes. Add the tofu. Stir together and then add in the whisked sauce. Cook 1 minute or until thickened. Serve over rice. *Yield:* Serves 2-3

Goulash

1 pack of Impossible brand ground, 1 medium onion diced small, 2 cloves minced garlic, 2 bay leaves, salt and pepper to taste, 1 tsp olive oil, 4 Tbs nutritional yeast, 3 Tbs Follow Your Heart brand vegan parmesan shreds, 1 cup dried uncooked macaroni noodles (I like Ronzoni brand Smart Taste noodles for the added fiber) **liquid ingredients:** 1.5 cups of your favorite store bought tomato sauce whisked together with 1.5 cups water, a 14.5 oz can of diced tomatoes, 1 Tbs of Better Than Bouillon brand No Chicken Base or Roasted Garlic Base, 1 Tbs soy sauce

Heat a large non stick pan or Dutch oven for 3 minutes on high and add in the olive oil and then the onions, garlic, Impossible ground and a pinch of salt and pepper. Cook for 3 minutes, breaking up the ground with a spatula. Add in the bay leaves and the liquid ingredients. Bring to a boil and add in the uncooked macaroni noodles. Boil it all together, stirring often until the macaroni is cooked, about 8 minutes. Remove the bay leaves, stir in the nutritional yeast and the parmesan. Enjoy. This is good with some shredded Daiya brand Farmhouse Block cheddar or Monterey Jack shredded on top. *Yield:* Serves 3-4

Sesame Japanese Eggplant, Chewy Tofu and Mixed Vegetable Stir Fry

2 Japanese eggplant cut into 1/2 inch pieces, cut on a bias (should yield about 3 cups of raw eggplant), 1 cup chopped broccoli, 1/4 cup diced onions
1 cup of cremini or button mushrooms that have been quartered
1/2 cup peeled carrots sliced on a bias angle
1/4 cup medium diced zucchini, 1/2 Tbs sesame oil, 2 Tbs toasted sesame seeds
1 recipe of the Pan Seared Chewy Tofu from this book, prepared
sauce:
1/4 cup soy sauce, 2 Tbs vegan oyster sauce
1/8 cup hoisin sauce
1/8 cup sweet chili sauce, 1/4 cup water
1 tsp rice wine vinegar, 1 tsp minced garlic
1 tsp minced ginger
2 Tbs sugar
1.5 Tbs cornstarch

For the sauce, mix the garlic, ginger, soy sauce, 1/4 cup water, sugar, cornstarch, vinegar, hoisin sauce and sweet chili sauce together with a whisk. Set aside.

Steam the eggplant pieces for 5 minutes in a steamer. Heat a large non stick pan over a high heat for about 3 minutes. Add in the sesame oil, then the carrots, onions, broccoli and mushrooms. Let them sit for 2 minutes and then stir them or flip the pan. Cook another 2 minutes and then add in the zucchini, steamed eggplant and pan seared tofu. Cook this all together for 3 more minutes and add in the sauce and the sesame seeds. Stir for 1 minute until the sauce has thickened. Serve over steamed rice.

Yield: Serves 2-4

Avocado Sweet Potato Tempura Sushi (gluten free)

This recipe requires a sushi mat.

1 cup of white sushi rice, a pinch of salt, 1.5 cups of water and a small 4 inch square of dried kombu (kombu is optional)
1 Tbs rice vinegar, cooled, 3 or 4 sheets of nori seaweed that have been cut in half, 1/2 a recipe of the prepared Tempura on page 45 made with sweet potatoes that have been peeled and cut into 2 inch long matchsticks about 1/8 of an inch thick before being battered and fried, 1 avocado peeled and thinly sliced, soy sauce, toasted sesame seeds or black sesame seeds and the Spicy Sweet Chili Mayo from this book for dipping

Cook the rice in a rice cooker with the 1.5 cups of water, pinch of salt and the optional kombu. Remove the kombu when the rice is cooked and stir in the vinegar. Bring it to room temperature. Place the sushi mat on a cutting board with the shorter side facing you Place a piece of nori on top with the longer side of the nori facing you. Wet your hands a little and grab about 4 Tbs of the cooked rice and flatten it onto the nori, leaving about 1/2 inch at the top of the nori bare. Place 3 pieces of cooked tempura and 3 avocado slices on top of the middle of the rice, spanning the entire length of the rice from left to right. Do not over fill it. Take the sushi mat and roll the bottom bare part of the nori over the avocado and tempura, pulling it in tight as you roll it over. Place a little water with your hands on the top bare end of the nori farthest from you so that it stays sealed as you roll up the sushi. Do not roll the mat up into the sushi, rather use it to keep the sushi in a rounded shape. Once rolled up, slice the roll into 6 pieces with a wet sharp knife. Repeat with the rest of the nori, rice and filling. Top with sesame seeds and dip into the soy sauce or spicy mayo. Enjoy.

Yield: Makes 4 sushi rolls that can each be cut into 6 pieces

French Toast

8 slices of your favorite sandwich bread
4 Tbs of Follow Your Heart brand Vegan Egg mixed with 1 1/4 cup plain rice milk, 1/2 tsp ground cinnamon, 2 Tbs sugar and a pinch of salt

Heat an electric griddle on high until ready. Dip your bread into the egg mixture, 1 piece at a time. Coat both sides and cook them all on the griddle until browned on both sides. Enjoy topped with some real maple syrup and Earth Balance brand buttery spread. *Yield:* Serves 3-4

Simple Sausage and Peppers

 This is great on it's own, on a fresh Italian warmed hoagie roll or mixed into red sauce and served over pasta. Keep the sausage links whole, pan searing them and saute the onions and peppers alone if you do it hoagie style, with a splash of balsamic stirred into the peppers and onions post cooking.

2 medium green peppers, cut the sides off so that you have 4 flat sides, lay each side flat and cut each side into long thin strips
1 medium onion cut into half moons, 3 cloves garlic, minced
1 package of Beyond Meat brand Italian sausage or Field Roast brand Itaian Sausage, each link sliced into 1 inch pieces on an angle
1/2 Tbs extra virgin olive oil
crushed red pepper flakes to taste (optional, if you want it spicy)
1/2 tsp salt or to taste, 1 tsp dried oregano,
1 tsp dried basil

 Heat a non stick saute pan for about 2 minutes on medium high heat. You want the pan very hot so that you get a nice sear on the sausage and vegetables. Add in the oil, then the peppers, onions, garlic and sausage. Let them sit for 30 or 40 seconds before stirring, let a nice color form on them, then stir around and repeat the browning process another minute and repeat once again until it all looks nicely browned (about 6 minutes total). Add salt, the oregano, basil and crushed red pepper to taste. *If you add 1/2 cup of sliced button mushrooms to the peppers and onions and let them all cook together, it makes a great hoagie sandwich on a fresh Italian roll too.

Yield: Serves 3-5   — 239 —

Smoky BBQ Pulled Seitan Sandwich

3 1/2 cups of your favorite seitan pulled into shreds, 1/2 cup small diced onion
4 of your favorite buns toasted with the insides face down in a hot non stick pan with a little melted Earth Balance buttery spread
for the sauce: whisk together 1/2 cup ketchup, 2 Tbs hoisin sauce, 1 tsp yellow mustard, 1 Tbs apple cider vinegar, 2 Tbs molasses, 2 Tbs sugar, 1/2 tsp garlic powder, 1 tsp smoked paprika, a pinch of salt, 1 tsp liquid smoke and a pinch of cayenne pepper (more if you want it spicier)

   Heat a large non stick pan for 3 minutes on high. Add in 1 Tbs vegetable oil and add in the onions. Cook 2 minutes and add in the shredded seitan. Cook 3 or 4 minutes, stirring often. Add in the sauce and stir often with a rubber spatula or wooden spoon for 5 minutes. Spoon onto a toasted bun and enjoy. This is good served with my Classic Cole Slaw recipe or even topped with it and a few dill pickle slices.

Yield: Makes 4 sandwiches

Pineapple, Chinese Broccoli and Green Bean Crunchy Katsu Tofu Topped Fried Rice

3 cups of cooked cold jasmine rice, 1/3 cup peeled diced carrots
1/2 cup fresh green beans cut into 1/2 inch pieces
1/2 cup small diced fresh pineapple, 1/3 cup sliced button mushrooms
3/4 cup Chinese broccoli with the hard bottoms cut off and cut into 1 inch pieces
2 cloves garlic, minced, 1 Tbs fresh ginger minced, 1/3 cup red bell pepper diced small
1/3 cup green peas, fresh or frozen, 1/3 cup small diced zucchini
1/3 cup baby corn cut into small pieces, 1 Tbs sesame oil, 2 Tbs soy sauce or to taste
1 recipe of my Katsu Tofu squares, cooked, 1/2 tsp garlic powder
hoisin sauce, sriraracha, chopped scallions and sweet chili sauce, all for topping

   Heat a large non stick skillet for 3 minutes on high. Add in the sesame oil, onions, garlic, carrots, Chinese broccoli, pineapple, ginger, green beans, red peppers and mushrooms. Cook for 3 minutes on high, stirring often. Add a pinch of salt and then add in the zucchhini, baby corn and peas. Cook 2 minutes and then add in the rice. Break up the rice with a spatula and add in the garlic powder and soy sauce. Cook all of this together for 2 more minutes. Taste for flavor. Add soy sauce or salt if needed. Arrange on a platter and topped with the Katsu tofu chopped into bite size pieces and season with hoisin, sriracha if desired, scallions and sweet chili sauce.

Yield: Serves 3-4

Meatball Sub

1 recipe of the Savory Meatballs from this book, 1/2 recipe of the Homemade Tomato Sauce from this book, 5 or 6 fresh Italian 6 inch long rolls, 1 block of Follow Your Heart brand soft block, shredded (make sure it is the soft and not the hard block, it melts best), a few pinches of salt, garlc powder, dried oregano and basil for the topping

Split the rolls but not all the way to the bottom. Mix the meatballs with the marinara and place as many sauced meatballs as you like in each roll. Place some shredded cheese on top as well as the salt, oregano, garlic powder and basil. Bake at 400 for 8 minutes on a foil lined sheet pan. Place under the broiler the last 2 minutes to melt the cheese completely. Watch carefully so you do not burn the bread (if you pull the foil up over the bread so that only the cheese is exposed to the broiler element, it will only melt the cheese and not burn the bread). Allow to cook 8 minutes out of the oven. Enjoy. *Yield:* Makes 5 or 6 sandwiches

Smoky Black Bean and Corn Tortilla Cakes

2 cans black beans, washed and drained
1 can plain corn, washed and drained
one bunch of scallions sliced thin
1/2 a large red pepper,
diced small, 1 Tbs chili powder, pinch of cayenne pepper
1 Tbs chilli powder, 1/2 Tbs garlic powder, 1 cup panko bread crumbs
1 tsp salt, 3/4 cup flour, 1.5 tsp liquid smoke, 1/2 tsp smoked paprika
3/4 cup flour, 1 tsp cumin powder, 3/4 cup crushed up salted tortilla chips

Mash the black beans in a food processor. Pour the mashed beans into a large bowl and add the rest of the ingredients. Use your discression here with the salt, flour and panko. You want a workable mix, not too wet, so add more bread crumbs or flour if it seems too wet to form into cakes. Taste to make sure the flavor is good too, it may need more garlic powder and chili powder.

Form into 3 inch cakes. Heat 1/2 inch of vegetable oil in a non stick pan. When you can dip a cake into it and bubbles form around it, it is ready to fry (usually takes 3 minutes on medium high to get hot enough). Cook each side 3 minutes or until a nice crisp crust forms. Drain and sprinkle with a little salt. Serve topped with your favorite homemade or store bought salsa and/or vegan sour cream.
Yield: Serves 4-6

Spicy Tofu Asparagus Scallion Cream Cheese Roll

This recipe requires a sushi mat.

1 cup of white sushi rice, a pinch of salt, 1.5 cups of water and a small 4 inch square of dried kombu (kombu is optional)

1 Tbs rice vinegar, 2 sheets of nori seaweed, cut in half so that you have 4 long rectangles, 1/2 a block of extra firm tofu that has been frozen, thawed and had all of the water squeezed out of the block until completely dry and then cut into 2 inch long 1/4 inch thick matchsticks, 2 Tbs soy sauce, 1 tsp water, 1 tsp sesame oil, 1 tsp hot chili oil

1 medium carrot, peeled and cut into 2 inch matchstiks about 1/8 inch thick, 5 individual asparagus stalks each cut into 2 inch pieces, 2 Tbs toasted sesame seeds

for the cream cheese: mix 1/2 a container of softened Tofutti brand cream cheese mixed with 1 Tbs minced scallions and a pinch of salt

Place the carrots and asparagus into a pot of boiling water for 1 minute. Drain and competely cool. Place the scallion cream cheese in a small plastic bag and cut a small end off the corner, making it into a pastry bag to squeeze the cream cheese out evenly. Cook the rice in a rice cooker with the 1.5 cups of water, pinch of salt and the optional kombu. Remove the kombu when the rice is cooked and stir in the vinegar. Bring it to room temperature. Take the soy sauce, sesame oil, hot chili oil and water and mix it together in a bowl. Pour it over the tofu matchsticks and allow them to marinate a few minutes. Take the sushi mat and cover it in plastic wrap. Take a sheet of the half cut nori and place it on the plastic wrap with the long end facing you. Wet your hands a little and take about 4 Tbs of the cooled rice and place it on the nori, flattening it out to fit the shape of the nori. Sprinkle a few sesame seeds on the rice. Now, pick up the sheet and flip it over so that the rice is now at the bottom, on the plastic, about a half inch from the bottom of the sushi mat, long end facing you. Take the cream cheese and squeeze out about 1/4 of the bag onto the nori, from left to right end, about a half inch away from the end facing you. Now, add 3 pieces of the tofu (be sure to squeeze the extra marinade out of the tofu pieces) 3 carrots and 2 asparagus stalks so that they run the length of the cream cheese.

Carefully take the sushi mat and roll it up over the filling, pulling it in tight as you roll. Do not roll the mat or plastic up into the rice, rather, use it to guide your roll. When you get to the end, unroll the mat and you will have 1 large sushi log. Take a wet sharp knife and slice the log into 6 rolls. Repeat the process with the rest of the nori and filling.
Enjoy dipped in soy sauce.

Yield: Serves 2-3

Spicy Buffalo Chicken or Tofu or Nashville Hot Chicken Sandwich

You can eat this as is or you can cut the tofu into 4 inch squares, pre breading, or bread whole vegan chicken patties. Cook and sauce them and then serve on a toasted bun with vegan mayo, lettuce, acvocado, pickles and onion for a Nashville hot chicken/tofu sandwich. You can also toss this in my BBQ sauce recipe instead of the Buffalo sauce if you want it less spicy.

if using tofu:
1 block extra firm tofu frozen overnight in package then thawed, opened and gently squeezed until no more water comes out of the tofu, then tear into bite size chunks (this freezing process makes the tofu extra chewy and delicious)

if using veggie chicken:
1 package Delight Soy or Maywah
brand soy chicken nuggets or patties pulled into chunks
2 cups flour
2 cups of panko bread crumbs mixed with 1 tsp salt+1 tsp garlic powder
1/2 cup Franks Red Hot sauce
4 Tbs vegan butter
canola oil to fry

Set up a breading station, put 1 cup flour in a flat casserole dish. In a bowl next to that, mix 1 cup flour with 1 cup water and whisk until a pancake type batter is formed and in another flat casserole dish add the bread crumb mixture. Dip each piece of tofu or chicken nugget into the flour, then the flour/water batter mix and then into the bread crumbs, coating completely. When every piece is breaded, set aside. Make the buffalo sauce by melting the Franks Red Hot with the vegan butter in a small sauce pan. Set aside. Now bring 1/2 inch of canola or vegetable oil to a medium heat in a non stick frying pan. When you can throw a bread crumb into it and it sizzles, it is ready to fry (usually takes 3 minutes to get hot enough to fry in). When ready to cook, simply slide the chicken or tofu carefully into the hot oil. Do no overcrowd the pan, cook in batches if needed. Cook each side 2-3 minutes and flip until golden brown. As soon as all are cooked and drained on a cookie cooling rack, place in a large bowl with the buffalo sauce. Toss until coated. I like to make a vegan ranch and serve with julienned carrots and celery. **Make the ranch dressing** by whisking all together 1/2 cup vegan mayo, 1 teaspoon red wine vinegar, 2 Tbs water, 2 Tbs chopped scallions, 1 teaspoon chopped fresh dill and a pinch of salt. Daiya also makes a great vegan blue cheese dressing.

Yield: Serves 4-6

Caramelized Leek Kidney Bean Cakes with Horseradish Cream Sauce (gluten free)

1 tsp fresh minced thyme
1 can of kidney beans,
drained and rinsed
5-7 Tbs chickpea flour
1/2 tsp salt or to taste
3/4 cup washed leeks
chopped into half moons
1 Tbs Earth Balance brand
buttery spread
3/4 tsp garlic powder, vegetable oil to fry

for the sauce: whisk together 1/2 cup Vegenaise brand mayo with 1/4 tsp minced fresh rosemary, 2 Tbs jarred horseradish, a pinch of salt and 1/2 tsp lime juice

Place the kidney beans in a food processor and process until smooth. Place them in a bowl. Heat a non stick skillet on high for 3 minutes. Add in the Earth Balance and the leeks. Add a pinch of salt and saute 3 minutes until a lightly browned. Add them to the mashed beans and add in the salt, thyme, garlic powder and chickpea flour. Add enough flour until you get a medium firm mixture, not too wet not too dry. Form into 2.5 inch cakes. It will make 6 cakes. Heat a large non stick skillet on high with 1/4 inch of vegetable oil inside for 3 minutes and then add in the cakes. Cook each side about 2 minutes until crisp and browned. Drain, top with the sauce. *Yield:* Makes 6 cakes

Thai Tofu and Mushroom Drunken Noodles

1 recipe of the Chewy Pan Seared Tofu recipe from this book, cooked and set aside 1.5 cups of Chinese or American broccoli, cut into bite size pieces
1/2 a cup of baby corn, 3 cloves minced fresh garlic
1 medium yellow onion cut into thin half moons
1/4 cup of scallions cut into 1 inch long pieces
1 tsp grated ginger, 1 Tbs sesame oil
2 fresh small red or green chiles, cut into small circles
2 cups of button mushrooms, sliced thin
1 packet of extra wide Rice Noodles, cooked and set aside still warm
1 cup of Thai basil, stems removed

for the sauce:
1/4 cup dark soy sauce, 3 Tbs soy sauce, 3 Tbs vegan oyster mushroom sauce
2 Tbs hoisin sauce, 1 Tbs rice wine vinegar

Mix all of the sauce ingredients together and set aside. Heat a large non stick pan for 3 minutes on high, then add in the sesame oil, the garlic, ginger and chiles or red pepper flakes. Cook 30 seconds, then add in the onions, cook 2 minutes and then add in the Chinese broccoli, mushrooms and baby corn. Cook 2 more minutes and then add in the tofu and scallions. Cook 1 minute more then add in the hot noodles and the sauce. Stir until well coated. Add in the basil and stir around until it wilts a little. Taste for flavor, if it needs more flavor, add in a little more hoisin or vegan oyster mushroom sauce. Enjoy.

Yield: Serves 4-6

Spicy Vietnamese Baby Bok Choy and Tofu Vermicelli Rice Noodle Soup

6 cups of cooked and cooled vermicelli rice noodles
3 baby bok choy, sliced in half from top to bottom leaving you with 6 pieces
1.5 blocks of extra firm tofu that have been frozen, thawed and had all of
the water completely squeezed out of the blocks between your palms (this
process creates an extra chewy tofu) cut into 9 even size rectangles
1 large peeled red onion that has been cut into 6 discs, toasted sesame oil

for the broth: whisk together 6 cups of water with 2 Tbs tomato paste, 1 tsp minced
ginger, 1 tsp minced garlic, 1 Tbs soy sauce, 1 Tbs hot chili paste or sriracha and
2.5 Tbs Better Than Bouillon brand No Chicken Base or Roasted Garlic Base
for garnish: sliced jalapeno peppers, sliced scallions, hot chili oil and fresh lime
slices

  For the broth, simply heat it to a boil and let it simmer on low while you prepare
the filling. Heat a large non stick skillet on high for 3 minutes. Add in a tsp of
sesame oil and then add in the bok choy face down. Cook about 3 minutes
and flip. Cook another 2 minutes. Add in a little dash of soy sauce. Remove from
pan. Wipe out the pan and heat for 2 minutes again. Add in a tsp of sesame oil
again and add in the onion discs and tofu. Cook each side about 3 or 4 minutes
until browned. Add in a few dashes of soy sauce at the end. Assemble the soups
by placing 1/3 of the noodles in each of 3 bowls (this recipe makes 3 large bowls of
soup). Add in 2 of the cooked bok choy to each bowl, 2 onions and 3 slabs of the
tofu to each bowl. Spoon over the hot broth evenly into each bowl. Top with the
garnish and enjoy.

Yield: Makes 3 large bowls of soup

Indian Butter Chickpeas, Tofu and Vegetables
(gluten free)

This is tasty with my Homemade Onion Naan Recipe, my Pakora recipe or my delicious Pea and Potato Samosas.

1 cup of cooked, drained and washed chickpeas, 3/4 cup each cauliflower and broccolini cut into bite size pieces, 2 cups baby spinach, 1/3 cup medium diced zucchini, 1.5 blocks of tofu that have been frozen, thawed and had all of the water squeezed out of the thawed blocks between your hands until completely drained (this process creates a delicious and chewy tofu) and torn into bite size pieces, 1/3 cup small diced onion, 1 tsp each roughly chopped garlic and fresh ginger, 3 Tbs Earth Balance brand buttery spread **for the sauce:** whisk together 1. 5 cups of plain tomato sauce whisked together with 1 can of coconut milk, 1 tsp garam masala, 1/2 tsp each garlic powder and cumin powder, 1/4 tsp cayenne pepper (more if you like it spicier), 2 Tbs Tofutti brand sour cream, 1 tsp tamarind sauce (not paste), 1/2 tsp salt and 1 tsp paprika

Heat 5 inches of water to a boil. Add in the spinach, cauliflower and broccolini. Cook 1 minute and then drain and cool completely. Heat a large non stick pan for 3 minutes. Add in 1 Tbs of the buttery spread and then the onions, ginger and garlic. Cook 2 minutes. Add in 1 more Tbs of the buttery spread and the tofu chunks. Stir and cook it all together for 2 minutes. Add in the sauce as well as the 1 more Tbs of buttery spread, cooked vegetables, the chickpeas and zucchini. Stir it all together and cook for 3 minutes, stirring often. Serve over basmati rice. *Yield:* Serves 2-3

Eggplant, Leek and Crispy
Bacon Deep Dish Sicilian Pizza

1 ball of my homemade dough, risen (my dough recipe from this book makes 2 balls of dough, but you will only use 1 ball of dough here)
1/2 a cup of my tomato sauce recipe from this book of your favorite store bought tomato sauce, 1/2 cup peeled and small diced eggplant, 1/3 cup small diced onion, 1/2 cup washed and half moon cut thinly sliced leeks, 2 cloves garlic, minced, 1/2 a package of Lightlife brand vegan bacon, cut into small cubes
1 block of Follow Your Heart brand soft block vegan mozzarella, shred it yourself (make sure it is the soft block, not the hard block or shredded cheese, the soft block is the only one that melts properly), fresh basil to top and vegan parmesan if desired

In a non stick saute pan, heat a tsp of olive oil over high heat for 2 minutes and then add in the onions, garlic, leeks and eggplant and a pinch of salt. Cook for 3 minutes. Remove them from the pan and add in a little more oil and add in the cubed bacon. Cook until crisp, about 3 minutes, adding in a pinch of salt. Set aside. Place the risen dough on a floured surface and push into an 8x12 inch rectangle. Take a good quality deep sided 8x12 inch pan (the size of the pan is important here to insure a thick Sicilian style crust) and brush 1/2 Tbs of olive oil on the inside of the pan and on the inside sides of the pan. Place your dough inside of the pan and cover, let it rise 1 hour. When risen, brush the crust with little more olive oil. Heat the oven to 440 degrees. Evenly spoon the sauce on top of the pizza, then the the the eggplant, onions, garlic, leeks and then the cheese with a few shakes of dried oregano and garlic powder. Top with the bacon. Place the pizza into the oven for 15 minutes and then under the broiler for 2 minutes to melt the cheese all the way and brown the crust. Brush the crust with a little more olive oil after you remove the pizza from the oven. Sprinkle with a little more salt, the fresh basil and parmesan, if using. Let this sit for 10 minutes before slicing. *Yield:* Serves 2-4

Spicy Chipotle Nachos

1/2 a large bag of your favorite salted tortilla chips
1 container of Tofutti brand sour cream
1 jar of your favorite salsa 1 recipe of Refried Beans from this book
1 recipe of Guacamole from this book
1 bag of So Delicious brand Cheddar Jack vegan cheese
2 links of Field Roast brand Chipotle Sausage, diced small
chopped scallions, pickled jalapenos and hot sauce for garnish (optional)

 Heat a non stick skillet over medium high heat for 2 minutes. Add a little
canola oil into the skillet and then add the diced sausage. Saute about 3 minutes
until slightly crisp. Set aside. Heat the refried beans, covered, in the microwave
for 1.5 minutes. Set aside. Place the guacamole and sour cream in different
Ziploc bags. Snip off the corners of the bags off once they are filled (these will
act as pastry bags). Place half of the tortilla chips on a large glass plate or platter.
Top with half of the cheese and then add more chips on top. Add the rest of the
cheese on top. Microwave the cheese topped tortilla chips for one minute or
until the cheese is melted (most vegan cheese melts much better in the
microwave as opposed to a regular oven). Next, top the nachos with the hot
refried beans, the sausage and as much salsa as you like. Using your homemade
pastry bags, pipe the guacamole and the sour cream onto the nachos. Garnish
with scallions, hot sauce and pickled jalapenos if you like your nachos spicier.

Yield: Serves 3-4

Crab Cakes with Spicy Cajun Horseradish and Caper Remoulade Sauce

2 cans of hearts of palm, washed and drained
1/3 cup flour plus 2 cups flour set aside
1/2 cup panko bread crumbs plus 2 cups panko set aside
2 Tbs vegan mayo, 1 tsp spicy brown mustard
3 Tbs each minced onion, green bell peppers and celery
1/4 tsp garlic powder
1 tsp Old Bay Seasoning
1/2 tsp salt

for the sauce:
simply whisk together 1/3 cup vegan mayo with a pinch of salt, 1/2 tsp grated
horseradish, a squeeze of Sriracha (depending on how spicy you want it), 1 tsp
minced capers and 1 tsp sweet relish

   Place the hearts of palm in a food processor and roughly chop them on pulse but
do not over chop them, just get them into small pieces. Place them in a bowl and
add in the peppers, celery, salt, onions, mayo, Old Bay, garlic powder, the 1/3 cup
flour, mustard and the 1/2 cup panko. Mix well with your hands. Form this mixture
into 2 inch patties about 1/3 of an inch thick. In a bowl, place in 1 cup of flour. In a
second bowl, whisk 1 cup of flour with 1 cup of water (this will act as your egg to
help the bread crumbs stick). In a flat glass sided dish, add in the 2 cups of panko
bread crumbs and mix them with 1/2 tsp each of salt, garlic powder and Old Bay.
Working from left to right, dip each patty, one at a time, into the flour, then the flour
and water mixture and then into the bread crumbs. Coat them completely with the
bread crumbs. Heat a large non stick pan with a half inch of vegetable oil for 3
minutes on high and then add in the cakes. Dip a cake in, if bubbles form, they are
ready to fry. Cook each side about 3 minutes or until golden. Drain them on a
cookie cooling rack placed on top of a foil lined cookie sheet (this way you can heat
them later without burning the bottoms since they will be elevated). Top with the
remoulade sauce and enjoy.

Yield: Makes 6 to 8 cakes

German Pretzel Bun Bratwurst Sandwich with Sauerkraut and Pickled Beets

4 of the prepared German Pretzel Buns recipe from this book, 1 cup sauerkraut, 4 pickled beets from the Pickled Beet recipe from this book, sliced thin after you pickle them, spicy brown mustard, 2 links of Beyond Meat brand Bratwurst sausages, cut in half into 2 round halves and then butterflied almost all the way through, letting the skin keep them held together

Heat a non stick skillet on high for 3 minutes. Lay the split sausages face down. Cook 2 minutes and flip them, cooking another 3 minutes. Split the pretzel buns in half and place a butterflied sausage on each bottom, then top with the sliced pickled beets, sauerkraut and mustard. Enjoy.

Yield: Makes 4 Sandwiches

Thai Black Bean, Eggplant, Seitan and Tofu Basil Red Curry

1 cup of seitan pulled into bite size chunks, 1 prepared recipe of the Chewy Pan Seared Tofu from this book, 1/3 cup onions thinly sliced into half moons, 1/2 cup cooked and drained black beans, 1 cup of bite size cut broccoli florets, 1/3 cup red bell pepper cut into 1 inch strips, 1 cup of Japanese eggplant cut into bite size shapes on an angle, 1/2 cup of button mushrooms cut into quarters, 1/2 cup peeled and thinly sliced carrots, 1/3 cup asparagus cut into 1 inch pieces, 2 cups raw baby spinach **for the sauce:** whisk together 2 cans of coconut milk with 2 Tbs red curry paste, 2 Tbs green curry paste, 1/2 tsp each fresh minced ginger and minced garlic, 5 Tbs brown sugar, 1 tsp soy sauce, 2 Tbs chopped fresh basil, 1 tsp hot chili paste (use more chili paste if you want it spicier) and 1/2 tsp dark soy sauce

Heat a large non stick pan on high for 3 minutes. Add in 1 Tbs of vegetable oil and add in the onions, seitan, mushrooms, eggplant and carrots. Cook and stir 2 minutes and then add in the red bell peppers. Cook this all 2 more minutes and then add in the broccoli, asparagus, baby spinach, beans and tofu. Cook for 1 minute and add in the sauce. Simmer it all together 3 minutes on a low boil. Serve over steamed rice and garnish with fresh chopped basil and sliced green onions.

Yield: Serves 3-5

Teriyaki Grilled Mushroom, Eggplant and Red Pepper Nigiri Sushi

1 cup of sushi rice placed in a rice cooker with 1.5 cups water and a pinch of salt and a 2 inch square of kombu seaweed (the kombu is optional) and then cooked, 1 Tbs rice vinegar, 1/2 of a medium Japanese eggplant cut into 1.5 inch long thin pieces with the skin left on (you will have about 16 pieces), 1 medium red bell pepper cut into 1.5 inch pieces (you will have about 16 pieces here too), 4 medium size button mushrooms, each cut into 4 thick pieces, 1 Tbs toasted sesame seeds, 1 sheet of nori seaweed cut in half and then each half cut into 10 thin pieces

teriyaki marinade: 2 Tbs dark soy sauce, 2 Tbs regular soy sauce, 1 Tbs brown sugar, 1 Tbs rice vinegar and 3 Tbs water

Whisk the marinade ingedients together. Toss the cut peppers, eggplant and mushrooms in the marinade. Heat a grill for 10 minutes on high. Grill each side of the vegetables 3 minutes and cool completely. When the rice is cooked, remove the optional kombu, stir in the rice vinegar. Let the rice cool to room temperature. Stir in the sesame seeds. Wet your hands and form about a 1.5 inch clump of rice into a football shape. Repeat with the rest. Keep your hands moist by dipping them in a little water so the rice does not stick to your hands. When you have them formed, place the pepper over the rice, then the eggplant and finally the mushroom. Take your cut nori pieces and wrap them around the sushi so that the vegetables are held in place. Enjoy dipped in soy sauce.   *Yield:* Makes about 16 pieces of sushi

Sweet Chili Summer Sausages

These go great with my Baked Macaroni and Cheese or with my Broccoli Cheddar Twice Baked Potato recipe, both from this book.

1 pack of Beyond Meat brand Bratwurst or Italian sausages or Lightlife brand Jumbo Hot Dogs
cut into 1/4 inch slices on a bias angle
1/4 cup sweet chili sauce
1 tsp vegetable oil

Heat a large non stick saute pan for 3 minutes on high. Add in the sausage slices or the hot dog slices, keeping them in a flat layer for 2 minutes in order to crisp them. Stir and flip them and cook for another 3 minutes until crisp. Add in a pinch of salt and then the sweet chili sauce and cook 30 more seconds. Enjoy.

Yield: Serves 3-5

Spinach, Marinated Artichoke and Garlic Mushroom Lasagna Roulades

1 recipe of the tofu ricotta from this book
8 long lasagna noodles, cooked and cooled (the Dreamfields brand makes one that is high in fiber but tastes like just regular white pasta)
1.5 small jars of marinated artichokes, chopped into small pieces
3 cups of flat leaf baby spinach, cleaned and rough chopped
1 tsp fresh garlic, chopped fine, 8 basil leaves, 1 cup sliced button mushrooms
2 cups of your favorite homemade or store bought tomato sauce
4 slices of Field Roast brand Chao cheese, cut in half to make 8 pieces
pinch of dried oregano

Heat a non stick pan over high heat for 2 minutes and then add in a tsp of olive oil and the garlic and mushrooms. Add a pinch of salt and oregano. Cook 2 minutes and then add in the spinach, another pinch of salt and the chopped artichokes. Cook 2 more minutes. Remove from heat and cool. When cooled, squeeze as much water as possible from this spinach/mushroom/artichoke mixture. Once done, add this mixture to the tofu ricotta. Stir until mixed well. Set aside.

  Cook the lasagna noodles for about 7 minutes and then drain and cool in cold water. Drain them again and lay the 8 noodles on a large cutting board. Take about 4 Tbs of the filling and spread it on each noodle, leaving about 3/4 of an inch of empty noodle at both ends. Roll them into roulades. Place about 3/4 cup of tomato sauce at the bottom of a baking dish. Lay each filled and rolled lasagna roulade in the sauce next to each other. Spoon about 2 Tbs of tomato sauce over each roulade. Place a leaf of fresh basil on top of each sauce topped roulade. Place the cheese slices on top of the basil of each roulade. Cover the baking dish with foil, making sure it is not touching the cheese. Bake at 380 degrees for 30 minutes covered. Once the cheese is melted, remove from the oven and serve hot. I like to make a little extra tomato sauce to pour on top of these once they are on the plate. Enjoy.

Yield: Serves 4-6

Spicy Thai "Peanut" Ramen Noodle, Mushroom, Baby Bok Choy and Black Bean Tofu Curry Soup

I use sunflower butter in this recipe in place of peanut butter due to an allergy, but you can use the same amount of peanut butter if you have no allergy.

3 cups of plain ramen noodles, cooked and cooled (available in Asian markets, they come in round disks, cook them yourself)
1 can of plain coconut milk mixed with 2 cups of water and 2 Tbs sugar
1 block of extra firm tofu, drained, pressed until dry and cut into bite size cubes
5 Tbs of Sun Butter brand sunflower butter, 2 Tbs hoisin sauce
3 Tbs red curry paste, 1/4 cup thin sliced red bell pepper
1.5 Tbs Better Than Bouillon brand No Chicken Base or Roasted Garlic Base
1/4 cup sliced
bamboo shoots
1 Tbs fresh lime juice
1 tsp soy sauce
1 cup cooked
black beans
1 tsp each minced fresh ginger and garlic
1 red onion cut into thin half moons
2 cups sliced cremini or button mushrooms
2 cups baby bok choy,
rough chopped
and washed
1 tsp sesame oil
scallions for garnish
hot chili oil to taste,
depending on your desired heat level
4 Tbs fresh basil chopped

In a large bowl, whisk together the coconut milk/water, hoisin, curry paste, No Chicken Base, sugar, soy sauce, hot chili oil and sunflower butter. Set aside. Heat a large non stick pan for 2 minutes on high, then add in the sesame oil, onions, ginger, red pepper, garlic and mushrooms. Cook 4 minutes and then add in the bok choy. Cook 3 more minutes and then add in the coconut milk broth and tofu. Heat to a boil and then add in the ramen noodles, lime juice, black beans, bamboo shoots and half of the basil. Cook 1 more minute and serve topped with the remaining basil and some fresh scallions. A few squeezes of fresh lime finishes this soup off nicely too.

Yield: Makes 2 entree size bowls of soup

Buffalo Cauliflower and Blue Cheese Street Tacos

1 recipe of Tempura Batter from this book, 2 cups of cauliflower cut into bite size florets (about 28 florets), 1 recipe of Guacamole from this book, Daiya brand vegan Blue Cheese dressing, 1/4 cup Earth Balance Soy Free Buttery Spread melted and mixed with 1/4 cup Franks Red Hot Sauce, 1 cup of So Delicious brand shredded Cheddar Jack cheese, 8-10 vegan taco size soft flour tortillas, shredded iceberg lettuce, fresh chopped tomatoes

Heat a 1/2 inch of canola oil in a large non stick pan over medium heat for 3 minutes. Flick a little tempura batter in the oil, and if bubbles form, it is ready to fry. Dip the cauliflower florets into the batter and then place them carefully into the oil, about 12 at a time. Cook both sides until golden (about 4-5 minutes total) and then drain on an elevated cookie rack on top of a foil lined cookie sheet (this way you can heat the cauliflower later if needed and it will stay crisp and not burn on the bottom). In a large bowl, toss the cooked cauliflower with the butter/Franks Red Hot Buffalo sauce mixture. Heat the tortillas in the microwave or wrapped in foil in the oven. Build your tacos with the Buffalo cauliflower at the bottom, then the guacamole, tomatoes, shredded lettuce, shredded cheese and the Daiya blue cheese dressing. Enjoy.

Yield: Serves 3-4

Stuffed Peppers with Creamy Bulgur and Provolone

1 cup bulgur wheat
2 cups water
1 Tbs Better Than Bouillon brand Roasted Garlic Base
6 Tbs vegan mayo
1/3 cup nutritional yeast
1 tsp salt
2 green peppers split in half to make 4 pepper pieces
4 slices Follow Your Heart brand Provolone slices or Field Roast brand Chao slices

Bring the water, a teaspoon of salt and the vegan chicken base to a boil, add bulgur wheat, stir and cover, turn to medium heat and cook 12 minutes. When cooked, cool completely.

When cooled, add the mayo, salt and nutritional yeast to the bulgur wheat. Taste to make sure the flavor is to your liking. Take this and stuff into the 4 pepper halves. Preheat oven to 375 degrees. Take a square casserole dish, put a quarter inch of water on the bottom. Place the stuffed peppers in the dish. Cover with foil and bake 30 minutes. Take out, place the cheese on top and cover again with foil completely, tenting it so that it does not touch the cheese. Sprinkle with a pinch of salt and bake another 12-15 minutes until the cheese is melted.

Yield: Serves 2-4

Garlic Broccoli Rabe and Provolone Stromboli

1 ball of dough from the Basic Dough recipe from this book, risen (the recipe makes 2 balls of dough, but you will only use 1 here)
1 prepared recipe of the Garlic Broccoli Rabe recipe from this book (page 102)
5 slices of Follow Your Heart brand provolone slices or 5 slices of Field Roast brand Chao slices, shredded on a box grater
tomato sauce for dipping (the one from this book is great)
1 tsp each black and white sesame seeds (optional)

Remove the dough from the bowl it has risen in but do not knead it again. Place it on a floured cutting board and push down on it into a large rectangle shape. Take a rolling pin and roll it into a larger about 16 inch by 10 inch rectangle. Place the broccoli rabe along the longer 16 inch side, the side closest to you. Leave about an inch of dough bare closest to you and about a half inch bare at the top and bottom. Sprinkle the cheese on top of the broccoli rabe. Roll the 1 inch bare side of dough that is closest to you up over the broccoli rabe and cheese and then keep rolling until you have a large log. Place it on a foil and parchment paper lined cookie sheet. Cover it and let it rise 1 hour. After it has risen, heat the oven to 440 degrees. If using the sesame seeds, brush the stromboli with a little water and sprinkle on the sesame seeds. If you are not using them, then brush the stromboli with a little olive oil. Bake for about 15 to 17 minutes or until golden. Brush the stromboli with a little olive oil out of the oven. Allow it to cool a few minutes, then slice and enjoy dipped in the tomato sauce.

Sweet and Sour Ham or Tofu and Vegetables

1 green pepper medium diced
1/2 cup asparagus cut in 1/2 inch pieces
1/2 cup zucchini diced small
1 cup quartered button mushrooms
2 carrots peeled and cut into half moons
3 cups chopped broccoli
1 cup vegan smoked ham cut into
triangles or chunks (Lam Sheng
Kee Vegetarian Ham or Maywah Vegan
Smoked Ham, available online or at
most Asian markets)
1 Tbs sesame oil
1 cup of sweet and sour sauce
 (you can use store bought or use the
homemade sweet and sour
sauce recipe in this book)

if using tofu:

1 block extra firm tofu, frozen overnight in the package then thawed, opened
and pressed gently with your hands until completely dry and no more water
comes out of the tofu block (this freezing prozess makes the tofu extra chewy)
1 cup cornstarch
3/4 cup flour
1/2 tsp salt
1/2 teaspoon garlic powder
canola/vegetable oil to fry

If you are using tofu, mix the flour, cornstarch, salt and garlic powder.
Take the thawed tofu block and tear it into about 15 medium sized chunks.
Dredge each chunk in the flour/cornstarch mixture until covered. Heat a
1/2 inch of canola or vegetable oil in a non stick pan for 3 minutes on high
and then add in the dredged tofu. Cook each side for a few minutes until
browned. Drain on a cookie rack that has been placed on top of a foil lined
cookie sheet (this way you can reheat the tofu later in the oven without the
bottom burning). Sprinkle with a little salt and set aside. Heat a non stick
pan or wok over high heat for 3 minutes, make sure it is very hot. Add a
Tbs of sesame oil and the ham. Brown the ham for a few minutes. Add in
the broccoli, carrots, mushrooms and peppers. Saute 4 minutes. Add the
zucchini, asparagus (add the tofu now if using) and your favorite sweet and
sour sauce. Cook 1 minute and serve over jasmine or brown rice.

Yield: Serves 2-3

Pesto Gnocchi with Sausage, Artichokes and Sun Dried Tomatoes

1 recipe of the Homemade Gnocchi from this book
1 recipe of the Basil Pesto recipe from this book
1 cup broccoli chopped into small florets, 2 cloves garlic minced, 1/2 cup sliced mushrooms, 3/4 cup cauliflower cut into small florets, 2 links of Beyond Meat brand Italian sausage cut into half moons, 1/3 cup asparagus cut into 1 inch pieces, 1/3 cup zucchini medium diced, 1/2 cup rough chopped marinated artichokes, 1/3 cup rough chopped oil cured sun dried tomatoes (the kind that are packed in a jar in oil)

Cook the gnocchi in boiling water until they float. Drain them and set aside. Heat a large non stick pan for 3 minutes on high. Add in 1 tsp of olive oil and then the broccoli, cauliflower, garlic, mushrooms and the sausage. Add a pinch of salt and cook about 4 minutes, stirring often. Now add in the zucchini, asparagus, artichokes and sun dried tomatoes. Cook for 2 more minutes and add in the cooked gnocchi. Add in the pesto and coat everything well. Serve topped with Follow Your Heart brand parmesan shreds.

Yield: Serves 2-3

Angel Hair Mushroom Scampi

1 box of cooked Barilla brand angel hair pasta or 1 lb of homemade angel hair (there is a great homemade pasta dough recipe in this book)
1 1/2 cups thinly sliced button or cremini mushrooms
8 basil leaves sliced thin
6 cloves of garlic sliced thin
3/4 cup grape tomatoes cut in half
1/2 cup Earth Balance brand buttery
spread melted and mixed with the juice of 1
medium lemon
1/2 tsp salt
dried red pepper flakes (optional)
1 tsp olive oil

Boil a large pot of water for the pasta. Heat a large non stick skillet for 3 minutes on high. Add the olive oil and then the garlic, mushrooms and tomatoes. Push them into a flat layer and cook 2 minutes. While this cooks, cook the angel hair for 3 minutes in the pot of boiling water and then drain it. Set aside. Add a pinch of salt to the mushroom mixture and then stir them and cook another 2 minutes. Add in the cooked pasta and the lemon and butter mixtute and the salt. Taste, if it needs more lemon or salt, add it now. Top with the fresh basil and red pepper flakes. Enjoy.

Yield: Serves 3-4

Sweet and Spicy Mock Duck Thai Coconut Milk Curry or Pan Seared Tofu Curry

2 cans drained vegetarian mock duck pulled apart aka shredded into chunks (available at most Asian markets, if you prefer tofu, use the Pan Seared Chewy Tofu recipe from this book)
1 cup broccoli chopped
1 red pepper large diced
3/4 cup carrots cut into large chunks
2 medium red potatoes, peeled and
cut into medium chunks
1/2 cup yellow onions cut into half moons

curry sauce:

2 cans plain coconut milk
1 small can or 1 small jar of vegan green curry paste
2 tsp hot chili paste
1/3 cup plus 1 Tbs sugar
pinch of salt
1 tsp fresh grated ginger
1 tsp soy sauce

chopped fresh basil for a topping garnish

Whisk sauce ingredients together and set aside.

For the vegetables, bring 3 cups water to a boil. Add in the chopped potatoes and carrots. Cook until just tender, 5 to 6 minutes. A minute before you drain them, add the peppers and broccoli. Drain all and cool by submerging them in cold water. Drain them again and set aside to cool completely.

Heat curry sauce over medium heat with the seitan mock duck or the chewy tofu and onions in the sauce. Once boiling, add the vegetables for another 3 minutes. Serve over steamed jasmine rice and garnish the curry with chopped fresh basil.

Yield: Serves 2-3

Grilled Eggplant Pesto Caprese Napoleon Stacks (gluten free)

1 medium eggplant cut into 12
1/4 of inch thick discs
1 medium red bell pepper with the 4
sides cut off into 4 flat pieces
1 large tomato cut into 4 thin slices
3 cups of raw baby spinach
1 clove fresh garlic minced
dried oregano
1 cup thin sliced button mushrooms
1 recipe of the Pesto from this book
8 slices of Field Roast brand Original
flavor Chao Cheese
1/2 cup balsamic vinegar mixed with
1/4 tsp salt, 1 Tbs sugar, 1/2 tsp basil
and 1 Tbs olive oil

Place the eggplant slices and the red peppers into a bowl and pour the balsamic mixture over them. Let them marinate 20 minutes. Heat a large non stick skillet for 3 minutes on high and add in a tsp of olive oil, the garlic and the mushrooms. Add a pinch of salt. Cook them 3 minutes. Add in the oregano and the spinach. Cook 2 more minutes. Taste, add a little salt if needed. Heat a grill for 15 minutes on high. Grill each side of the eggplant and peppers about 3 minutes. Spread some pesto on the largest 4 eggplant discs and top them each with a slice of cheese and a grilled red pepper piece. Place the next largest eggplant disc on top of this. Top these 4 smaller discs with the tomato and the spinach and mushroom mixture and then top those with the smallest eggplant disc and half a piece of the cheese on top. Break some wooden skewers in half and push them down into each stack so they stay together. Place the top down on the grill for another minute until the cheese is melted. Remove the skewers and enjoy.

Yield: Makes 4 stacks

Grilled Sunflower Butter, Jelly and Banana Sandwich

2 slices of your favorite bread
Sun Butter brand sunflower butter
1/2 a banana, sliced
1 Tbs Earth Balance buttery spread
any jelly you like best

Place sunflower butter on one half of the sandwich, jelly on the other and the sliced bananas in the middle. Assemble the sandwich. Heat a non stick skillet on high for 2 minutes. Add in the buttery spread, let it melt and add in the sandwich. Cook each side until golden. Slice and enjoy.

Yield: Makes 1 sandwich

Thai Cilantro Basil Tofu With Spicy Hoisin Peanut Sauce or Sunflower Sauce

1 block of extra firm tofu drained
1 cup white flour
1/2 cup cornstarch
1/2 tsp salt
1/2 tsp garlic powder
3 Tbs each: chopped
fresh basil,
cilantro and scallions
1/4 tsp red pepper flakes
vegetable oil or canola oil

for the sauce:
4 Tbs peanut butter (if you
are allergic to nuts,
you can use 4 Tbs
of smooth sunflower butter)
1 Tbs hoisin sauce
water to thin
2 Tbs chopped scallions
2 Tbs sugar
1 tsp Sriracha

   Chop the tofu into 6 rectangles. Soak it in water after you chop it. In a flat casserole dish mix the flour, fresh herbs, garlic powder, salt, red pepper flakes and cornstarch. Take the tofu out of the water and dredge it in the flour mixture. Get as thick of a coating on each piece as you can.

   Heat a non stick pan over medium high heat with 1/4 inch oil in it for 3 minutes. Dip a corner of a tofu piece in, if bubbles from around it, it is ready to cook. Place each piece in and cook each side about 5 minutes until crisp and golden. Drain and top with peanut sauce.

   For the sauce, place the sauce ingredients in a food processor except the water. Turn on the food processor and slowly add water until you get the consistency you desire, it should be a tiny bit thinner than pancake batter. If you like it spicier, add more Sriracha.

Yield: Serves 2-4

Fried Green Tomato and Smoked Gouda Egg Biscuit

6 Tbs of Follow Your Heart brand Vegan Egg mixed with 1.5 cups of water and prepared
4 slices of Follow Your Heart brand gouda slices
1/2 a prepared recipe or the Extra Crunchy Fried Green Tomato recipe from this book with
the Sour Cream and Onion Dip
biscuits:
2 cups King Arthur brand flour, sifted
1/2 Tbs baking powder
1/2 teaspoon salt
8 Tbs vegan shortening
1 1/4 cup freshly opened club soda mixed with 1 tsp apple cider vinegar

Preheat oven to 450 degrees. Mix flour with salt and baking powder and soda in a large
bowl. Put the shortening into the bowl and cut it into the flour with a pastry cutter until it
looks like pea sized balls in the flour. Add the club soda/vinegar mixture into the flour.
Carefully mix and knead by folding the dough over itself over and over. If the dough
seems too dry, add more soy milk before folding it over on itself. This is a very important
step, it creates layers and makes a fluffy, better biscuit. If the dough seems too wet, add
more flour. Do not over knead the dough or the biscuits will be tough. When mixed into a
nice dough, flatten the dough out to about 1/2 inch thick. Cut into biscuits with a biscuit
cutter. Refold the leftover dough and cut more biscuits. Place each biscuit into a non stick
cake pan sprayed with non stick spray. Make sure the biscuits are touching each other, this
makes them bake softer and more tender. Bake for 18 minutes or until risen and browned
on top. Remove from the oven and brush with a little melted Earth Balance buttery spread.
Split the biscuit and add in the fried tomato, egg, cheese and the sour cream dip. Enjoy.

Yield: Makes 4-6 biscuits

Thanksgiving Vegan Sliced Turkey and Gravy

I serve this every year for the holidays with vegan mac and cheese, green beans, garlic broccoli, spaghetti squash, mashed potatoes and cranberry sauce. This recipe is simple and delicious. You can also use tofu bought in bulk from an Asian market (it has a much better texture than other tofu for this) that has been frozen, thawed and squeezed completely dry and sliced into 1/4 inch triangles).

2 packs Maywah brand or Delight Soy brand chicken steaks very carefully sliced in half the so that you have 2 thin sliced rounds of the patties. if they are not perfect and if you get random size pieces, it is ok, preferred in fact

for the gravy:

1.5 cups water with 1.5 Tbs Better Than Bouillon dissolved into it with a whisk
1/2 teaspoon salt, 3 Tbs nutritional yeast, 1 tsp Gravy Master (in spice isle at store)
1 tsp fresh dill, 1/4 tsp fresh chopped fresh sage, a little less that 1/2 cup flour
3 Tbs Earth Balance brand Soy Free vegan butter spread, 1.5 cups plain rice milk

In a medium to large saucepan, heat the vegan butter over medium heat. When the butter is melted, add the flour. Whisk around for 30 seconds, then add the remaining ingredients. Whisk for a few minutes until thickened into a gravy. Taste to make sure the flavor is good. If it seems too thick, add more rice milk.Take a 9x13 inch glass casserole dish, spray with non stick spray and layer afew ladles of gravy on the bottom to cover it completely. Layer the sliced vegan chicken slices so that only about half an inch of them touch each other.You should end up with about 3 rows. If you are using tofu, heat an electric griddle and cook each side until slightly browned first and then layer it like the vegan chicken slices. Ladle the remaining gravy over the layered sliced patties or tofu. Cover with foil, bake at 375 for 20 minutes.

Japanese Style Eggplant Fish

3 Japanese eggplant that are about 8 or 9 inches long, 2 Tbs vegetable oil, 1/2 cup cornstarch, a few sesame seeds, scallions and small cut nori pieces for garnish **for the sauce:** whisk together 2 Tbs each of soy sauce, dark soy sauce and vegan oyster sauce

Cut a half inch off of the top and bottom of the eggplant. Make a cut down the eggplant from top to bottom, but do not cut all the way through the skin. Open it up and lay it flat on the cut open side (you are making a butterfly cut here). Steam each eggplant for 5 minutes. Once all are steamed, place the eggplant skin side down, make cross marks into the eggplant flesh and then dust the flesh of each eggplant with a third of the cornstarch. Heat a large non stick pan on high for 3 minutes and add in the oil. Place the eggplant, flesh side down, and cook each side about 2 or 3 minutes or until golden (you will only be able to fit 1 at a time in the pan). Flip it and brush 1/3 of the sauce onto each flesh side of the eggplants and cook the skin side another 2 minutes. Serve over rice garnished with sesame seeds, scallions and nori pieces. *Yield:* Serves 2-3

Crispy Pineapple Seitan, Green Beans and Broccoli

1 cup of green beans cut into bite size pieces, 1 cup of Chinese broccoli or broccolini cut into bite size pieces, 1/2 cup each medium diced yellow onions, peeled fresh pineapple and red bell peppers, 1/3 cup peeeld and sliced carrots, 1 tsp each fresh rough chopped garlic and ginger
1.5 cups of seitan torn into bite size chunks that have been tossed in a mixture of 1/2 cup flour, 1/4 cup cornstarch, 1/2 tsp salt and 1/2 tsp garlic powder
for the sauce: whisk together 1/2 cup pineapple juice witih 1/4 cup water, 1 Tbs soy sauce, 2 Tbs hoisin sauce, 1 tsp rice vinegar, 1 Tbs brown sugar, 1/2 tsp Better Than Bouillon brand No Chicken Base or Roasted Garlic Base and 1.5 Tbs cornstarch

Heat about 1 inch of vegetable oil in a non stick skillet on high for 3 minutes. Add in the coated seitan and cook for about 4 minutes or untill crisp. Drain. Heat a large non stick skillet on high for 3 minutes again. Add in 1 Tbs vegetable oil and then the green beans. Cook 1 minute and then add in the garlic, ginger, onions, chinese broccoli, peppers and carrots. Cook 2 minutes and add in the fresh pineapple. Cook 1 more minute and then add in the crispy seitan and the whisked sauce. Stir it all together for a minute until the sauce thickens. Serve over steamed rice. Enjoy. Yield: Serves 2-3

Tofu, Ham or Chicken Hoisin Topped Fried Rice

1.5 cups uncooked jasmine rice, cook it in a rice cooker or pot with a pinch of salt and completely cool it (yields about 4-5 cups rice when cooked)
1 cup of vegan ham, small diced (Lam Sheng Kee Vegetarian Ham or Maywah Vegan Smoked Ham are my favorite brands. They are available online or at some Asian markets) or 3/4 cup chopped Gardein brand vegetarian chicken strips, 3 Delight Soy brand chicken or Maywah brand vegan chicken steaks, small diced

if using tofu, use the chewy pan seared tofu recipe from this book and add it in at the end

2 carrots peeled and small diced
1 onion small diced
1 cup broccoli florets chopped small
1/2 cup small diced zucchini
1 tsp minced garlic
1 tsp minced ginger
1 cup thawed green peas
2 Tbs soy sauce
1 tsp mushroom powder
or 1 tsp garlic powder, 2 Tbs sesame oil, hoisin sauce

Heat a non stick pan on medium high heat for 3 minutes. Add the sesame oil, carrots, onions, garlic, ginger, ham or chicken and broccoli. Stir and cook about 3 minutes. Add zucchini, cook one minute, then add the cooled cooked rice, breaking it up with a spatula constantly until coated with the oil and mixed well. When warmed, add the peas (if using pan seared tofu, add it in now), mushroom or garlic powder, salt and soy sauce, to your taste liking. Mix well and serve hot. Top with hoisin sauce and, if you want it spicy, some Sriracha or hot chili oil. A combination of the tofu and chicken is my favorite. This is also very tasty if you add some scrambled Follow Your Heart brand Vegan Egg into it, cooked according to the package directions.

Yield: Serves 4-6

Char Grilled Hamburger Steaks

1 package of Impossible brand ground, 1/2 tsp dried cumin powder,
1/2 tsp garlic powder, 1/2 tsp chili powder, 1/2 tsp dried oregano

Mix all of the ingredients in a bowl together with your hands. Form this into 3
even size balls and form them into 1/3 of an inch thick size steak shapes. Heat a
grill for 12 minutes. Spray the grates with a little non stick spray and grill each side
for 2 or 3 minutes. Do not grill any longer or they may dry out, you want
them to be nice and juicy. Top with steak sauce and enjoy.   *Yield*: Makes 3 steaks

Parmesan Basil Bread Crumb Stuffed Tomatoes

4 medium sized tomatoes with a quarter of the top cut off and the
insides scooped out with a spoon
1 Tbs fresh chopped basil
1.5 cups panko bread crumbs, 4 Tbs olive oil, 1/2 tsp each garlic powder and
and dried oregano, 1/4 tsp salt
3 Tbs Follow Your Heart brand parmesan shredded cheese
3 slices of Field Roast brand Original Flavor Chao Cheese cut into small pieces

Put a little pinch of salt in each tomato after you have scooped out the inside and
turn the tomatoes upside down for 10 minutes, this will remove all the liquid. Mix
the bread crumbs, olive oil, salt, basil, cheeses, oregano and garlic powder and
stuff each tomato with this filling. Bake in a 400 degree oven until the filling has
browned on top, about 13 minutes.

Yield: Serves 2-4

Vietnamese Tofu Vermicelli Pho Soup

This is a delicious Asian inspired entree style soup. I kept it very simple here. You can add as many or whatever ingredients you like to make it as authentic as you desire. This is still my favorite version, as good or better than Pho I have had in any restaurant.

8 cups water with 3 Tbs of Better Than Bouillon brand roasted garlic base, 1 tsp grated fresh ginger, 1/2 tsp fresh minced garlic, 1 tsp of soy sauce and 1 Tbs vegan oyster sauce all whisked into it
1 cup fresh enoki mushrooms
4 cups raw flat baby spinach and/or chopped baby bok choy
3/4 cup small cubed extra firm tofu
2.5 cups of cooked and cooled Asian rice noodles (sometimes called rice vermicelli)
chopped scallions, fresh basil, sprouts, toasted sesame oil, fresh lime wedges, sriracha or hot chili oil and hoisin sauce for garnish

Heat the water/bouillon/garlic/ginger/soy sauce mixture until boiling. In 3 large bowls, place the tofu, raw enoki mushrooms, raw baby spinach and/or baby bok choy and cooked noodles in the bottom. Ladle the hot broth over the ingredients. Top with scallions, hot chili oil or sriracha, sprouts, hoisin sauce, a tiny bit of sesame oil, a squeeze of lime and fresh basil. Serve hot. This makes a delicious meal.

Yield: Makes about 3 large bowls of Pho

Vodka Sausage Pizza

1 ball of the Basic Dough recipe from this book, risen (the recipe makes 2 balls of dough but you will only use 1 here)
2 links of Beyond Meat brand bratwurst sausage with the skin peeled off by running it under warm water that have been broken up in a hot non stick pan until crumbled & brown 1 soft block of Follow Your Heart brand Mozzarella (make sure it is the soft block and not the hard, the soft melts better) that you have shredded yourself, few pinches dried oregano

for the vodka sauce:
1 cup of your favorite tomato sauce
1/4 cup Vegenaise brand Soy Free vegan mayo, 2 Tbs Tofutti brand cream cheese, 1/2 a small jar of marinated artichokes, 1 tsp lemon juice, 4 Tbs nutritional yeast, 1 /2 tsp salt, 1/8 cup vodka, 3 Tbs rice milk. 2 cloves minced garlic, 1 Tbs Earth Balance brand buttery spread, 2 Tbs Follow Your Heart brand parmesan shreds

Take the dough out of the bowl and do not knead it again. Place it on a floured cutting board and flatten it into a 14 to 16 inch circle (you can use a rolling pin too) and press it into a 14 to 16 inch non stick sprayed deep dish pizza pan. Cover and let it rise an hour. While it rises, **make the sauce** by first placing the mayo, cream cheese, artichokes, salt, lemon juice, salt, nutritional yeast and rice milk in a blender and blend until smooth. Heat the Earth Balance in a pan on medium high for a minute and add in the garlic. Cook 1 minute and add in the tomato sauce and then the vodka. Cook and stir 2 minutes and add in the cream sauce from the blender. Add in the parmesan and cook 2 more minutes until thickened a bit. Cool it completely and then spread this on the risen dough. Heat the oven to 440 degrees. Sprinkle on the sausage and then the shredded cheese. Sprinke on a few shakes of dried oregano and a pinch of salt. Bake 15 minutes. Place under the broiler 1 more minute to melt the cheese completely. Remove from oven. Brush the crust with a little olive oil. Top pizza with fresh basil if desired. Let it cool 10 minutes before slicing.

Yield: Serves 3-4

White Bean Asparagus Cakes with Basil Aioli

These won me the "2008 Best Chef on Campus Award" at Cornell University. They are well deserving and very tasty. I like to serve these over my Two Tomato, Artichoke and Pepperoncini Pasta Salad recipe from this book.

2 cans navy or cannellini
beans drained,
washed and mashed
in a food processor into a
chunky paste
1/2 cup panko bread crumbs
3/4 cup nutritional yeast
1/2 cup plain flour

1 tsp salt
1 tsp fresh sage chopped
1 tsp fresh dill chopped
8 individual stalks asparagus sliced into thin circles
1 onion small diced, sauteed in a pan with a tsp of olive oil until browned

Place the food processed mashed beans and the rest of the ingredients in a bowl. Put on food safe gloves and mix all together. If too wet, add more bread crumbs and flour. It should be the consistency of a medium firm dough.

Form into individual sized cakes about 2 inches across. Heat a non stick pan with a half inch canola or vegetable oil for 3 minutes over medium high heat. When you can dip a cake into it and it sizzles, it is ready to go. Slide about 6 to 8 cakes a time carefully into the hot oil. Cook 3 to 5 minutes per side. Drain on a cookie cooling rack placed on top of a foil lined cookie sheet. Serve with vegan basil aioli sauce. **Aioli recipe follows:**

1/3 cup vegan mayonaise
1 tsp red wine vinegar
pinch of salt
1 Tbs water
pinch dried basil or 3 leaves minced fresh basil

Whisk all together, serve over cakes.

Yield: Serves 4-6

Aglio e Olio Pasta with Zucchini and Asparagus

1 box Barilla brand White
Fiber Spaghetti
5 cloves garlic minced
1/4 cup chopped parsley
1/4 cup extra virgin olive oil
1 Tbs red wine vinegar
1 medium zucchini cut
into matchsticks
1 bunch of asparagus with the
hard bottoms trimmed off,
sliced into 1/2 inch pieces
1 tsp salt

Heat the olive oil and garlic over medium heat until the garlic starts to barely brown. Set aside.

Cook the spaghetti 7 minutes. Add the zucchini and asparagus directly into the pasta that is cooking and cook for 30 more seconds. Drain well and add this to a bowl and mix in the rest of the ingredients. Top with Follow Your Heart brand vegan parmesan cheese.

Yield: Serves 4-6

Beyond Simple Meatloaf

1.5 packs of thawed Impossible brand ground
1 cup plain bread crumbs
3 Tbs ketchup, 1 tsp garlic powder
2 Tbs Go Veggie Brand
vegan Parmesan
1 Tbs Follow Your Heart brand
Vegan Egg mixed with 1/4 cup water
2 Tbs flour (you can add more
if the mix seems too wet)
1/2 tsp salt or to taste, black
pepper to taste
1/2 tsp each dried oregano and basil
1/2 cup ketchup for topping , 1/4 cup chopped fresh parsley, 1/2 cup minced onion

Mix everything besides the 1/2 cup of ketchup in a large bowl. Taste a little for seasoning. If it needs more salt, pepper, parmesan or garlic powder, add it now. Heat the oven to 375 degrees. Push the meatloaf mix into a non stick sprayed baking loaf tin. Spread the ketchup on top and bake for 35 to 40 minutes. Let it cool a bit and remove from pan. Slice and serve with my Spinach Mushroom Gratin Bake or my Garlic Mashed Potato recipe and my Salt and Pepper Blanched Vegetable recipe.

Yield: Serves 3-6

Cajun Sausage and Red Bean Jambalaya

1/3 cup red onion, 2 cloves minced garlic,
3/4 cup sliced mushrooms, 1/4 cup
each medium diced red bell pepper &
green bell pepper, 1 cup cooked kidney
beans and 2 links of Beyond Meat
brand Bratwurst cut into half
moons, 1 Tbs Earth Balance
brand buttery spread

for the rice:
1 cup jasmine rice mixed
with a pinch of salt,
1.5 cups of water that has 1.5
Tbs of Better Than Bouillon brand
Roasted Garlic Base or No Chicken
Base whisked into it

for the spice mix:
mix together 1 tsp chili powder,
1/8 tsp cayenne pepper, 1/2 tsp
garlic powder, 1/4 tsp salt, 1/4 tsp
dried oregano and 1/2 tsp cumin powder

Place the rice ingredients in a rice cooker, cook it and then completely cool it
on a flat plate (make sure it is cooled down or the recipe will not work right).
Heat a large non stick skillet for 3 minutes. Add in a Tbs of olive oil and the
onions, peppers, garlic, sausage, mushrooms and a pinch of salt. Cook for 5
minutes and add in the cooked cooled rice, the beans, the spice mix and the
Earth Balance. Break it up well with a spatula until all is mixed well. Heat
through, stirring often. Taste for flavor, add salt or spices if needed. Serve
topped with hot sauce and a spoon of Tofutti brand sour cream. Enjoy.

Yield: Serves 3-4

Bowtie Pasta with Sausage and Broccoli Rabe

1 box farfalle pasta
3 Tbs Earth Balance spread, 3 cloves minced garlic
3 links of Field Roast brand Chipotle sausage cut into half
moons and browned in a non stick pan in a little olive oil
1 tsp salt, 1 cup cliced mushrooms, 2 Tbs lemon juice
1 bunch broccoli rabe cut into 1/2 inch pieces, 3 Tbs nutritional yeast

Heat Earth Balance and garlic in a medium sized pot until the garlic is just
starting to brown. Set aside. Cook the pasta 9 minutes, then add to the pasta
water the broccoli rabe, mushrooms and red peppers. Cook the pasta and
vegetables together in the water another minute and then drain. Add back
to the empty pasta cooking pot and add the sausage and the rest of the
ingredients. Stir in some dried red pepper flakes if you like. Enjoy topped
with Follow Your Heart brand vegan parmesan cheese.

Yield: Serves 6-8

Eggplant Cutlet Sandwiches with Spinach Artichoke Dip on Homemade Focaccia

1 recipe of the homemade focaccia from this book, warm and sliced in half for sandwiches,

1 recipe of the Spinach Artichoke Dip from this book, baked and warm,

1 medium eggplant, peeled and sliced into thin circles,

3 cups of panko bread crumbs, 1 tsp garlic powder, 1 tsp salt,

2.5 cups flour, 1/2 tsp dried basil, 1 1/4 cup water,

1/2 inch of vegetable oil in a non stick pan,

lettuce and tomato for the sandwiches

Dip the sliced, peeled eggplant into 1 1/4 cup of the flour, covering each piece until covered. Take the other 1 1/4 cup of flour and mix it with the water, whisking until smooth. Now, dip the coated eggplant into this (it will act as the egg so the panko will stick). Lay your panko, garlic powder, salt and dried basil in a flat casserole dish, mixing it well. Lay the eggplant into this now, coating it with the panko. When they are all coated, heat the oil in the non stick pan on high for 3 minutes. Fry the eggplant, about 6 at a time, until golden on each side, about 3 minutes per side. Drain and spread some of the artichoke dip on both sides of the focaccia bread, then stack a few pieces of the eggplant, lettuce and tomato on top of the bottom piece of the focaccia. Place the top on and enjoy warm.

Roasted Red Pepper Pasta Sauce (gluten free)

A nice alternative to tomato pasta sauce. It is creamy, rich and delicious.

2 large red bell peppers, 1 cup thinly sliced yellow onions, 2 cloves rough chopped garlic, 1/4 tsp dried red pepper flakes, 2 Tbs tomato paste, 1/2 cup nutritional yeast, 4 Tbs Follow Your Heart brand shredded parmesan, salt and pepper to taste, 2 Tbs Earth Balance brand buttery spread, 1 to 2 cups coconut milk, 3 Tbs lemon juice

Place the red peppers under the broiler and watch carefully, turning them until the skin is blackened on all sides. Remove them from the broiler and place them in a large bowl covered in plastic wrap while they are still hot. Let them sit 10 minutes and then remove the plastic and peel the skin off of them. Remove the seeds and cut the peeled peppers into thin slices. Heat a large non stick skillet on high for 3 minutes. Add in 1 Tbs of the buttery spread and add in the onions and garlic. Cook 3 minutes, stirring often. Add in a pinch of salt and pepper and then the red pepper slices, red pepper flakes and tomato paste. Cook 2 more minutes, stirring often. Add in 1 cup of the coconut milk and the rest of the buttery spread, parmesan and nutritional yeast. Cook 1 more minute. Transfer the mixture to a blender and blend until smooth. Add a little more coconut milk if it is too thick. Add the lemon juice and salt and pepper to taste. Mix some with your favorite cooked pasta topped with a little more shredded parmesan and fresh basil. *Yield:* Serves 2-3

Pancakes/ Waffle Batter For a Waffle Machine

2 cups King Arthur brand flour, sifted, 3 Tbs sugar, a pinch of salt, 1 Tbs ground flax seed, 1 tsp baking powder, 1/2 tsp baking soda, 4 Tbs vegan shortening
2 cups freshly opened plain club soda mixed with 1/2 Tbs apple cider vinegar

Mix the flax with 2 Tbs water. Place flour, sugar, salt, baking soda and baking powder. Cut in the shortening with a pastry cutter until it forms small balls. Cutting in the shortening means placing the shortening onto the flour mixture and pushing down over and over with the pastry cutter until the shortening is mixed into the flour mixture completely. You can use a fork for this if you have no pastry cutter, it just takes a little longer. Whisk in the club soda/vinegar and the flax seed and water mixture. Do not over mix. Heat an electric griddle. Spray with non stick spray and pour about 1/3 cup of the batter on the griddle at a time. When the tops bubble, flip them and cook another two minutes. You can also add fresh blueberries, strawberries, minced pineapple or chocolate chips to the batter. Serve warm topped with real maple syrup and vegan buttery spread.

Yield: Serves 6-8

Falafel with Cucumber Yoghurt Sauce (gluten free)

1 cup dried chickpeas, soaked 8 hours (do not use canned chickpeas)
1/2 cup onion, roughly chopped
1.5 cups parsley, roughly chopped, 1 clove garlic, 1/4 tsp garlic powder
1 tsp cumin, 1 tsp salt
a pinch of cayenne pepper (optional), black pepper to taste
2 to 3 Tbs chickpea flour
1/2 tsp baking soda
vegetable oil for frying
for the sauce:
1/2 cup of your favorite plain vegan yoghurt, 1/2 of a medium cucumber, peeled,
pinch of salt, 2 Tbs chopped scallions, 1/2 tsp lemon juice

 After the dried chickpeas have soaked 8 hours, drain them and add them into the
food processor along with the parsley, onion, garlic, cumin, garlic powder, salt and
optional cayenne pepper. Pulse this mixture until it resembles a coarse texture, not
too wet not too dry. Scrape the sides down a few times. Place it into a large bowl.
Add in the baking soda and a little chickpea flour. Mix until it all comes together,
if it seems too wet, add a little more chickpea flour, if it seems too dry, add a little
water. Taste and add salt if needed. Let it sit for 20 miutes covered and then form
into balls a little smaller than a golf ball or you can flatten them a little to make
them easier to brown each side. Heat an inch of vegetable oil in a non stick pan
for 4 minutes on medium high. Dip in a falafel, if bubbles form, they are ready to
fry. Cook about 6 to 8 at a time until golden brown, stirring occasionally. Drain
and sprinkle with a little salt. You can sprinkle them with a few sesame seeds out of
the oil too if you like. Serve with the cucumber sauce. **For the sauce**, simply place
the sauce ingredients into a blender or food processor until mixed. You can eat
these as is or on warm pita with hummus, shredded lettuce, tomato, the cucumber
sauce and a little tahini. Enjoy.

Yield: Makes 22 falafel

Tortellini in Brodo

28 of my Homemade Tortellini from this book, fresh, not frozen, 3 cups water mixed with 1.5 Tbs of Better Than Bouillon brand Roasted Garlic Base, salt and pepper to taste, 1 tsp each chopped parsley and chives 1/3 cup each thinly sliced peeled carrots and celery

Simply heat the water, carrots and celery to a boil. Add in the tortellini, parsley and chives. Cook for 2 more minutes, season with salt and pepper and serve hot topped with Follow Your Heart brand vegan parmesan. Enjoy. *Yield:* Makes 4 normal sized bowls of soup or 2 entree size bowls.

Lemon Chicken or Tofu

6 patties Delight Soy brand or Maywah brand plain vegan chicken steaks or 1 block of extra firm tofu, frozen, thawed and all of the water squeezed out of the block with your hands and then cut into 6 large triangles (this process makes the tofu extra chewy), 1 cup cornstarch mixed with 1 cup plain flour, 1 tsp salt, 2 Tbs chopped parsley, 1/2 tsp black pepper and 1 tsp garlic powder, canola or vegetable oil to saute chicken or tofu **lemon sauce:** 1/4 cup lemon juice, 3/4 cup water, 1 Tbs Earth Balance brand buttery spread, pinch of salt, 3 Tbs sugar, 1/2 tsp basil, 1 Tbs cornstarch dissolved in 1/4 cup water by stirring quickly with a fork

Heat the lemon juice, salt, water, buttery spread, sugar and basil over a medium heat until about to boil. Slowly add in the cornstarch mixture, whisking the sauce quickly as you do. When thickened, turn off heat and set aside. If too thick, add a little more water. For the chicken or tofu, dip the steaks or tofu into a bowl of water and then into the cornstarch/ flour seasoned mix, make sure to coat well. Heat 1/8 inch of canola or vegetable oil in a non stick pan and when hot (you will know if it is ready by flicking some of the cornstarch/ flour mixture into the oil, if it sizzles, it is ready to cook. Add in the chicken steaks or tofu and cook on each side 3 minutes until browned. Drain and top with the lemon sauce.

Yield: Serves 4-6

Ricotta Stuffed Shells

16 cooked large stuffing shell pasta, cooked and cooled
1 block firm tofu, 1/2 tsp salt, 1/2 cup nutritional yeast
3 leaves fresh basil, juice of half a lemon
1/2 teaspoon garlic powder
8 slices of Chao brand Original flavor vegan cheese slices, cut in
half lengthwise
3 cups of your favorite homemade or store bought marinara sauce

Place tofu, nutritional yeast, lemon juice, basil, salt and garlic powder in a
food processor. Process until smooth. Spoon into a medium size ziploc bag.
Take a large pyrex casserole dish, spray with non stick spray and line the
bottom with some marinara sauce. Cut the tip off the bottom corner off the
ricotta filled ziploc bag and pipe the ricotta into each shell, placing next to
each other in the pyrex after filled. When all are filled, spoon marinara over
the tops of the shells, then lay the Chao cheese slices across each row of
stuffed shells. Sprinkle the cheese with a little salt, garlic powder and dried
basil. Cover, tented with tin foil. Make sure it does not touch the cheese
and shells. Preheat oven to 375 degrees and bake 35 minutes or until cheese
is melted. I like to serve these with the vegan meatballs from this book in
extra marinara sauce or Beyond Meat Italian sausage links, salad and the
homemade rolls recipe from this book.

Yield: Serves 4-8

Wild Mushroom Steak Fajitas

These are great served with guacamole, Tofutti brand vegan sour cream,
saffron rice and refried beans.

1.5 cups sliced cremini baby portabella mushrooms
1 cup king mushrooms cut into long thin strips
1.5 cups sliced white button mushrooms
1 cup chopped oyster mushrooms
2 green peppers, sides cut off and then julienne cut the sides into thin strips
1 onion cut into half moons, 1 cup of seitan torn into bite sized chunks
spice mix:
1 Tbs chili powder, 1/2 tsp garlic powder, 1/2 tsp salt, 1/2 tsp dried oregano,
1/2 Tbs sugar, pinch of cayenne pepper

Mix all the spice mix ingredients together in a bowl. Set aside.

Heat a large saute pan over high heat 3 minutes. Add 1 Tbs of canola oil. Add all
of the mushrooms, peppers, seitan and onions. Add a pinch of salt. Stir and saute
5 minutes or until the mushrooms are cooked. Add the spice mix. Serve inside of
a warm flour tortilla.

Yield: Serves 4-6

Schezwan Eggplant, Tofu and Mushrooms

1.5 cups of quartered button mushrooms, 1 prepared recipe of the Pan Seared Chewy Tofu from this book that has been cut into triangles before cooking it according to the recipe, 1 tsp each rough chopped fresh garlic and peeled ginger, 2 cups baby bok choy cut into bite size pieces, 1.5 cups of broccolini cut into 1 inch pieces, 1 long Japanese eggplant cut into 3/4 inch chunks, 1/2 cup each plain flour and cornstarch mixed with 1/2 tsp each garlic powder and salt **for the sauce:** whisk together 1/8 cup dark soy sauce, 1/8 cup regular soy sauce, 1 tsp rice vinegar, 1 Tbs brown sugar, 1 Tbs cornstarch, 2 Tbs vegan oyster sauce, 1 tsp sesame oil, 2 tsp chili garlic paste and 1/2 cup water plus 2 Tbs water water

Place about a half inch of vegetable oil in a large non stick pan. Heat for 3 minutes on high. As it heats, place the eggplant and the cornstarch/flour/garlic powder mixture into a large plastic bag and shake the bag to coat the eggplant. Drop the eggplant into the hot oil and cook the eggplant about 3 minutes until crisp. Drain the eggplant. Heat another large non stick pan on high for 3 minutes. Add in 1 Tbs of vegetable oil. Add in the mushrooms, garlic, baby bok choy, ginger and broccolini. Cook about 3 minutes, stirring often. Add in the tofu and cook 1 more minute. Add in the crispy eggplant and the whisked sauce. Stir it all together another minute until the sauce thickens. Serve ove rice. *Yield:* Serves 2-3

Sesame Hoisin Grilled Tofu /Chicken

2 blocks of extra firm tofu that have been frozen and then thawed with all of the water squeezed out of the block after thawed (this leaves you with extra chewy, delicious tofu) or 8 patties of Maywah brand or Delight Soy brand vegetarian chicken steaks, 1/2 cup hoisin sauce, 1 Tbs rice vinegar, 1 Tbs sugar, 1/2 cup sweet chili sauce, 1 tsp sesame oil, 2 Tbs sesame seeds

Heat a grill on high for 15 minutes. Cut each block of tofu half, and then each half into 2 equally thick pieces (this will leave you with 8 total pieces from the 2 blocks). Whisk together the hoisin sauce, sesame oil, sweet chili sauce, sugar, vinegar and sesame seeds. Lay the tofu or the chicken in a casserole dish and pour the sauce over the tofu or chicken, coat both sides. When the grill is hot, spray the grates very well with non stick spray and grill each side about 4 minutes.

Yield: Serves 3-6

All Purpose Tomato Sauce (gluten free)

3 28 oz cans San Marzano plum tomatoes (Cento brand are good) with juices crushed with your hands as fine as you
can get them, 1/2 tsp salt, 1 small can of tomato paste
1/2 Tbs balsamic vinegar, 1/2 cup Montepulciano D'Abruzzo red wine or your favorite red wine, 4 cloves garlic minced
1/2 tsp dried oregano, 1/4 cup water, 1 Tbs sugar (optional, I like a little sweetness to my tomato sauce), 8 fresh basil leaves minced
1 medium white onion diced small

  Heat a large pot over medium heat, add the 1/4 cup of water. When it looks about to boil, add the onions and garlic. Water saute for 4 minutes (this keeps a greasy film from being on top of your finished sauce, which oil tends to do). Add the red wine and reduce for another 3 minutes, then add the rest of the ingredients and turn the heat to medium low. Stir often, do not let it burn on the bottom of the pot. If you have a flame diffuser, you can place it under the pot to keep from having to stir as much. Cook for 30 minutes, stir often. Season with more salt, fresh basil or sugar if needed after the cooking time is up.

Yield: Makes sauce for 3 or 4 meals

Butternut Basil Homemade Gnocchi

2 cups of peeled medium cubed butternut
squash, 1 1/2 cups flour, 1/2 tsp salt, 1 tsp minced fresh basil, 1 tsp olive oil

  Boil the squash cubes for 13 minutes or until tender but not mushy. Place the flour, salt, basil and oil in a large bowl. Drain the squash and using a potato ricer, rice the squash into the flour (this recipe only works if you have a ricer). Knead it all together until you have a smooth ball of dough. Divide into 5 balls and roll each one into about a 15 inch long rope. Cut a little less than 1/2 inch pieces off of the dough and roll each piece into a little ball. Using a fork or ghocchi board, roll each ball along the fork or board to form lines in the gnocchi. When all are done, cook them in boiling water until they float, usually about 2 or 3 minutes (they are not done until they float). You can also freeze them before cooking them and use them later. If you cook them from frozen, they will need to boil them for about 5 or 6 minutes until they float. Toss the hot cooked gnocchi in a little Earth Balance brand buttery spread and fresh lemon juice.

Yield: Serves 3-4

Salisbury Steak

for the steak:
1 pack of Impossible brand groundless beef
1 tsp garlic powder, 1/2 tsp cumin powder
1/2 tsp salt
1 Tbs finely ground flax seed mixed with 2 Tbs warm water
1 Tbs ketchup, 1 tsp dijon mustard
1/4 cup panko bread crumbs, 1/4 tsp black pepper
for the gravy:
3/4 cup each plain rice milk whisked together with 3/4 cup water, 1 Tbs Better Than Bouillon brand Roasted Garlic Base, 1 tsp Gravy Master (brand available in spice isle of grocery stores), salt and pepper to taste, 1 tsp nutritional yeast, 1 Tbs ketchup and 2 Tbs plain white flour

1 Tbs Earth Balance brand buttery spread
1 cup thin sliced cremimi mushrooms

   For the steak, mix the steak ingredients together and form into 4 half inch thick flat football shaped steaks. Heat a non stick pan on high for 3 minutes and add in 1 tsp of vegetable oil and then the steaks. Cook each side 3 minutes and remove from pan and set aside. **For the gravy**, place the Earth Balance buttery spread into the same pan still on the high heat. Add in the mushrooms and a pinch of salt and pepper. Cook 3 minutes and then add in the whisked gravy ingredients. Cook 3 minutes on low, whisking until thickened. Add in the steaks and cover them with the gravy. Serve hot with the Garlic Mashed Potato or Baked Mac and cheese recipes from this book.

Yield: Makes 4 steaks

Avocado BLT on Homemade Focaccia Bread

1 recipe of homemade Garlic Parmesan Focaccia Bread from this book, freshly baked and warm
1 package of Lightlife brand Smart Bacon, cook it according to package directions
lettuce, tomato and peeled sliced avocado
Vegenaise brand vegan mayo
salt and pepper to taste

Slice the warm focaccia bread into 4 large pieces and then slice them in half width wise. Fill the sandwiches with the mayo, bacon, lettuce, tomato, avocado and a pinch of salt and pepper. Enjoy with my Minaste Beans and Potato soup recipe from this book.

Yield: Serves 2-4

Garlic Buttered Mushroom and Spinach Risotto

1.5 cups white Arborio rice, 3 Tbs Earth Balance brand buttery spread
3 cloves minced garlic, 1 mdium onion diced small, 2 cups sliced cremini mushrooms
3 cups or fresh and cleaned chopped baby spinach, 3 Tbs nutritional yeast
8 cups of water with 2.5 Tbs of Better Than Bouillon No Chicken Base whisked into it, kept on a low simmer on the stove
Follow Your Heart brand parmesan cheese, salt andn pepper to taste, dried oregano

Heat a non stick saute pan for 2 minutes on high. Add in the Earth Balance, the mushrooms, garlic and onions. Add in a little salt and pepper and a pinch of dried oregano. Saute for 3 minutes. Add in the rice and coat the rice in the buttery mushrooms. Turn the heat to medium high and spoon in about half a cup of the stock. Stir it around with a wooden spoon until the rice soaks up the stock, then, add another half cup of stock and stir until absorbed. Repeat this process about 5 to 8 times until the rice is soft and creamy (it takes about 20 minutes total to achieve this). Taste it to make sure the rice is fully cooked. When cooked, stir in the spinach until it wilts, then add in the nutritional yeast and a little more butter if desired. Top with the parmesan.

Yield: Serves 3-4

Hoisin Grilled Tofu Banh Mi Sandwich with Pickled Carrots, Bok Choy and Sweet Chili Mayo

This is a deliciously light and crispy sandwich with a ton of flavor. It goes great with any one of my Pho recipes from this book.

1 cup shredded peeled carrots, 1/8 cup rice vinegar, 1 Tbs sugar
2 fresh 12 inch long baguettes from the Asian market (these are very light and delicious), 1 recipe of the Sweet Chili Mayo from page 93,
1 recipe of the Scsame Hoisin Grilled Tofu recipe from page 275, but made with no sesame seeds
fresh cilantro, 1 cup bok choy greens, shredded thin with a knife

  Cut each loaf into two 6 inch sandwiches then slice in half so that you have 4 tops and 4 bottoms. Take your shredded carrots and mix them in a bowl with the 1/8 cup rice wine vinegar and the Tbs of sugar. Let them chill in the fridge. Brush the inside of the bread with a little vegetable oil or sesame oil and grill the bread face down on a hot grill for 30 seconds. To assemble, spread a little of the sweet chili mayo on each side of the bread. Lay 3 pieces of grilled tofu on the bottom piece of each of the 4 sandwich bottoms. Top this with some shredded bok choy and some of the pickled carrots (be sure to squeeze the liquid out of the pickled carrots first). You can add a little plain sweet chili sauce and fresh chopped cilantro on now too if you want. Place the top of the bread on the sandwich and enjoy hot.

Yield: Makes 4 sandwiches   — 279 —

Baked Cheese Manicotti

10 tubes of Barilla brand manicotti, cooked and cooled
1 recipe of tofu ricotta from this book
3 cups of the Homemade Tomato Sauce recipe from this book or your
favorite store bought tomato sauce
6 slices Field Roast brand Chao Cheese or Follow Your Heart brand
provolone slices, each slice cut in half or 3/4 a soft block of Follow Your
Heart brand Mozzarella, shred it yourself
dried oregano, salt and pepper to taste
fresh basil for garnish

Preheat the oven to 385 degrees. Place the tofu ricotta in a plastic seal top
bag. Cut the tip off of the bag (making it into a pastry bag, this makes it easy
to fill the manicotti tubes). Pipe out the filling evenly into all of the cooked
tubes. Place about a cup of the tomato sauce at the bottom of a glass casserole
dish. Place the filled tubes into the sauced dish in 2 or 3 rows. Evenly spoon
the rest of the sauce over the filled tubes. Place the sliced Chao or provolone
cheese across the filled tubes evenly until they are covered (the ends of each
tube will not be completely covered with the cheese) or sprinkle the Follow
Your Heart shredded mozzarella over the tubes evenly. Sprinkle the cheese
with a little dried oregano, salt and pepper. Cover the dish with foil and bake
about 25 to 30 minutes until the cheese is melted. Uncover, remove from
oven and garnish with a little fresh basil and Go Veggie brand vegan
parmesan cheese, enjoy.

Yield: Serves 3-5

Ratatouille

1 medium onion, diced small, 3 cloves of garlic, minced
4 medium tomatoes, medium diced, 1 large red pepper, medium diced
1 medium eggplant, medium diced
1 medium yellow and 1 medium green squash, medium diced
3 Tbs fresh chopped basil, 1/2 tsp fresh thyme
1/2 cup water, 1/2 tsp red wine vinegar
3/4 tsp salt, pepper to taste, a few pinches of dried red pepper flakes

Heat a large saute pan or Dutch oven for 3 minutes on high. Add in 1 tsp of
olive oil and then add in the garlic and onions. Cook 3 minutes and then add
in the tomatoes, water and vinegar with a pinch of salt. Cook for 5 minutes
and then add the yellow and green squash, eggplant and the peppers. Stir
until mixed and cook this all together with the rest of the salt, pepper and red
pepper flakes for 10 minutes or until the vegetables soften but are not mushy.
Stir in the basil and thyme. Taste for flavor. Adjust the salt and pepper if needed.

Yield: Serves 4-6

Spicy Burokkori and Pickled Red Pepper Sushi

This recipe requires a sushi mat.

1 cup of white sushi rice, a pinch of salt, 1.5 cups of water and a small 4 inch square of dried kombu (kombu is optional)
1 Tbs rice vinegar, 2 sheets of nori seaweed, cut in half so that you have 4 long rectangles, 1/2 cup of red bell peppers sliced thin and tossed in 1 Tbs rice vinegar and 1 tsp sugar and left to marinate 20 minutes, a few green scallion tops cut into about 4 inch pieces, 8 individual stalks of Chinese broccoli that has been dropped in boiling water for 1 minute and then drained and completely cooled **mix together:** 1 tsp soy sauce, 1 tsp sesame oil, 1 Tbs hot chili paste and toss the cooked broccolini in it

   Cook the rice in a rice cooker with the 1.5 cups of water, pinch of salt and the optional kombu. Remove the kombu when the rice is cooked and stir in the sugar/vinegar mixture. Bring it to room temperature. Take the sushi mat and cover it in plastic wrap. Take a sheet of the half cut nori and place it on the plastic wrap with the long end facing you. Wet your hands a little and take about 3/4 of the cooled rice and place it on the nori, flattening it out to fit the shape of the nori. Sprinkle a few sesame seeds on the rice. Now, pick up the sheet and flip it over so that the rice is now at the bottom, on the plastic, about a half inch from the bottom of the sushi mat, long end facing you. Take 2 pieces of the broccolini, the bell peppers (squeeze the marinade out from the peppers the best you can) and a few scallion tops and place them from left to right end, about a half inch away from the end facing you. Carefully take the sushi mat and roll it up over the filling, pulling it in tight as you roll. Do not roll the mat up into the rice, rather, use it to guide your roll. When you get to the end, unroll the mat and you will have 1 large sushi log. Take a wet sharp knife and slice the log into 6 rolls. Repeat the process with the rest of the nori and filling. Enjoy dipped in soy sauce or topped with my Spicy Mayo recipe.

Yield: Serves 4-6

Pumpkin Seed Sage Crusted Chicken Cutlets or Tofu Cutlets Topped with Baked Spinach Artichoke Dip

6 Maywah brand or Delight Soy brand unbreaded vegetarian chicken patties, or, if using tofu, take 1 block of extra firm tofu that has been frozen, thawed and had all of the water squeezed out of the block (this leaves you with an extra chewy block of tofu) and cut into 6 triangles, 3 cups of panko bread crumbs mixed with 3/4 cup of rough chopped salted green toasted pumpkin seeds, 1 tsp garlic powder, 1 tsp chopped fresh sage and 3/4 tsp salt, 3 cups of flour, 1 1/2 cups water, 1 recipe of the Spinach Artichoke Dip from this book, baked and warm, vegetable oil to fry

Put 1 1/2 cups of the flour in a bowl. In another bowl, mix the other 1 1/2 cups of flour with the 1 1/2 cups of water with a whisk (this will act as the egg to make the bread crumbs stick to the chicken or tofu). In another flat Pyrex type dish, place the panko/sage / pumpkin seed mixture. Dip all of the tofu or chicken into the flour, then into the flour / water mixture and then into the panko/sage/pumpkin seed mixture. Coat the tofu or chicken completely with the bread crumb mixture. Heat a half inch of canola or vegetable oil in a large non stick pan for 3 minutes over medium high heat. Dip a piece of the tofu or chicken into the oil. If bubbles form around it, it is ready to fry. Cook each side for 2-3 minutes or until golden. Drain the cutlets on a foil lined cookie sheet that has been topped with a cookie cooling rack. Sprinkle them with a little salt right out of the oil and top with some of the artichoke dip. *Yield:* Serves 3-4

Leek, Kale, Olive, Caper and Artichoke Greek Spinach Feta Pasta

1 package of Ronzoni brand Smart Taste rotini pasta (this pasta has extra fiber but tastes like regular white pasta), 1 Tbs olive oil, 1/3 cup cleaned leeks sliced into half moons 1/2 cup chopped pitted small Greek green olives, 1/3 cup small diced red bell pepper 3 cups raw baby spinach and 1 cup raw stemmed kale rough chopped into small pieces 1/2 cup marinated artichokes rough chopped, 2 Tbs capers, 3 cloves chopped garlic 1 to 2 Tbs lemon juice, 1 tsp fresh chopped oregano 1/2 a container or Follow Your Heart brand vegan feta cheese crumbles, 1 tsp salt or to taste

Cook the rotini for 5 minutes. As it cooks, heat a large non stick pan for 3 minutes on high. Add in the olive oil and then the garlic, leeks, red pepper, spinach, kale and a pinch of salt. Stir and cook 4 minutes. Add in the artichokes, capers and olives. Drain the pasta and add it to the pan with the cooking vegetables. Turn off the heat and add in the lemon juice, feta, oregano and salt. Taste, add more salt if needed. Enjoy.

Yield: Serves 3-4

Baked Feta and Grape Tomato Penne

1 container of Follow Your Heart brand feta cheese, 3/4 a container of grape tomatoes, each tomato cut in half, 1/2 tsp dried oregano, 4 peeled and chunky chopped cloves of garlic, a few pinches of salt and pepper to taste, 3 Tbs olive oil, 5 basil leaves rough chopped, 1 box of Ronzoni brand Smart Taste Pasta (this pasta has added fiber but tastes like normal white pasta), 3 Tbs nutritional yeast, 3 Tbs Follow Your Heart brand shredded parmesan, 3 Tbs fresh lemon juice, 1 tsp garlic powder

Heat the oven to 400. Take a non stick sprayed glass baking dish, mix the feta and permesan and pour this in the middle of the baking dish. Arrange the tomatoes and garlic around the feta. Sprinkle on the salt, pepper and oregano and then pour the olive oil over all of the ingredients. Bake for 18 minutes. Cook the pasta for 7 minutes in boiling water and then stir this into the baked feta mixture along with the nutritional yeast, garlic powder and fresh lemon juice. Stir in the basil. Add salt if needed. Enjoy. *Yield:* Serves 3-4

BBQ Grilled Tofu or BBQ Chicken (gluten free)

If using tofu, drain a block of extra firm tofu and freeze overnight and then thaw, this gives it a better, more chewy texture or use 6 Delight Soy brand or Maywah brand vegan chicken steaks.
1 recipe of the homemade BBQ sauce from this book

Completely squeeze all of the water out of the tofu block, cut into 6 rectangles and marinate in the BBQ sauce. If using the vegan chicken, just marinate it 15 minutes. Heat a grill for 15 minutes and then spray the grates with non stick spray. Place the tofu or chicken on the grill. Grill each side about 3 minutes. This goes great with my vegan mac and cheese.

Yield: Serves 3-5

Chicken Fried Steak with Mushroom Gravy

1 recipe of the Mushroom Gravy from this book, prepared and warm
1 pack of Impossible brand ground mixed together with 1 tsp garlic powder, 1/4 tsp black
pepper, a pinch of salt and 1/2 tsp cumin and flattened into 5 individual 1/4 inch thick
patties, 3/4 cup flour whisked together with 3/4 cup water **for the coating:** 1.5 cups flour
mixed with 1/2 cup cornstarch, 1 tsp garlic powder, 1/4 tsp each black pepper and oregano

   Dip the steak patties, one at a time, in the dry flour mixture, then into the flour/water
mixture. Repeat the process again, so that each patty is double battered, lastly dipping it
into the dry flour mixture. Repeat with the rest of the patties. Heat 1/2 inch of of
vegetable oil in a non stick pan for 3 minutes and then add in the patties. Cook each side
about 4 minutes or until golden. Drain them and serve topped with the mushroom gravy.
Yield: Makes 5 steaks

Beyond Simple Dijon Grilled Chicken or Tofu

6 Delight Soy brand vegan chicken steaks or Maywah brand vegan chicken
steaks or 2 blocks of extra firm tofu that have been frozen, thawed and
gently squeezed until all of the water is pressed out of them, cut into 4
triangles per block, for a total of 8 triangles (this gives the tofu a chewy,
chicken type texture)
1/4 cup dijon mustard
3 Tbs maple syrup, 1 tsp dried basil, 1/2 tsp garlic powder
1 tsp olive oil, salt to taste

   Preheat the grill for 15 minutes. While preheating, mix the maple syrup,
the mustard, olive oil and the salt, whisk well. Pour it over the chicken or
tofu, coating both sides well. Once the grill is heated, spray the grates with
non stick spray and grill each side of the chicken or tofu for 3-5 minutes.
Spoon a little extra of the marinade on the chicken or tofu as it grills. This
goes great with smoky red beans and rice (from this book) and some grilled
vegetables.

Yield: Serves 3-6

Oyster Mushroom and Broccolini Beef Pho

8 cups water with 3 Tbs of Better Than Bouillon brand roasted garlic base, 2 Tbs vegan oyster sauce, 1 tsp fresh ginger, 1/2 tsp fresh minced garlic and 1 tsp of soy sauce all whisked into it, 1 cup fresh oyster mushrooms roughly chopped, 2 chopped baby bok choy, 1 cup of broccolini cut into 1/2 inch pieces, 2 cups seitan pulled into bite size pieces, 2.5 cups of cooked and cooled Asian flat rice noodles, chopped scallions, fresh basil, sprouts, toasted sesame oil, fresh lime wedges, sriracha or hot chili oil and hoisin for garnish

Steam the broccolini and oyster mushrooms for 1 minute, set aside. Heat a large non stick pan on high for 3 minutes, add in 1 tsp of vegetable oil and then the seitan. Let it sit in a flat later for 1 minute so that it gets some color on it. Stir and cook 1 more minute and then add a tsp of soy sauce. Set aside. Heat the water/bouillon/garlic/ginger/soy sauce mixture until boiling. In 3 large bowls, place the seitan, raw bok choy, seitan, mushrooms and broccolini and the cooked noodles in the bottom. Ladle the hot broth over the ingredients. Top with scallions, hot chili oil or sriracha, sprouts, hoisin sauce, a tiny bit of sesame oil, a squeeze of lime and fresh basil. Serve hot.   *Yield:* Serves 2-3

Smoky Cabbage and Bratwurst Sausage Roll

1 recipe of the Spicy Smoked Paprika Garlic Cabbage and Mushrooms from this book, prepared and cooled, 2 links of Beyond Meat brand Bratwurst sausages that have been pan seared 5 minutes and cut into half moons once cooled
1 ball of the Basic Dough recipe from this book, risen (the recipe makes 2 balls of dough, but you will only use 1 here), sesame seeds for topping the bread

Remove the risen dough from the bowl and do not knead it again. Place it on a floured surface and push it into a large rectangle shape. Take a rolling pin and roll it into about a 18 inch by 12 inch larger rectangle. Take the cabbage filling and run it along the longer side of the dough closest to you. Leave a half inch of non covered dough from the top and the bottom and at the edge closest to you. Place the sliced sausage on top of the cabbage. Roll the dough over the filling and then into a large log. Place it on a foil lined cookie sheet that has been sprayed with non stick spray. Cover the dough roll for 1 hour. After an hour, brush the top of the dough with a little water and then sprinkle about a Tbs of sesame seeds on top. Heat the oven to 440 degrees. Bake it for about 16 to 18 minutes or until golden. Remove from the oven and brush with a little olive oil. Cool a few minutes and then slice and enjoy.

Yield: Serves 2-4

Mapo Tofu

1 block of soft tofu cut into 1/3 inch cubes, 1.5 Tbs Doubanjiang broad bean paste, 2 links of Beyond Meat brand bratwurst links that have had the skin removed by running them under warm water, 1 1/2 cups water, 8 sichuan peppercorns, 1/2 of a small dried red pepper minced, 2 cloves rough chopped garlic, 1 tsp minced fresh peeled ginger, 1 tsp sugar, 3 Tbs chopped scallions, 1 Tbs soy sauce, 1 tsp vegetable oil, 1/4 tsp sesame oil, 1 Tbs cornstarch whisked into 2 Tbs water

  Heat a large non stick pan for 2 minutes. Add in the peppercorns and stir them around for about 2 minutes. Remove them and finely mince them or crush in a mortal & pestle. Heat the pan again for 2 minutes. Add in the vegetable oil and then 2 Tbs of the scallions, the ginger and garlic. Cook 30 seconds, stirring often. Add in the broad bean paste and minced red pepper. Add in the sausages and break it up. Cook the sausage until it browns. Add in the ground peppercorns, the 1 1/2 cups water, the sugar, tofu, sesame oil and the soy sauce. Allow it to barely come to a boil. Add in the cornstarch/water mixture. Stir carefully so the tofu does not break up until the sauce thickens. Serve over steamed rice topped with the rest of the chopped scallions. Enjoy. *Yield:* Serves 2-3

Chewy Tofu/Pan Seared Tofu (gluten free)

  This is a technique to get a delicious texture for your tofu. After using this technique you can grill, pan sear, marinate, bake, saute or fry the tofu.

1 block extra firm tofu

  Take the tofu out of the package and drain. Place the tofu in a plastic bag and freeze 6 to 8 hours. Take it out of the freezer and thaw on the counter. Once completely thawed, carefully squeeze all of the water out of the tofu completely. You are left with tofu that now has almost a chicken type texture. It is delicious torn into chunks and pan seared or grilled and chopped up into pasta or any other way you desire. I like to get a non stick pan searing hot, break the thawed, squeezed out tofu into chunks, add a little oil to the pan and pan sear each side of the chunks until they are golden. I then season the seared chunks in the hot pan with either soy sauce, balsamic vinegar or lemon pepper seasoning, depending on which cuisine I will use the tofu for. This is great on a salad too.

Yield: Serves 2-4

Chicken and Dressing Casserole

This is a very simple and satisfying recipe.

1 recipe of the homemade Herb Stuffing recipe from this book, cooled or 2 boxes of your favorite store bought vegan stuffing mix, prepared and cooled (if you use a store bought mix, add 1/4 cup each of finely chopped onions and celery once cooled)
1 recipe of the vegan chicken gravy recipe from this book
1 cup of Maywah brand veggie chicken, Delight Soy brand veggie chicken or Gardein brand chicken strips, cut into small cubes

Preheat the oven to 375 degrees. Spray a 9x13 inch glass casserole dish with non stick spray. Mix the chicken with the gravy and pour it all into the casserole dish. Cover the gravy/chicken mixture with all of the stuffing. Bake for 25 minutes. Serve hot.

Yield: Serves 4-6

Garlic Spinach and Creamy Chao Cheese Grilled Panini

4 slices of sourdough bread or whole grain bread
4 slices of Field Roast brand Chao Cheese Original Creamy flavor
4 cups fresh baby spinach
2 cloves garlic minced
few pinches salt
non stick spray
1 tsp olive oil

Heat a non stick pan for one minute on medium high, then add the olive oil, garlic, spinach and salt. Saute until wilted down. Set aside. Take the 4 pieces of bread, lay 2 slices of Chao Cheese on one side of each of the sandwiches and top with the sauteed spinach. I like to place the sandwiches open faced in the microwave for 30 seconds to get the cheese starting to melt good. Remove from microwave, heat a non stick pan for one minute on medium high or a panini maker until ready to cook. Assemble the sandwiches. Spray the non stick pan or the panini maker with the non stick spray and cook each side of the sandwiches until crisp and golden. Serve w/ tomato basil soup.

Yield: Makes 2 sandwiches

Chicken or Seitan Cheesesteak

use either 3 cups or Maywah brand or Delight Soy brand non breaded
vegan chicken nuggets, cut into strips, or, if you prefer seitan, cut the seitan
into 3 cups worth of chunks (you can use homemade or store bought seitan)
1 cup of green peppers cut into thin strips
1 cup of onion cut into thin strips
1/2 a recipe of the Nacho Cheese Sauce from this book, warmed
vegetable oil
salt and pepper to taste
1/2 tsp garlic powder
4 of your favorite 6 inch Italian hoagie rolls

If you are using seitan, toss it in 1 Tbs of soy sauce mixed with 1 Tbs of rice
wine vinegar before cooking. Heat a large non stick pan for 3 minutes on
high and then add in about a teaspoon of vegetable oil and then the onions,
peppers and chicken or seitan. Spread it into a flat layer and let it sit for a
minute and a half before stirring. Add a little salt and pepper and then stir or
flip the pan. It will start to brown nicely. Cook for another 4 minutes. Add in
the 1/2 tsp garlic powder. Stir well and taste for seasoning. Warm your
bread in an oven at 350 degrees for 3 minutes. Spread a little of the warmed
cheese sauce in each of the rolls, then add in your cheesesteak filling, evenly
into the 4 rolls. Top with more cheese sauce and enjoy hot.

Yield: Makes 4 sandwiches

Crispy Asian Style Tofu Nuggets

This is a technique for getting crunchy tofu nuggets which can be used in my
General Tso Tofu recipe, Sweet and Sour Tofu Recipe or any stir fry dish.

1 block of tofu that has been frozen, thawed and then squeezed with
your hands until no more water comes out of the tofu block (this
freezing prozess makes the tofu extra chewy)
1 cup cornstarch
3/4 cup flour
1 teaspoon salt
1/2 tsp garlic powder
canola/vegetable oil to fry

Mix the flour, cornstarch, salt and garlic powder. Take the thawed tofu
block and tear it into about 15 medium sized chunks. Dredge each chunk
in the flour/cornstarch mixture until covered. Heat a 1/2 inch of canola
or vegetable oil in a non stick pan for 3 minutes on high and then add in
the dredged tofu. Cook each side for a few minutes until browned. Drain
on a cookie rack that has been placed on top of a foil lined cookie sheet,
this way you can reheat the tofu later in the oven without the bottom
burning. Sprinkle with a little salt. Enjoy.

Yield: coats 1 block of tofu

Chicken Salad Sandwich Filling or Salad Topping

1 pack of Maywah brand or Delight Soy brand non breaded Chicken Nuggets
4 Tbs Soy Free Veganaise
1/2-1 tsp salt
1/4 tsp black pepper
2 Tbs sweet relish
1/4 cup minced celery
1/4 cup minced onion
1/2 tsp garlic powder

Place the chicken nuggets, salt, pepper, garlic powder and mayo in a food processor. Pulse the machine until it is mixed well but not mushy. Place this into a large bowl and add the rest of the ingredients. Add in more mayo if it seems dry and more salt if it is bland. Stir well and serve chilled on your favorite bread, toast or on top of a mixed greens salad. This is also great on a griddled sandwich with vegan Follow Your Heart brand American cheese slices on it.

Yield: Makes about 5 sandwiches

Avocado, Scrambled Egg and Cheddar Jack Breakfast Quesadillas

4 flour tortillas, the 8 inch ones work well here
2 ripe avocados, peeled and sliced into half moons
1 package of So Delicious brand Cheddar Jack cheese shreds
your favorite salsa
Tofutti brand sour cream
6 servings worth of the Follow Your Heart brand Vegan Egg, cooked and kept hot (these are great, they scramble up just like real eggs)
your favorite hot sauce (optional)
Lay the tortillas flat. Spread the cheese evenly over them. Lay the hot, prepared Vegan Egg over half of the cheese and then some avocado slices (the hot eggs will get the cheese to start melting). Add a few pinches of salt and fold them into half moon quesadilla shapes. Heat a large non stick pan for 3 minutes. Spray with non stick spray and cook 2 quesadillas at a time. Cook each side until crisp and golden. Slice in half and top with salsa, sour cream and hot sauce, if you like.

Yield: Serves 3-4

Teriyaki Marinated Grilled Tofu

2 blocks of extra firm tofu that have been frozen, thawed and had all of the water completely squeezed out of the blocks between your palms (this process leaves you with an extra chewy and delicious tofu)
teriyaki marinade: simply whisk together
1/3 cup soy sauce plus 2 Tbs soy sauce, 1/8 cup water, 2 Tbs brown sugar, 1 Tbs sesame oil, 1/2 tsp each minced fresh ginger and minced fresh garlic, 2 Tbs maple syrup, 1 Tbs rice wine vinegar

   Cut each block of the chewy tofu into 6 rectangles or 6 triangles each (you will have 12 total pieces of tofu). Place them in a flat glass sided dish and pour the marinade over them all. Cover and marinate 2 hours. Heat a grill for 15 minutes, then spray it very well with non stick spray. Grill each side of the tofu on the heated grill for about 3 minutes per side. Enjoy with one of my Fried Rice reipes, Peanut Noodle Salad or my Grilled Vegetables.

Yield: Serves 4-5

Classic Beef Tacos

1 package of Boca Burger brand Beef Crumbles or Beyond Meat Beefless Ground or Impossible Meat Ground

spice mix:
1 tsp chili powder mixed with 1/2 tsp salt, 1/2 tsp garlic powder, 1/2 tsp paprika, 1/2 tsp sugar and 1/2 tsp dried oregano.
1 recipe of the Guacamole from this book
your favorite salsa, homemade or store bought
2 cups of feather shredded iceberg lettuce
chopped tomatoes and onions
1 container of Tofutti brand sour cream placed in a squeeze bottle to make it easier to put on top of your taco
1 package of So Delicious brand Cheddar Jack vegan cheese
1 tsp vegetable oil
1 tsp soy sauce
Cholula brand hot sauce (optional)
1 package of hard corn taco shells (you can use soft taco shells too if you prefer)

Heat a large non stick pan for 2 minutes on high. Add in the vegetable oil and then the bag of the thawed vegan beef crumbles. Cook 5 minutes and then add in the soy sauce and the spice mix. Stir and taste for flavor. It should be rich and meaty. Place the taco shells in the oven for 2 minutes on 375 degrees and then assemble your tacos with the beef on the bottom, then the guacamole, salsa, lettuce, cheese, tomatoes, onions and optional hot sauce. Enjoy.

Yield: Serves 4-6

Crispy Fried Cauliflower Steaks with Mushroom Gravy

1 recipe of the Mushroom Gravy from this book
2 heads of cauliflower cut into 4 or 5 flat, 1/2 inch thick steaks each (you will get about 4 or 5 steaks per head of cauliflower, so 8 or 10 total)
3 cups panko bread crumbs mixed with 1 tsp garlic powder, 1/2 tsp each dried oregano and basil, 1/4 tsp black pepper and 1 Tbs nutritional yeast
3 cups flour, 1 1/2 cups water
1/2 inch of vegetable oil in a large non stick pan

Take 1.5 cups of the flour and mix it with 1.5 cups of water. Whisk well, this will act as the egg to make the bread crumbs stick to the cauliflower. Place the other 1.5 cups of flour in a flat glass baking dish. Working from left to right, dip the cauliflower steaks into the flour first, then the flour/ water mixture and lastly into the bread crumbs. Coat them completely. Heat the oil for about 3 minutes on high. Dip one of the steaks into the oil and when bubbles from around it, they are ready to fry. Cook 4 at a time until each side is golden. Drain and serve hot topped with the mushroom gravy. If you drain them on a sheet pan topped with a cookie cooling rack, you can crisp them in the oven again later without burning the bottoms.

Yield: Serves 3-5

Coconut Crusted Chicken, Vegan Shrimp or Tofu

6 Delight Soy brand or Maywah brand vegan chicken steaks or 15
Maywah brand vegan shrimp
If using tofu, 1 block of extra firm tofu, drained and squeezed dry and cut into
6 large triangles
2 cups panko bread crumbs
1 tsp garlic powder
1 Tbs sugar
1 tsp salt
1/4 cup sweetened coconut flakes
2 cups flour
1 cup water
canola or vegetable oil to fry

Place one cup of flour into one bowl, in a second bowl, whisk the other 1 cup of flour with 1 cup of water until you get a pancake batter type consistency and then in a flat casserole dish, mix the panko, salt, sugar, garlic powder and coconut.

Working from left to right, dip the chicken, shrimp or tofu pieces into the flour, then the flour/water mixture (this acts as the egg and helps the panko stick) and finally into the panko/coconut mixture. Once all pieces are coated, heat 1/4 inch of oil in a non stick frying pan over medium high heat for 3 minutes. Dip a piece of the tofu, shrimp or chicken in, if bubbles form around it, they are ready to fry. Cook each side 2-3 minutes or until golden. Drain on a foil lined cookie sheet topped with a cookie cooling rack. Sprinkle with salt and top with sweet chile sauce (available in most grocery stores and Asian markets).

Yield: Serves 3-6

Creamy Rich Penne Primavera

This is tasty served with a few pan seared Beyond Meat brand Italian Sausages.

1 box of Dreamfields brand penne (I like this brand becauase it has extra fiber but looks and tastes like regular white pasta)
1 cup mushrooms sliced thin
1 cup broccoli chopped into small florets
1 cup cauliflower chopped into small florets
1/2 cup asparagus cut into 1 inch pieces
1/2 cup small diced zucchini
2 Tbs lemon juice
1 tsp garlic powder
2 Tbs Earth Balance buttery spread
1/2 cup Vegenaise brand vegan mayo
1 tsp salt or to taste
black or red pepper flakes to taste
1/3 cup nutritional yeast

Bring a large pot of water to a boil. Add in the pasta and cook it for 6 minutes. In the same water, as the pasta is still boiling, add in the zucchini, cauliflower, asparagus, cauliflower and broccoli and cook them with the pasta for another minute. Drain the pasta and vegetables and add them into the drained pasta pot. Add in the rest of the ingredients. Stir, taste for flavor, adjust seasonings if needed and top the pasta with Follow Your Heart brand parmesan and some fresh basil. Enjoy.

Yield: Serves 4-5

Crispy Tofish Fillet Sandwich

3/4 of a block of extra firm tofu , drained and cut into 4 squares 1/4 inch thick, that have been frozen, thawed and had all the water squeezed out
2 cups panko bread crumbs mixed with a tsp black pepper, a teaspoon of garlic powder and a teaspoon of dried dill
1 1/2 cup flour
1/2 cup shredded lettuce
4 slices Follow Your Heart brand American cheese slices or Chao Tomato Cayenne slices (optional)
4 hamburger buns, dill pickle slices

tartar sauce:

mix 1/2 cup vegan mayo with 1/4 tsp fresh chopped dill and 3 Tbs sweet relish

  Take the tofu squares and dip them into 3/4 cup of the flour. Take the other 3/4 cups of flour and whisk it with 3/4 cups of water. Dip the floured tofu in this mixture and then finally into the panko bread crumb mixture. Coat it well with the panko and heat 1/4 inch of vegetable oil into a non stick saute pan. Heat over high heat for about 3 minutes then add the tofu. Cook each side until golden brown, about 2 minutes per side. Drain and set aside. Toast the buns in the oven with the cheese on the top part of the buns, about 2 minutes at 375° if you are adding cheese. Remove from the oven and then assemble the sandwich with the tofu, then the lettuce, pickles & tartar sauce. If you are not using cheese, simply toast the buns in the oven for a minue or two or on a griddle. Enjoy.

Yield: Makes 4 sandwiches   — 293 —

Italian Wedding Soup

5 cups of water with 2.5 Tbs of Bettter than Bouillon brand No Chicken Base or Roasted Garlic Base and 1 Tbs nutritional yeast dissolved into it, 1/2 recipe of the Savory Meatball recipe from this book, rolled into tiny meatballs about the size of a normal size marble & cooked, 1/2 cup sliced celery, 1/2 cup small diced white onion, 2 cloves garlic, minced, 1 Tbs fresh minced dill, 1 cup of cooked and cooled baby bowtie vegan pasta or ditalini, 1 cup peeled sliced carrots

Heat about 1/4 of an inch of water in the bottom of a large pot to a boil. Add in the garlic, onions, celery and carrots. Saute in the water for 5 minutes (the water saute method cuts down fat and will not leave an oily film on your soup like oil would). Add in the rest of the ingredients, bring to a boil and serve warm topped with some Follow Your Heart brand vegan parmesan cheese and my Rustic Olive Bread recipe or my Pesto Bread Stick recipe. *Yield:* Serves 3-4

Egg Salad Sandwich Filling (gluten free)

2 blocks of silken extra firm tofu (make sure it is the kind of silken tofu that comes in a cardboard box, cut into small cubes (it has a nice hard boiled egg texture)
1 Tbs fresh parsley, 1 tsp fresh dill, 1 tsp turmeric powder
1/4 cup minced onion 1/4 cup minced celery, 1 Tbs yellow mustard
1/2 tsp garlic powder
1/4 cup vegan mayo
1 tsp black salt (it has an egg type flavor, available in health food stores or spice stores)
3 Tbs sweet relish
3 Tbs nutritional yeast
salt and pepper to taste

Simply stir all of the ingredients together gently, try not to break up the tofu too much. If it is too dry or bland, add more mayo and salt. Chill in fridge and serve on your favorite bread or toast.

Yield: Makes about 6 sandwiches

Artichoke, Broccolini and Italian Sausage Stromboli

1 ball of the Basic Homemade Dough from this book, risen (the dough recipe makes 2 balls of dough, but you will only use 1 ball here)
1 large or 2 small bunches of broccolini with 1 inch cut off of the bottom and discarded
2 links of Beyond brand Italian sausage with the skin peeled off by running the links under warm water and peeling off the skin
2 cloves rough chopped garlic, 1/2 cup of drained marinated artichokes cut in half from top to bottom, a few pinches of salt, 5 slices of Field Roast brand Chao cheese cut in half

 Drop the broccolini into a large pot of boiling water. Cook 1 minute, drain, cool and squeeze all of the water out of it. Heat a non stick pan for 2 minutes on high. Add in a tsp of olive oil and add in the artichokes, garlic and drained broccolini with a few pinches of salt. Cook in a flat layer 1 minute, stir and cook another minute. Cool completely on a plate. Clean the pan and heat the pan again on high for 2 minutes, add in the sausage, break it up as it browns for about 3 minutes with a pinch of salt. Cool completely, dab the oil off of it and mix with the broccolini and artichokes. Remove the dough from the bowl it rose in but do not re knead it. Place it on a floured surface and push it into about an 18 inch by 10 inch rectangle. You can use a rolling pin if you want. Place the 18 inch side of the dough facing you and place 5 slices of the cheese running the length of the 18 inches, leaving about 1 inch of bare dough facing you. Place the broccolini/artichoke/sausage mixture on top of the cheese, running the whole length of the cheese. Place the rest of the cheese on top of the broccolini mixture and then fold the dough over the top of all of the filling and roll it into a large log shape. Place it on a foil lined cookie sheet and let it rise an hour covered. Heat the oven to 420 degrees. Brush the dough with a little olive oil and bake it about 18 minutes until golden. Brush with a little more olive oil, cool 5 minutes. Serve with my Tomato Sauce recipe.

Yield: Serves 2-3

Crispy Avocado Po Boy Sandwich with Spicy Cajun Remoulade Sauce

3 of your favorite 6 inch hoagie rolls
1 recipe of the Avocado Fries recipe from this book, cooked and warm
1 cup of shredded iceberg lettuce, 3 Tbs melted Earth Balance brand buttery spread, sliced dill pickles, thinly sliced tomatoes, salt and pepper
remoulade sauce: whisk together 3/4 cup Vegenaise brand vegan mayo with 1 Tbs chopped capers, 2 Tbs Franks brand or Louisiana hot sauce, 1/4 tsp salt, 1 tsp lime juice, 1 Tbs chopped scallions, 1 Tbs sweet relish and 1 tsp dijon mustard

Slice the rolls in half and lengthwise and brush each half with the melted Earth Balance. Heat a grill or a large non stick skillet for a few minutes on high and then place the buttered rolls face down on the grill or in the skillet. Brown for a minute until warmed. Remove from the heat and place some of the remoulade on the top and bottom of the rolls. Place 5 to 7 of the fried avocado pieces on the bottom half of each roll and top with the shredded lettuce, tomato, salt, pepper and pickles and place the top half of the roll on the sandwich. Cut the sandwiches in half. Enjoy.

Yield: Makes 3 sandwiches

General Tso's Tofu

1 block extra firm tofu, frozen overnight in the package then thawed, opened and pressed gently with your hands until completely dry and no more water comes out of the tofu block (this freezing prozess makes the tofu extra chewy)

1 cup cornstarch
3/4 cup flour
1/2 tsp salt
1/2 tsp garlic powder
2 cups broccoli florets
vegetable oil to fry

General Tso sauce:
1/3 cup soy sauce
3/4 cup water
1/2 tsp minced garlic
3 Tbs sugar
1/2 Tbs sriracha sauce
3 Tbs hoisin sauce
1 tsp rice vinegar

Bring the General Tso sauce ingredients to a boil, turn down to a simmer. Mix 2 Tbs of cornstarch into 1/4 cup cold water. Dissolve cornstarch very well by stirring quickly with a fork, then pour this little by little into the simmering sauce. Use a whisk and whisk the sauce until thickened. Remove from heat. If too thin still, mix more cornstarch with water and add slowly to the sauce while whisking.

Tear bite sized chunks off of the block of tofu, about 18 total. Put the flour, cornstarch, salt and garlic powder in a big bowl. Add in the tofu and stir around to coat tofu entirely. Remove the tofu. Heat a half inch of oil in a non stick frying pan over medium high heat for 3 minutes. Test to see if it is hot enough by dipping a piece of tofu in. If it bubbles around it, it is ready. Place all of the tofu in and cook 5-7 minutes until browned. Drain on a cookie rack that has been placed on a foil lined cookie sheet (this allows you to heat the tofu in the oven later if you needed to cook the tofu ahead of time, without burning the bottoms). Sprinkle with a little salt.

Bring a pot of water to a boil and drop in the broccoli for 1 minute. Drain and set aside. When the tofu is all cooked, remove from oil, drain and mix the tofu with the General Tsos sauce. Serve over jasmine rice next to the broccoli and top with a little hot chili oil.

Yield: Serves 2-3

Tofu Palak Paneer (gluten free)

1 block of tofu that has been frozen, thawed and had all of the water squeezed from the thawed block between your palms (this process creates an extra chewy tofu), 1/2 cup small diced yellow onions, 2 Tbs Earth Balance brand buttery spread, 2 Tbs vegetable oil whisked together with 1/4 tsp each cumin powder and garlic powder and 1 Tbs tamarind sauce (not paste) **for the sauce:** place in a blender 4 cups of tightly packed fresh baby spinach, 1 tsp garam masala powder, 2 cloves fresh garlic, 1 tsp peeled fresh ginger, 1/4 tsp salt or to taste, a few pinches of cayenne pepper depending on how spicy you like it, 1 medium sized tomato with the top stem cut out, 1 can of coconut milk, 1 tsp sugar

Blend all of the sauce ingredients in the blender until smooth. Set aside. Cut your tofu into 1/2 inch cubes and toss in the oil/cumin/tamarind mixture. Heat a large non stick pan on high for 3 minutes. Add in the Earth Balance and let it melt. Add in the onions and cook 2 minutes. Add in the tofu and cook it all for 3 minutes. Add in the sauce and stir well, cooking it together for about 5 minutes. Stir it often. Serve over basmati. *Yield:* Serves 2-3

Seitan Beef, Cabbage and Mushroom Stir Fried Rice Noodles

4 cups of cooked and cooled wide rice noodles and tossed in a little sesame oil, 1/2 cup thin sliced onions, 1 cup of seitan pulled into bite size chunks
1 cup mushrooms quartered, 1 cup shredded green cabbage
1 tsp each fresh minced garlic and minced ginger, 1 Tbs sesame oil
1/2 cup sliced asparagus cut into 1 inch pieces
sauce: whisk together 2 Tbs soy sauce with 2 Tbs dark soy sauce, 1 tsp rice vinegar, 1 Tbs of hoisin sauce, 1.5 Tbs brown sugar, 2 Tbs vegan oyster sauce, 6 Tbs water and 1 tsp cornstarch **garnish:** chopped scallions and fresh bean sprouts

Heat a large non stick pan for 3 minutes on high. Add in the sesame oil and the cabbage, onions, seitan and mushrooms. Cook 3 minutes, stirring often. Now, add in the garlic, ginger and asparagus. Cook 2 more minutes. Add in the cooked noodles and pour the sauce over the top. Cook 2 more minutes. Garnish with scallions and bean sprouts if desired. Enjoy hot. *Yield:* Serves 2-3

Hard or Soft Taco Salad or Corn Tostadas

4 hard, soft or Azteca brand tortilla bowls (the Azteca bowls are the ones you bake yourself, they are very light, crispy and delicious). You can also use 4 flat, hard corn tostadas for this recipe if that is all you can find.
3/4 bag of thawed Boca Burger brand beef crumbles or Beyond Meat or Impossible Burger Meat, thawed
1/2 tsp soy sauce
1/2 cup small diced onion
2 cloves garlic, minced
1 tsp chili powder, 1 tsp garlic powder, 1/2 tsp salt, small pinch of sugar, 1/4 tsp paprika, 1/2 tsp dried oregano
1 cup of your favorite homemade or store bought salsa
1 recipe of the guacamole from this book
1 cup So Delicious brand shredded Cheddar Jack cheese
1 cup iceberg lettuce, shredded
1 large tomato, diced small
3/4 container of Tofutti brand sour cream
1 recipe of refried beans from this book, warmed
sliced black olives to top (optional)
hot sauce to top (optional)

Heat a teaspoon of olive oil in a non stick pan for a minute on high. Add in the onions and garlic. Saute one minute. Add in the beef crumbles, soy sauce, the chili powder, garlic powder, salt, sugar, oregano and paprika. Cook it all together for a few minutes. Keep warm. Take your tortilla bowl or tostada and place the warmed refried beans on the bottom. Next, add the beef, then the salsa, lettuce, tomatoes, sour cream, cheese, hot sauce and olives.

Yield: Serves 4

American Cheese Omelette (gluten free)

4.5 Tbs Follow Your Heart brand Vegan Egg powder whisked together with 1 cup of very cold water, a pinch of salt and pepper, 1 Tbs minced red pepper and 1 Tbs sliced green onion
1 slice of Follow Your Heart brand American cheese cut in half

Heat a 6 or 8 inch non stick pan for 3 minutes on high. Add in some non stick spray and pour in the egg mixture. Let it sit about 3 minutes until it starts to firm a little on the top. Take a plastic spatula and flip it over, or flip it with the pan if you know how. Add the cheese on top and let it cook 2 to 3 more minutes. Fold in half or into a roll and enjoy warm.

Yield: Makes 1 omelette

Homemade Bagels

You can make these plain or you can sprinkle them with sesame seeds or some "everything bagel" seasoning right after you boil them, right before they go in the oven. These are best eaten right out of the oven, they do not even need to be toasted when eaten this way. I like to slice and top them with Tofutti brand vegan cream cheese or Earth Balance buttery spread. Eating them fresh is when they are tastiest, hot and crispy.

One full recipe of the basic dough recipe from this book, risen

Remove the dough from the bowl it has risen in and carefully transfer it to a lightly floured cutting board, re knead the dough. Divide the dough into 7 equal sized balls. Place them in 7 small bowls, covered, this gives them a round shape. Let rise 1 hour and then, with your finger, create a bagel hole in the middle of each risen ball and pull it gently and evenly to a half inch wide hole. Heat the oven to 450 degrees and bring a large pot of water to a boil. When all are complete, drop 4 bagels at a time into the boiling water. Cook one side 30 seconds and then flip and cook the other side 30 seconds. Remove bagels from the water with a slotted spoon. Drain on a cookie cooling rack on top of a foil lined cookie sheet. If you are going to add sesame seeds or everything bagel seasoning, do it now. Transfer and then bake them directly on top of a cookie sheet lined with foil and parchment paper for 20 minutes or until golden. I place them under the broiler for the last minute to get them extra golden.

Yield: Makes 7 bagels

Homemade From Scratch Seitan (Wheat Meat)

Seitan is "wheat meat". It has a meaty texture and has been made for hundreds of years by Buddhist monks. This method of making seitan is the way it was traditionally made in the past, from whole wheat flour, soy sauce and water. It takes a little longer than just using wheat gluten but the taste and texture is far superior. It makes 2 giant roast size chunks of seitan that you can slice like a Sunday roast or slice and grill like steak. You can also dust slices in flour to pan sear or bread some slices in panko and make seitan parmesan (just substitute slices of it for the vegan chicken in my chicken parm recipe from this book). You can also cut bite size pieces of the cooked seitan and make my Mongolian Beef and Broccoli or Steak Tips with it too.

8 cups of whole wheat flour
5-7 cups of water
broth for simmering:
12 cups water mixed with 1/2 cup soy sauce and 4 dried shitake mushrooms

Mix the whole wheat flour with water (start with 5 cups, if it seems too dry, add more). You want to form a basic dough that feels like a bread dough. Now, get 2 large bowls. Put regular cold tap water in one and hot tap water in the other. Submerge the dough in the cold water and knead and squeeze under the water. Take it out and now submerge the dough in the hot water and squeeze and knead in the hot water. Remove the dough, empty the hot and cold water from the bowls and fill them again, one with hot water, one with cold water. Submerge the dough in the cold water, squeeze and knead again, and then in the hot water again, squeezing and kneading. You will repeat this process about 8 to 10 times total until the water is no longer cloudy when you squeeze the dough submerged in it. What you are left with is pure gluten. It will be very stretchy and sponge like, chewy looking. Cut this into 2 equal sized chunks.

Heat the water/soy sauce/shitake simmering broth in a very large pot until boiling. Add in your two balls of gluten dough. Turn the heat to medium and simmer the seitan for an hour and twenty minutes on a very slow boil, turning the pieces over a few times during simmering for even cooking. Remove from the water and cool the seitan chunks down to cook with later or slice it into pieces like a roast with mushroom gravy and roasted potatoes and carrots. Also works great for my Seitan Piccata recipe from this book.

Yield: Serves 8-12

Sri Lankan Green Bean Pineapple Curry with Pan Seared Tofu

1 recipe of my Pan Seared Tofu from this book
1 medium sized pineapple, peeled and cut into
 medium sized chunks
1 tsp curry powder, 1/2 tsp turmeric powder
1 tsp mustard seeds, 1/2 tsp ground cloves
1/2 tsp ground cardamom, 2 Tbs green curry paste
1 medium onion, medium diced
1 tsp minced fresh ginger, 2 minced garlic cloves
1/2 of a small thin hot red pepper, seeded and
choped finely, 1 small green bell pepper, medium diced
1 cup of green beans, cleaned with the ends snipped
1/2 tsp garlic powder, 3/4 cup water
1 can coconut milk, 1 tsp salt, 1 Tbs Better Than
Bouillon brand No Chicken Base, 2 Tbs sugar
1 tsp vegetable oil, chopped scallions to garnish

Dry roast the curry powder, cardamom, mustard seeds, turmeric and cloves in a dry non stick pan over medium heat, stirring often, for 3 minutes until fragrant. Set aside. Heat a large non stick pan for 2 minutes on high. Add in the oil, red peppers, green peppers, green beans, ginger, onion and garlic and a pinch of salt. Saute 2 minutes and add in the pineapple. Cook 2 more minutes and then add in the rest of the ingredients and toasted spices (do not add the seared tofu in yet though). Bring to a boil and simmer on medium high for 15 minutes. Add in the tofu. Taste for flavor. If you like it a little sweeter, add a little more sugar. Simmer 2 more minutes and serve over steamed basmari rice. This dish is very tasty with my Broccoli Pakora recipe.

Yield: Serves 3-5

Iowa Corn Pancakes

2 cups King Arthur flour, sifted
3 Tbs sugar, pinch of salt, 4 Tbs vegetable shortening
1 tsp baking powder, 1/2 tsp baking soda
2 cups freshly opened plain club soda mixed with 1/2 Tbs apple cider vinegar
1/2 cup fresh or canned corn kernels

Place flour, sugar, salt , baking soda and baking powder in a large bowl. Cut in the shortening with a pastry cutter until it forms small balls. Cutting in the shortening means placing the shortening onto the flour mixture and pushing down over and over with the pastry cutter until the shortening is mixed into the flour mixture completely. You can use a fork for this if you have no pastry cutter, it just takes a little longer. Whisk in the club soda/vinegar and the corn kernels. Do not over mix. Heat an electric griddle. Spray with non stick spray pour on about 1/3 cup of the batter on the griddle at a time. When the tops bubble, flip them and cook another two minutes. Serve warm topped with Earth Balance vegan buttery spread. Real maple syrup is good too.

Yield: Serves 3-5

Jumbo Chili Cheese Dogs

1 pack of Lightlife brand Jumbo Dogs (there are 5 in a pack) or 1 pack
of Beyond Meat brand Bratwurst Sausages
5 vegan hot dog buns
1/2 recipe of the nacho cheese sauce from this book, warmed
for the chili:
1 cup of your favorite homemade or store bought tomato sauce
3/4 cup of Boca Burger brand vegan beef crumbles or Impossible
brand vegan crumbles browned in a non stick pan 4 minutes
1/2 tsp each of chili powder, paprika, salt, cumin and liquid smoke
1/2 tsp hot sauce (optional)
1/4 tsp dried oregano
2 Tbs water
1/2 tsp soy sauce

   For the chili, simply place the chili ingredients in a pot and simmer over
medium heat for 10 minutes, stirring often. Heat a non stick pan on high for
2 minutes and spray it with a little non stick spray. Brown the hot dogs
slightly for a few minutes. Toast your buns in the oven at 375 for 3 minutes.
Lay a hot dog in the warmed bun and then top it with some chili and some of
the warmed nacho cheese sauce. Enjoy.

Yield: Makes 4-5 hot dogs

Baked Balsamic Tofu Cacciatore

1 tsp Better Than Bouillon
brand No Chicken Base
a double batch worth of my Chewy
Tofu recipe from this book, tossed in
3 Tbs of balsamic vinegar after cooked
1 can of San Marzano tomatoes,
crushed by hand with the juices
2 medium green peppers, seeds
removed and cut into thin rings
1 medium onion, diced
3 cloves of garlic, minced, 1 bay leaf
1/2 cup red wine
1 tsp olive oil, 1/2 tsp each dried
basil, garlic powder and dried oregano
1 tsp sugar, 1 tsp salt, fresh basil to top

 Spray non stick spray in a large, flat sided glass bakig dish and then lay
the tofu in the bottom and the green pepper rings on top. In a non
stick saute pan, add in the olive oil and heat for 2 minutes. Add in the onions,
garlic and bay leaf. Cook 3 minutes, then add in the wine, tomatoes, garlic
powder, dried basil, oregano, the No Chicken base, sugar and salt. Cook for 3
minutes and then pour this over the tofu and peppers. Bake, uncovered, at 400
degrees for 20 minutes. Top with the fresh basil, remove the bay leaf, enjoy.

Yield: Serves 4-5

Chicken Fried Steak Cheddar Chive Biscuits

1 prepared warm batch of the Cheddar Chive biscuits from page 114
1 pack of Impossible brand ground mixed together with 1 tsp garlic powder, 1/4 tsp black pepper, a pinch of salt and 1/2 tsp cumin and flattened into 6 individual 1/4 inch thick patties
3/4 cup flour whisked together with 3/4 cup water **for the coating :** 1.5 cups flour mixed with 1/2 cup cornstarch, 1 tsp garlic powder, 1/4 tsp each black pepper & dried oregano

Dip the steak patties, one at a time, in the dry flour mixture, then into the flour/water mixture. Repeat the process again, so that each patty is double battered, lastly dipping it into the dry flour mixture. Repeat with the rest of the patties. Heat 1/2 inch of of vegetable oil in a non stick pan on high for 3 minutes and then add in the patties. Cook each side about 4 minutes or until golden. Drain them. Split your biscuits and serve with the patties. *Yield:* Makes about 6 biscuit sandwiches

Crispy Corn Dog Bites

1 pack of Lightlife brand Jumbo Dogs vegan hot dogs, each link cut into 3 equal size pieces, or 4 Beyond Meat brand Bratwurst Sausage links, each cut into 3 equal size pieces
1 cup yellow cornmeal, 1 cup plain flour, 1 Tbs sugar, 1 tsp salt
1 tsp garlic powder, 1/2 tsp baking powder
1.5 cups freshly opened plain club soda, 1 cup plain flour
1 inch of canola oil for frying

In a large bowl, whisk together the cornmeal, the flour, salt, sugar, baking powder and garlic powder. Whisk in the club soda until you have a smooth, medium thick batter. Heat the canola oil in a non stick pan for 3 or 4 minutes on high. When you can flick a little batter into the oil and it bubbles, you are ready to fry. Dip the hot dog or sausage pieces, one by one into the batter. Coat them completely. Drop them carefully into the oil. If any hot dog is showing, you can carefully add a little more batter to the tops after frying has begun. Cook each side about 3 minutes or until golden. Sprinkle with a little salt right out of the oil. Drain on a cookie cooling rack that has been placed on top of a foil lined cookie sheet. This way you can crisp up the leftovers later without burning the bottoms.

Yield: Makes 12-15 bites

Philly Style Tomato Pie

Tomato Pie is a delicious Philly deep dish Sicilian style pizza topped only with a rich, sweet and thick tomato sauce. Enjoy cold or hot.

for the dough:

3 1/2 cups King Arthur brand Flour
1 tsp yeast
1 tsp extra virgin olive oil
1/2 tsp salt
1 3/4 cups water

for the sauce:

1 29 oz can of San Marzano tomatoes, pureed
3 cloves minced garlic
3 Tbs tomato paste
3 Tbs sugar
1 Tbs balsamic vinegar
1/2 tsp salt
few pinches of dried basil and dried
oregano, 1/2 tsp extra virgin olive oil

Begin with the dough since it requires time for the starter to mature. Mix 1 3/4 cup of the flour with 1 1/2 cups of water that has 1/2 tsp of the yeast stirred into it. Stir well and cover for 4-6 hours or overnight. After 4-6 hours, mix the remaining 1 3/4 cup flour with the 1/2 tsp salt (do NOT forget the salt). Take the remaining 1/2 tsp yeast and mix it with 3 Tbs of water and the tsp of olive oil. Pour this into the starter that just sat 4-6 hours. Mix in the flour too and knead it all together until you have a dough ball. If it is too wet, add more flour. Cover this and let it rise 45 minutes, then punch it down and let it rise another 45 minutes covered or you can cover it and let it sit in the fridge overnight or up to 3 days. When it is risen, take a 12 x 17 inch sheet pan and grease it with a 1/2 Tbs olive oil. Take your risen dough and place it on a floured cutting board. Do not re knead it, simply push it into a large rectangle shape with your hands. Use a rolling pin to make it large enough to fit the sheet pan. Transfer it to the sheet pan and cover, letting it rise an hour. As it rises, make the sauce.

Place the 1/2 tsp olive oil into a pan and heat for 2 minutes on high. Add the minced garlic. Cook 20 seconds and then add in the rest of the sauce ingredients. Simmer 30 minutes, stirring often, until thick. Cool the sauce a few minutes in the fridge. When the dough has risen, pre heat the oven to 425 degrees. Spread the sauce evenly over the risen dough. Brush the edges with a little olive oil. Bake the topped tomato pie for 18 to 22 minutes or until the crust is golden on the bottom and sides. Remove from the oven and brush a little more olive oil onto the crust sides. You can top this with Follow Your Heart brand vegan parmesan cheese if you like. Enjoy.

Yield: Serves about 6 or 7 people

Spicy Sweet and Sour Ham, Asparagus and Broccolini

1 Tbs vegetable oil, 1 cup of Maywah brand vegan ham cut into thin triangles, 1 cup each of broccolini and asparagus with the woody bottoms removed and discarded, cut into 1 inch pieces, 1 cup chopped baby bok choy, 1/2 cup peeled sliced carrots, 1/3 cup each medium diced onion and green pepper, 1 tsp each minced garlic and ginger, 3/4 cup of homemade or your favorite sweet and sour sauce mixed with 2 tsp hot chili paste, 1 tsp sesame oil and 1 tsp hoisin sauce

Heat a half Tbs of the vegetable oil in a non stick pan for 2 minutes on high. Add in the ham triangles and brown each side about 2 minutes, flipping once until crisped. Remove them from the pan and add in the other half Tbs of vegetable oil. Add the ginger, bok choy, garlic, broccolini, carrots, onions and peppers. Let them sit in a flat layer for 30 seconds, then add in the asparagus and then stir around for 3 more minutes. Add in the crisped ham and the sauce. Stir until heated through. Serve over steamed rice. *Yield:* Serves 2-3

Spaghtetti Primavera with Mushrooms, Broccoli, Cauliflower and Garlic Butter

1 box of Dreamfields brand spaghetti or Barilla brand White Fiber spaghetti (these are high fiber pastas that taste like regular white pastas)

1.5 cups of sliced button or cremini mushrooms

1/2 cup zucchini cut into thick 1 inch strips

3/4 cup each broccoli and cauliflower cut into bite sized chunks

4 Tbs of fresh lemon juice, 1/3 cup each red bell pepper cut into strips and asparagus cut into 1 inch pieces, 2 Tbs nutritional yeast,

2 Tbs fresh basil, 1/2 cup Earth Balance Buttery Spread

1 Tbs fresh minced garlic

1 tsp garlic powder, 1 tsp salt or to taste

Follow Your Heart brand Parmesan Cheese and fresh basil to garnish

Heat the buttery spread over medium heat in a small pan. Add in the fresh garlic and cook for one minute after the butter is melted. Set aside. Bring a large pot of water to a boil. Add in the spaghetti. Stir often with tongs. Cook 6 minutes. After 6 minutes, throw the zucchini, mushrooms, spinach, asparagus, cauliflower, broccoli and mushrooms right into the water with the pasta. Cook it all together for 1.5 more minutes. Drain it all, place it back into the pot and add in the garlic butter and the rest of the ingredients. Stir well, taste for seasoning. Adjust with lemon juice or salt if needed. Top with the vegan parmesan and fresh basil.

Yield: Serves 3-5

Chinese Broccoli and Tofu in Black Bean Garlic Sauce

1 bunch of broccolini or Chinese broccoli with 1 inch of the tough bottoms cut off 1/2 cup carrots peeled and cut into thick 2 inch matchsticks, 1/2 cup sliced mushrooms, 1 block of tofu that has been frozen, thawed and had all of the water squeezed out of the block between your palms (this creates an extra chewy tofu) and torn into bite size chunks, 1/3 cup each red bell pepper, zucchini and asparagus cut into thick 2 inch matchticks and 1 tsp fresh peeled grated ginger, 1 Tbs sesame oil **sauce:** blend in a blender 1/3 cup soy sauce, 1 clove fresh garlic, 1/3 cup water, 1 tsp hot chili paste, 1 Tbs rice vinegar, 1 Tbs brown sugar, 4 Tbs hoisin sauce and 1/2 Tbs cornstarch and 3 Tbs cooked black beans, set aside

Heat a large non stick pan for 3 minutes on high. Add in the sesame oil then the tofu, broccoli, carrots, ginger, mushrooms and red peppers. Let it sit in a flat layer for about a minute and then stir it around. Let it sit another minute, stir and let sit another minute. Add in the zucchini and asparagus. Cook it all together 2 more minutes, stir the sauce and pour it in and stir until thickened. Enjoy over steamed rice.   *Yield:* Serves 2

Parmesan Mushroom Risotto Cakes

2 cups water whisked together with 1.5 Tbs of Better Than Bouillon brand No Chicken Base or Roasted Garlic Base, 1 cup arborio risotto rice, 2 cups sliced button mushrooms pinch of salt + salt to taste, 1/2 container of Go Veggie brand vegan parmesan cheese, 1/4 cup nutritional yeast, 3 cups flour 1 box of panko bread crumbs mixed with 1 tsp salt, 1 tsp each garlic powder and oregano

Heat a non stick saute pan for 3 minutes over medium high heat, then add a tsp olive oil, then the sliced mushrooms. Add a pinch of salt and a pinch of dried oregano. Saute 3 minutes. Heat the 2 cups of water/bouillon mixture with a pinch of salt. When boiling, add the arborio risotto rice. Stir, cover and turn to low and cook 15 to 20 minutes until cooked. Cool completely. Add to the cooled rice, 3/4 cup of flour, the vegan parmesan cheese, nutritional yeast, cooked mushrooms and salt to taste. You want a consistency that can easily be formed into cakes. If it seems too wet, add more flour. Taste for salt and cheesy flavor, it may need more salt, parm or nutritional yeast. Form into 2.5 inch cakes. Fill a bowl with 1 cup flour and coat the cakes. Take a second bowl and whisk together one cup of flour with one cup of water, whisk well and then dip the cakes into this, and finally into a flat dish filled with the panko mixture. Coat cakes completely. Heat a 1/2 inch of vegetable oil in a non stick pan over medium heat for 3 minutes. When you can dip a cake into it and bubbles form around it, it is ready to cook. Cook each side about 3 minutes until golden.

Yield: Serves 6-8

Cajun Spicy Mustard Blackened Tofu

2 blocks of extra firm tofu that have been frozen, thawed and had all of the water completely squeezed out of the blocks between your palms (this creates an extra chewy tofu)
marinade: whisk together 2 Tbs spicy brown mustard with 1 tsp vegetable oil, 2 Tbs water, 1 tsp soy sauce, 1 tsp liquid smoke, 1 Tbs maple syrup, 1 tsp apple cider vinegar and a pinch of salt
spice mix: mix together in a flat dish 3 Tbs chili powder, 2 Tbs smoked paprika, 1 tsp garlic powder, 1 tsp sugar and a pinch of salt

Cut each block of tofu into 6 squares. Brush each side with the marinade and then dip each piece into the spice mix, coat both sides. Heat a large non stick or cast iron pan on high for 3 minutes. Place the tofu flat in the hot pan and let each side blacken for about 2 minutes. It will make some smoke, so make sure the oven fan is on. I like to serve these with my Ranch recipe from this book.   *Yield:* Serves 4-5

African Ground Nut Stew

1 medium onion diced small
1 can tomato paste
1 tsp each minced fresh ginger and garlic
1/2 a bunch of cilantro chopped
3 cups stemmed, chopped collard greens
1 medium red bell pepper medium diced
1 tsp fresh lime juice
1 medium sweet potato peeled and medium diced
1 recipe of the Pan Seared Tofu from this book
1/2 cup smooth peanut
butter (I use sunflower butter due to a nut allergy)
1 tsp each dried cumin and garlic powder a pinch of cayenne pepper to taste if you want it spicy
1.5 Tbs green curry paste
6 cups of water mixed with 2 Tbs of Better Than Bouillon brand Roasted Garlic Base,
2 Tbs sugar and 1 tsp soy sauce
salt and pepper to taste
chopped peanuts as an optional garnish

Heat 1 tsp of vegetable oil in a large pot for 2 minutes on high. Add in the onions, garlic and ginger. Cook 2 minutes and add in the sweet potato and collard greens. Add in a few pinches of salt. Cook 2 more minutes and then add in the rest of the ingredients. Stir well and bring to a boil. Turn down the heat and simmer to 20 minutes, stirring often, then add the lime juice. If it is too thick, you can add a little more water.

Yield: Serves 3-4

Garlic Broccolini and Spicy Sausage Mushroom Pizza

1 risen ball of dough from the Basic Dough recipe from this book (the recipe makes 2 balls, but you will only use 1 ball here), 1 pack of Follow Your Heart brand soft block mozzarella (you will need to shred it yourself, make sure it is the soft block, it melts best), 2 links of Beyond Meat brand Italian sausage with the skin peeled off (running it under cold water makes it peel easier), 1/2 cup broccolini chopped into half inch pieces, 1/2 cup sliced mushrooms, 1 tsp rough chopped garlic, 1/4 cup of your favorite homemade or store bought tomato sauce, 1 tsp olive oil, a few shakes of dried red pepper flakes

Remove the risen dough from the bowl but do not knead it. Place it on a large floured cutting board and simply press it down gently and evenly into a 16 inch circle shape. You can use a floured rolling pin to get it stretched out easier. Place it in a non stick sprayed 16 inch round pan and allow it to rise for 1 hour. Heat a large non stick pan for 3 minutes on high. Add in the peeled sausage and break it up with a spatula and brown it. Sprinkle a few red pepper flakes into it. Remove from the pan and drain it on a paper towel lined plate. Heat the pan another minute on high and add in the oil, mushrooms, garlic, broccolini and a pinch of salt. Saute about 3 minutes, stirring often and then cool them. Heat the oven to 430 degrees. Spread the tomato sauce on the risen dough. Brush the dough edges with a little olive oil. Place the sausage, mushrooms and broccolini on top of the sauce. Cover it all with the cheese and a pinch of salt, dried oregano and garlic powder. Bake about 15 minutes. Place it under the broiler for 2 more minutes to brown the crust and melt the cheese fully. Remove from oven and let it sit 10 minutes before cutting. Enjoy.   *Yield:* Serves 2-3

Pesto Pasta

1 box of your favorite shaped pasta (I like Ronzoni brand Smart Taste pasta), 1 recipe of the Basil Pesto from this book (page 82), prepared

Bring a large pot of water to a boil, add your favorite pasta. My rule of thumb is to always cook my pasta 2 to 3 minutes less than the box suggests for the best al dente texture since it continues to cook after drained. Drain the pasta. Coat with as much pesto as you like, a few pinches of salt, 2 Tbs nutritional yeast and 2 Tbs of Earth Balance Buttery Spread. I like the non soy version the best. Top with some Go Veggie brand vegan parmesan cheese or Follow Your Heart brand shredded parmesan.

Yield: Serves 4-6

Artichoke Garlic Spinach and Mushroom White Pizza

1 ball of the Basic Dough recipe from this book, risen (the dough recipe makes 2 balls of dough, you will only use 1 here), 2 cups of sliced button or cremini mushrooms, 2 cloves minced garlic, 1/4 tsp dried oregano, 3 cups fresh baby spinach, 1/4 tsp salt **the artichoke white sauce:** blend in a food processor until smooth 3 Tbs Tofutti brand cream cheese, 4 Tbs soy free Veganaise brand vegan mayo, 1 small jar of drained marinated artichokes, 1/4 tsp salt, 1 tsp lemon juice, 3 Tbs water and 4 Tbs nutritional yeast

Remove the risen dough from the bowl and place it on a large floured cutting board. Do not knead it. Place a little flour on top and gently press it into a flat circle. Take a rolling pin, roll into a 16 inch circle. Place it in a non stick sprayed non stick pizza pan. Cover it, allow it to rise 1 hour. While it rises, heat a large non stick pan on high for 3 minutes. Add in 1 tsp olive oil, the garlic, mushrooms, oregano and salt. Saute them, stirring often, for 3 minutes. Add the spinach. Saute 2 more minutes and then cool it down. Take the now risen pizza dough and spread the artichoke sauce evenly over the top. Place the spinach and mushroom mixture over the sauce. Heat the oven to 430 degrees and bake about 16 minutes. Place it under the broiler for another minute so that the top and crust get a little more browned. Remove from the oven, brush the crust with a little olive oil. Enjoy. *Yield:* Serves 3-4

Bean Curd and Vegetables in Garlic White Sauce

1 cup broccoli florets cut into bite size pieces, 1/3 cup peeled sliced carrots, 1/2 cup sliced mushrooms, 1/2 cup cauliflower cut into bite size pieces, 1/3 cup each zucchini and asparagus cut into bite size pieces, 1/2 tsp each rough chopped ginger and garlic, 1 prepared recipe of the Pan Seared Chewy Tofu from this book, 1 Tbs vegetable oil **for the sauce:** 1.5 cups of water whisked together with 1 tsp soy sauce, 1 Tbs Better Than Bouillon brand Roasted Garlic Base, 1 tsp sesame oil, 1 Tbs vegan oyster sauce, 1 tsp sugar, 1 tsp rice vinegar and 1.5 Tbs cornstarch

Heat a large non stick skillet on high for 3 minutes. Add in the vegetable oil and the garlic, ginger, broccoli, carrots and cauliflower. Cook in a flat layer for 1 minute and then stir. Cook it 2 more minutes, stirring often. Add in the zucchini and asparagus. Cook 1 more minute and then add the tofu. Stir and cook 1 minute and add in the whisked sauce. When it thickens (after 30 seconds or so) stir it well and serve over steamed rice.

Yield: Serves 3-4

Rich and Smooth Indian Butter Chicken (gluten free)

If using chicken, dice up 1 cup of Maywah brand or Delight Soy brand non breaded chicken nuggets. **If using tofu**, freeze one block of extra firm tofu, thaw it and completely squeeze all of the water out of it (this creates a chewy, chicken type texture for the tofu) and tear it into bite size chunks.
1.5 cups plain tomato sauce
1.5 cups coconut milk
6 Tbs Earth Balance brand Buttery Spread
3 Tbs Tofutti brand vegan sour cream
1/2 Tbs garam masala powder
1 tsp fresh grated ginger
1 tsp garlic powder
1/4 tsp cumin powder
1/2 tsp paprika
1 Tbs tamarind sauce
salt and pepper to taste
1/4 tsp cayenne pepper (more or less depending on desired spice level)
1/2 cup medium diced onion
2 cloves minced garlic

Heat a non stick pan over high heat for 3 minutes. Add in 2 Tbs of the butter and the chicken or tofu. Season with a little salt and pepper. Cook a few minutes until golden. Add in the rest of the butter and the onions, garlic and ginger. Cook 3 minutes more. Add in the rest of the ingredients. Whisk well. Simmer for 6 minutes, stirring often. Add more salt, tamarind or spices if needed. Serve over steamed basmati rice and my Onion Naan recipe from this book and top with my Indian Smoked Paprika Onion Chutney recipe. Enjoy.

Yield: serves 3-5

Radiatore Pasta with Chicken, Leeks, Peas and Kale

The radiatore pasta here holds the sauce and other ingredients nicely in this dish. If you can not find radiatore, you can use fusilli pasta or even vegan egg noodles if you can find those.

1 lb of radiatore pasta cooked 5 minutes, then drained and cooled in cold water to stop the cooking, 2 cloves chopped garlic, 1/2 cup cleaned leeks cut into half moons, 1/3 cup green pitted olives cut in half, 1 cup kale stemmed and finely chopped, 1/2 cup thawed or fresh peas, 1 large tomato diced, 1/2 cup Maywah brand or Delight Soy brand chicken nuggets cut into bite size cubes (you can use my Pan Seared Tofu recipe for this instead if desired), juice of 1 medium lemon, 4 Tbs Earth Balance brand buttery spread, 1/2 tsp salt or to taste, 3 Tbs nutritional yeast

Heat a large non stick pan for 3 minutes on high and then add in 1 Tbs of the Earth Balance. Melt it and add in the chicken, kale, leeks, garlic and olives. Spread it all in a flat layer and let it all sit for 2 minutes. Add a pinch of salt and stir. Let it sit another minute until the kale is wilted. Add in the peas and tomatoes. Cook 1 minute and then add in the pasta, lemon juice, nutritional yeast, the rest of the Earth Balance and salt. Stir all together until the Earth Balance melts. Enjoy topped with some Follow Your Heart brand shredded parmesan. *Yield:* Serves 3-4

Mushroom Stroganoff

4 cups button or cremini mushrooms, sliced
1 cup plain rice milk whisked together with 1 tsp soy sauce and 2 Tbs flour
1/2 cup small diced onion
2 cloves garlic, minced
a few small thyme leaves removed from stem, chopped
1/4 tsp dried oregano
1/2 tsp garlic powder
2 Tbs Earth Balance buttery spread
1/2 tsp salt, black pepper to taste
1/2 container of Tofutti brand vegan sour cream
2 Tbs nutritional yeast
1 package of vegan egg noodles cooked or rotini noodles

Bring a large non stick pan to high heat for 2 minutes. Now, add in the butter and the mushrooms, minced garlic and onions. Cook for 2 minutes, add in the thyme, salt and oregano. Cook 4 more minutes and then add in the non dairy milk mixture, nutritional yeast, black pepper and garlic powder. Cook 30 seconds then add in the sour cream, stir well. If it seems too tight, add in a little non dairy milk to loosen the mixture up. If it seems too loose, add more sour cream. Taste for flavor, add salt and pepper if needed. Serve it over cooked noodles with an extra topping of sour cream if desired.

Yield: Serves 2-3

Penne with Sun Dried Tomatoes, Chicken, Mushrooms, Broccoli and Marinated Artichokes

1 box cooked Dreamfields or Barilla White Fiber Penne Pasta drained
and cooled completely in cold water then drained again
1/2 jar of oil cured sun dried tomatoes, the ones packed in oil, not the dried
1 cup chopped cauliflower florets, 2 small jars marinated artichokes drained
2 cups sliced white or cremini mushrooms
1.5 cups chopped broccoli florets, 2 cups flat leaf baby spinach
1 cup diced Delight Soyfoods brand or Maywah brand vegetarian chicken
steaks (if you prefer, you can use the chewy tofu recipe from this book
instead of the vegan chicken), 1 Tbs balsamic vinegar
3 cloves chopped garlic, 1 tsp dried oregano, juice of 1 large lemon
1/3 cup nutritional yeast, 6 leaves chopped fresh basil
3 Tbs Earth Balance soy free buttery spread, 1 tsp salt

Heat one tablespoon of olive oil over medium high heat 1 minute then add
the mushrooms, broccoli, cauliflower, sun dried tomatoes and vegan
chicken or tofu. Cook 3 minutes, then add the spinach, cook 1 minute,
then add salt, the basil, artichokes, lemon juice and the cooked pasta. Stir
until heated and coated well. Add nutritional yeast, buttery spread,
balsamic and oregano, remove from heat. If too bland, add more lemon
juice and salt. Top with Follow Your Heart brand parmesan.

Yield: Serves 3-4

Seitan, Tofu or Chicken Piccata

if using tofu, freeze a block of extra firm tofu, thaw it and completely squeeze all
of the water out of the block and cut into 6 large triangles (this freezing process
creates an extra chewy, delicious tofu)

if using seitan, make my Homemade Seitan recipe from this book and
slice into cutlet sized 1/4 inch thick slices

if using chicken, use 5 Maywah brand non
breaded chicken patties
1 cup of flour mixed with 1/2 cup
cornstarch, 1 tsp garlic powder, 1/2 tsp
salt and 1/2 tsp dried basil and oregano
piccata sauce:
1/2 cup melted Earth
Balance brand buttery spread
2 Tbs fresh lemon juice
3 Tbs capers, rough chopped
pinch of salt, 1 clove minced garlic

Dip the tofu, seitan or vegetarian chicken in the flour/cornstarch mixture. Coat
completely. Heat a large non stick skillet with a 3 tablespoons of vegetable oil over
medium high for 3 minutes. Add in the coated seitan, tofu or vegetarian chicken.
Cook each side about 3 minutes or until browned. Sprinkle with a little salt straight
out of the oil. For the sauce, simply heat it in a small sauce pan for 2 minutes until it
comes to a boil. Spoon the sauce over the cooked tofu, seitan or vegetarian chicken.
Garnish with chopped basil.

Yield: Serves 3-4

Sesame Orange Tofu or Chicken

1 block of extra form tofu that
has been frozen, thawed and had
all of the water squeezed out of
the block (this will leave you with an
extra chewy and delicious tofu) or 1 pack
of Maywah or Delight Soy brand
non breaded chicken nuggets cut in half
1 Tbs sesame seeds, toasted in a dry
non stick skillet on medium heat
until slightly browned
3/4 cup of flour mixed with 1/2
cup cornstarch, 1 tsp garlic
powder and 1/2 tsp salt
1 medium white onion, diced
into medium size chunks, 1 tsp
freshly grated ginger
1 medium red bell pepper diced
into medium size chunks
1 green pepper diced into
medium size chunks
1 cup broccoli florets, 1/2 cup sliced
mushrooms, 1/2 Tbs sesame oil
1/2 inch vegetable oil to fry

sauce:
1 cup fresh orange juice
1 Tbs soy sauce
2 Tbs sugar
2 Tbs hoisin sauce
1/4 tsp minced garlic
1.5 Tbs cornstarch

For the sauce, whisk all of the sauce ingredients together and set aside.
Break the tofu into bite size chunks. Toss the chicken or tofu (whichever you
are using) in the seasoned flour/cornstarch mixture. Heat the 1/2 inch of
vegetable oil in a large non stick skillet for 4 minutes on medium high. Dip a
piece of tofu or chicken in, if bubbles form, it is ready to fry. Cook each side
until golden and drain on a cookie cooling rack that has been place on a foil
lined cookie sheet. Sprinkle tofu or chicken with a little salt. Discard the oil
and heat the non stick skillet on high for 3 minutes. Add in the sesame oil,
onions, broccoli, mushrooms, ginger and peppers. Saute 4 minutes and add
in the chicken or tofu. Cook a minute more and then add in the sauce
ingredients to coat the tofu or chicken and vegetables until it thickens (about
30 seconds). Add in the toasted sesame seeds. Serve over steamed jasmine or
brown rice.

Yield: Serves 2-4

Spicy Rice Noodle, Japanese Eggplant, Mushroom and Tofu Coconut Ginger Soup

2 cups of water whisked together with 2 Tbs Better Than Bouillon brand No Chicken Base or Roasted Garlic Base until dissolved

1 can plain coconut milk, 2 Tbs sugar

1 tsp turmeric powder

1 recipe of the Pan Seared Tofu from this book

2 tsp toasted sesame oil

1 or 2 tsp of Sriricha or hot chili paste (depending on spice level desired)

1 cup of sliced button mushrooms

1/2 cup white onions cut into thin half moons

1 tsp soy sauce

2 Tbs green curry paste

1 tsp each minced garlic and minced ginger

1 cup of Japanese eggplant, cut on a bias angle into bite size chunks

1/2 cup bite size chopped broccoli

fresh scallions, basil and cilantro (optional garnish)

2 cups of cooked and cooled flat medium thin rice noodles

2 cups fresh baby spinach

Heat a non stick pan for 3 minutes on high. Add in the sesame oil, garlic, ginger, onions, eggplant, broccoli and mushrooms. Saute for 3 minutes. Mix the coconut broth mixture with the sugar, turmeric powder, curry paste, soy sauce, Sriracha and a pinch of salt. Add this into the vegetables with the spinach and simmer for 4 minutes. Add in the cooked rice noodles and tofu. Garnish with the fresh scallions, basil and cilantro if desired. Enjoy.

Yield: Serves 3

Szechuan Cabbage, Asparagus and Ginger Tofu

3 cups of cabbage cut into half inch cubes, 3/4 cup broccoli cut into bite size pieces
1 cooked recipe of the Pan Seared Tofu from this book, 1/3 cup peeled carrots sliced
1/2 cup asparagus cut on an angle, 1/2 cup cremini mushrooms quartered
2 cloves garlic minced and 1 Tbs of fresh grated ginger, 1 Tbs sesame oil
for the sauce: whisk together 1/3 cup soy sauce with 1/2 cup water, 2 Tbs sweet
chili sauce, 1 tsp hot chili paste or sriracha (more if you want it spicier), 1 Tbs sugar,
1 Tbs hoisin sauce, 1 tsp rice vinegar, 1 tsp Better Than Bouillon brand No
Chicken Base or Roasted Garlic Base and 1 Tbs cornstarch

Heat a large non stick pan for 3 minutes on high. Add in the sesame oil and then
the mushrooms, cabbage, broccoli and carrots. Push it into a flat layer and let it
cook 2 minutes undisturbed. Stir after 2 minutes and let cook another 4 minutes,
stirring often. Add in the garlic, ginger tofu and asparagus. Cook it all together 2
more minutes. Whisk the sauce again and add it in. Cook about 30 seconds
until the sauce thickens as you stir. Serve over steamed rice. Enjoy.

Yield: Serves 2-3

Crispy Sesame Beef and Tofu with Vegetables in Black Bean Garlic Sauce

1 cup of seitan, homemade or store bought, torn into chunks
1 block extra firm tofu, frozen and then thawed with all of the water
squeezed from block (this gives the tofu an extra chewy texture) torn into chunks
1 cup flour mixed with 1/2 cup cornstarch, 1 tsp garlic powder and 1/2 tsp salt
1/2 cup asparagus cut into 3/4 inch pieces
1/2 cup peeled carrots, sliced on a bias angle, 1 cup broccoli cut into bite size pieces
1/2 cup black cooked beans, 1/2 cup sliced button mushrooms
1/3 cup small diced onions, 1/2 cup baby corn cut in half
for the sauce:
1/2 cup soy sauce
1.5 Tbs cornstarch, 3/4 cup water
2 Tbs toasted sesame seeds, 3 Tbs hoisin sauce
3 Tbs sugar, 1 Tbs rice wine vinegar
1/2 tsp each minced ginger and garlic

For the sauce, whisk the sauce ingredients together in a sauce pan and heat
over medium heat until thickened. Add a little more waer if it seems too thick. Set
aside. Dredge the tofu and seitan in the flour/cornstarch mixture. Heat a large
non stick skillet with a 1/2 inch of vegetable oil inside for 3 minutes on high.
Add in the dreged tofu and seitan. Cook until crisped. Drain and drain the oil as
well. Heat the empty skillet back up for 2 minutes on high. Add in 1 Tbs of
sesame oil and add in the broccoli, onions, mushroom, corn and carrots. Cook
for 3 minutes, stirring often, then add in the asparagus, then add in the cooked
tofu and seitan. Cook this for 2 more minutes and add in the black beans and as
much or as little sauce that you want. Heat for 2 minutes and then serve over
cooked brown or jasmine rice, topped with sesame seeds.

Yield: Serves 3-4

Spicy Pan Seared Tofu and Vegetable Pad Thai

4 cups of flat rice noodles, cooked and tossed in a little sesame
oil to prevent sticking , 1 Pan Seared Tofu recipe from this book
1/2 cup shredded bok choy

1/2 cup carrots shredded, 1 tsp each minced ginger and garlic

1 cup broccoli chopped into small florets

1 medium onion cut into half moons, 3/4 cup bean sprouts

1/2 cup red bell pepper cut into thin strips, toasted sesame oil

1/2 cup cooked black beans, 3/4 cup enoki mushrooms

1/2 cup of chopped fresh scallions and a few sliced basil leaves

for the sauce:
1/2 cup soy sauce, 2 Tbs sugar, 3 Tbs hoisin sauce, 1/2 cup water
2 Tbs sweet chili sauce
1 tsp hot chili paste, 1 Tbs dark soy sauce
1 Tbs rice wine vinegar, 1 Tbs tamarind sauce
2 Tbs of cornstarch whisked into 1/4 cup of water

For the sauce , mix all of the sauce ingredients except for the water/cornstarch
mixture in a small pot over medium high heat until boiling and then slowly add
in the cornstarch/water mixture, whisking until the sauce is thickened. Once
thickened, set aside. Het a large non stick skillet over high for 3 minutes and then
add in 1 Tbs of sesame oil, the ginger, garlic, mushrooms, broccolli, peppers, bok
choy, onions and carrots. Let them sit in a flat layer 2 minutes and then stir and
let sit another 2 minutes. Add in the sprouts, black beans and tofu, cooking 1
more minute and then add in the sauce and noodles. Stir it all together until the
noodles are heated. Serve topped with more sprouts, chopped scallions, fresh
basil and crushed peanuts or more chili paste and hoisin sauce if desired.

Yield: Serves 2-4

Creamy Pasta Verde

Packed with flavor and vitamins from the delicious green vegetables in the sauce.

1 box of Dreamfields brand Fusilli Pasta (this brand has added fiber but still tastes like traditional pasta) cooked al dente (about 5 minutes) and cooled
1 Tbs Earth Balance brand buttery spread
3 Tbs Follow Your Heart brand parmesan shreds
3 Tbs nutritional yeast

for the verde sauce:
1 cup chopped broccoli rabe or broccolini with the hard bottoms cut off and discarded, 1 cup stemmed chopped kale, 1 cup raw baby spinach, 1/2 cup plain rice milk, 1/2 a peeled avocado

for the cream sauce:
1/2 cup Vegenaise brand vegan mayo (I like the soy free version)
1 small jar of drainied marinated artichokes
3 Tbs Tofutti brand cream cheese
4 Tbs nutritional yeast, 1/2 of a ripe peeled and pitted avocado, 1 tsp lemon juice
1 tsp salt, 1 Tbs Follow Your Heart brand parmesan shreds
1/2 to 3/4 cup plain rice milk

For the verde sauce, boil the kale, broccoli rabe and spinach for 4 minutes. Drain and cool. Add to a blender with the rice milk, avocado and a pinch of salt and blend until very smooth. If it seems too thick to blend, add a little water. **For the cream sauce**, add all of the cream sauce ingredients into a blender and blend until it is about as thick as alfredo sauce and very smooth. Add more rice milk if needed. Pour this and the verde sauce together into a large non stick pan and heat until bubbling. Add in the buttery spread, the remaining parmesan and nutritional yeast for 20 seconds, stirring often, then add in the cooked pasta. Mix well and enjoy.

Yield: Serves 4-6

Zucchini Corn Fritters

2 medium sized zucchini, shredded, 1/4 cup onion finely minced, 1 cup flour mixed with 1 tsp baking powder, 1/3 cup Follow Your Heart brand shredded parmesan, 1/2 tsp garlic powder, 1/2 cup drained canned or fresh corn kernels, 1/4 tsp each salt and pepper, 2 Tbs finely ground flax seed whisked together with 5 Tbs water

Mix the zucchini and onion with a pinch of salt and allow it to sit in a strainer for 3 minutes. Squeeze all of the water completely out of the zucchini and onions after the 3 minutes. Mix all of the ingredients together. Heat about 1/8 of an inch of vegetable oil in a non stick pan for 3 minutes on high. Take about 2 Tbs of the mixture at a time, flatten it a little and place into the oil. Cook about 8 at a time, cooking each side about 2 minutes or until golden. Serve with my Ranch Dressing recipe on page 72. *Yield:* Serves 4-5

Sausage, Pesto, Provolone and Broccoli Rabe Hoagie

1 bunch of broccoli rabe, 2 cloves fresh minced garlic, 1/2 cup roasted red pepper strips, extra virgin olive oil, 4 links of Beyond Meat brand Italian Sausages or Field Roast Italian Sausages 4 slices of Follow Your Heart brand vegan Provolone slices, 4 rolls of your favorite 6 inch Italian hoagie bread, 1/2 a batch of the Pesto recipe from this book, red pepper flakes

Heat a large pot of water to a boil. Trim off about 3/4 of an inch off of the bottom of the broccoli rabe and discard. Place the broccoli rabe in the water and simmer for 2 minutes. Drain well and squeeze it dry. Heat the garlic over medium high heat in a large non stick pan in a tsp of olive oil.
After 30 seconds of the garlic browning a bit, add in the broccoli rabe, a pinch of dried red pepper flakes and a pinch or two of salt. Cook until heated. Remove from pan and add in the sausages. Cook them about 6 minutes until crisp on all sides. Heat your hoagie rolls in the oven for 3 minutes at 350 degrees. Remove from oven, spread some pesto inside of the warm bread. Cut each piece of provolone in half. Lay 2 half slices on top of the pesto, then place the sausage inside and top it with some of the roasted red peppers and then some of the broccoli rabe. You can add a little olive oil on top if you like.

Yield: Makes 4 hoagies

Spinach, Corn and Black Bean Cheddar Jack Quesadillas

4 flour tortillas, the 8 inch ones work well here
4 cups of baby spinach, dropped in hot water for 30 seconds, drained, cooled and squeezed until very dry
1 cup cooked, drained black beans
1 cup cooked, drained canned corn
1 pack of So Delicious brand Cheddar Jack cheese shreds
a few pinches of salt
the guacamole recipe from this book
Tofutti brand sour cream
your favorite salsa
your favorite hot sauce (optional)

Heat the tortillas for 30 seconds in the microwave, then lay them flat and evenly spread cheese on each one (the hot tortillas help the vegan cheese melt easier). Lay the spinach, corn and black beans on one side of the cheese topped tortillas. Sprinkle a little salt on them and then fold them into half moon quesadilla shapes. Heat a large non stick pan over high heat for 2 minutes. Spray with non stick spray. Add in 2 quesadillas at a time. Cook each side until golden. Cut in half and serve topped with salsa, guacamole, sour cream and hot sauce, if desired.

*You can add whatever you like to quesadillas once you have the basic procedure down. You can leave off the spinach, corn and black beans and opt for vegan chicken, tofu, vegan ground beef, cooked mushrooms, seitan etc. Endless possible combinations.

Yield: Serves 2-4

Apricot Basil Glazed Grilled Tofu or Chicken

2 blocks of extra firm tofu that have been frozen, thawed and had all of the water completely squeezed from the blocks between your palms (this creates a very tasty and chewy tofu) or 8 Maywah or Delight Soy brand veggie chicken patties
1/2 cup apricot jelly mixed together with
1 Tbs each sugar, red wine vinegar, water, vegetable oil and minced fresh basil and a pinch of salt

Cut each block of thawed, squeezed tofu into 4 large triangles (you will have 8 total). Place them in a flat sided glass dish, or place the veggie chicken in the dish if using, and pour the apricot mixture over them. Coat both sides of each piece. Heat a grill for 15 minutes on high. Spray the grill very well with non stick spray and cook each side about 4 minutes. Enjoy.

Yield: Serves 3-4

Tandoori Chicken or Tofu and Vegetable Curry (gluten free)

Serve this over steamed basmati rice and with my Homemade Onion Naan Bread or Broccoli Pakoras. The Tandoori paste, curry and tamarind sauce are available at Indian markets or some grocery stores.

sauce:

1/2 jar of Patak's Jalfrezi Curry sauce, 1/2 tsp garam masala
2 cups of plain tomato sauce
1/2 can coconut milk
2 Tbs Earth Balance brand buttery spread
1 teaspoon salt
1/4 teaspoon cayenne pepper
2 Tbs tamarind sauce (not paste)
1 Tbs tandoori paste

vegetables:

1 green pepper diced medium
1 large russet potato peeled and medium diced
2 carrots peeled and medium diced
1 cup cauliflower cut into medium florets
1/2 cup thawed frozen peas

1 cup Maywah brand or Delight Soy brand vegan chicken cut into chunks (if you prefer, you can use the chewy tofu recipe from this book instead of the vegan chicken)

Mix the sauce ingredients, set aside.

Bring a large pot of water to a boil, add the potatoes and carrots. Cook 7 minutes. Add the cauliflower and cook another minute. Drain and cool in cold water.

Heat the sauce in a large pot over medium heat. Add the cooked vegetables and vegan chicken or chewy tofu. Simmer 5 minutes then add the thawed peas and peppers and cook another minute. Serve over Basmati rice with my Onion Naan recipe.

Yield: Serves 2-3

Tofish Fillets with Vegan Tartar Sauce

These go good with my Pommes Frites French Fry recipe for a tasty fish and chips dinner with some malt vinegar to dip the fries into.

1 1/2 cups plain flour
1/2 cup cornstarch
1 teaspoon salt
1/2 teaspoon garlic powder
1 Tbs freshly chopped dill
1 3/4 cup freshly opened club soda
1/2 inch canola or vegetable oil
1 block extra firm tofu completely drained, then cut into 6 large triangles

Mix the flour with salt, cornstarch, dill and garlic powder. Add club soda and whisk very fast until a pancake type batter forms. If it seems way too thick, add more club soda. Heat oil in a non stick frying pan for 3 minutes on medium high heat. Test if it is hot enough by flicking some batter into it, if, if bubbles form around it, it is ready to fry. Dip each tofu piece into the batter a few at a time and quickly but carefully place into the hot oil. Cook each side until golden brown (3-4 minutes per side). Flip and cook the other side. Drain on a cookie cooling rack placed on a cookie sheet lined with foil. You can also cook ahead and reheat on the cookie rack/sheet set up. This will keep it from getting soggy when reheating. **Make a vegan tartar sauce** by whisking together 1/3 cup vegan mayo with 2 Tbs sweet relish.

Yield: Serves 4-6 — 322 —

Dijon Grilled Tofu and Provolone Muffaletta

The tang from the mustard and the olive tapenade make this a delicious sandwich.

1 recipe of the Olive Tapenade from this book, 1 block of extra firm tofu that has been frozen, thawed and had all of the water squeezed out of the thawed block (this creates an extra chewy tofu) cut unto 6 triangles, shredded fresh baby spinach, tomato, Vegenaise brand vegan mayo, onions and avocado for topping, 4 slices of Follow Your Heart brand provolone slices cut in half, two 6 inch hoagie rolls
the marinade: 4 Tbs dijon mustard, 3 Tbs A1 brand steak sauce and 1 tsp vegetable oil whisked together

Brush the marinade over the tofu and on the bottom of the tofu. Heat a grill for 15 minutes. Spray it with non stick spray. Cook each side 2 minutes. When you flip it, place the cheese on top of the tofu. Close the grill and let the cheese melt. Place the hoagie rolls on the grill and toast them a few seconds. Spread the mayo on the rolls, then the olive tapenade, then place on the tofu with the melted cheese and the onion, tomato, shredded spinach and avocado slices. Enjoy. Yield: Makes 2 sandwiches

Thai Sunflower Butter Grilled Leek Tofu Kebabs

2 blocks of extra firm tofu that have been frozen, thawed and had all of the water squeezed out of the blocks (this process makes the tofu extra chewy and delicious) torn into medium sized chunks
1 cup of cleaned leek bottoms that have been cut into 1/4 inch thick chunks
marinade:
1/2 cup Sun Butter brand smooth sunflower butter,
1 cup coconut milk, 1/4 cup water, 1 Tbs red curry paste, 2 Tbs hoisin sauce, 1 Tbs rice wine vinegar, 2 Tbs sugar, 1 small thin Thai spicy green pepper, seeds removed, 2 cloves garlic, 1 tsp fresh ginger, 1 tsp soy sauce

For the marinade, add all of the ingredients into a food processor and blend until smooth. If it seems way too thick to marinate the tofu and leeks, add a little water. When ready, toss this carefully with the leeks and tofu. Let them marinate an hour and then place the tofu and leeks onto skewers (soak the skewers in water first so they do not burn when grilling), 4 pieces of tofu and 4 leeks per skewer. Save the leftover marinade for brushing. Heat a grill for 15 minutes on high and then spray it with non stick spray. Grill the kebabs about 5 minutes per side, brushing them with the extra marinade. You can spoon a little more over the top when you serve them. Enjoy with steamed rice, fried rice or ramen noodles and a nice salad.
Yield: Makes 8 to 10 kebabs   — 323 —

Wild Rice, Pear and Vegan Provolone Stuffed Delicata Squash or Zucchini (gluten free)

4 zucchini split in half lengthwise with the insides carefully scooped out with a spoon leaving enough skin to support the filling or 2 delicata squash, seeds removed, baked face down in a glass dish with a half inch of water until soft (400 degrees for 25 minutes)
1 box store bought wild rice mix (any vegan brand)
2 pears peeled, small dice
5 Tbs vegan mayo
1 tsp garlic powder
1 tsp salt
3 Tbs nutritional yeast
8 slices Follow Your Heart Vegan Provolone or Field Roast brand Chao cheese

Cook the rice as instructed on the box, drain completely if any liquid is leftover. Cool completely then mix in the pears, vegan mayo, garlic powder, nutritional yeast and salt. Fill each zucchini cavity or each cooled, cooked delicata squash cavity with the rice mixture. Preheat oven to 400 degrees. Place the filled zucchini or delicata in a non stick sprayed baking dish and bake covered 15 minutes. Uncover and slice the cheese in half lengthwise and top the squash boats with the cheese. Place back in the oven and bake another 10 minutes covered. Enjoy.

Yield: Serves 3-4

Meaty Mushroom Marinara Sauce (gluten free)

3 28 oz cans San Marzano whole plum tomatoes with juices crushed with your
hands as fine as you can get them (I like Cento brand San Marzano tomatoes the best)
1/2 of a small can of tomato paste, 1/2 cup of your favorite red wine
1 tsp salt, 1/2 Tbs balsamic vinegar
4 cloves garlic minced, 2 cups thinly sliced button mushrooms
1/2 cup medium diced
peeled carrots, 1/4 cup water, 1 medium whice onion diced small, 1 pack of Impossible
brand groundless beef, 1 tsp dried oregano, 1 Tbs sugar, 8 fresh basil leaves chopped

Heat a large pot over medium heat, add the 1/4 cup of water. When it looks about to
boil, add the onions, mushrooms, carrots, a pinch of salt and the garlic. Water saute for 2
minutes (this keeps a greasy film from being on top of your finished sauce, which oil tends
to do). Add in the Impossible and cook 3 minutes, breaking it up with a spatula. Add the
red wine and reduce for another 3 minutes, then add the rest of the ingredients and turn
the heat to medium low. Stir often, do not let it burn on the bottom of the pot. If you
have a flame diffuser, you can place it under the pot to keep from having to stir as much.
Cook for 15 minutes. Season with more salt, fresh basil or sugar if needed after the
cooking time is up. Serve over your favorite pasta. *Yield*: Serves 6-7

Basil Monterey Jack Sausage Rolls

4 full links of Beyond Meat brand Bratwurst Sausages, cooked 5 minutes
until crisp and browned
2 sheets of vegan puff pastry, 1 Tbs toasted sesame seeds
1 cup of Daiya brand Farmhouse Block Monterey Jack cheese, shredded
2 Tbs fresh basil, sliced thin

Roll out the puff pastry on a lightly floured cutting board until it is about
25% larger than it was originally. Lay 2 of the cooked links, half of the basil
and half of the shredded cheese on each roll on the edge closest to you. Roll
the dough up, around the sausage, basil and cheese. Preheat the oven to 425
degrees. Place the stuffed rolls on a sheet pan that has been lined with foil
and parchment paper. Brush the rolls with a litte olive oil. Sprinkle on some
sesame seeds, Bake for 20-25 minutes or until golden. Cool 5 minutes, enjoy.

Yield: Serves 4-6

Aloo Matar, Spiced Peas and Potatoes (gluten free)

3 Tbs Earth Balance brand buttery spread
2 medium russet potatoes peeled and cut into 1/2 inch cubes, 1 cup frozen thawed peas, 1/2 cup small diced onions, 1 tsp each minced garlic and peeled minced fresh ginger, 5 cups raw baby spinach, 1/4 cup fresh chopped cilantro
sauce: 2 cups of water with 3 Tbs of tomato paste, 1 Tbs of Better Than Bouillon brand No Chicken Base and 2 Tbs tamarind sauce (not the paste) whisked into it
spices: mix together 1 tsp ground cumin, 1 tsp garlic powder, 1 tsp garam masala, 1/2 tsp salt and a few pinches of cayenne pepper depending on how spicy you like it

  Heat a large non stick pan for 2 minutes on high. Add in 1 Tbs of the Earth Balance buttery spread. Add in the potatoes, onions, garlic and ginger. Cook together 3 minutes. Add in the spices. Stir for 1 minute and then add in the spinach. Cook 1 minute and add in the sauce ingredients. Cover and simmer on a low boil for 12 minutes. Add in the peas and let it simmer 4 more minutes or until the potatoes are soft. Add in the rest of the buttery spread and stir in the cilantro. Enjoy over steamed basmati rice with my Onion Naan recipe.

Yield: Serves 3-4

Mushroom, Artichoke and Spinach Puff Pastry

2 sheets thawed puff pastry, 6 cups raw baby spinach
3 cups sliced mushrooms, 2 cloves minced garlic
1 cup drained marinated artichokes, salt and pepper
2 cloves garlic minced

 Bring a teaspoon of olive oil to a high heat for 2 minutes. Add the garlic and mushrooms. Cook 3 minutes. Add a few pinches of salt and add the spinach. Cook until wilted. Add the artichokes and more salt and pepper to taste. Drain completely, gently squeezing out the excess liquid. Cool it. Now, on a floured surface, roll out the puff pastry a little flatter and longer than it is when you remove it from the package. Preheat the oven to 425 degrees. Line the edge of the puff pastry closest to you with half the mixture, then do the same with the second sheet, using up the other half of the mixture. Roll the sheets away from you into a log. Place on a parchment paper lined cookie sheet sprayed with non stick spray. Bake 25-35 minutes.

Yield: Serves 4-8

Savory Meatballs

These come out the tastiest using Impossible brand vegan ground.

1 pack of thawed Impossible brand ground or 1 tube of vegan Lightlife brand
Gimme Lean Beef mixed with 1/2 a tube of Gimme Lean Sausage
2 Tbs Go Veggie brand vegan parmesan cheese, 1 Tbs finely ground flax seed
mixed wih 2 Tbs hot water, 1/2 tsp each dried oregano, basil, garlic powder, salt
1/2 - 3/4 cup vegan bread crumbs or panko bread crumbs

Mix all of the ingredients together with your hands. If it seems too wet, add
a little more bread crumbs. Taste and add more salt or parmesan if bland.
Form into balls about 3/4 the size of a golf ball. Heat a non stick skillet for 3
minutes. Spray with a little non stick spray. Add in the meatballs. Cook
about a minute per side, flipping them with a fork for about a 5 minute total
cooking time until crisped and brown. If you make these using the
Impossible meat, make sure they are finished off in the oven for 8 minutes at 375
degrees on a non stick cookie sheet. These are great with
marinara sauce and Barilla brand White Fiber Spaghetti or with the Baked
Ziti recipe from this book. Makes about 20-24 meatballs or 50 tiny
meatballs for the Italian Wedding Soup recipe in this book.

Yield: Serves 4-8

Hamburger, Oyster Mushroom and Kalamata Olive Pizza

one ball of homemade dough from this book, risen (the dough recipe makes 2 balls of dough, but you will only use one here)
1/2 a package of Impossible brand ground
1 medium onion, diced small
2 cloves minced garlic
1 cup oyster mushrooms, rough chopped (discard any hard stems before chopping)
3/4 cup pitted kalamata olives, rough chopped
1 soft block of Follow Your Heart brand Mozzarella, shredded (you will need to shred it yourself, make sure it is the soft block and not the hard block, the soft melts better)
a few pinches of salt, dried oregano and garlic powder
1/4 cup of Follow Your Heart brand Parmesan
1/4 cup of your favorite homemade or store bought tomato sauce

Take your dough, place it on a floured cutting board and do not knead it again, simply push it down a little with your hands into a circle and roll it out to fit a 14 inch round pizza pan. Spray the pan with non stick spray. Place the dough inside and cover it with a towel, letting it rise for an hour. While it rises, heat a non stick saute pan on high for 2 minutes. Add in the beef and break it up with a spatula. Cook it until it is browned and resembles ground beef. Season with a little salt and oregano. Drain the beef crumbles on a paper towel. Heat the pan again for 2 minutes on high, add in a 1/2 teaspoon of olive oil, then the mushrooms, onions and garlic. Add in a pinch of salt and saute for 4 minutes. Add in the chopped kalamata olives. Set aside. When the dough is risen, brush around the rim of the crust with a little olive oil. Place the tomato sauce on the dough and spread it evenly. Place the onion, olive and mushroom mixture on top of the sauce. Top this with the mozzarella and parmesan cheeses and finally the beef. Add a few pinches of salt, oregano and garlic powder on top. Place the pizza into a 425 degree pre heated oven. Cook for 15 to 18 minutes. Place it under the broiler for a minute or so to brown the crust and melt the cheese fully. Remove from oven and sprinkle with a little more salt and oregano. Allow it to cool 10 minutes before slicing.

Yield: Serves 3-4

Desserts

Italian Olive Oil Amaretto Semolina Cake

A deliciously moist Italian cake. The cake will become even more moist the longer that is sits from the delicious simple syrup glaze finding its way deeper into the cake.

dry ingredients: 1.5 cups King Arthur brand flour mixed with 1/2 tsp salt, 1 tsp baking soda, 1 1/4 cup sugar and 1/4 cup semolina flour **wet ingedients:** mix together with a whisk 1/3 cup non extra virgin olive oil, 1 tsp vanilla extract, 3 Tbs Amaretto and 1 1/4 cup plain freshly opened club soda **for the simple syrup glaze:** place 1/2 cup of sugar and 1/2 cup of water in a small sauce pan and whisk constantly until it comes to a boil and then cool and set aside

Heat the oven to 375 degrees. Cut a 9 inch circle out of parchment paper and place it in the bottom of a 9 inch non stick cake pan. Spray the paper and sides with non stick spray. Place the dry ingredients into a large bowl and pour the wet ingredients into the dry. Whisk until smooth and pour the batter into the cake pan. Bake for about 28 minutes or until golden on top. Do not open the oven until the cake is risen and golden on top or the cake may fall. Remove the cake from the oven and allow it to sit a few minutes and then remove it from the pan, placing it on a cookie cooling rack, parchment paper side up. Remove the parchment paper. Poke several holes in the cake where you removed the parchment from with a fork and then evenly pour the simple syrup over the cake. Allow to cool completely, dust with powdered sugar and serve. *Yield:* Serves 5-8

Chocolate Chip Banana Bread

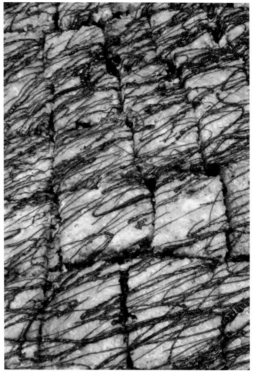

dry ingredients:
2 cups King Arthur flour
2 cups sugar
1 tsp baking powder
1 tsp baking soda
pinch of salt
2 cups vegan chocolate chips
wet ingredients:
2 mashed bananas
4 Tbs vegetable oil
1 1/2 cups rice milk

Mix the wet ingredients with the dry. Whisk well. Pour into a non stick spray sprayed 9x13 inch pan and bake at 375 degrees for 30-35 minutes or until it springs back when pressed in the middle. Melt 1/2 a cup of vegan chocolate chips in the microwave or a double broiler and drizzle over the top of the bread with a fork for extra decadence.

Yield: Serves 8-12

Chocolate Mousse (gluten free)

1/2 a cup of Guittard brand semi sweet chocolate chips
1 container of So Delicious brand Coco Whip coconut whipped cream, thawed,
1 tsp vanilla extract

Heat an inch of water in a pot with a large bowl placed on top of it that is filled with the chocolate chips. This is called a double broiler, the steam from the boiling water in the pot will melt the chocolate chips without burning them. Add in a pinch of salt and stir with a rubber spatula until the chocolate is melted. Remove from the heat and add in the coco whip and vanilla. Fold it all together gently until mixed well. Transfer it to a flat glass casserole dish and let it cool until firm and then cover. Enjoy. You can also spoon this into a graham cracker pie crust before cooling it if you want to make it into a chocolate mousse pie or layer it with So Delicious brand Coco Whip in a glass for a tasty dessert.. *Beat the mousse with an electric hand blender before cooling it for an extra light, whipped texture. *Yield:* Serves 3-5

Classic Crisp and Chewy Chocolate Chip Cookies

  Chewy, crispy, sweet and chocolatey with a little hint of salitiness, leaving you
wanting more. I like serving these with an ice cold glass of vanilla rice milk.
You can bake as few or as many as you like and store the rest of the dough in the fridge.

2 cups King Arthur brand flour
3/4 cup brown sugar, 1 tsp vanilla extract
3/4 cup natural cane sugar
1/2 tsp salt, 1 tsp baking soda
3 Tbs Earth Balance brand buttery spread, 3 Tbs vegan shortening
2 Tbs finely ground flax seed mixed with 10 Tbs hot water (this acts as the egg, do
not skip this ingredient)
1 cup vegan chocolate chips

  Cream the butter, shortening, sugars, vanilla and flax seed mixture together with
a hand beater, stand mixer or a whisk. Once creamed together, add in the rest of
the ingredients. Stir together well, you can add a little water if it is too dry. When it
forms into a cookie dough, heat the oven to 375 degrees. Roll the dough into a
large log shape and cut 1/4 inch thick circles off into cookie shapes. Place about 8 at a
time on a cookie sheet lined with parchment paper and bake about 12 minutes or
until browned. If you like them a little more brown and crisp, put them under the
broiler for a minute, watching them carefully. You can place a few more chocolate
chips on top of them when they are still warm for extra decadence. Cool them a
few minutes and enjoy. — 332 — *Yield:* Makes about 24 cookies

Simple Sunflower Butter Parfait

   These are so easy to make, impress anyone and taste incredible. You can use peanut butter if desired.

1 thawed container of So Delicious brand Coco Whip
3/4 of a can of coconut milk
1 small box of vegan vanilla instant pudding mix
4 Tbs creamy sunfower butter
1/2 a batch of the Crispy Chocate Bark recipe from this book crushed into small pieces

   In a large bowl, whisk the pudding mix with the coconut milk for 3 minutes until smooth. Add in the sunflower butter. Whisk 1 more minute. Place about 2 Tbs in the bottom of a serving glass. Top it with 2 Tbs of the coco whip, then a few bark pieces. Top this with 3 Tbs of the pudding mix and then 3 Tbs of the coco whip and a few more bark pieces. Enjoy cold.

Yield: Makes about 5 parfaits

Tres Leches Cake

1.5 containers of So Delicious
brand Coco Whip
dry ingredients:
2 cups King Arthur brand flour
1 tsp baking soda
pinch of salt
1 tsp baking powder
1 1/2 cups sugar
wet ingredients:
1/3 cup+2 Tbs vegetable oil
1 Tbs vanilla extract
1 tsp apple cider vinegar
1 1/2 freshly opened club soda
the tres leches topping:
3/4 cup vanilla rice milk
1/2 cup Natures Charm brand evaporated coconut milk
1/2 cup Natures Charm brand sweetened condensed coconut milk

For the cake, pre heat the oven to 375 degrees. Spray a glass 9x13 inch glass sided baking dish with non stick spray. In a large bowl, combine the wet and dry ingredients but not the topping. Whisk well and pour into the glass baking dish. Bake for about 25 minutes or until golden and firm in the center. Do not open the oven until at least 25 minutes or the cake may fall in the center. Remove cake from oven and let cool completely. Poke little tiny holes all over the cake with a tooth pick or fork. Whisk the topping ingredients together and slowly pour it over the whole cake so that it absorbs into the holes you poked. Let it absorb 30 minutes and then spread the 1.5 containers of So Delicious brand Coco Whip over the top of the cake, like icing. A few fresh pitted cherries or cinnamon are good on top as well. Enjoy.

Yield: Serves 8-10

Chocolate Peanut Butter or Sunflower Butter Eggs

1 cup smooth peanut butter or smooth Sun Butter brand sunflower butter
2 Tbs brown sugar, 1 tsp vanilla extract, pinch of salt
1/4 cup melted Earth Balance brand buttery spread, 2 cups powdered sugar
1.5 bags of Guittard brand semi sweet chocolate chips

Mix all of the ingredients besides the chocolate chips. You want an almost dough like texture. If it seems too wet, add more powdered sugar. Roll about 1/4 an inch thick into a large rectangle. Place in the freezer for 30 minutes and then cut this into egg shapes with an egg shaped cookie cutter (you can just cut them into 2 inch squares or circles if you have no egg shaped cutter). Use the leftover scraps to form into a ball to flatten and make more eggs. Place them back in the freezer for 20 minutes while you melt the chocolate by placing the chips in a large bowl that is placed on top of a pot that has 1 inch of water in the bottom of it (this is called a double broiler, the steam from the water boiling will melt the chocolate without burning it). Turn the heat on high under the pot and let the water boil until the chocolate is melted, stirring the chocolate often. When melted, dip the frozen eggs into the chocolate. Coat them completely and cool them on parchment paper in the fridge. Enjoy.

Yield: Makes about 14 eggs

Old Fashioned Fresh Ginger Molasses Cookies

These are great for the holidays. Soft and chewy with a ton of flavor. They make your house smell great while they bake in the oven.

1 1/4 cup King Arthur brand flour mixed with 1/4 tsp salt and 1/2 tsp baking soda
cream together in a large bowl with a whisk:
1/2 cup softened Earth Balance brand buttery spread, 1 tsp vanilla extract, 1/8 cup dark molasses, 1/2 cup dark brown sugar, 1/4 cup sugar, 1/2 tsp ground cinnamon, 1 tsp fresh peeled grated ginger and 1 Tbs finely ground flax seed meal that has been mixed with 2 Tbs water (the flax acts as the egg binder, do not skip this ingredient)

After the creamed ingredients are smooth, add in the flour mixture. Stir together until you have a uniform soft cookie dough ball. Heat the oven to 375. Roll into balls about 3/4 the size of a golf ball and then roll each ball into plain sugar. Place about 4 inches apart on a parchment lined cookie sheet, 7 or 8 per sheet. Bake about 11 minutes or until flattened and golden. Enjoy.

Yield: Makes about 18 cookies

Pepita Pumpkin Seed Chocolate Dipped Ramen

Ramen for dessert? Works great in this simple and tasty dish.

1 cup of uncooked ramen noodles that you have crushed up in a plastic
bag with a rolling pin
1.5 Tbs Follow Your Heart brand Vegan Egg powder whisked together
with 1/4 plus 2 Tbs cup water
1/3 cup sugar
1 package of Guittard brand semi sweet chocolate chips mixed with a pinch of
salt
1/3 cup roasted salted green pumpkin seeds

  Mix the ramen with the sugar and egg/water mixture. Spray a 12 tin
muffin tin with non stick spray and push about a 1/4 thick layer of the
ramen mixture into each tin. Bake them at 375 degrees for about 13
minutes or until crisped a little. Remove from the oven and let them
completely cool. Place the chocolate and pinch of salt in a medium size
bowl. Microwave them for 1 minute, stir them, microwave another
minute, stir and then microwave 1 more minute until completely melted
and smooth. Remove the ramen from the tins with a butter knife. Dip
the tops of each one into the chocolate and then sprinkle the pumpkin
seeds over the top. Let the chocolate harden and enjoy.

Yield: Makes 12

Cinnamon Streusel Topped Coffee Cake

This cake is incredible.

dry cake ingredients:
2 cups King Arthur Flour
1 1/4 cup sugar, pinch salt
1 tsp baking soda

wet cake ingredients:
2 tsp vanilla extract
1/3 cup + 2 Tbs
vegetable oil
1 tsp apple cider vinegar
1 1/4 cups plain club
soda freshly opened

topping ingredients:
1.5 cups flour
1 cup brown sugar
1.5 tsp ground cinnamon
a pinch of salt
1/2 cup Earth Balance
Balance buttery spread

filling:
1 cup brown sugar,
1/2 Tbs ground cinnamon, 1 teaspoon unsweetened cocoa powder

 Preheat oven to 375 degrees. Spray an 8x12 inch glass rectangle baking dish or non stick baking pan with non stick spray. In a large bowl, mix the topping ingredients together, squeezing them together with gloved hands until it is uniformly mixed and small beads of crumbs start to come together. Set aside.

 In another large bowl, pour the wet cake ingredients into the dry cake ingredients. Whisk them well together and pour half of the batter into your sprayed baking dish or pan. Spread the filling over the batter and then top the filling with the remaining batter. Sprinkle the topping evenly over the batter and bake the cake for 35 minutes or until the topping is golden. Enjoy warm. You can rewarm individual slices in the microwave for 20 seconds, they are very delicious this way. Ice your warmed individual slices as you serve them. The icing is simply 2 cups powdered sugar mixed with 2 Tbs melted Earth Balance buttery spread and a splash or two of rice milk, whisk well and then drizzle over individual servings. If the icing is too thin, add more powdered sugar. If it is too thick, add more rice milk. Drizzle the icing over the warmed slices with a fork, moving in a zig zag pattern.

Yield: Serves 8-10

Double Chocolate Chip Whoopie Pie

Soft, pillowy homemade cookies with deliciously creamy coconut whip sandwiched in between.

1 1/2 cup King Arthur brand flour
1/3 plus 1 Tbs cocoa powder
1/2 tsp each baking powder and baking soda
a pinch of salt
1 1/8 cup sugar
1/3 cup vegan semi sweet chocolate chips
1 tsp vanilla extract
2 Tbs Earth Balance buttery spread
3 Tbs vegan shortening
1 Tbs finely ground flax seed mixed with 2 Tbs water
3/4 cup freshly opened club soda mixed with 1 tsp red wine vinegar
1 container of So Delicious brand coconut whipped cream

   Place the butter, shortening, sugar, vanilla and flax mixture in a bowl. Beat with a hand blender until creamed together. Mix the flour, cocoa powder, chocolate chips, salt, baking soda and baking powder together and add then into the mixture. Add in the club soda/vinegar mixture, a little at a time, until a thick, semi moist dough forms. Add more liquid if needed. Heat the oven to 375 degrees. Place golf ball sized pieces of the dough in perfect balls on a parchment lined cookie sheet, about 6 per sheet pan, spaced a few inches apart. Do not bake more than 1 tray at a time or they will not cook evenly. Bake about 12 minutes or until they look done. Pull them from the oven, cook the remaining batches of dough. Cool the cookies completely and then place a liberal amount of the whipped cream on the flat side of half of the cookies and top with the remaining halves. Store covered or wrapped in the fridge. Enjoy.

Yield: Makes 8 whoopie pies   — 338 —

Coconut Layer Cake

*Line the baking pan w parchment paper cut into the shape of your pan to keep the cake from sticking.

dry ingredients:
2 cups King Arthur Flour
1 1/4 cup sugar, pinch salt
1 tsp baking soda

wet ingredients:
2 tsp vanilla extract
1/3 cup + 2 Tbs vegetable oil
1 Tbsp apple cider vinegar
1 1/4 cups freshly opened
plain club soda

icing:
5 cups powdered sugar
6 Tbs melted Earth Balance
Soy Free Buttery Spread
1 tsp vanilla extract
rice milk (4 Tbs or more)
1 cup So Delicious brand Coco
Whip, 3 cups shredded
sweetened coconut

 Preheat the oven to 375 degrees. Spray a non stick 9 inch cake pan lined with parchment paper cut into a circle to fit the pan very well with non stick spray. This prevents the cake from sticking to the pan. Mix your dry ingredients (NOT the coconut though) together. In a measuring cup, mix the wet ingredients together. Mix the dry and wet ingredients together in a large bowl and whip with an electric hand beater until mixed well. Pour the batter into the non stick pan. Bake for 30 minutes or until you can push on the middle of the cake and it pushes back and it is browned on top (do NOT open the oven until the cake looks browned on top or it will fall). Remove the cake from the oven and carefully remove the cake from the round pan. Remove the parchment paper. Cool it on a cookie rack. Do not ice the cake until it is completely cooled or the icing will become runny! With an electric hand beater, mix the icing ingredients together. Only add a little rice milk in at a time until you get a good icing consistency. If it seems too runny, add more powdered sugar to thicken it and beat again. Whisk in the Coco Whip until smooth. When the cake is completely cooled, take a serrated knife and carefully cut the cake in half, across, so that you have 2 even sized circles. Place the flat side (which was the bottom of the cake when it was in the pan) flat side down on a large plate or cake dome bottom. Spread 1/4 of the icing and then about a cup of coconut onto the cake. Place the other cake half on top, rounded side up. Spread the remaining icing on the top and sides and then the rest of the coconut. Enjoy.
Yield: Serves 6-8

Salted Caramel Chocolate Butter Bars

These are incredible. Melty caramel and chocolate baked on top of a rich shortbread crust and topped with a buttery crisp crumble.

1.5 cups King Arthur brand flour, 3/4 cup powdered sugar, 1/2 cup sugar, a pinch of salt, 3/4 cup Earth Balance buttery spread, 1 tsp vanilla extract, 1 package of Cocomels brand salted caramel candies, removed from the wrappers and pulled in half, 3/4 cup Guittard brand semi sweet chocolate chips

Add the softened buttery spread, vanilla, salt and sugars into a large bowl. Whisk it all together until smooth. Add in the flour and stir until you have a crumbly mixture. Press half of this mixture evenly into a 9 by 9 inch glass baking dish and bake at 375 for 17 minutes. Remove from the oven. Spread the caramels and chocolate chips over the baked dough. Top this all by sprinkling the remaining crumbles over the chocolate and caramels. Bake for 15 more minutes or until the crumbles brown a little. Cool it and cut into squares. Enjoy. *Yield:* Serves 5-7

Crispy Peanut Butter or Sunflower Butter Ball Candies (gluten free)

1 16 oz jar of peanut butter or sunflower butter 1-2 cups powdered sugar
2 bags of Guittard brand semi sweet dark chocolate chips
2 cups crispy rice cereal
vegan white chocolate (optional, usually available at Whole Foods or online)

In a large bowl with gloved hands, mix the jar of peanut or sunflower butter with a cup of powdered sugar. You are looking for a less sticky texture than peanut butter but not completely dry either. Add more powdered sugar if needed to reach this consistency. Roll into as many one inch balls as possible. Roll each ball into the crispy cereal to completely coat. When all are coated, roll each ball into the melted chocolate (melt chocolate chips by placing an inch of water in a pot then placing a bowl on top and turning the burner on high with the chocolate chips in the bowl with a tsp of vegetable oil, stir until melted, this is called a double broiler). Set each chocolate dipped ball on a foil covered cookie sheet and cool in the fridge until hardened. Melt some of the vegan white chocolate and drizzle over the top of the candies and harden again in the fridge. Enjoy.

You can make reverse candies by dipping the peanut butter balls or sunflower balls into chocolate crisped rice cereal and then dipping them into melted white chocolate, like I did in the picture.

Yield: Serves 10-15

Boston Cream Pie

I like to place each slice in the microwave for 12 seconds before serving so
that the chocolate is a little melty and the cake is warm and extra soft.

dry cake ingredients: 1 3/4 cup King Arthur brand flour mixed with 1 cup sugar, a pinch
of salt and 1 tsp baking soda
wet cake ingredients: 1/3 cup vegetable oil, 1 tsp vanilla extract, 1 tsp apple cider vinegar
and 1 1/8 cup freshly opened club soda
for the filling: whisk together 1 package of your favorite store bought vanilla instant
pudding powdered mix with 3/4 cup of Silk brand vanilla creamer until thickened
and then cover it, stored in the fridge
for the ganache topping: mix 1/2 plus 2 Tbs of semi sweet vegan chocolate chips with
1/3 cup of full fat coconut milk in a microwave safe bowl

For the cake, heat the oven to 375 degrees. Line the bottom of a 9 inch round cake pan
with a piece of parchment paper that you have cut in the shape of the pan. Spray the
parchment paper and sides of the pan with non stick spray (the parchment will allow the
cake to remove from the pan easily and not stick to the pan). Whisk the wet cake
ingredients into the dry cake ingredients in a large bowl until uniform. Pour the batter into
the cake pan, right on top of the parchment paper. Bake it for 30 minutes or until golden
on top. Do not open the oven before 30 minutes or the cake may fall in the middle. When
the cake springs back a little when pushed in the middle, remove it from the oven. Cool 10
minutes and then remove it from the pan, bottom side up on a cooling rack. Remove the
parchment paper. Allow the cake to cool completely. You can cool it faster by placing it in
the freezer 30 minutes. When cooled, take a bread knife and carefully cut the cake evenly
in half across the cake so that you have 2 equal size circles of cake. Spread the pudding
filling on the half of the cake that did not have the parchment on it, making sure to spread
it on the inside cut portion of the cake. Place the other half on top of the pudding so that
the top of the cake is the part that had the parchment peeled off of it. Place the chocolate
chips and coconut milk mixture in the microwave for 30 seconds. Stir it and microwave
another 30 seconds. Repeat again but only for 15 seconds. Stir until a chocolate ganache
forms. Cool it in the fridge 20 minutes and then spread it over the top of the cake. Cool the
cake in the fridge 30 minutes. Slice and enjoy.

Crispy Sea Salted Corn Crisp Chocolate Bark or Toasted Pumpkin Seed Bark (gluten free)

Simple and addictive, decadent and delicious. I could and do eat this almost every day. A personal favorite.

1 bag of Guittard brand semi sweet chocolate chips (these are by far the creamiest vegan chocolate chips, available at Whole Foods or Sprouts) 1 cup of sea salt flavored Pop Corners chips crushed in a plastic bag with your hands into small pieces or 1/2 cup of toasted, salted green pumpkin seeds, 1/2 tsp vegetable oil, a pinch of salt

Bring a half inch of water to a boil in a medium sized pot. Place a large glass bowl on top of the pot of water but not touching the water, then fill the glass bowl with the chocolate chips, the sea salt and vegetable or canola oil (this is called a double broiler, the steam from the water melts the chocolate). Stir around the chocolate until it is melted and smooth.

Add in the crushed Pop Corners chips or toasted pumpkin seeds. Stir into the chocolate until combined and then pour this mixture onto a large sheet of tin foil on top of a sheet pan. Spread into a large thin rectangle. Let cool until hardened in the fridge or freezer for a few minutes, remove from foil in one large sheet of bark and then cut into bite size pieces. With the Pop Corners, these taste like a Kit Kat bar, and with the pumpkin seeds, they taste like a Mister Goodbar. Store these in the refrigerator, it keeps the chocolate from getting cloudy or drying out.

Yield: Serves 6-8

Chocolate Dipped Crispy Rice Treats (gluten free)

1 bag of Guittard brand semi sweet chocolate chips mixed with a pinch of salt
1 prepared recipe of the Crispy Rice Treats from this book cut into 3 inch squares

Place a large bowl on top of a pot filled with an inch of water on top of the stove, this is called a double broiler. Place the chocolate chips and the salt in the bowl that is on top of the pot and turn on the heat to high. Let the steam from the boiling water in the pot melt the chocolate, stirring often. Once melted, dip the bottom half of each crispy treat into the chocolate and let them cool on a parchment paper lined cookie sheet. You can dip a fork into the leftover melted chocolate and form zig zag patterns across the top of them to make them look nice. Enjoy.

Yield: Serves 8-10

Double Chocolate Chip Brownie Cookies

1.5 cups King Arthur brand flour
6 Tbs Earth Balance brand buttery spread, softened to room temperature
1 tsp vanilla extract
1 1/4 cups sugar
pinch of salt
1/2 cup cocoa powder
1 tsp baking soda (not baking powder)
1 cup vegan chocolate chips
1/3 to 1/2 cup plain rice milk

In a large bowl, whisk together the softened butter with the sugar, salt and vanilla. In another bowl, mix the flour, baking soda, chocolate chips and cocoa powder. Pour this into the butter/sugar mixture and add a little rice milk at a time, stirring until you have a medium firm cookie dough. Heat the oven to 375 degrees and drop Tbs size balls of cookie dough on a parchment paper lined cookie sheet about 3 inches apart. You can fit 8 on a sheet pan. Bake 5 minutes, then flatten each cookie slightly with a spatula and bake 4 more minutes. Remove from the oven and cool them a few minutes and enjoy.

Yield: Makes about 16 cookies

Apple Blueberry Crumble Cake

topping:

1 1/2 cup King Arthur flour

1 1/2 cup sugar

1/2 cup Earth Balance brand soy free buttery spread

dry cake ingredients:

2 cups King Arthur flour, sifted

pinch of salt, 1 3/4 cup sugar, 1 tsp baking powder, 1 tsp baking soda

wet cake ingredients:

1/4 cup canola oil, 1 3/4 cup vanilla rice milk

1 cup fresh blueberries, 1 large apple diced small

For the topping, cut all topping ingredients together w a pastry cutter or squeeze it all together with gloved hands until it is mixed together into small crumbs. Set aside.

Add the wet ingredients to the dry ingredients. Whisk together and place the batter in a non stick spray sprayed 9x13 inch casserole dish or pan. Spread the topping over the batter, covering entirely.

Bake in a preheated oven at 375 for 40 to 45 mins or until it springs back in the middle and the crumbs are browned. Serve warm with vegan vanilla ice cream or So Delicious brand Coconut vegan whipped topping.

Yield: Serves 8-12   — 345 —

Apple or Blueberry Fritters

These have a great old fashioned cake doughnut feel to them. Be sure and cook these long enough so they are all the way cooked and not doughy in the center.

2 cups King Arthur brand flour
pinch of salt
1/4 cup sugar
1 tsp baking powder, 1/2 tsp cinnamon, 1/2 tsp baking soda
1/4 cup melted Earth Balance brand buttery spread
1 tsp vanilla extract
1/2 cup peeled apples cut into small cubes or 1/2 cup fresh blueberries
1/2 cup rice milk or soy milk
1/2 inch vegetable oil for frying

for the glaze:
simply whisk together 2 cups of powdered sugar with a few Tbs of rice milk or soy milk until a thick glaze forms and set aside

In a large bowl, mix the flour, cinnamon, baking soda, salt, sugar, apples or blueberries and baking powder. In a measuring cup, mix the melted butter, vanilla and rice milk or soy milk. Stir this into the flour/apple mixture until a moist dough forms. Heat the oil in a large non stick pan for 4 minutes over medium high heat. Break off pieces of the dough a little bigger than a golf ball and flatten them evenly. Dip one into the oil, if bubbles form, they are ready to fry. Cook about 4 at a time until each side is golden, being careful not to burn them. Drain them on a cookie cooling rack placed on top of a sheet pan, and while they are still hot, drizzle some of the glaze over them with a spoon. Enjoy.

Yield: Makes 12 fritters

Harvest Apple Crisp

5 granny smith apples, peeled with
4 sides cut off and each side sliced
into thin half moons
1 tsp cinnamon
pinch of salt
2 cups sugar
4 Tbs flour
1 tsp vanilla extract

topping:

2 cups flour
2 cups sugar
pinch of salt
1 tsp cinnamon
3/4 cup Earth Balance brand
buttery spread

Heat an oven to 375 degrees. In a large bowl, mix the apples, cinnamon,
2 cups of sugar, salt, the 4 Tbs of flour and vanilla extract. Place this
mixture in a non stick sprayed glass baking dish in an even layer. Mix all of
the toppings together by squeezing it all between your fingers until you
have a crumbly mixture. Spread it evenly over the top of the apple filling
and bake for about 30 minutes or until browned on top. Enjoy topped with
some vegan vanilla ice cream or So Delicious brand Coco Whip.

Yield: Serves 8-10

Crispy and Chewy Corn Flake Cookies

1/2 cup Earth Balance Soy Free Buttery Spread, softened
2/3 cup sugar
1 Tbs Follow Your Heart brand Vegan Egg
whisked with 3 Tbs water, 1 tsp vanilla extract
3/4 cup flour
1 1/2 cups crunched up corn flake type cereal

Heat the oven to 350 degrees. In a large bowl, mix together the
vegan egg, buttery spread , sugar , water and vanilla . Add in the flour
and stir it in. Add in the corn cereal and mix well. Roll into golf ball
sized slightly flattened balls and place on a parchment paper lined
cookie sheet. Bake about 12 minutes until flat and crisped.

Yield: Makes 15 cookies

Pineapple Pina Colada Cake

dry ingredients:
2 cups King Arthur brand flour, 1 tsp baking soda, pinch of salt and 1 1/2 cups sugar
wet ingredients:
1/3 cup+2 Tbs vegetable oil, 1 Tbs vanilla extract, 1 tsp apple cider vinegar and 1 1/2 cups freshly opened club soda
pineapple mix:
1/2 cup pineapple diced small and soaked in 1/2 cup of rum for 20 minutes and then drained
filling/topping:
1 container of So Delicious brand plain Coco Whip whipped cream whipped or whisked together with 1 can of Natures Charm brand condensed sweetened coconut milk for 4 minutes and chilled in the fridge 6 hours

  For the cake, mix the dry ingredients with the wet ingredients in large bowl. Whisk well and then add in the pineapple. Heat the oven to 375 degrees. Line a 9 inch non stick pan with parchment paper that has been cut into a circle to fit the pan (do not skip this step or the cake will stick to the bottom of the pan). Spray the pan with non stick spray, pour the batter inside. Bake for about 25 minutes or until golden on the top and firm in the middle. Do not open the oven until it has baked at least 25 minutrs or it may fall in the middle. Remove the cake from the pan and remove the parchment paper. Allow to cool completely and then carefully cut the cake in half width wise with a bread knife so you have 2 even circles. Lay the more rounded top side of the cake face down on a large plate. Spread half of the chilled coconut cream icing on this and then place the other half of the cake on top and spread the remaining icing on rop and the sides if you want the sides iced. Enjoy each slice with some more small diced pineapple on top if you wish. Store the cake in the fridge.

Yield: Serves 4-8

Crispy Banana Tempura

  These are great on their own topped with
  powdered sugar and dipped in
  pure maple syrup or as a decadent topping
  for some vegan vanilla ice cream.

  1 cup plain flour mixed with 1/2
  cup cornstarch , 2 Tbs sugar and
  a pinch of salt
  placed in a large bowl
  1 to 1 1/4 cup plain freshly opened club soda
  3 peeled bananas sliced into 1/2 inch chunks
  1/2 inch of vegetable oil in a non stick skillet

  Slowly add the club soda into the flour mixture. You want it to look like a thick pancake batter. Add more club soda if it is too thick. Heat the oil on the stove top on high for 3 minutes and then flick a little of the batter into the oil. If bubbles form, they are ready to cook. Dip the bananas into the tempura batter and then into the hot oil. Cook each side until golden. Drain them on a cookie cooling rack that has been placed on top of a foil lined cookie sheet so that you can heat these again later if needed without burning the bottoms. Enjoy.

Yield: Serves 3-4

Italian Pizzelle Cookies

These gorgeous and delicious Italian cookies require a pizzelle maker.

1 Follow Your Heart Vegan Egg,
 prepared but not cooked
1/3 cup sugar
1/4 cup melted Earth Balance
soy free vegan butter
1 teaspoon anise extract
1 teaspoon whole anise seed
3/4 cup king arthur flour
1/4 teaspoon vanilla
1/2 teaspoon baking powder
pinch salt

Heat the pizzelle maker according to directions. In a medium mixing bowl add the egg and sugar, and whisk for about 1 minute, until the sugar is incorporated. Whisk in the melted butter, vanilla, anise seed and anise extract. In a medium mixing bowl, sift together the flour, baking powder, and salt. Fold the flour mixture into the egg mixture until combined into a smooth dough. To make larger pizzelles, use a rounded tablespoon of the dough, and to make the smaller ones, use a leveled off tablespoon. Place the desired amount of the dough in the center of each round iron on your pizzelle maker, then close and lock it. Cook for 25-30 seconds, until there is slight browning all around. Remove and let completely cool on a wire rack.
Yield: Serves 3-5

Chocolate Coated Coconut Candy (gluten free)

3 cups sweetened coconut flakes
2 cups powdered sugar
1/2 cup melted Earth Balance
brand buttery spread
1 1/2 bags of Guittard brand
semi sweet chocolate chips

Mix all of the ingredients besides the chocolate in a bowl. Form this mix into 4 inch candy bar shapes. Freeze them for 1 hour. Place a large bowl on top of a pan filled with an inch of water. Place the chocolate chips and a pinch of salt into the bowl that is sitting on top of the pan (this is a double broiler, the steam from the water in the pan will melt the chocolate). Place this all on a stove and turn the heat to high and stir until the chocolate melts. Place each coconut candy, 1 at a time, into the chocolate until coated. Cool them on a foil lined sheet pan in the fridge. Enjoy.

Yield: Makes 12 candy bars

Lemon Loaf with Vanilla Lemon Glaze

1 1/2 cups King Arthur brand flour
1 1/4 cups sugar
1/4 tsp salt
1 tsp vanilla extract
1/3 cup vegetable oil
1/3 cup fresh lemon juice
1 tsp baking soda, 1/2 tsp turmeric powder (for color) 3/4 cup freshly opened plain club soda
3 Tbs water mixed with 2 Tbs finely ground flax seed left to sit 5 minutes
for the icing: 1 1/2 cups powdered sugar, 1 Tbs melted Earth Balance brand buttery spread, 1 to 3 Tbs plain rice milk, 1 tsp vanilla extract, 1 Tbs fresh lemon juice

For the icing, whisk all of the icing ingredients together, adding a little rice milk at a time until you have a glaze. Set aside. Heat the oven to 375. Line the bottom of a 9 inch non stick loaf pan with parchment paper you have cut to fit the bottom and spray the loaf pan with non stick spray. In a large bowl, mix the flour, sugar, turmeric, salt and baking soda. In another bowl, mix the oil, tsp of vanilla, lemon juice, flax/water mixture and club soda. Whisk this into the flour mixture and when you have a smooth batter, pour it into the loaf pan or you can use a sprayed non stick bundt pan too. Bake for about 1 hour minutes or until it pushes back in the center. Do not open the oven before 1 hour, bake it until it looks risen and firm and browned on top first. When cooked, allow to cool 30 minutes in the pan and then remove from the pan, remove the parchment paper and place the loaf on a cookie cooling rack that has been placed on top of a foil lined cookie sheet. With a spoon or fork, drizzle the icing over the loaf. Allow it to cool completely, then slice and enjoy.

Yield:. Serves 4-8

Peppermint Patties (gluten free)

3 cups powdered sugar
1/4 cup melted Earth Balance brand buttery spread
1/4 cup plain white corn syrup or 1/4 cup light colored maple syrup (the corn syrup will keep the filling whiter)
1 tsp peppermint extract
1 package of Guittard brand dark chocolate chips
pinch of salt
1/2 tsp vegetable oil

In a large bowl, mix the powdered sugar, peppermint extract, melted Earth Balance and the corn syrup or maple syrup with a hand beater. When it comes together, form the mixture into 1 inch discs. Keep them in the fridge or freezer for 30 minutes. Make a double broiler by filling a large pot with an inch of water, then place large mixing bowl on top of this, fill the mixing bowl with the chocolate chips, oil and pinch of salt. Place this double broiler set up on the stove and turn the heat to high, the steam from the water boiling under the bowl will melt the chocolate chips. Once melted, remove from the heat and dip the peppermint discs into the chocolate, a few at a time. Coat them and place them on a parchment paper lined cookie sheet until they are all coated. Cool them in the fridge until hardened. Enjoy.

— 350 —

Yield: Makes 24-30 candies

Sweet Potato Pie

A delicious Southern classic made vegan.

for the crust: 1 cup of King Arthur Flour, 1 tsp baking powder, 3 Tbs sugar, a pinch of salt and 4 Tbs vegan shortening

for the filling: 2 medium sweet potatoes (about 1.5 lbs) peeled and cut into 1/4 inch thick half moons and boiled 15 minutes until tender and then drained and cooled, 1 cup brown sugar, 1.5 cups sugar, 1 tsp vanilla extract , a pinch of salt , 1/2 cup cornstarch , 4 Tbs Follow Your Heart brand Vegan Egg whisked with 3/4 cup water and 1/2 tsp each ground cinnamon, ground allspice and ground cloves

  For the crust, place the flour, baking powder, salt and the 3 Tbs sugar in a large bowl. Add in the shortening. Using a pastry cutter or a fork, press the shortening into the flour mixture over and over until small beads form in the flour. Now, add about 1/3 cup of cold water until a shaggy dough forms. Fold it over on itself several times but do not knead it like bread dough. Be gentle with it or it will be tough when baked. Wrap it in plastic and let chill in the freezer for 30 minutes. **For the filling**, place the cooked, cooled, drained sweet potatoes in a large food processor with the remaining filling ingredients. Blend until very smooth. Take your dough and roll it thin on a large floured cutting board into the shape of a 9 or 10 inch pie pan. Spray the pie pan with non stick spray and press the dough into the pie pan. Heat the oven to 375 degrees. Pour the filling into the crust, use a crust shield around the pie edges just to make sure the crust will not burn if you want. Bake about 1 hour or a little longer, until firm in the middle. Allow to cool completely and serve slices topped with some So Delicious brand Coco Whip. Enjoy.

Yield: Serves 6-8

Sunflower Butter Cookies

These are so delicious. They are rich, buttery, soft, chewy and
incredibly satisfying. They are similar to Peanut Butter cookies. You
can use peanut butter instead if you like.

1 cup sugar
1 cup brown sugar
2 Tbs finely ground flax seed mixed with 4 Tbs water (this acts as the egg, do
not skip this step)
2 1/2 cups King Arthur brand flour
1/2 tsp baking powder
1/2 tsp baking soda
1/4 tsp salt
1 cup Sun Butter brand sunflower butter
3/4 cup Earth Balance brand buttery spread, softened
1 tsp vanilla extract

In a large bowl, mix the sugar, brown sugar, vanilla, softened butter,
sunflower butter and the flax/water mixture. Cream them together with a
whisk. When uniform and smooth, add in the flour, salt, baking powder and
baking soda. Mix until you have a medium soft dough. Chill an hour in the
fridge, covered. Heat the oven to 375 degrees. Line a cookie sheet with
parchment paper. Drop Tablespoon sized cookies on the sheet in a ball
shape, about 8 per sheet. Make a cross pattern with a fork to flatten them a
little. Bake about 12 minutes or until golden. Enjoy.

Yield: Makes about 28 cookies

Rich and Decadent Tripple Chocolate Fudge Brownie Cake

You can bake this in a glass casserole dish or a round 9 inch baking tin as well, just line the bottom of the 9 inch tin with parchment paper to avoid sticking. No parchment is needed if you bake in the glass dish.

dry ingredients for cake:

1 cup King Arthur brand flour
3/4 cup sugar mixed with
1/4 cup powdered sugar
pinch of salt
1 tsp baking soda
(NOT baking powder)
1/4 plus 3 Tbs cocoa powder
1 cup vegan dark chocolate chips

wet ingredients for cake:

3/4 cup freshly opened club soda
1 tsp vanilla extract
1/4 cup vegetable oil+1 tsp apple cider vinegar

Spray a 9 inch square glass casserole dish with non stick spray or use a parchment paper lined 9 inch baking tin, preheat oven to 375 degrees. Mix the dry ingredients for the cake in a large bowl. In another measuring cup, mix the wet ingredients for the cake.
Pour wet ingredients into dry. Whisk well and pour into sprayed glass dish or the parchment lined tin. Bake at 375 for 30 to 35 minutes or until firm in the center and it bounces back if you gently press the center of cake. Do not open the oven during baking or the cake will fall in the center, wait at least 30 minutes before opening the oven to check firmness. Cool completely before icing. Leave the cake in the glass dish to ice or remove the cake from the 9 inch baking tin, remove parchment paper, cool and ice the top and sides.

chocolate frosting:

Melt 1/4 cup Earth Balance Soy Free buttery spread, add 3 Tbs vanilla rice milk. Pour into a bowl that contains 2 1/4 cups powdered sugar and 1/3 cup plus 2 Tbs cocoa powder. Whisk all until smooth. If it seems too thick, add a little more rice milk until it is spreadable. If it seems too thin, add more powdered sugar to thicken and whisk agin. Cool the cake completely (if the cake is warm at all, the icing will run, so cool it completely) and spread the icing liberally over the cake. Goes great microwaved 15 seconds to melt the chocolate chips again and then topped with So Delicious brand Coco Whip vegan coconut whipped cream.

Yield: Serves 4-8

Lemon Bars with Shortbread Crust

A tasty and rich sweet lemon filling baked in a
crisp and buttery crust. One of my favorite desserts.

crust: with a pastry cutter or fork, mix together 1 1/4 cups flour, 1/2 cup powdered
sugar, a pinch of salt and 9 Tbs of Earth Balance brand buttery spread untl small
beads form all throughout the flour
filling: whisk together 6 Tbs of Follow Your Heart brand Vegan Egg with 1 1/2 cups
cold water and then whisk it in large bowl with the juice of 2 lemons, 1/4 tsp lemon
zest, 1 cup sugar, 3 Tbs flour and 1 tsp baking powder

Push the crust mixture into a 9 by 9 inch glass baking dish that has been sprayed
with non stick spray until firmly packed. Bake this at 375 degrees for 12 minutes.
Remove from oven and pour the filling evenly over the crust. Bake about 25 to 28
minutes ar 375 or until the filling is set and firm. Do not open the oven before 25
minutes or the filling may fall. Allow to cool completely and then dust some
powdered sugar on top. Slice and enjoy.

Yield: Makes about 12 bars

Simple Chocolate Dipped Strawberries (gluten free)

1 pint of fresh strawberries
1 bag of high quality vegan semi sweet dark chocolate chips (I like Guittard brand semi sweet dark chocolate chips, available at Whole Foods)
1 tsp vegetable oil

   Bring an inch of water to a boil in a medium sized pot. Place a larger bowl on top of the pot of boiling water with the chocolate chips and oil placed in the bowl (this is called a double broiler, the steam from the water melts the chocolate gently). Stir the chocolate chips around until they are completely melted. Turn off the heat and dip the strawberries until covered in chocolate and cool on an aluminum foil lined cookie sheet. Take a fork and slowly shake the leftover melted chocolate in a zig zag pattern over the strawberries to make the design in the picture. Cool in fridge until chocolate has hardened and enjoy.

Yield: Serves 6-8

From Scratch Cinnamon Rolls

1 1/4 cup King Arthur brand flour mixed with 1 cup of water that has 1 tsp of yeast mixed into the water and left to sit 6 hours or overnight
another 1 1/4 cup King Arthur brand flour mixed with 1/3 cup sugar and a pinch of salt and set aside
another 1 tsp yeast and 1 Tbs vegetable oil
for the filling:
3/4 cup brown sugar, 1 Tbs cinnamon, 1/4 cup melted Earth Balance brand buttery spread
for the glaze:
2 cups powdered sugar whisked together with 1 Tbs melted Earth Balance buttery spread, 2 to 5 Tbs of rice milk and 1 tsp vanilla extract until you get a thick but spreadable icing

After your flour, water and yeast mixture has sat 6 hours or overnight, add in the other tsp of yeast and the vegetable oil. Mix and add in the other 1 1/4 cup flour, the 1/3 cup sugar and pinch of salt. Mix them together well and knead into a smooth dough, it will be a soft dough. Add more flour if it seems too wet. Cover and let it rise 1 hour in the fridge (the dough is easier to work with when it is a little cold). When risen, remove from rising bowl but do not knead it. Place it on a very well floured surface, push it into a flat, even rectangle about 10 inch by 16 inches. Brush the melted 1/4 cup Earth Balance buttery spread on top and then evenly sprinkle on the brown sugar and the cinnamon. From the shorter 10 inch side, roll it into a large tube. Take a large sharp knife and forcefully cut about 3/4 inch thick circles out of the rolled tube, giving you about 7 to 9 pieces. Line a round 9 inch baking tin with parchment paper (cut the parchment paper into a circle shape to fit the pan before placing the paper into the pan). Spray the sides of the tin with non stick spray and place your rolls inside, make sure they are all just barely touching each other (this way they rise into each other and become very soft and tender). Let them rise covered 1 more hour. Heat the oven to 400 degrees and bake these about 16 to 18 minutes or until golden. Remove from oven and drizzle the icing over the hot rolls, spreading it evenly with the bottom of a spoon. Enjoy hot.

Yield: Makes 7-9 rolls

Strawberry Shortcake

*If you cut your parchment paper into the shape of the pan before you pour the batter into the pan, the cake will not stick to the pan after baking.

dry ingredients:

1 and 3/4 cups King Arthur Flour
1 cup sugar
1 tsp baking soda
1/2 tsp salt

wet ingredients:

2 tsp vanilla extract
1/3 cup vegetable oil
1 Tbsp apple cider vinegar, 1 1/8 cup fresh plain club soda (freshly opened because this helps make the cake very light)

topping:

1 container of So Delicious brand whipped cream
8 large strawberries, each one sliced into 5 slivers

Preheat the oven to 375 degrees. Spray a non stick 9 inch cake pan very well with non stick spray. You do not want your finished product to stick. Mix your dry ingredients together. In a measuring cup, mix the wet ingredients (not the whipped cream or strawberries). Mix the dry and wet ingredients together and whip with an electric hand beater in a large bowl until mixed well. Pour the batter into the non stick pan. Bake for 25 minutes or until you can push on the middle of the cake and it pushes back and it is slightly browned (do NOT open the oven until the cake looks browned on top or it will fall). Remove from the oven and carefully remove the cake from the pan. Remove parchment paper. Cool it on a cookie rack and once cooled, very carefully slice the cake in half width wise, so that you have 2 even circles. On the bottom circle, spread on half of the whipped cream and half of the strawberry slivers. Place the other cake circle on top of the whipped cream/strawberry topped bottom piece. Spread the rest of the whipped cream on top of the top round. Save the rest of the strawberries to top each slice when you serve the cake so that the fruit does not run all over the cake. Enjoy.

Yield: Serves 5-7 — 357 —

Banana Cream Pie

One 3.4 oz box of Jell-O brand banana cream pudding mix
One 14 oz can of Aroy-D brand coconut milk
One pre made vegan graham cracker crust
One container of So Delicious brand Coco Whip vegan whipped cream
3 bananas sliced into 1/8 inch circles

Make the banana pudding filling by whisking the coconut milk into the
pudding mix. Whisk 2 minutes. Place half of the sliced bananas at the bottom
of the pie crust. Spread the pudding over the bananas. Let the pudding set,
covered for an hour in the fridge, then add the rest of the bananas on top of
the pudding and cover them with the coconut whipped topping. Serve cold,
enjoy.

 *You can add melted chocolate to the top of you want a banana chocolate
cream pie.

Yield: Serves 6-8

Italian Sweet Amaretto Polenta Fritters

1/2 inch of vegetable oil for frying in a large non stick pan
powdered sugar for dusting

dry ingredients:
1/2 cup of instant polenta
1/2 cup King Arthur
brand flour
1 tsp baking powder
2 Tbs sugar
pinch of salt

wet ingredients:
1/4 cup amaretto liquer
1/4 cup plus 2 Tbs freshly
opened club soda
1 tsp vanilla extract
1/2 tsp grated orange rind

   Whisk the dry and wet ingredients together so that you have a thick batter. If it is too thick to whisk, add a tiny bit more club soda. Heat the oil on high for 3 minutes. Flick a little batter into the oil. If bubbles form, they are ready to cook. Spoon Tbs sized pieces of the batter into the oil with a spoon, about 10 at a time. Cook each side about 3 minutes until golden. Remove from the oil, drain on a paper towel lined plate and immediately dust with the powdered sugar. Serve warm.

Yield: Serves 4-6

Hello Dolly Bars

1.5 cups of vegan graham cracker crumbs (if you can not find any, just put some vegan graham crackers in a food processor until you have crumbs)
1/2 cup Earth Balance Soy Free Buttery Spread, melted
2 cups vegan chocolate chips
optional 1 cup chopped salted peanuts (if you are allergic to nuts, you can use 1 cup of chopped toasted salted green pumpkin seeds)
1 cup shredded sweetened coconut
3/4 a can of 11.25 oz sweetened vegan condensed coconut milk

Preheat the oven to 325 degrees. Mix the melted butter and the graham cracker crumbs. Press them into a 9x9 inch glass casserole dish that has been sprayed with non stick spray. Place the peanuts or pumpkin seeds (if you are using either, if not, go straight to the chocolate chips) on top of the graham cracker crust, then the chocolate chips and the coconut. Pour the condensed coconut milk evenly over the top. Press down a little to make sure the condensed milk is covering all of the ingredients. Bake for 30 minutes or until firm and golden. Cut into squares once cooled and enjoy.

Yield: Serves 6-10

Holiday Pumpkin Pie

dough:

1 cup sifted King Arthur brand flour
4 Tbs vegan shortening
1 tsp baking powder
pinch salt
3 Tbs sugar

for the filling:

2 15 oz cans of pumpkin puree (not the pie mix)

4 Tbs Follow Your Heart brand Vegan Egg whisked into 3/4 cup water

1.5 cups sugar and 1 cup brown sugar

1/2 teaspoon each cinnamon and ground nutmeg

1 teaspoon vanilla extract, 1/2 cup cornstarch

For the dough, place the dough ingredients in a large bowl. With a pastry cutter, cut in the shortening until little beads form in the flour. Take about 1/3 cup of cold water and add it in. Stir it all together with a rubber spatula until a shaggy dough forms. Fold the dough gently over onto itself about 8 times (this will create layers). Place in plastic wrap and place in the fridge about 30 minutes. Roll it out flat on a floured cutting board into a flat 10 inch circle. Place it into a non stick sprayed 9 inch pie tin. **For the filling,** place the filling ingredients into a food processor and blend until very smooth. Pour this into the pie shell and bake at 375 degrees for about an hour or until you can shake the pie and it does not jiggle in the middle. Let cool one hour before slicing. Enjoy topped with some So Delicious brand Coco Whip.

Yield: Serves 6-8

Ice Box Pie

2 packages of vegan chocolate instant pudding mix
2 cans of Aroy-D brand coconut milk (it is important to use this brand becuase it is thick enough to set up the pudding, it is available in Asian markets) or you can use my Chocolate Mousse recipe from this book instead that you have prepared (if you use the mousse, go straight to the spreading step), a pinch of salt, 1 tsp vanilla extract
one container vegan So Delicious brand Coconut Whiped Cream
half a box of vegan graham crackers

 Whisk the pudding mix together with the coconut milk until you get a smooth pudding texture. Place a layer of graham crackers at the bottom of a 9 inch glass casserole dish. Spread half of the chocolate pudding over the crackers, then add another layer of graham crackers on top of the pudding and then cover them with the rest of the chocolate pudding. Chill in the fridge covered for 2 hours. Once it has chilled, spread a container of the whipped cream over the top. Keep chilled until ready to eat.

Yield: Serves 4-8

Pineapple Sorbet (gluten free)

 This recipe is beyond simple and very tasty.

1 medium pineapple, peeled and cut into medium size chunks
1 tsp each vanilla exract and lemon juice and 1/3 cup sugar

 Freeze the pineapple chunks on a sheet pan and then place them in a food processor with the rest of the ingredients and process until smooth. Enjoy. Store leftovers in the freezer, covered.

   Yield: Serves 4-6   — 362 —

Simple Cookies and Cream Ice Cream Cake

2 pints of Tofutti vanilla flavored vegan ice cream (this is the smoothest
and creamiest vegan ice cream, tastes like soft serve)
3 cups of chopped up Oreo brand cookies or your favorite sandwich cookies
vegan chocolate syrup (squeeze container style, most grocery store
brands are vegan)
1 tub of So Delicious brand Coco Whip whipped cream, thawed

Let the ice cream sit on the counter 30 minutes to soften. With gloved
hands, take a 9x9 inch glass pyrex dish and push the softened ice cream into
the dish, filling the bottom. Spread half of the cookies over the top, then
squirt some chocolate syrup over the cookies. Take the defrosted Coco Whip
and spread this over the ice cream and cookies. Top the whipped cream with
the remaining cookies, then drizzle more chocolate syrup over the top.
Freeze for an hour or overnight, slice into squares and enjoy.

Yield: Serves 4-6

Pineapple Upside Down Cake

If you cut parchment paper into the shape of your baking pan and line
the pan before you pour the batter into the pan, the cake will not stick to
the pan.

dry ingredients:
1 and 3/4 cups King Arthur Flour, sifted
1 cup sugar
1 tsp baking soda
1/2 tsp salt
wet ingredients:
2 tsp vanilla extract
1/3 cup vegetable oil
1 Tbs apple cider vinegar
1 1/8 cup fresh plain club soda (freshly opened because this helps
make the cake very light)
bottom/top:
1/4 cup melted Earth Balance brand Buttery Spread
6 to 9 fresh pineapple rings with the core center pieces removed
6 to 9 pitted and stemmed cherries
2/3 cup brown sugar

Preheat the oven to 375 degrees. Spray a parchment lined 9 inch square
baking tin or round pan with non stick spray. Place in the melted butter on
the bottom, then the brown sugar. Lay down the pineapple rings and the
pitted cherries in the center of the pineapple holes. Mix the dry cake
ingredients in a large bowl with the wet ingredients. Whisk well and pour
batter over the pineapples. Bake for 35-45 minutes or until firm and golden
on top. Remove from pan and remove parchment paper. Flip over. Enjoy.

Yield: Serves 4-8

Crisp and Buttery Peach Cobbler

4 cups frozen peaches, thawed or 4 cups fresh peaches, pit removed, peeled and sliced
1/4 cup flour plus 1.5 cups flour
2.5 cups sugar
1/2 cup Earth Balance brand soy free buttery spread
1 tsp vanilla extract
few pinches of salt

Mix the peaches with 1 cup of sugar, a pinch of salt, the vanilla extract and 1/4 cup of flour. Spray a 9 inch glass baking dish with non stick spray and place the peach mixture in the bottom. Heat the oven to 400 degrees. In a large bowl, mix the remaining 1.5 cups of flour with the extra 1.5 cups of sugar and a pinch of salt. Take the buttery spread and mash it into the flour/sugar mixture between your hands until you have tiny beads of buttery flour. It will be crumbly and loose. This takes about 3 minutes. With your hand, spread this evenly over the top of the peaches. Bake for about 30 minutes or until the topping is golden. This is great topped with Tofutti brand Vanilla Ice Cream or So Delicious brand coconut whipped cream. You can substitute blueberries for peaches if you prefer, the amounts are the same. *Yield:* Serves 4-6

Southern Style Banana Pudding

So easy and so tasty, a great summer after dinner treat.

2 packages of vegan instant banana pudding mix (many brands in any grocery store are vegan)
2 cans of Aroy-D brand coconut milk (this is important because this brand thickens the best, available in Asian markets)
1 bag of vegan vanilla style mini wafer cookies
3 ripe peeled bananas sliced into thin circles
1 container of thawed So Delicious brand Coco Whip whipped topping

Take a 9x9 inch square glass casserole dish. Place about 18 cookies at the bottom. Spread on half of the pudding. Put 18 more cookies on top of the pudding, the sliced bananas and then spread the rest of the pudding on top. Spread the coco whip on top of this final pudding layer. Decorate the sides of the pudding by placing cookies around the edges, placed sticking half way out of the pudding. Enjoy chilled.

Yield: Serves 4-8

Tripple Berry Cobbler

2 cups fresh blueberries
3 cups stemmed and chopped fresh strawberries
2 cups fresh blackberries
1.5 cups sugar
4 Tbs flour
1 tsp vanilla extract
pinch of salt

for the topping:

2 cups King Arthur Flour

1.5 cups sugar

8 Tbs Earth Balance Soy Free Buttery Spread

1 tsp baking powder

pinch of salt

2 cups vanilla rice milk

1 tsp vanilla extract

Preheat the oven to 375 degrees. In a large bowl mix all the berries with the sugar, salt, flour and vanilla extract. Spray a 9x13 inch pyrex baking dish with non stick spray and pour the berry mixture inside. It will seem dry, that is ok. Melt the buttery spread in the microwave then mix it with the rice milk and vanilla. In a different bowl mix the flour, sugar, salt and baking powder. Pour in the butter/rice milk, vanilla mixture and whisk until a nice batter forms. Pour this evenly over the berry mixture and bake for 45 minutes or until firm and golden.

Yield: Serves 6-8

Chocolate Chip Blondies

1 cup King Arthur brand flour, a pinch of salt. 1/2 tsp baking soda
3 Tbs Earth Balance buttery spread and 3 Tbs vegetable shortening
1/2 cup sugar, 1/4 cup dark brown sugar, 1 tsp vanilla extract
1 1/2 cups vegan chocolate chips
1 Tbs finely ground flax seed powder mixed with 3 Tbs hot water

Place the buttery spread and shortening in a large bowl. Add in the sugars, vanilla and flax/hot water mixture. Beat with a hand mixer or a whisk until creamed together. Add in the flour, salt, baking soda and chocolate chips. Mix until you have a thick dough. Push this into an 8 by 8 inch baking pan or glass baking dish that has been sprayed well with non stick spray, forming it to the shape of the baking dish.. Sprinkle a few extra chocolate chips on top and bake at 375 degrees from about 15 minutes. Remove from oven and allow to cool slightly before cutting. Enjoy.

Yield: Serves 3-4

Vanilla White Layer Cake with Vanilla Icing

*Line baking pan with parchment paper cut into the shape of your pan to avoid sticking.

dry ingredients:
2 cups King Arthur Flour, sifted
1 1/4 cup sugar, pinch salt
1 tsp baking soda

wet ingredients:
2 tsp vanilla extract
1/3 cup + 2 Tbs vegetable oil
1 Tbsp apple cider vinegar
1 1/4 cups plain club soda, freshly opened

icing:
5 cups powdered sugar
6 Tbs melted Earth Balance Soy Free Buttery Spread
1 tsp vanilla extract
rice milk (2 Tbs or more)

Preheat the oven to 375 degrees. Spray a non stick 9 inch cake pan lined w parchment very well with non stick spray. If you want to make a sheet cake, use an 13x9 inch non stick rectangle pan, sprayed very well with non stick spray. Mix your dry ingredients together. In a measuring cup, mix the wet ingredients together. Mix the dry and wet ingredients together in a large bowl and whip with an electric hand beater until mixed well. Pour the batter into the non stick pan. Bake for 25 minutes or until you can push on the middle of the cake and it pushes back and it is browned on top (do NOT open the oven until the cake looks browned on top or it will fall). Remove the cake from the oven and carefully remove the cake from the round pan, remove parchment paper. Cool cake on a cookie rack. If you made a sheet cake, you can cool it in the pan. Do not ice until the cake is completely cooled or the icing will be runny! With an electric hand beater, mix the icing ingredients together. Only add a little rice milk in at a time until you get a good icing consistency. If it seems too thin, add more powdered sugar to thicken and beat again. With a serrated knife, carefully slice the cake in half, width wise, so that you have 2 even circles. Place the flat side of the bottom circle on a large plate or cake dome bottom. Spread 1/4th of the icing onto this circle and then place the other half, regular side up, on top of the iced bottom half so that the top of the layer cake will be rounded. Ice the rest of the cake and sides with the rest of the icing. If you made a sheet cake, ice the top or the top and sides, if you removed it from the pan. If not, just ice the top.

Yield: Serves 4-8

Hot Cocoa (gluten free)

Rich, comforting and delicious. Made with real chocolate chips.

2 1/2 cups vanilla rice milk or whatever non dairy milk you prefer, 1. 5 Tbs unsweetened cocoa powder, 3 Tbs semi sweet chocolate chips, 3 Tbs sugar, 1/2 tsp vanilla extract **optional garnish:** a few vegan marshmallows and So Delicious brand coconut whipped cream

In a sauce pan, heat the milk, cocoa powder, vanilla and sugar. When boiling, turn to a simmer and add in the chocolate chips. Whisk until they are melted. Enjoy with the optional topping if desired.

Yield: Serves 2

Marshmallow Crispy Rice Treats (gluten free)

4.5 cups of crispy rice cereal, 1 package of small vegan marshmallows
4 Tbs Soy Free Earth Balance Buttery Spread

Melt the buttery spread in a large non stick pan. Add in the marshmallows and stir constantly with a rubber spatula. Once it is melted together, stir in the rice cereal. Mix well and push this mix into a non stick sprayed glass 9x13 inch casserole dish. Cool until firm.

Yield: Serves 8-12

Simple Sunflower Butter Fudge (gluten free)

3/4 cup Earth Balance brand
buttery spread, 1 jar of smooth Sun Butter brand sunflower butter
3 1/3 cup powdered sugar

Melt the Earth Balance in a large pot, remove from heat, stir in the Sun Butter until completely smooth. Add in the powdered sugar and mix it all together with gloved hands. Press into a 9x9 casserole dish. Chill in fridge, covered with plastic, for 2 hours. Cut into small squares. Store in fridge.

Yield: Serves 4-8

Chef's Bio

Peter Tarantelli first got into vegan cooking in 1993. He realized quickly that if he wanted to eat, he had to do the work. Back in those days, vegan products were sparse at best and restaurants hardly offered anything vegan, not on purpose anyways, so a lot of trial and error went into his cooking.

He attended the Vega Institute in Oroville, CA in 1995 for a macrobiotic disease healing through food course. He has worked as a chef in several vegetarian and non vegetarian restaurants. All of them have helped him develop as a better all around chef.

He is currently a private chef in Philadelphia as well as doing caterings and cooking classes upon request.

He encourages people, vegan, vegetarian or meat eater, to "strive for five", to try and get five different vegetables into their diet a day. He also believes that cooking your own nutritious meals is the most important investment that you can make for your future well being.

Index

Butternut Basil Homemade Gnocchi, 276

Butternut Squash Caramelized Leek Ravioli in Sage Butter Sauce, 196

Banh Mi Ginger Soy Marinated Grilled Tofu Sandwich with Pickled Carrots, Bok

Choy & Sweet Chili Mayo, 279 Beyond Simple Meatloaf, 268

Baked Cheese Manicotti, 280 Baked Basamic Tofu Cacciatore, 303

Baked Leek and Oyster Mushroom Creamy Ziti Pasta, 183

Beef and Cheese Crunch Wraps, 203

Bruschetta Topped Pesto Grilled Tofu, 216 Homemade Farfalle Pasta 183

Bangers and Mash with Sauteed Onion Brown Gravy, 185

Basil Monterey Jack Sausage Rolls, 325 Brunswick Stew, 179

Beyond Simple Dijon Grilled Chicken or Tofu, 284

Biscuits and Sausage Gravy, 187 Bolognese Sauce, 221

Bowtie Pasta with Spicy Sausage and Broccoli Rabe, 269

Buffalo Cauliflower&Blue CheeseTacos, 253 Cajun Sausage&Red Bean Jambalaya, 269

Caper, Mushroom and Olive Pizza Puttanesca, 191 Cajun Mustard Blackened Tofu, 308

Caramelized Onion & Pesto Sausage Pizza, 193 Cacio e Pepe, 201 Cauliflower Parm,
218 Char Grilled Hamburger Steaks, 264 Caramelized Leek Kidney Bean Cakes, 244

Classic Double Cheeseburger, 228 Chili Garlic Home Style Tofu and Vegetables, 236
Crispy Asian Style Tofu Nuggets, 288 Chewy Tofu / Pan Seared 286

Curried Onion and Egg Sandwich with Tamarind Tofu and Mango Chutney Mayo, 232
Eggplant Cutlet Sandwich with Spinach Artichoke Dip, 270

Chicken Salad Sandwich Filling, 289 Chicken Fried Steak with Mushroom Gravy, 284

Chicken Fried Steak Cheddar Chive Biscuits, 304 Chicken Tenders Tofu Tenders, 197
Chicken and Dressing, 287 Chinese Broccoli & Tofu in Black Bean Garlic Sauce, 307
Chicken or Eggplant Parmesan, 195 Cornmeal Johnny Cakes, 220

Chicken or Seitan Cheesesteak, 288 Chinese Eggplant & Tofu in Garlic Sauce, 194
Crispy Pineapple Seitan, Green Beans and Chinese Broccoli

Classic Beef Lasagna, 199 Crispy Sesame Beef and Tofu in Black Bean Sauce, 316

Classic Beef Tacos, 290 Crispy Fried Cauliflower w Mushroom Gravy, 291 Classic
Grilled Cheese Sandwich, 201 Classic Macaroni Salad, 126

Coconut Crusted Chicken, Vegan Shrimp or Tofu, 291 Crab Cakes, 248

Creamy Paste Verde, 318 Creamy Rich Penne Primavera, 292

Crispy Cauliflower Pakora Sandwich on Homemade Naan, 178

Creamy and Rich Penne Vodka Pasta 203 Crispy Avocado Po Boy Sandwich, 296
Crispy Tofish Fillet Sandwich, 293 Eggplant Leek & Crispy Bacon Sicilian Pizza, 246
Crunchy Southern Style Fried Chicken or Tofu, 205, Egg Foo Young, 226
Dijon Grilled Tofu and Provolone Muffaletta, 323
Egg Salad Sandwich Filling, 294 Fluffy Pancakes/Waffle Batter, 271
Feta Spinach Topped Balsamic Grilled Tofu, 189
French Toast, 238 Garlic Broccoli Rabe and Provolone Stromboli, 254
Garlic Spinach and Creamy Chao Cheese Grilled Panini, 287 Goulash, 236
Garlic Broccolini and Spicy Sausage Mushroom Pizza, 309
Greek Kale, Olive, Caper, Leek and Artichoke Spinach Pasta, 282
General Tso's Tofu, 297 Falafel with Cucumber Yoghurt Sauce, 272
German Pretzel Bun Bratwurst Sandwich with Sauerkraut and Pickled Beets, 249
Grilled Chicken Caesar Bowtie Pasta Salad, 112 Grilled Sunbutter and Jelly 258
Grilled Eggplant Pesto Caprese Napoleon Stacks, 258
Grilled Polenta with Mushroom Marsala Sauce, 207
Hard or Soft Taco Salad or Corn Tostadas, 299
Hamburger, Oyster Mushroom and Kalamata Olive Pizza, 328
Hoisin Ginger Beef Stuffed Cabbage Rolls, 224
Homemade Artichoke Chicken Ravioli in Lemon Butter Sauce with Spinach
and Broccoli, 209 Grilled Sweet and Sour Pineapple Tofu Skewers, 186
Homemade Bagels, 300 Homemade Spicy Gnocchi with Garlic Kale,
Asparagus, Broccoli and Sausage, 216 Homemade Sloppy Joes, 220

Homemade Moo Shu Tofu and Vegetables, 234

Homemade Omelette and Cheese Avocado Bagel Sandwich, 188
Homemade Egg Pappardelle Pasta with Garlic Spinach, Mushrooms &
Asparagus in White Wine Butter Sauce, 211

Homemade Flaky Chicken Pot Pie, 213   Homemade Gnocchi, 230

Homemade From Scratch Sausage, Egg and Cheese Biscuits, 215

Homemade From Scratch Seitan (Wheat Meat), 301

Homemade Jumb Ricotta Beef Fresh Ravioli, 217

Homemade Pesto Beef Cannelloni Baked in Artichoke Cream Sauce, 219

Iowa Corn Pancakes, 302   Indian Butter Chickpeas, Tofu & Vegetables, 246
Fried Green Tomato and Smoked Gouda Egg Biscuit, 260

Italian Hoagie, 221 Italian Wedding Soup, 294
Italian Sausage and Cheese Baked Ziti, 223   Japanese Eggplant Fish, 262
Jumbo Chili Cheese Dogs, 303 Jamaican Beef Patties, 182

Crispy Corn Dog Bites, 304   Kofta Kebabs with Tahini Garlic Sauce, 179
Korean Spicy BBQ Tofu and Vegetables, 225 Kung Pao Tofu, 208
Lemon Chicken or Tofu, 273   Kimchi and Scrambled Egg Fried Rice, 226
Philly Style Tomato Pie, 305 Japanese Tofu Katsu with Tonkatsu Sauce, 180
Mile High Crispy Chicken Fillet Sandwich, 227 Mushroom Stroganoff, 312
Meatball Sub, 241   Meaty Mushroom Marinara Sauce, 325 Moo Goo Gai Pan,
214 Mapo Tofu, 286   Mee Siam, 212

Mushroom, Artichoke and Spinach Puff Pastry, 326
Mushroom Scallion Crusted Tofu or Eggplant w/ Spinach Artichoke Dip, 229
Spaghetti Primavera with Mushrooms, Broccoli, Cauliflower and Garlic
Butter , 306 Creamy Sesame Beef and Vegetables over Brown Rice, 198
New England Style Lobster Roll, 231 Oyster Mushroom Broccolini Beef Pho, 285
Parmesan Mushroom Risotto Cakes, 307 Parmesan Basil Stuffed Tomatoes, 264
Pesto Gnocchi w Sausage, Artichokes and Sun Dried Tomatoes, 256
Penne with Sun Dried Tomatoes, Chicken, Mushrooms, Broccoli and
Marinated Artichokes, 313   Pesto Pasta, 308
Pineapple Chinese Broccoli Green Bean Tofu Katsu Fried Rice, 240
Pesto Beef Homemade Agnolotti Pasta with Eggplant, Mushrooms, Kale
and Oil Cured Sun Dried Tomatoes in Sage Butter Sauce, 204 Pickled Beet,
Scallion Avocado Topped Dragon Roll, 235
Pumpkin Seed Sage Crusted Chicken Cutlets or Tofu Cutlets Topped with
Baked Spinach Artichoke Dip, 282 Ratatouille, 280
Radiatore Pasta with Chicken, Leeks, Peas and Kale, 312
Rich and Smooth Indian Butter Chicken, 311
Rich and Decadent Vegan Stromboli, 233
Roasted Red Pepper Pasta Sauce, 271
Ricotta Stuffed Shells, 274 Sausage Rice, 212
Savory Meatballs, 327 Spicy Buffalo Chicken or Tofu, 243
Hamburger, Kale and Mushroom Calzone, 184
Sslisbury Steak, 277   Seitan, Tofu or Chicken Piccata, 313
Sesame Hoisin Sweet Chili Grilled Tofu, 275
Seitan Beef, Cabbage and Mushroom Rice Noodle Stir Fry, 298
Szechuan Cabbage, Asparagus and Ginger Tofu, 316
Sesame Japanese Eggplant, Chewy Tofu and Mixed Vegetable Stir Fry,
237 Sesame Orange Tofu or Chicken, 314 Smoky Pulled BBQ Seitan, 240
Simple Sausage and Peppers, 239
Casserole, 232 Sri Lankan Green Bean Pineapple Curry w Pan Seared Tofu, 302
Spicy Rice Noodle, Japanese Eggplant, Tofu, Mushroom and Coconut Ginger
Curry Soup, 315 Spicy Sweet and Sour Ham, Asparagus and Broccolini. 306
Saffron Cauliflower Raisin Penne, 218 Schezwan Eggplant, Tofu+Mushrooms. 275
Smoky Black Bean and Corn Tortilla Cakes, 241 Spaghetti Alla Puttanesca, 208

Smoky Cabbage and Bratwurst Sausage Stuffed Bread, 285
Sauteed BBQ Tofu, Vegetables, Black Beans and Kidney Beans, 206
Spicy Chipotle Sausage Nachos, 247 Spicy Black Pepper Sweet&StickyAsian Wings, 224
Spicy Miso Tofu Vegetable Ramen Bowl, 231 Sun Dried Tomato Pesto Baked
Penne, 188 Shepherds Pie, 192 Spanakopita Hand Pies, 222 Spicy Beef+Broccoli, 186
Southern Style Pimento Cheese, 94 Spicy Burokkori and Pickled Red Pepper Sushi, 281
Spicy Pan Seared Tofu Pad Thai, 317 Spinach Florentine Artichoke Pizza, 228
Spicy Tofu Asparagus Scallion Cream Cheese Roll,242 Spicy Korean Beef
and Rice Bowl, 234 Spicy Sausage, Pesto, Provolone and Broccoli Rabe Hoagie, 319
Spinach, Corn and Black Bean Cheddar Jack Quesadillas, 320
Spinach, Marinated Artichoke and Garlic Mushroom Lasagna Roulades,
251 Stuffed Peppers with Creamy Bulgur and Provolone, 253
Sweet and Sour Ham or Tofu + Vegetables, 255 Sweet Chili Summer Sausages, 250
Sweet and Spicy Mock Duck Thai Coconut Milk Curry or Pan Seared
Tofu Curry, 256 Tarragon Maple Dijon Black Bean, Tofu and Eggplant, 214
Thai Sunflower Butter Grilled Leek and Tofu Kebabs, 323
Tandoori Chicken or Tofu and Vegetable Curry, 321 Teriyaki Grilled Tofu, 290
Thai Black Bean and Eggplant Seitan and Tofu Basil Red Curry, 249
Thai Cilantro Basil Tofu With Spicy Hoisin Peanut Sauce or
Sunflower Sauce, 259 Thai Tofu and Mushroom Drunken Noodles, 244
Thanksgiving Vegan Sliced Turkey and Gravy, 261 Tofu Sushi Fashion Sandwich, 206
Teriyaki Grilled Mushroom, Eggplant and Red Pepper Nigiri Sushi, 250
Tofish Fillets with Vegan Tartar Sauce, 322 Tofu Palak Paneer, 298 Tortellini, 210
Tofu, Ham or Chicken Hoisin Topped Fried Rice, 263 Tortellini in Brodo , 273
Vietnamese Tofu Vermicelli Pho Soup, 265 Vodka Sausage Pizza, 266
Zucchini Corn Fritters, 319 White Bean Asparagus Cakes with Basil Aioli, 267
Wild Mushroom Steak Fajitas, 274
WildRice, Pear and Provolone Stuffed Delicata Squash or Zucchini, 324
Spicy Thai "Peanut " Ramen Noodle , Mushroom , Baby Bok Choy and Tofu
Curry Soup, 252 Spicy Vietnamese Bok Choy Tofu Vermicelli Rice Noodle Soup, 245
Garlic Buttered Mushroom and Spinach Risotto, 278

SALADS, SIDES & STARTERS
Antipasto, 78 Avocado White Bean Hummus, 34 Arancini Rice Balls, 28
Asian Baby Corn and Cucumber Fresh Cherry Salad, 142
Avocado Rice with Sour Cream and Fresh Chives, 13
Bacon and Cheddar Crispy Potato Skins,110 Baked Steak Fries, 79
Baked Thick Cut Potato Chips, 15 Baba Ganoush, 159
Balsamic Spicy Grilled Cauliflower Steaks with Green Goddess Dressing, 44
Balsamic Grilled Cauliflower Lemon Pepper Avovado Salad, 165
Balsamic Reduction Tomato Basil Salad, 152 Balsamic Reduction Dressing, 152
Balsamic Tofu, Broccoli, Kidney Bean, Mango and Monterey Jack Mixed
Greens Salad, 80 Balsamic Watermelon, Cucumber and Arugula Salad, 134
Basic Dough for Bread, Pizza, Rolls, Focaccia, 81
Basil Pesto, 82 Banana, Sunflower Butter, Kale and Avocado Smoothie, 90
Basil Roasted Red Potatoes, 153
Beet, Avocado, Red Bean and Spicy Sesame Tamari Tofu Baby Bibb Lettuce
Salad, 17 Beet Avocado Salad with Lemon Pepper Chive Aioli, 49
Beyond Simple Fruit Salad, 153 Bloody Mary, 34
Beet, Kale and Cabbage Borscht, 66
Beyond Simple Low Fat Vegetable Soup, 83 Buffalo Brussel Sprouts, 154
Black Bean, Spinach, Avocado Kale Salad, 130
Borlotti Beans with Fresh Thyme and Rosemary, 136

Mushroom Gravy, 165 Mushroom and Leek Wild Rice, 16

Nacho Cheese Sauce, 74 Nordic Root Vegetable Soup, 62

Navy Bean Corn Chowder, 51 Nut Free Peanut Sauce, 144

Oil Cured Sun Dried Tomato, Cannellini Bean, Red Grape and Pan Seared Tofu Baby Greens Salad, 123

Olive Oil Roasted Brussel Sprouts, 126

Olive Oil and Garlic Green Beans, 124

Olive Oil and Garlic Roasted Cremini and Button Mushrooms, 125

Olive Tapenade, 165

Onion Naan Bread, 75 Orange Citrus Couscous with Chickpeas & Vegetables, 41

Pasta Dough, 53 Barley Black Bean Vegetable Salad in Smoked Paprika Maple Dijon Dressing, 70 Panzanella Salad, 47 Pesto Bread Sticks, 127

Poor Man's Caviar (Simple Spicy Black Bean and Corn Salad), 128

Pear, Golden Raisin and Cabbage Vinaigrette Slaw

Parmesan Crusted Avocado Fries, 36 Parsnip Cauliflower Mushroom Bake, 92

Pork and Japanese Eggplant Gyoza Dumplings or Steamed Dumplings, 52

Potato Leek Soup, 129 Potato Latkes, 50

Potato, Mushroom and Broccoli Hash, 55

Potato, Spinach and Mushroom Gratin Cassoulet, 57

Pumpkin Seed Pesto Rice, 166 Purple Carrot and Caramelized Onion Horseradish Hummus, 20

Grilled Broccoli with Creamy Dijon Caper Sauce, 130 Ranch Dressing, 72

Rosemary, Grape Tomato, Olive and Caper Focaccia, 13

Rich and Creamy Potato Salad, 61 Roasted Cauliflower and Kale, 166

Rosemary Ginger Roasted Parsnips and Carrots, 152

Roasted Vegetables, 131 Roasted Beet Salad with Mandarin Oranges and Kalamata Olives, 22 Rich and Creamy Tahini Goddess Dressing, 87

Rustic Truffle Oiled Olive Bread, 132 Sausage Breakfast Patties, 114

Saffron Yellow Rice, 167 Sesame Five Spice Asian Roasted Red Potatoes, 61 Sesame Crusted Pickle Fried Beets with Green Goddess Dressing, 30 Savory Sausage Ball Cookies, 167

Sesame Ginger Grilled Leeks, 64 Sesame Seed Braided Golden Bread, 63

Sesame Stick, Chocolate Chip, Cashew, Dried Cherry and Toasted Pumpkin Seed Snack Mix, 168 Savory Italian Fennel Seed Tiralli, 118

Sicilian Olive and Truffle Oil Roasted Garlic Lemon Spaghetti, 133

Sicilian Potato Salad, 26 Silky Smooth Butternut Squash Bisque, 65

Simple BBQ Baked Beans, 168

Simple BBQ Sauce, 169 Simple Balsamic Vinaigrette, 23

Simple Bruschetta Topping, 134

Simple Caesar Salad, 135 Simple Cheese Grits, 136

Simple Chicken Gravy, 137

Corn, Cherry, Asparagus and Avocado Salad, 138

Simple Fresh Summer Rolls with Sweet Chili Hoisin Dipping Sauce, 139

Simple Garlic Roasted Asparagus, 169

Simple Garlic Sauteed Spinach, 170

Simple Guacamole, 140 Simple Garlic Sauteed Vegetables, 97 Simple Herb Garlic Compound Butter, 170

Simple Olive Oil and Herb Dip For Bread, 171 Spicy Olive Oil Grilled Eggplant, 86

Simple Salt and Black Pepper Blanched Vegetables, 141

Simple Southwestern Kale, Sweet Potato, Pinto Bean, Mushroom and Rice Soup, 142 Simple Salt and Pepper Butter Blanched Broccoli, 106

Smoky Coconut Crusted Avocado Cocktail, 10 Smoked Paprika Pickled Beets, 32

Simple Steamed Bulgur Wheat, 98 Simple Indian Smoked Onion Chutney, 89

Smashed Baked Crispy Red Potatoes, 171 Simple Vegetable Stock, 63

Smoky Mozzarella Penne Pasta Salad, 143 Smoked Paprika Avocado Raisin Salad, 156

67 Smoky Red Beans and Rice, 144   Smoky Southern Style Collard Greens, 124

Smoky Oyster Mushroom and Scallion Cream Cheese Fried Wontons,
Homemade Spicy Chili Garlic Biang Biang Noodles, 26

Soba Noodle Salad in Spicy Sunflower Butter "Peanut" Sauce Dressing,
145 Sour Cream and Onion Dip, 172 Soft Pretzels, 14   Spicy Italian Pickled Veg, 90

Spanish Steamed Bulgur Wheat, 172 Spiced Green Pea and Potato Samosas, 60

Spicy Asian Baked Black Beans, 173 Spicy Sausage, Kale and Mushrooms, 67

Spicy Kidney Bean Shaved Brussel Sprout Avocado Salad, 30 Spicy Korean Fire Noodles, 47 Spicy Chipotle Dressed Green Beans, 82 Spicy Sweet Chili Mayo, 93

Spinach Artichoke Dip, 76   Spicy Smoked Paprika Garlic Cabbage and Mushrooms, 40

Spinach, Mozzarella and Tomato Basil Caprese Salad, 147 Spinach Pasta Dough, 77

Split Pea Basil Soup, 148 Sriracha Sausage and Spinach Potato Hash, 24

Stuffed Twice Baked Broccoli and Cheddar Potatoes, 69 Stracciatella, 24

Sun Dried Tomato Basil Dip, 77 Sun Dried Tomato Pesto, 120

Sweet and Sour Sauce, 173 Steamed Asparagus with Creamy Saffron Aioli, 116

Spaghetti al Limone, 148 Sun Dried Tomato Vinaigrette, 99

Spicy Mushroom and Onion Tofu Sambal Buns, 54

Tabouli Salad, 149 Thyme Maple Buttered Roasted Carrots, 117

Teriyaki Grilled Pineapple, 28 Thyme and Olive Oil Roasted Beet Root, 174

Toasted Whole Grain Pita Points, 174 Tofu Ricotta, 175

Tofu or Chicken Noodle Soup, 150 Tuscan White Bean Kale Soup, 103

Cooked Kale, Cauliflower, Mango and Papaya Black Bean Salad, 151

Vinegar Cherry Pepper, Sicilian Olive, Red Radish, Kidney Bean & Toasted Green Pumpkin Seed Salad, 71

Simple Sesame Soy and Ginger Roasted Vegetables, 107

Simple White or Brown Rice in a Rice Cooker, 85

Two Tomato, Artichoke and Pepperoncini Pasta Salad,
101   Vegn Egg Pasta Dough, 56 Vietnamese Avocado Smoothie, 131

Tuscan Kale with Sauteed Garlic Mushrooms, Cauliflower and
Klamata Olives, 115 Vegetable Steamed Dumplings or Gyoza/Potstickers, 119

Watermelon Feta Salad w/ Mint Vinaigrette, 55 Watermelon Red Pepper Vinaigrette, 135 Whole Wheat Wreath Bread, 125 Wonton Soup, 66

Zucchini Bread Muffins, 48

Made in the USA
Monee, IL
29 August 2021

c3f848dd-0daf-4d10-a459-cf83cd0e9e5fR01